Spiral-Bound
(top secret summer)

 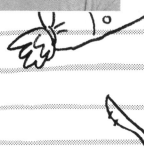 

Spiral-Bound (Top Secret Summer) © & ™ 2005 Aaron Renier

Edited by Chris Staros. Copyediting by Robert Venditti.

Published by Top Shelf Productions, PO Box 1282, Marietta, GA 30061-1282, USA. Publishers: Brett Warnock & Chris Staros. Top Shelf Productions ® and the Top Shelf logo are registered trademarks of Top Shelf Productions, Inc. All Rights Reserved. No part of this publication may be reproduced without permission, EXCEPT for small exerpts for purposes of review. This is a work of fiction. Names, characters, places, and incidents are the creations of the author's imagination. Any resemblance to actual events, locales, or persons, living or dead, is entirely coincidental. Visit our online catalog at www.topshelfcomix.com.

Renier, Aaron

Spiral-Bound (Top Secret Summer) / Aaron Renier

ISBN 1-891830-50-3

First Printing, August 2005. Printed in Canada

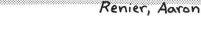

Spiral-Bound
(top secret summer)

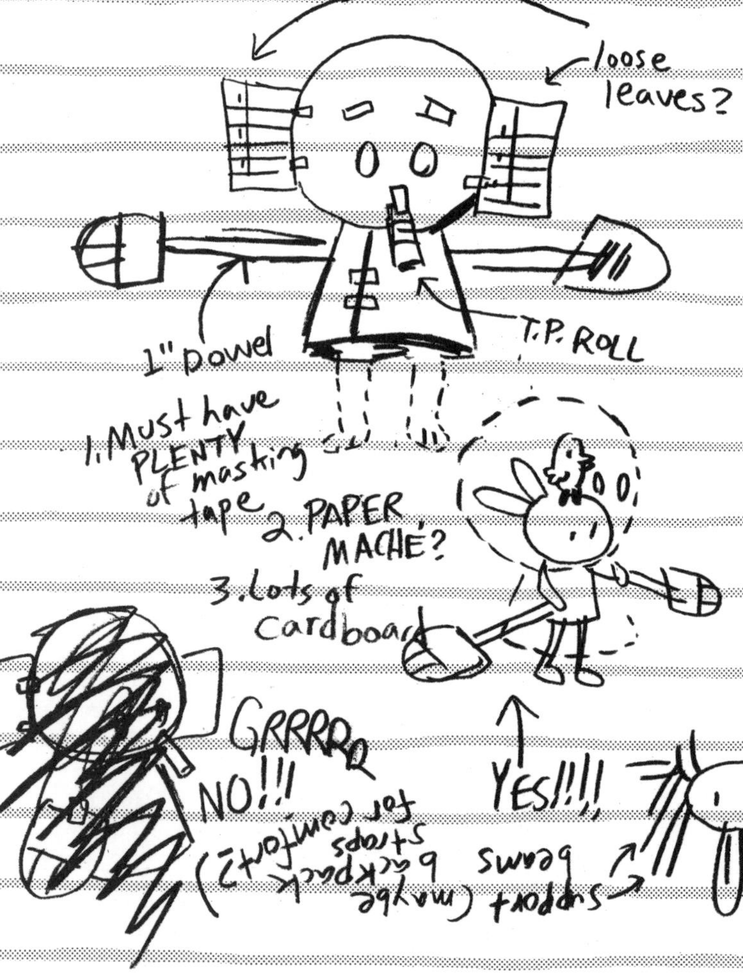

loose leaves?
1" Dowel
T.P. ROLL
1. Must have PLENTY of masking tape
2. PAPER MACHÉ?
3. Lots of cardboard
GRRRRR
NO!!!
YES!!!!
support beams (maybe backpack straps for comfort?)

Aaron Renier

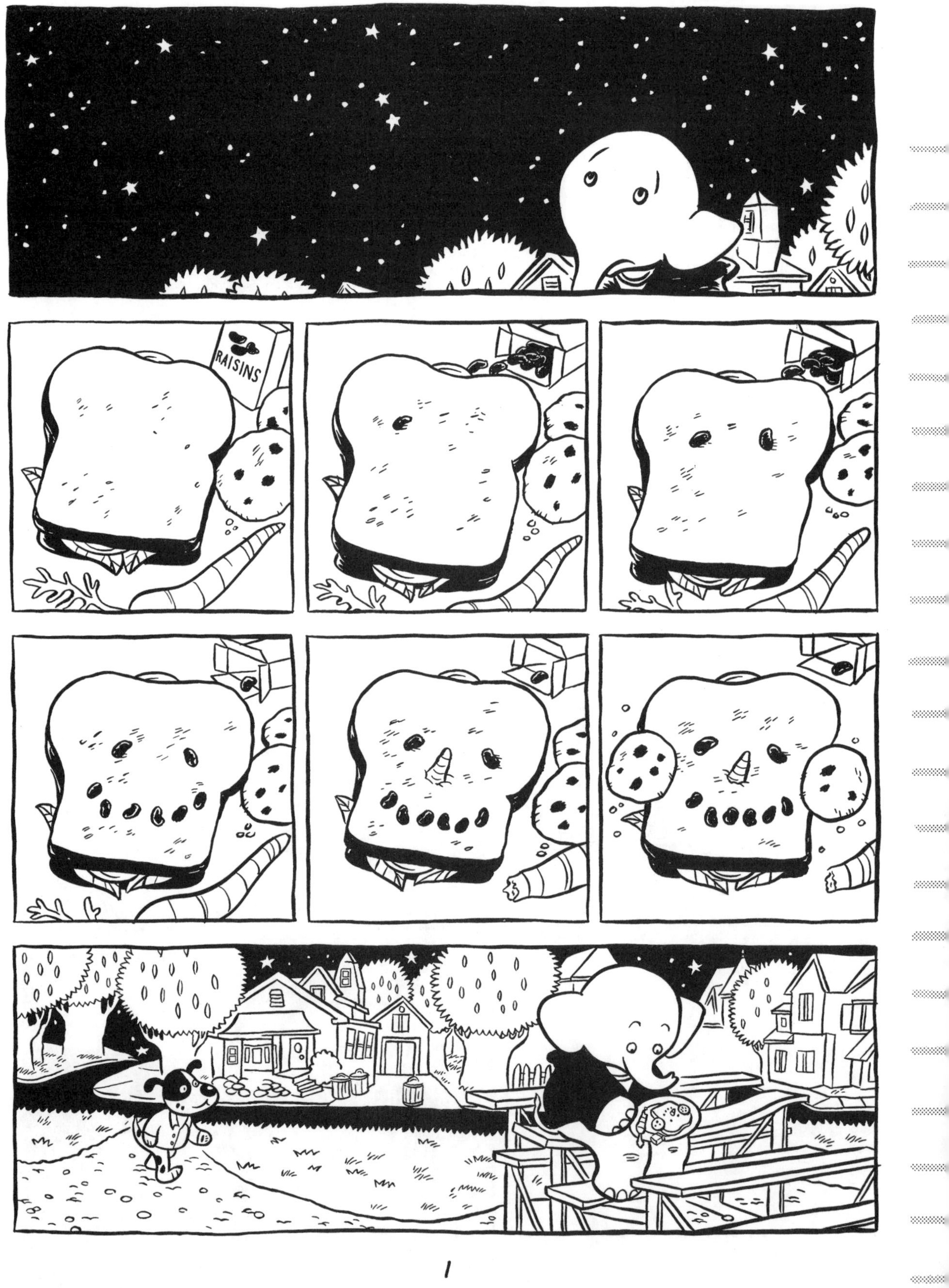
RAISINS

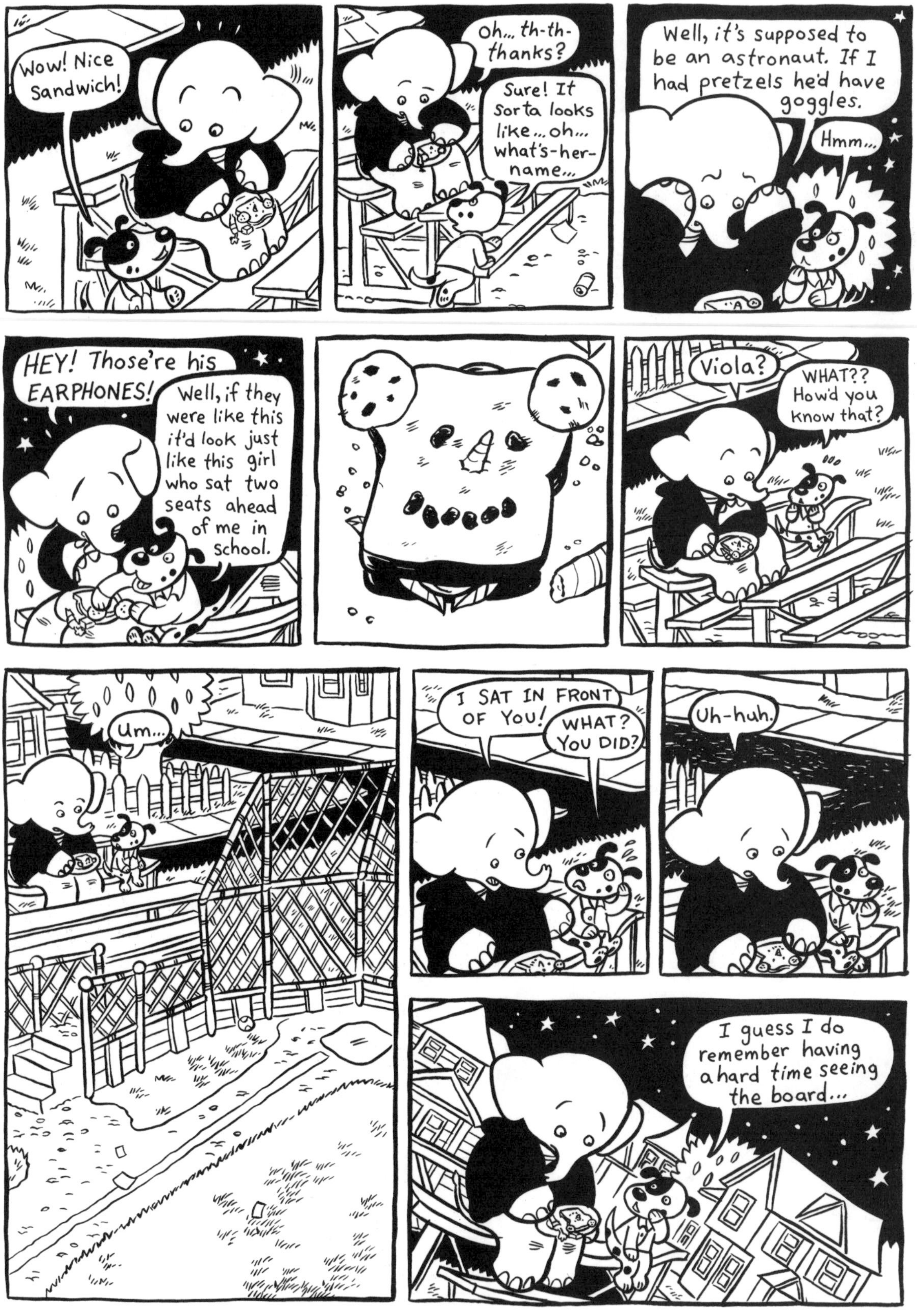
Wow! Nice sandwich!
Oh... th-th-thanks?
Sure! It sorta looks like... oh... what's-her-name...
Well, it's supposed to be an astronaut. If I had pretzels he'd have goggles.
Hmm...
HEY! Those're his EARPHONES!
Well, if they were like this it'd look just like this girl who sat two seats ahead of me in school.
Viola?
WHAT?? How'd you know that?
Um...
I SAT IN FRONT OF YOU!
WHAT? YOU DID?
Uh-huh.
I guess I do remember having a hard time seeing the board...

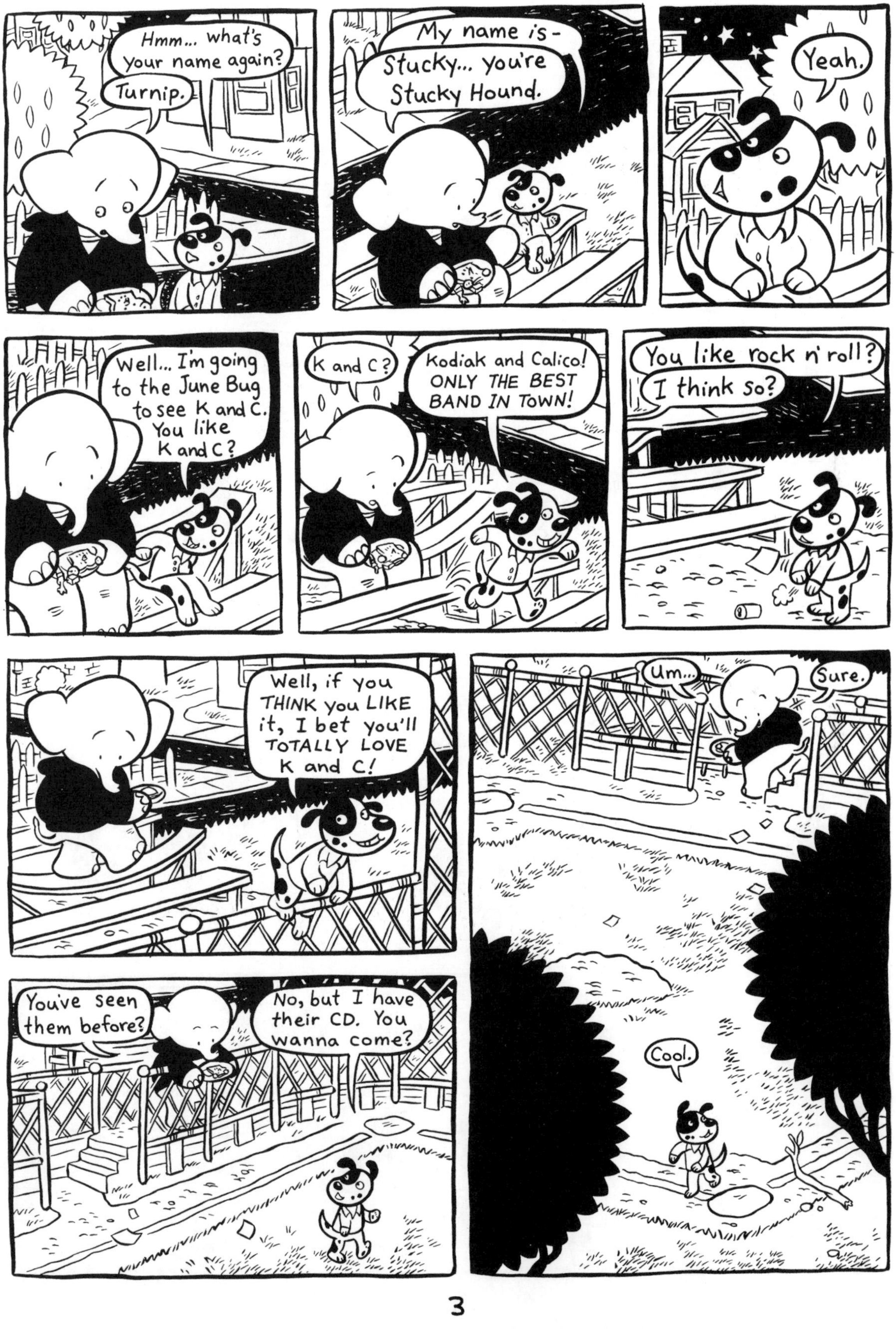
Hmm... what's your name again?
Turnip.
My name is-
Stucky... you're Stucky Hound.
Yeah.
Well... I'm going to the June Bug to see K and C. You like K and C?
K and C?
Kodiak and Calico! ONLY THE BEST BAND IN TOWN!
You like rock n' roll?
I think so?
Well, if you THINK you LIKE it, I bet you'll TOTALLY LOVE K and C!
You've seen them before?
No, but I have their CD. You wanna come?
Um...
Sure.
Cool.

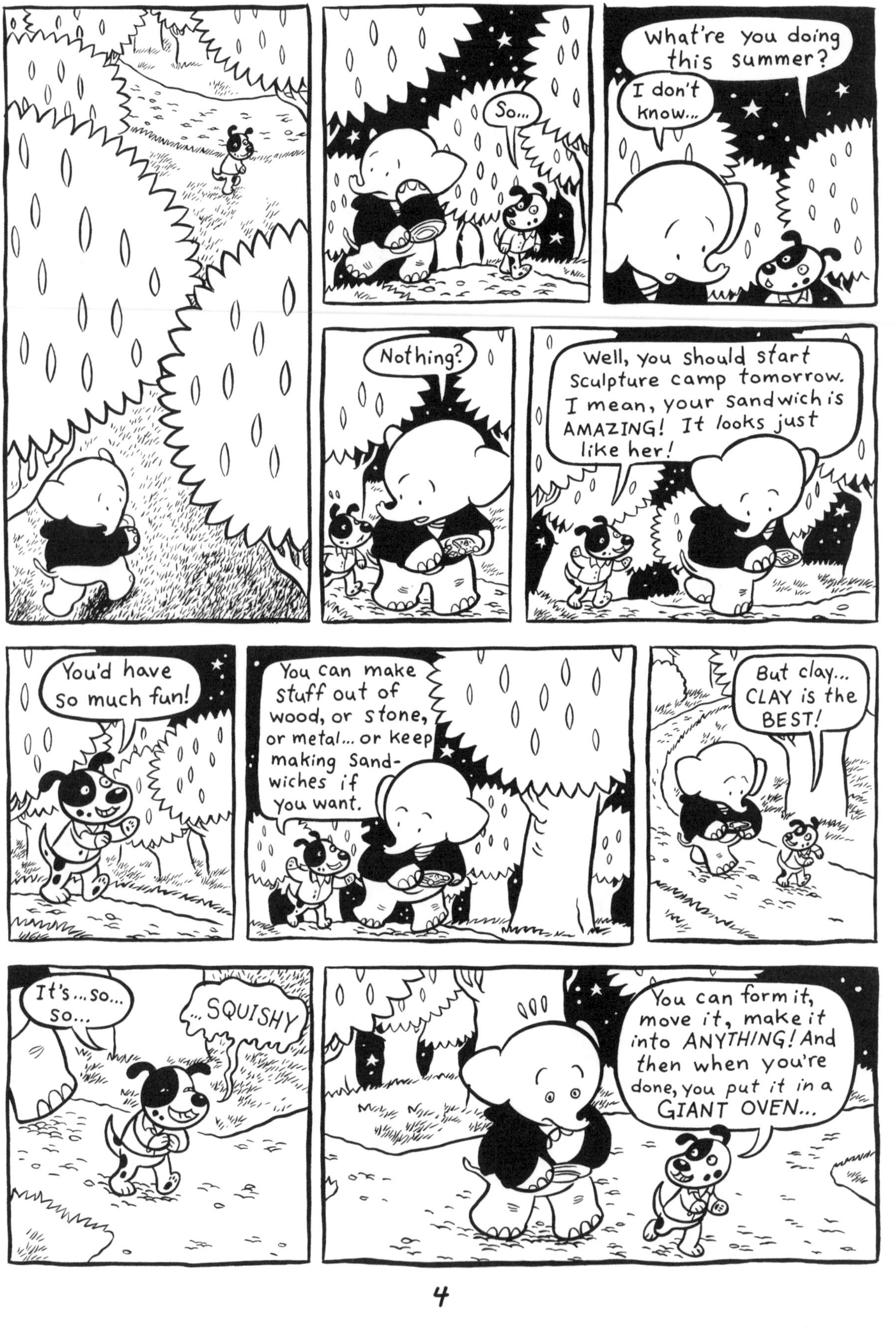
So...
What're you doing this summer?
I don't know...
Nothing?
Well, you should start Sculpture camp tomorrow. I mean, your sandwich is AMAZING! It looks just like her!
You'd have so much fun!
You can make stuff out of wood, or stone, or metal... or keep making sand-wiches if you want.
But clay... CLAY is the BEST!
It's... so... so...
...SQUISHY
You can form it, move it, make it into ANYTHING! And then when you're done, you put it in a GIANT OVEN...

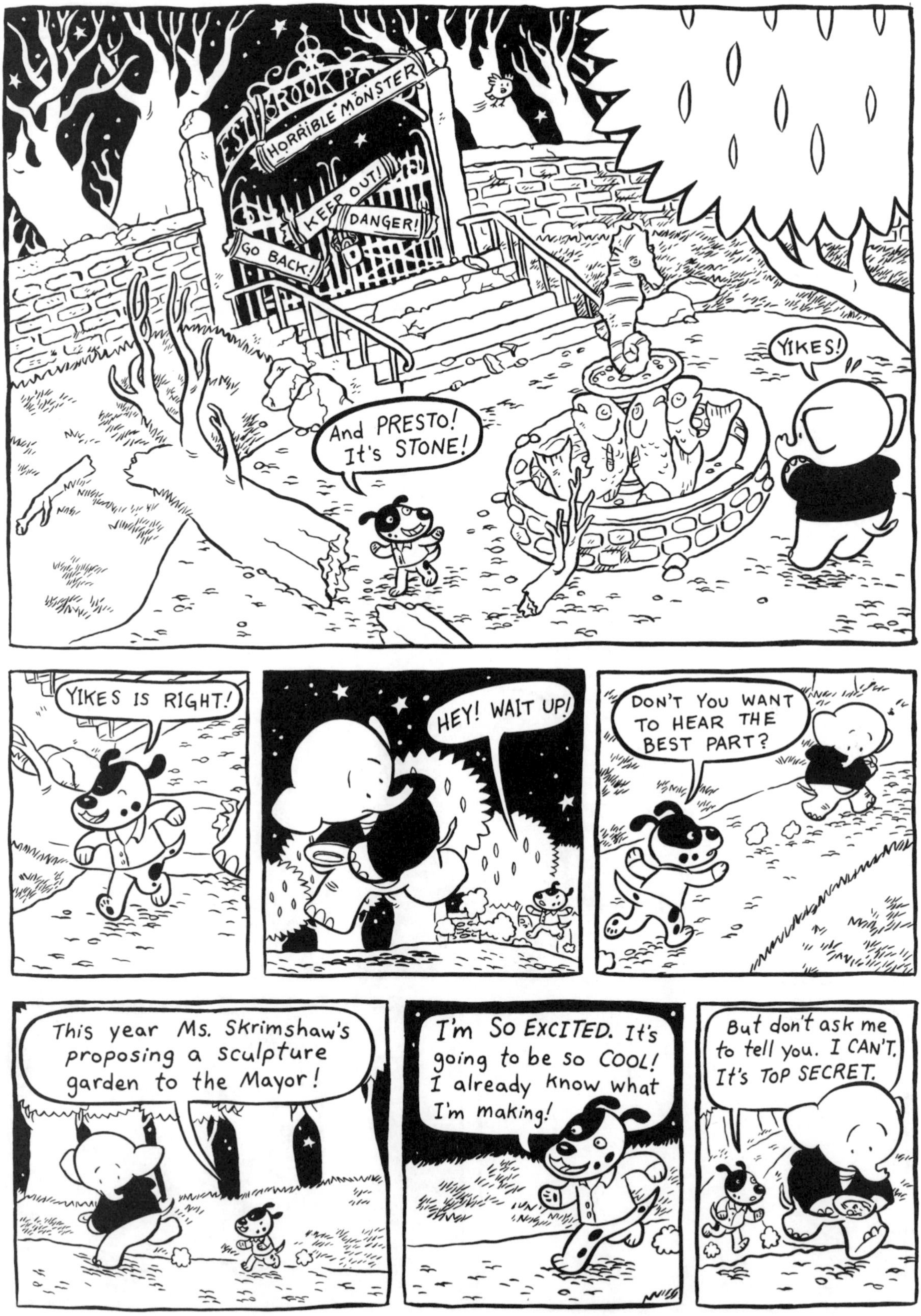

HORRIBLE MONSTER
KEEP OUT!
DANGER!
GO BACK!
YIKES!
And PRESTO! It's STONE!
YIKES IS RIGHT!
HEY! WAIT UP!
DON'T YOU WANT TO HEAR THE BEST PART?
This year Ms. Skrimshaw's proposing a sculpture garden to the Mayor!
I'm SO EXCITED. It's going to be so COOL! I already know what I'm making!
But don't ask me to tell you. I CAN'T. It's TOP SECRET.

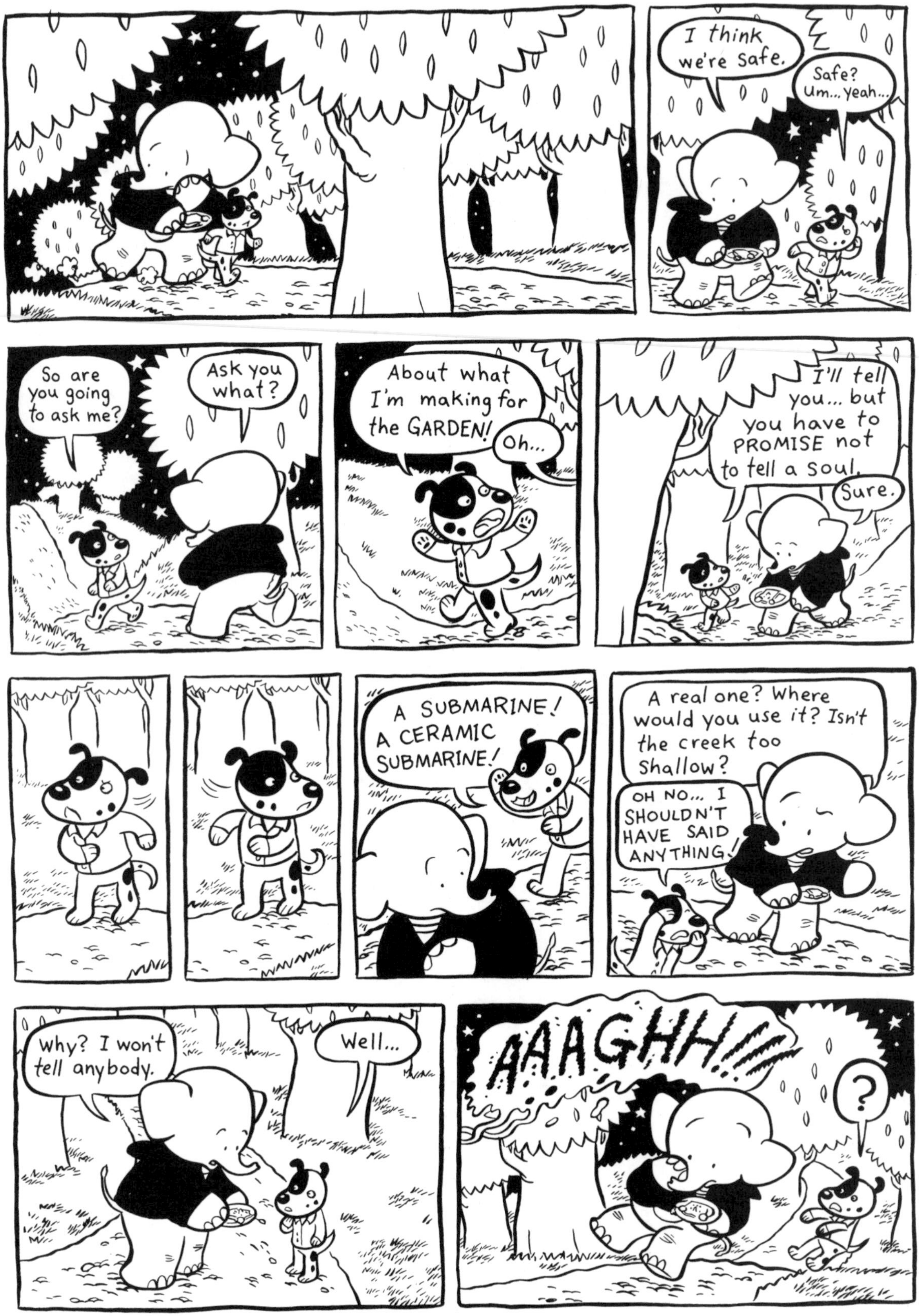
I think we're safe.
Safe? Um... yeah...
So are you going to ask me?
Ask you what?
About what I'm making for the GARDEN!
Oh...
I'll tell you... but you have to PROMISE not to tell a soul.
Sure.
A SUBMARINE! A CERAMIC SUBMARINE!
A real one? Where would you use it? Isn't the creek too shallow?
OH NO... I SHOULDN'T HAVE SAID ANYTHING!
Why? I won't tell anybody.
Well...
AAAGHH!!!
?

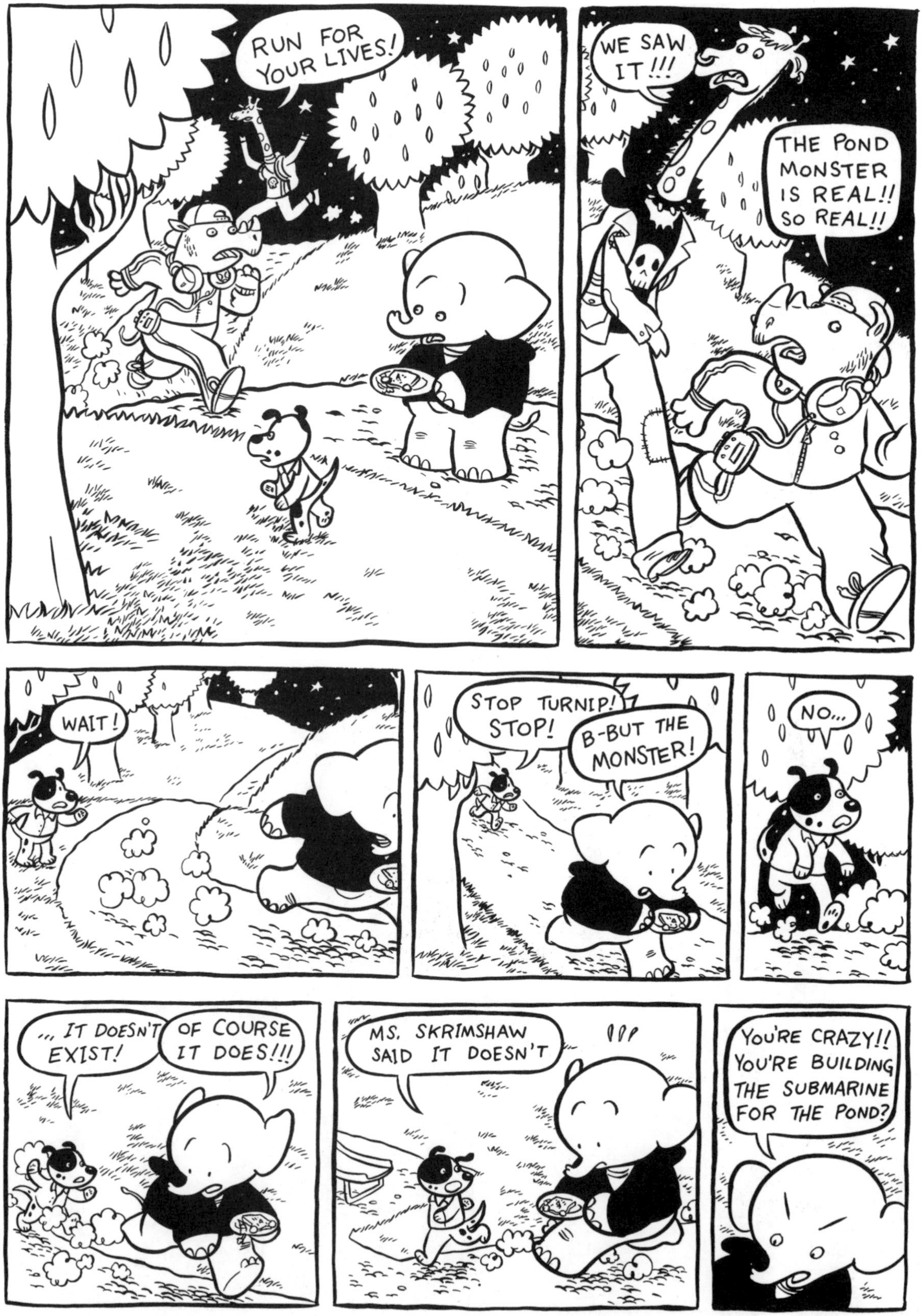

RUN FOR YOUR LIVES!
WE SAW IT!!!
THE POND MONSTER IS REAL!! SO REAL!!
WAIT!
STOP TURNIP! STOP!
B-BUT THE MONSTER!
NO...
... IT DOESN'T EXIST!
OF COURSE IT DOES!!!
MS. SKRIMSHAW SAID IT DOESN'T
YOU'RE CRAZY!! YOU'RE BUILDING THE SUBMARINE FOR THE POND?

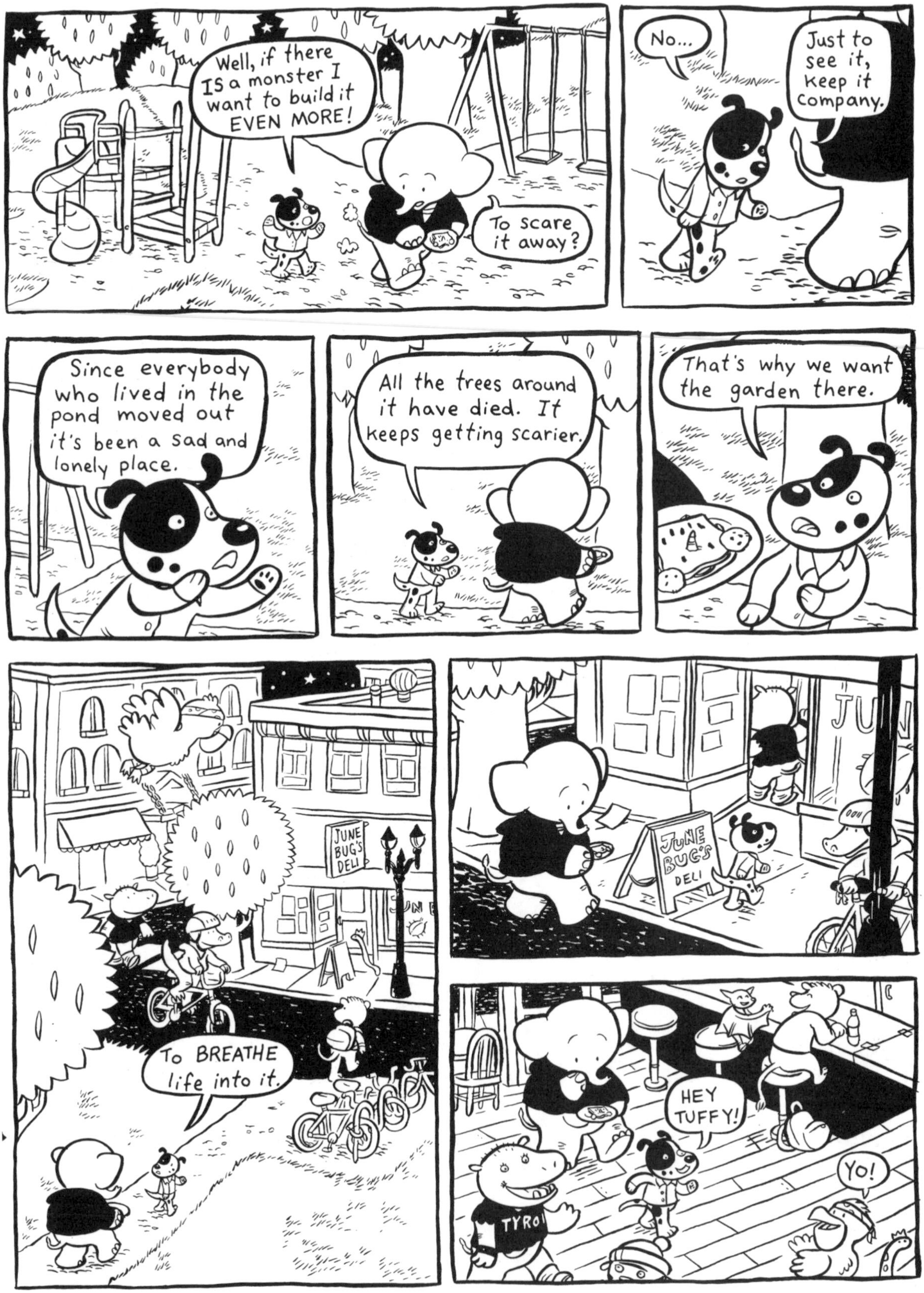
Well, if there IS a monster I want to build it EVEN MORE!
To scare it away?
No...
Just to see it, keep it company.
Since everybody who lived in the pond moved out it's been a sad and lonely place.
All the trees around it have died. It keeps getting scarier.
That's why we want the garden there.
JUNE BUG'S DELI
To BREATHE life into it.
JUNE BUG'S DELI
HEY TUFFY!
YO!
TYRO

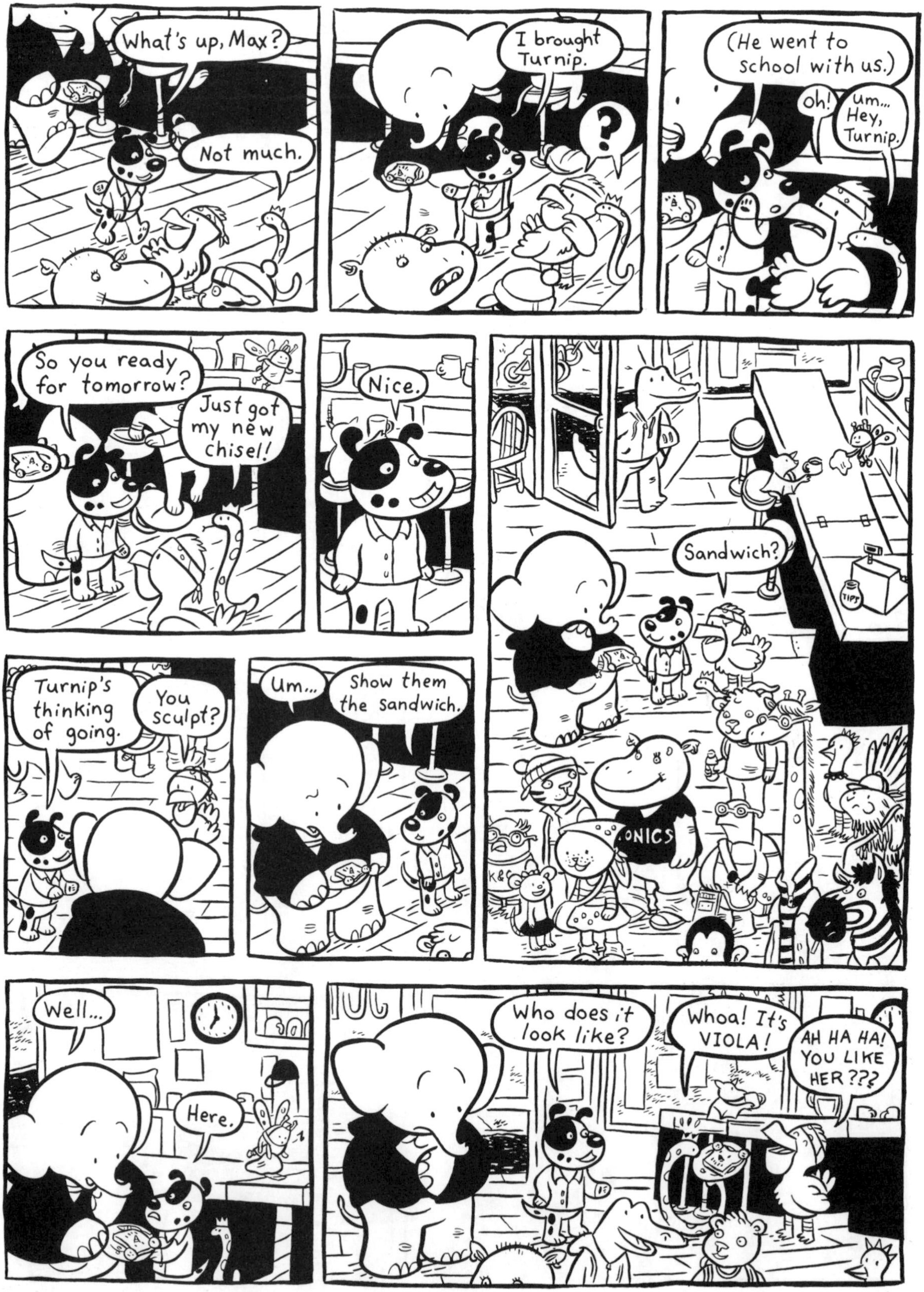

What's up, Max?
Not much.
I brought Turnip.
?
(He went to school with us.)
Oh!
Um... Hey, Turnip.
So you ready for tomorrow?
Just got my new chisel!
Nice.
Sandwich?
TIPS
ONICS
K&C
Turnip's thinking of going.
You sculpt?
Um...
Show them the sandwich.
Well...
Here.
Who does it look like?
Whoa! It's VIOLA!
AH HA HA! YOU LIKE HER???

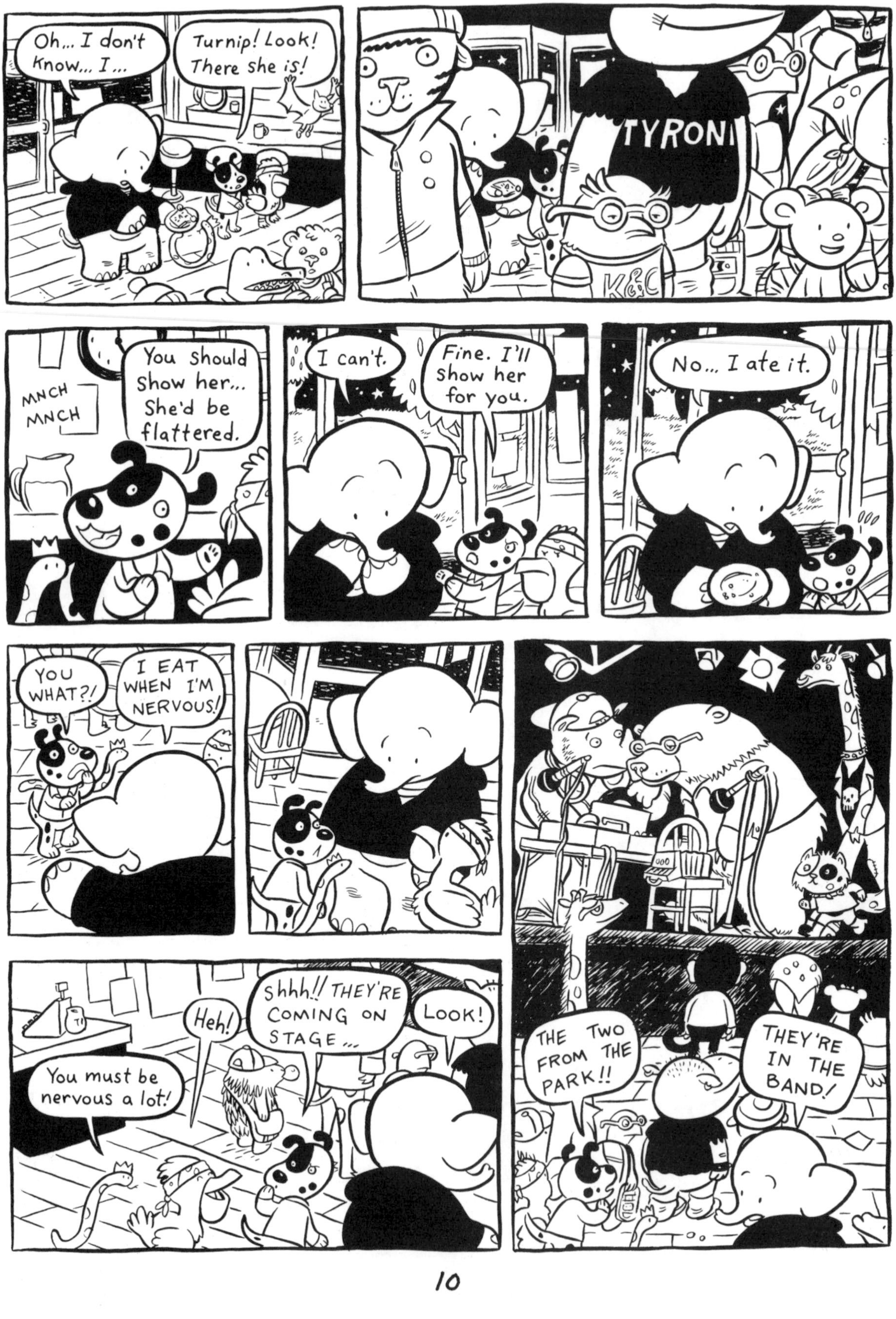

Oh... I don't know... I...
Turnip! Look! There she is!
TYRONI
K&C
MNCH MNCH
You should show her... She'd be flattered.
I can't.
Fine. I'll show her for you.
No... I ate it.
YOU WHAT?!
I EAT WHEN I'M NERVOUS!
You must be nervous a lot!
Heh!
Shhh!! THEY'RE COMING ON STAGE...
LOOK!
THE TWO FROM THE PARK!!
THEY'RE IN THE BAND!

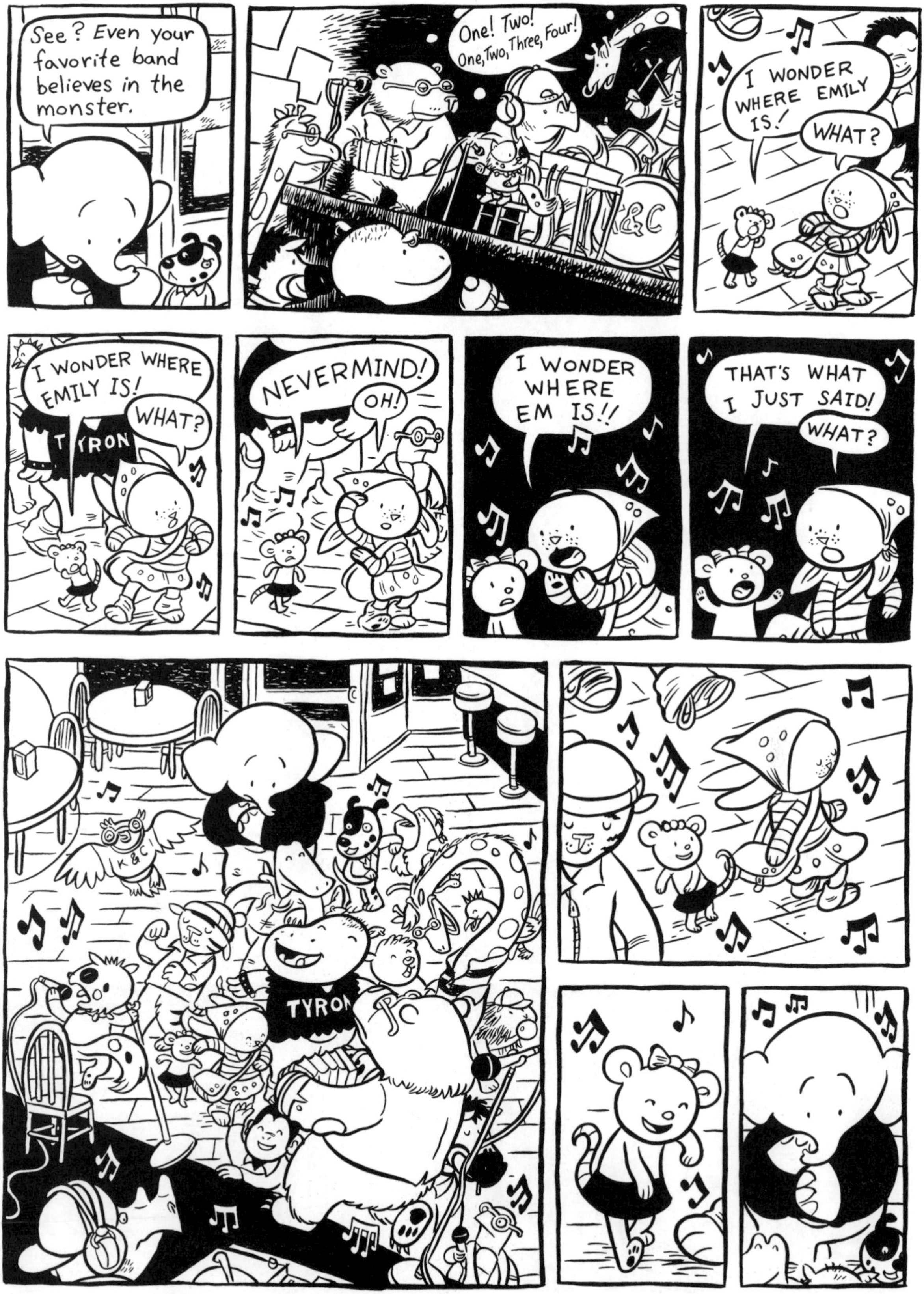
See? Even your favorite band believes in the monster.
One! Two! One, Two, Three, Four!
K&C
I WONDER WHERE EMILY IS!
WHAT?
I WONDER WHERE EMILY IS!
WHAT?
TYRON
NEVERMIND!
OH!
I WONDER WHERE EM IS!!
THAT'S WHAT I JUST SAID!
WHAT?
K&C
TYRON

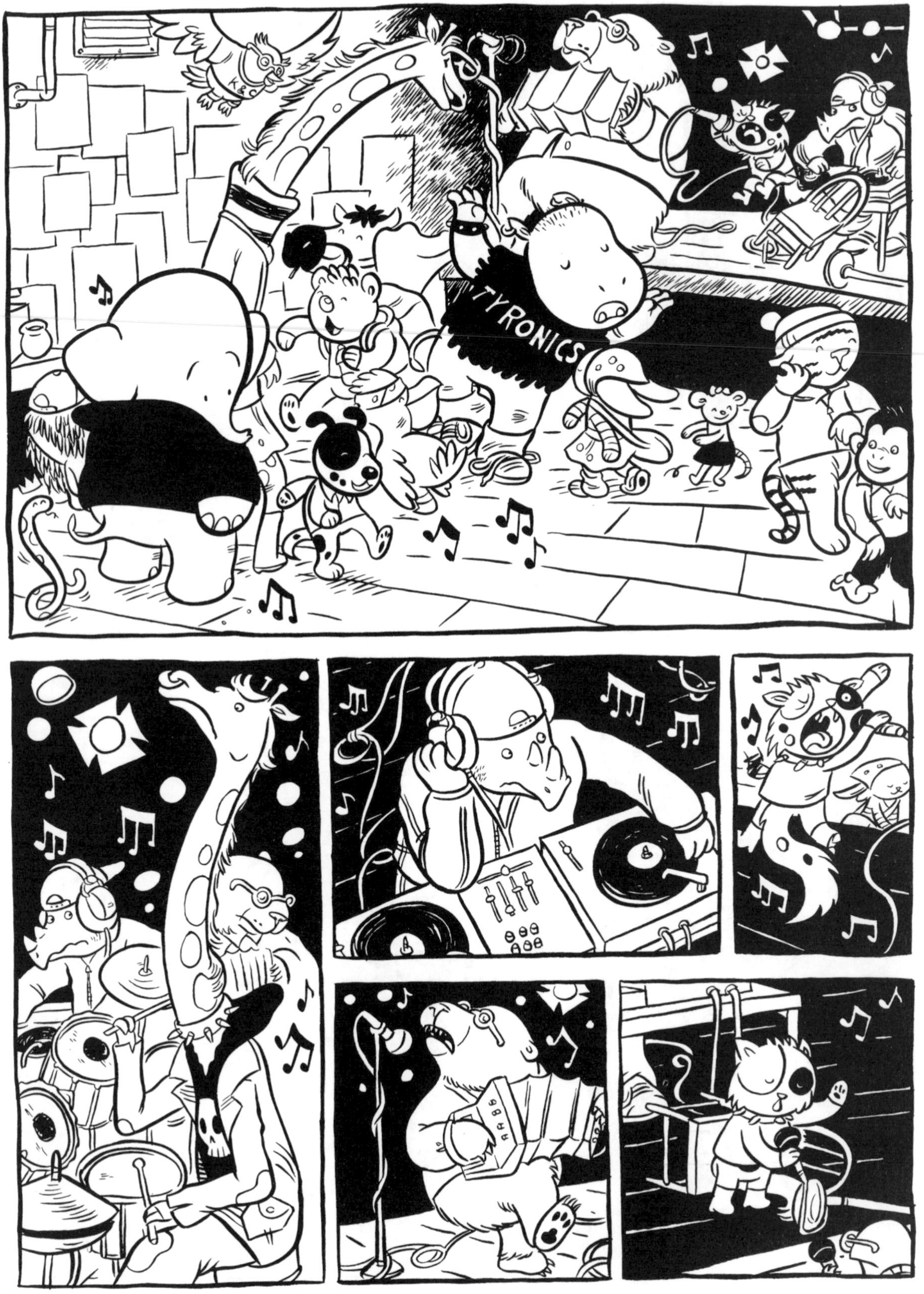
TYRONICS

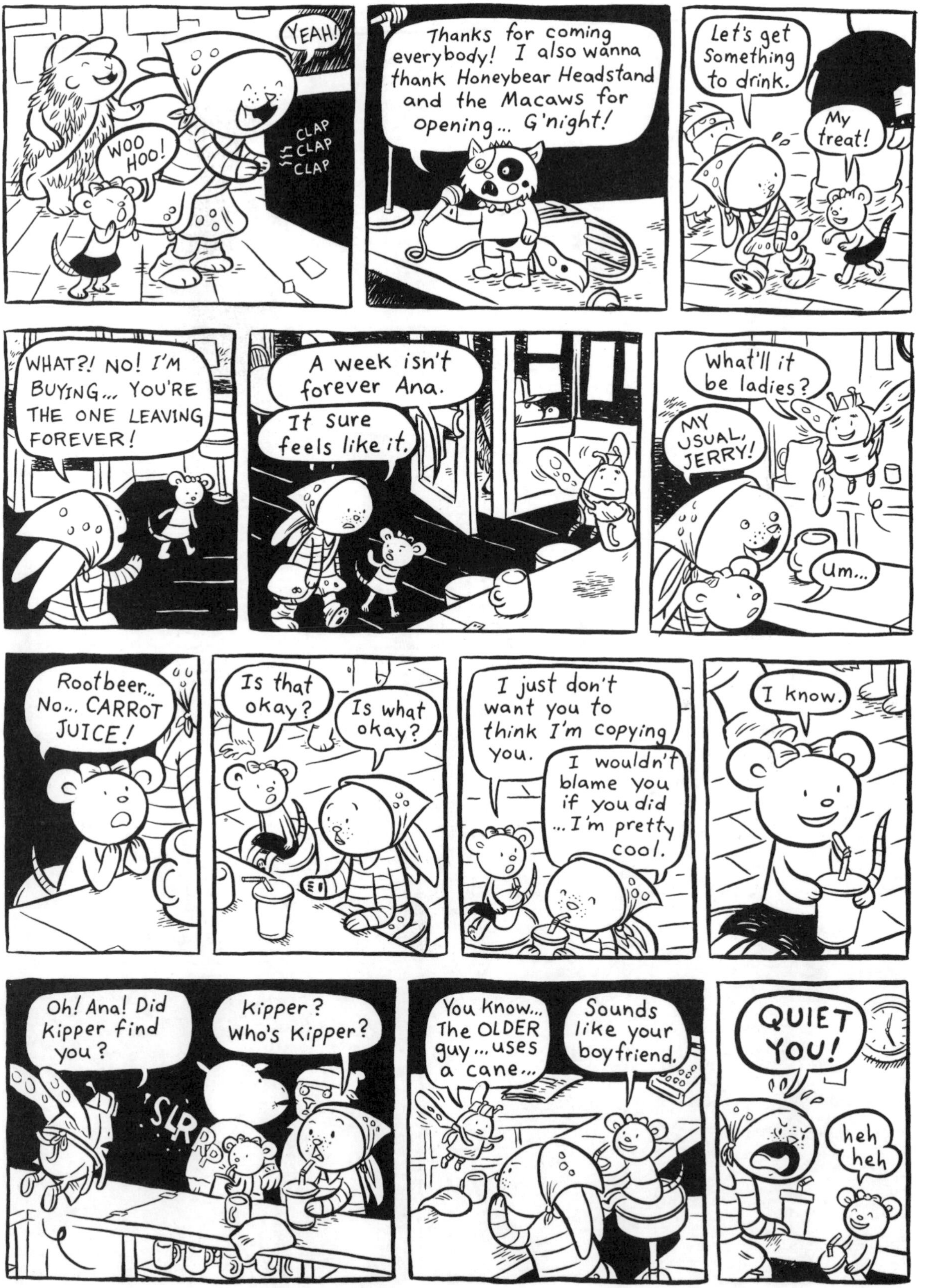
YEAH!
WOO HOO!
CLAP
CLAP
CLAP
Thanks for coming everybody! I also wanna thank Honeybear Headstand and the Macaws for opening... G'night!
Let's get something to drink.
My treat!
WHAT?! NO! I'M BUYING... YOU'RE THE ONE LEAVING FOREVER!
A week isn't forever Ana.
It sure feels like it.
What'll it be ladies?
MY USUAL, JERRY!
Um...
Rootbeer... No... CARROT JUICE!
Is that okay?
Is what okay?
I just don't want you to think I'm copying you.
I wouldn't blame you if you did ...I'm pretty cool.
I know.
Oh! Ana! Did Kipper find you?
Kipper? Who's Kipper?
SLRRP
You know... The OLDER guy... uses a cane...
Sounds like your boyfriend.
QUIET YOU!
heh heh

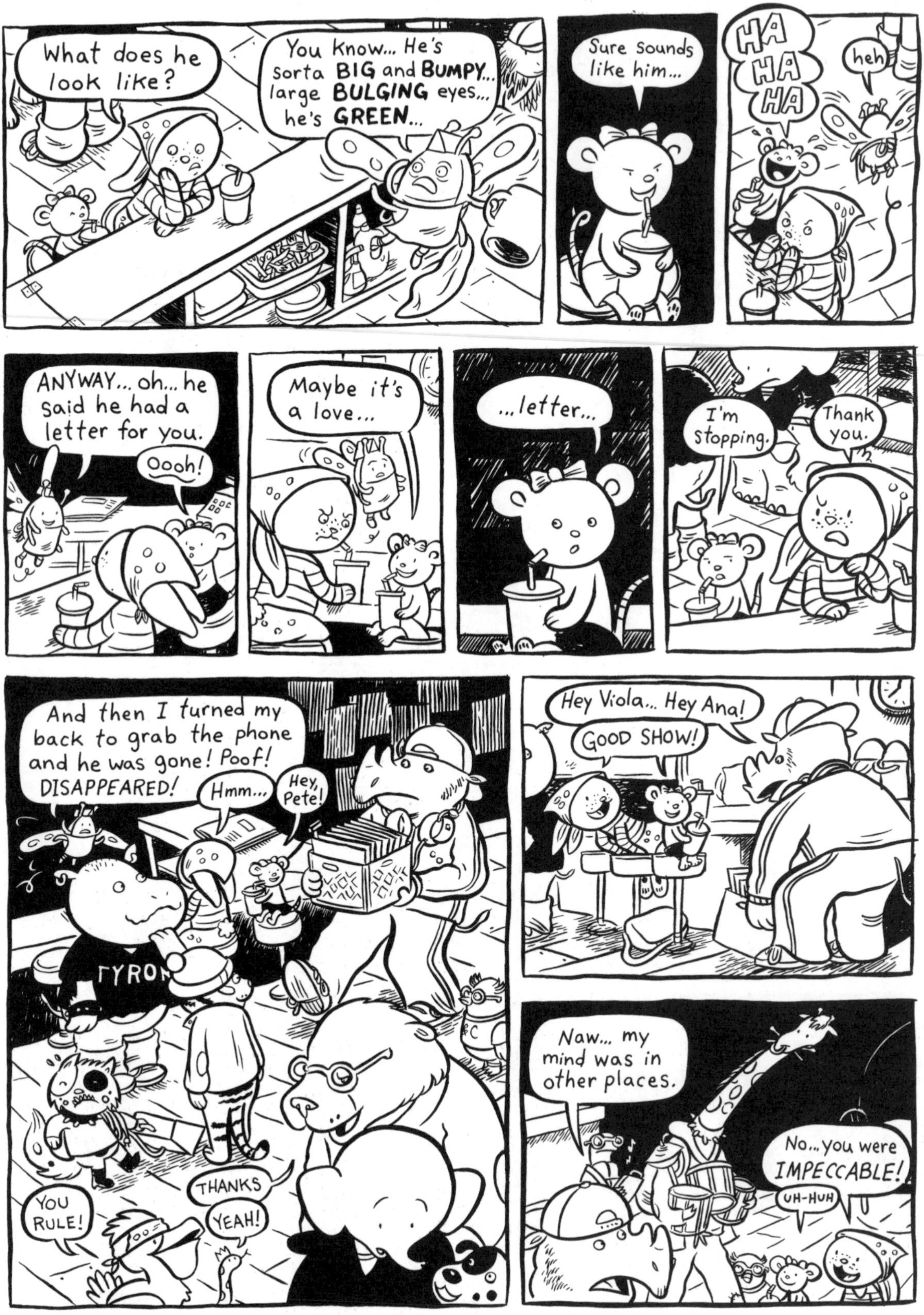
What does he look like?
You know... He's sorta BIG and BUMPY... large BULGING eyes... he's GREEN...
Sure sounds like him...
HA HA HA
heh
ANYWAY... oh... he said he had a letter for you.
Oooh!
Maybe it's a love...
...letter...
I'm stopping.
Thank you.
And then I turned my back to grab the phone and he was gone! Poof! DISAPPEARED!
Hmm...
Hey, Pete!
TYRO
YOU RULE!
THANKS
YEAH!
Hey Viola... Hey Ana!
GOOD SHOW!
Naw... my mind was in other places.
No... you were IMPECCABLE!
UH-HUH

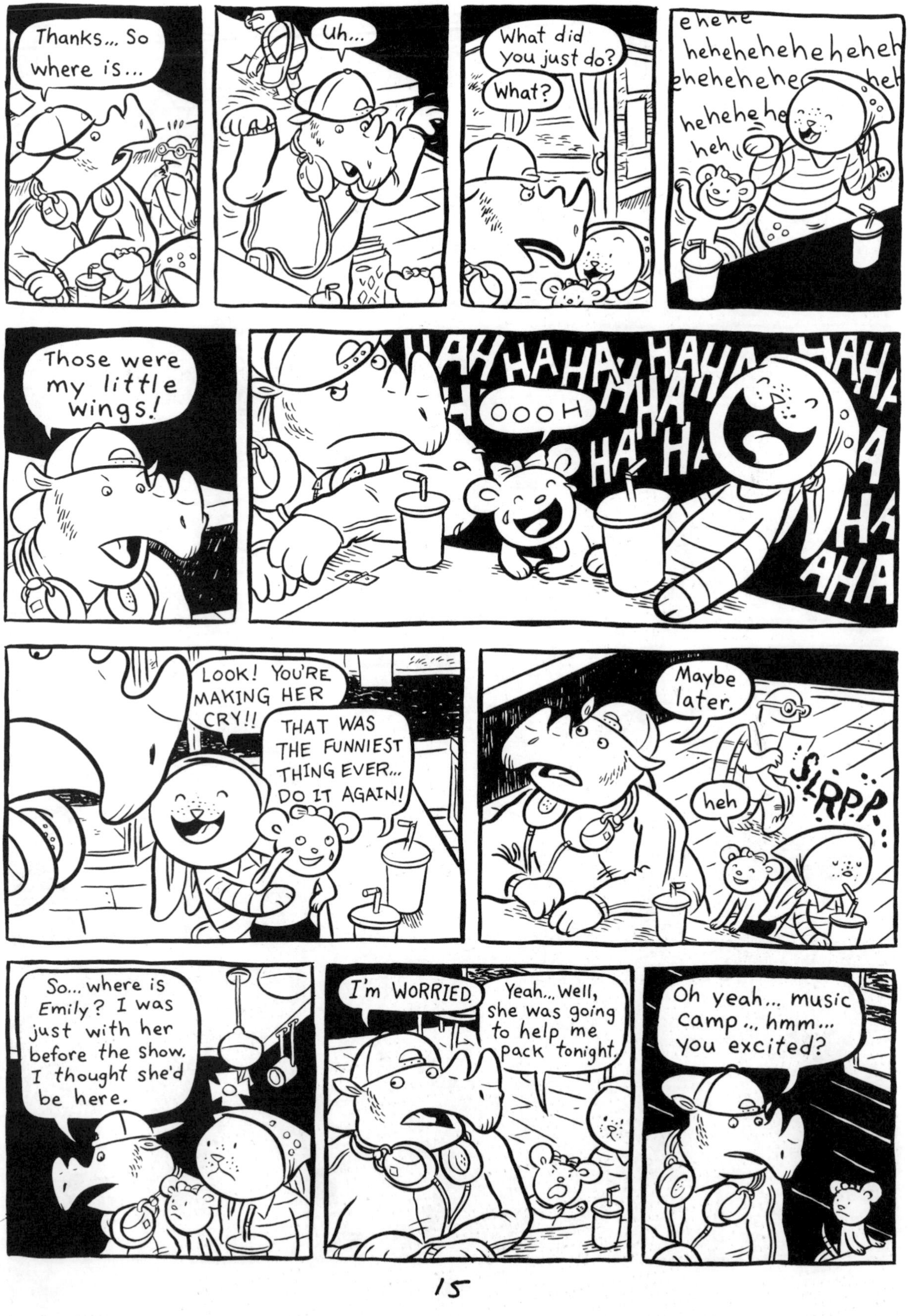
Thanks... So where is...
Uh...
What did you just do?
What?
ehehe hehehehehehehehehehehe hehehehe heh
Those were my little wings!
HA HA HA HA HA HA HA HA HA HA HA HA HA HA AHA
OOOH
LOOK! YOU'RE MAKING HER CRY!!
THAT WAS THE FUNNIEST THING EVER... DO IT AGAIN!
Maybe later.
heh
SLRPP
So... where is Emily? I was just with her before the show. I thought she'd be here.
I'm WORRIED.
Yeah... Well, she was going to help me pack tonight.
Oh yeah... music camp... hmm... you excited?

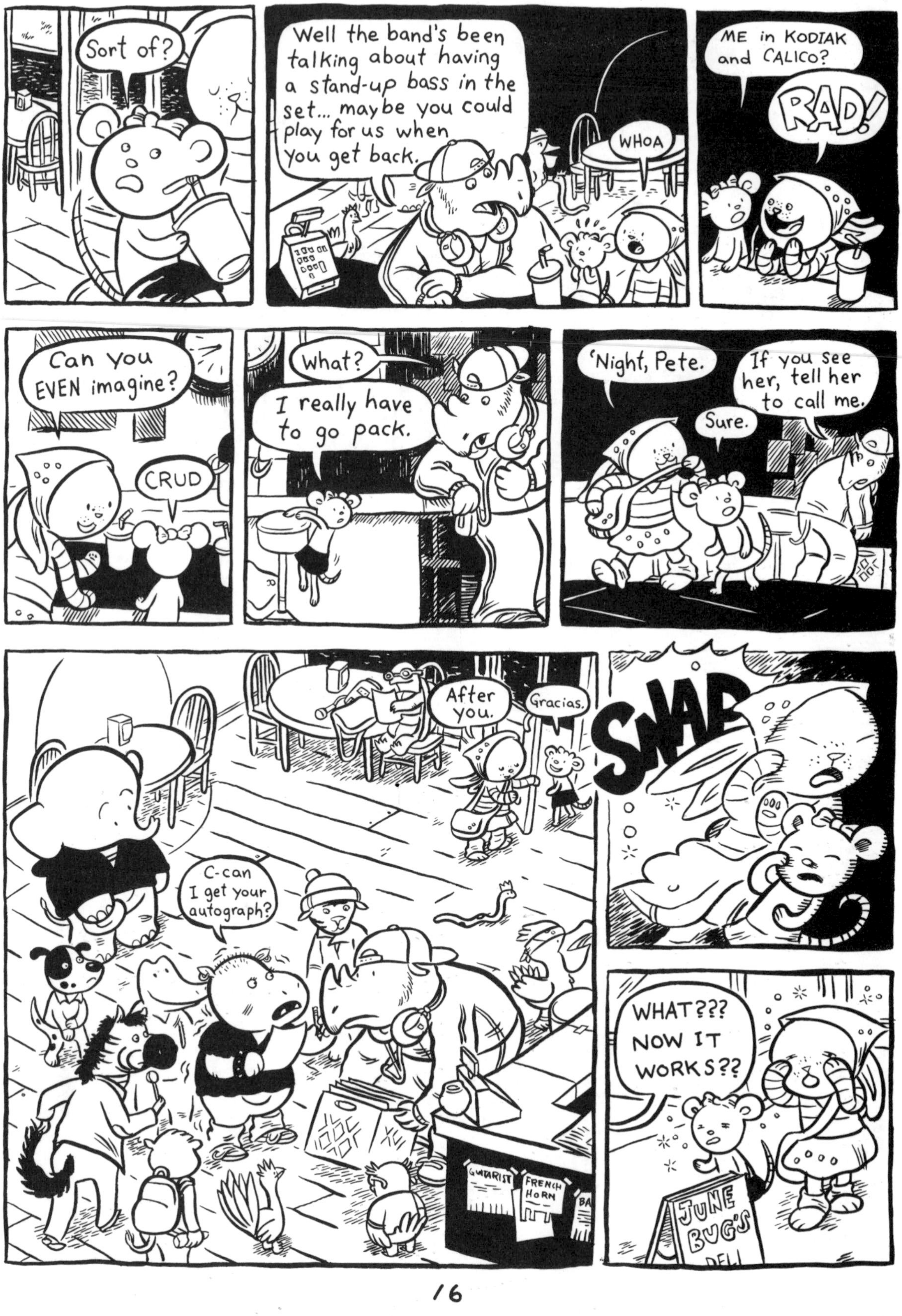

Sort of?
Well the band's been talking about having a stand-up bass in the set... maybe you could play for us when you get back.
WHOA
ME in KODIAK and CALICO?
RAD!
Can you EVEN imagine?
CRUD
What?
I really have to go pack.
'Night, Pete.
If you see her, tell her to call me.
Sure.
After you.
Gracias.
C-can I get your autograph?
GUITARIST
FRENCH HORN
SNAP
WHAT??? NOW IT WORKS??
JUNE BUG'S

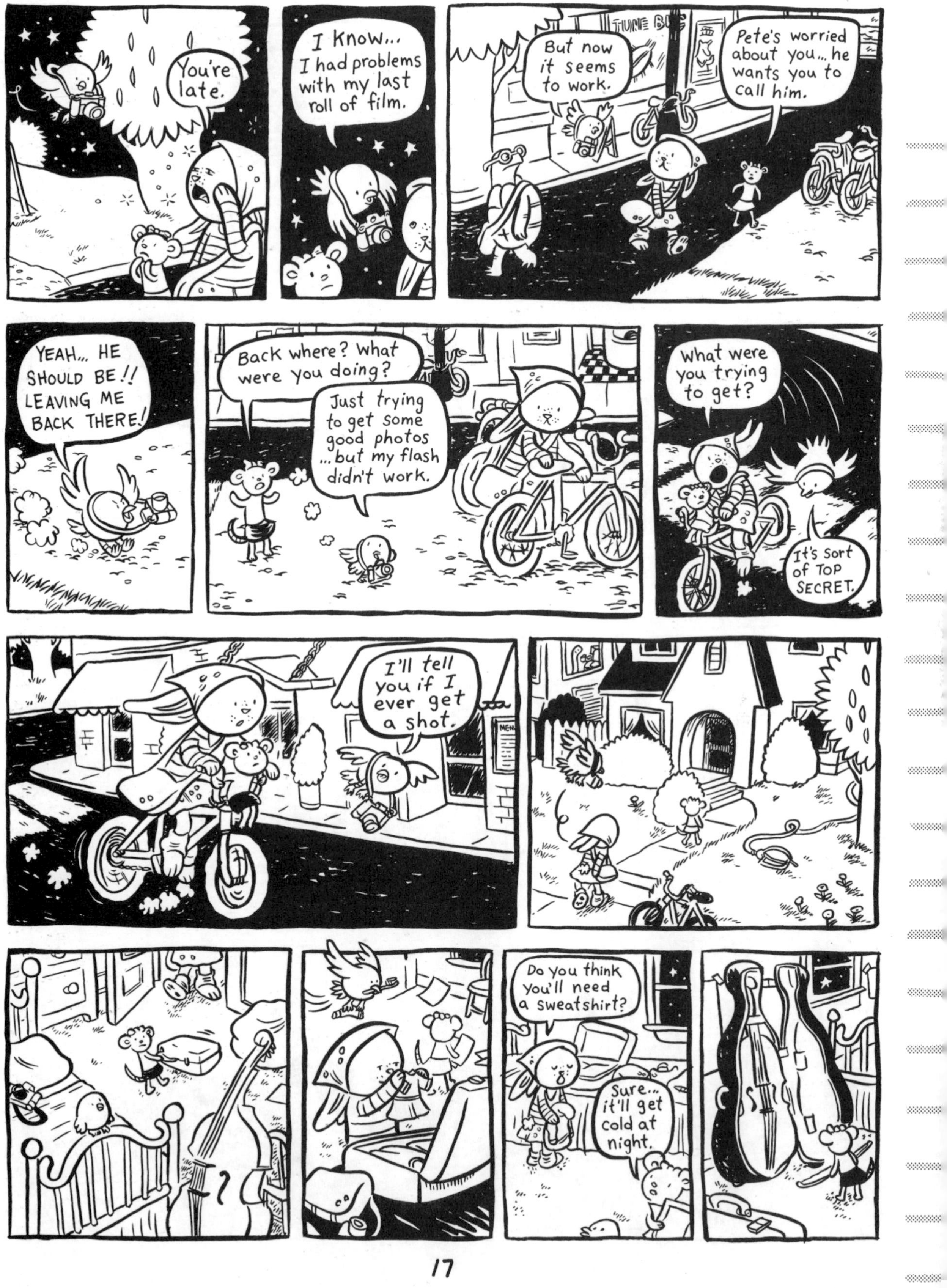
You're late.
I know... I had problems with my last roll of film.
But now it seems to work.
Pete's worried about you... he wants you to call him.
YEAH... HE SHOULD BE!! LEAVING ME BACK THERE!
Back where? What were you doing?
Just trying to get some good photos ...but my flash didn't work.
What were you trying to get?
It's sort of TOP SECRET.
I'll tell you if I ever get a shot.
Do you think you'll need a sweatshirt?
Sure... it'll get cold at night.

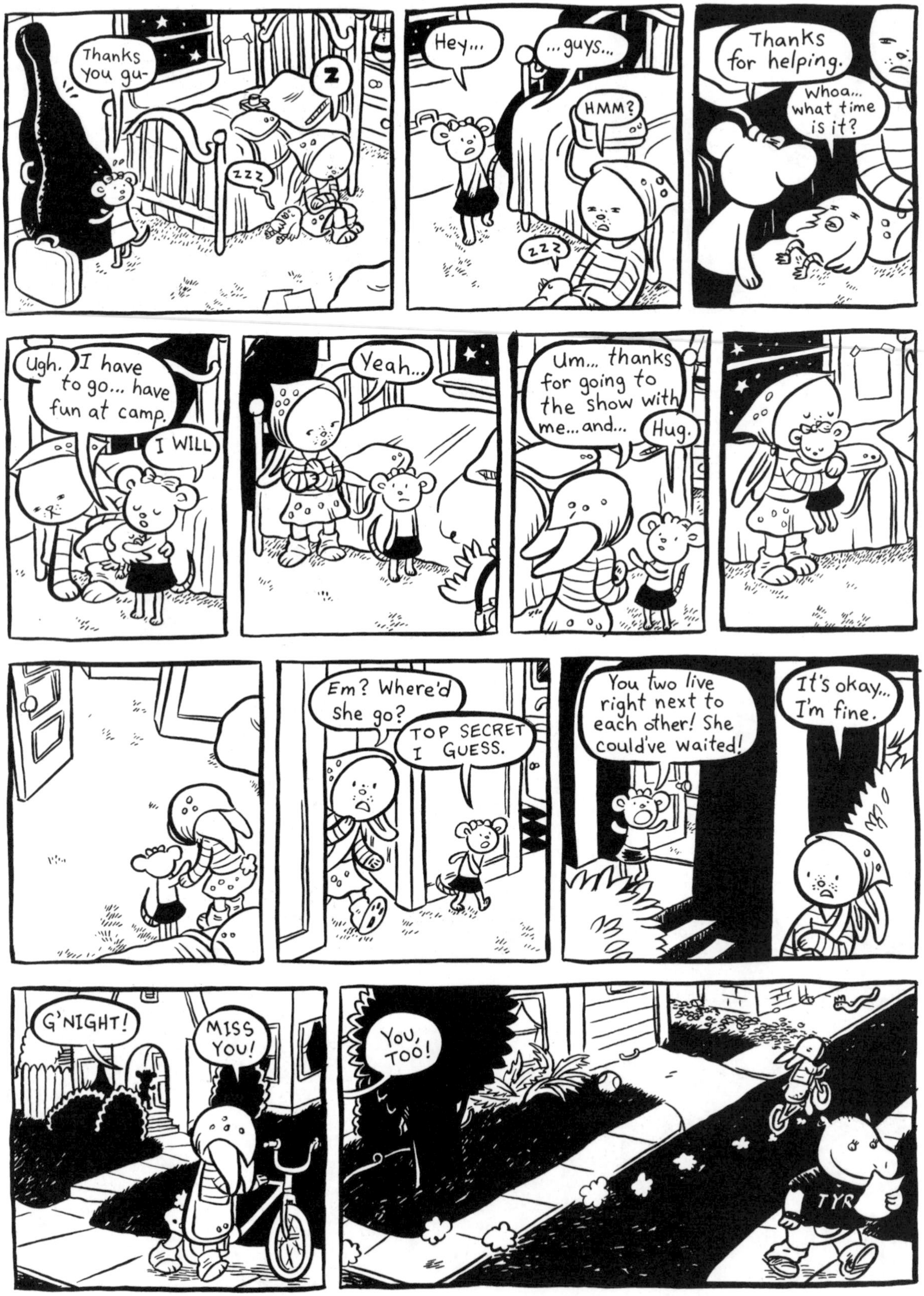
Thanks you gu-
Z
ZZZ
Hey...
...guys...
HMM?
ZZZ
Thanks for helping.
Whoa... what time is it?
Ugh. I have to go... have fun at camp.
I WILL
Yeah...
Um... thanks for going to the show with me... and...
Hug.
Em? Where'd she go?
TOP SECRET I GUESS.
You two live right next to each other! She could've waited!
It's okay... I'm fine.
G'NIGHT!
MISS YOU!
YOU, TOO!
TYR

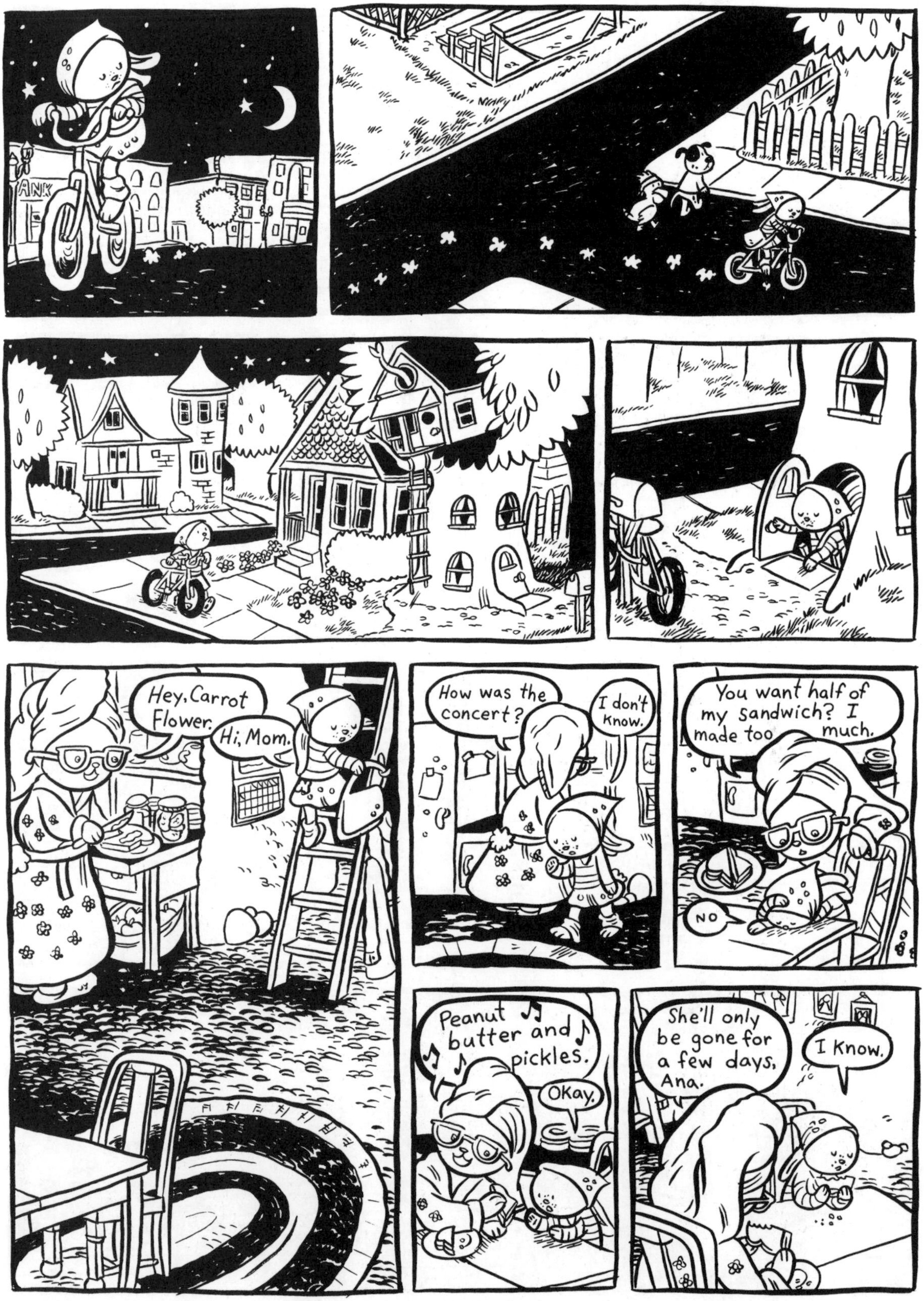
Hey, Carrot Flower.
Hi, Mom.
How was the concert?
I don't know.
You want half of my sandwich? I made too much.
NO
Peanut butter and pickles.
Okay.
She'll only be gone for a few days, Ana.
I know.

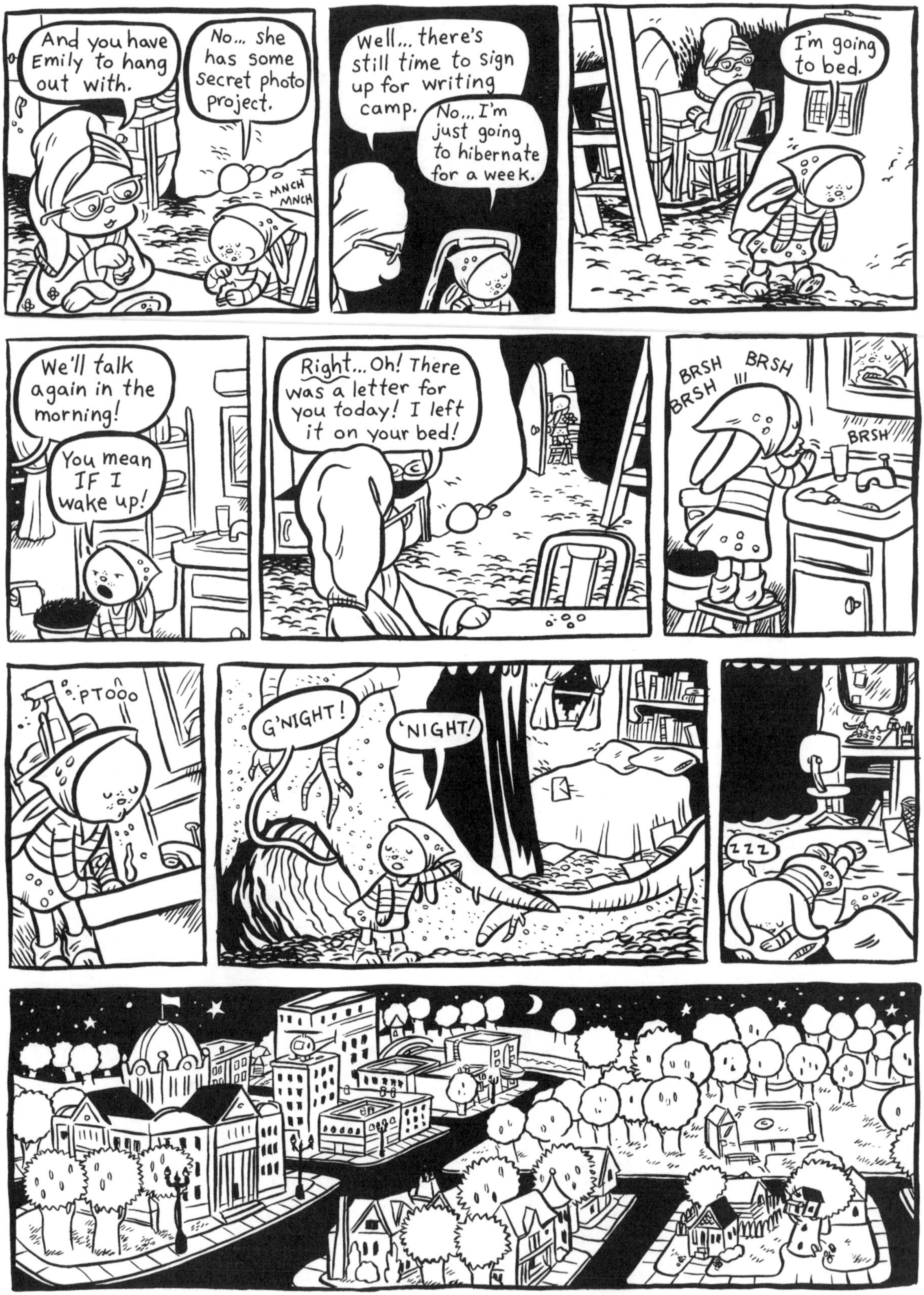
And you have Emily to hang out with.
No... she has some secret photo project.
MNCH MNCH
Well... there's still time to sign up for writing camp.
No... I'm just going to hibernate for a week.
I'm going to bed.
We'll talk again in the morning!
You mean IF I wake up!
Right... Oh! There was a letter for you today! I left it on your bed!
BRSH BRSH BRSH
BRSH
PTOOO
G'NIGHT!
'NIGHT!
ZZZ

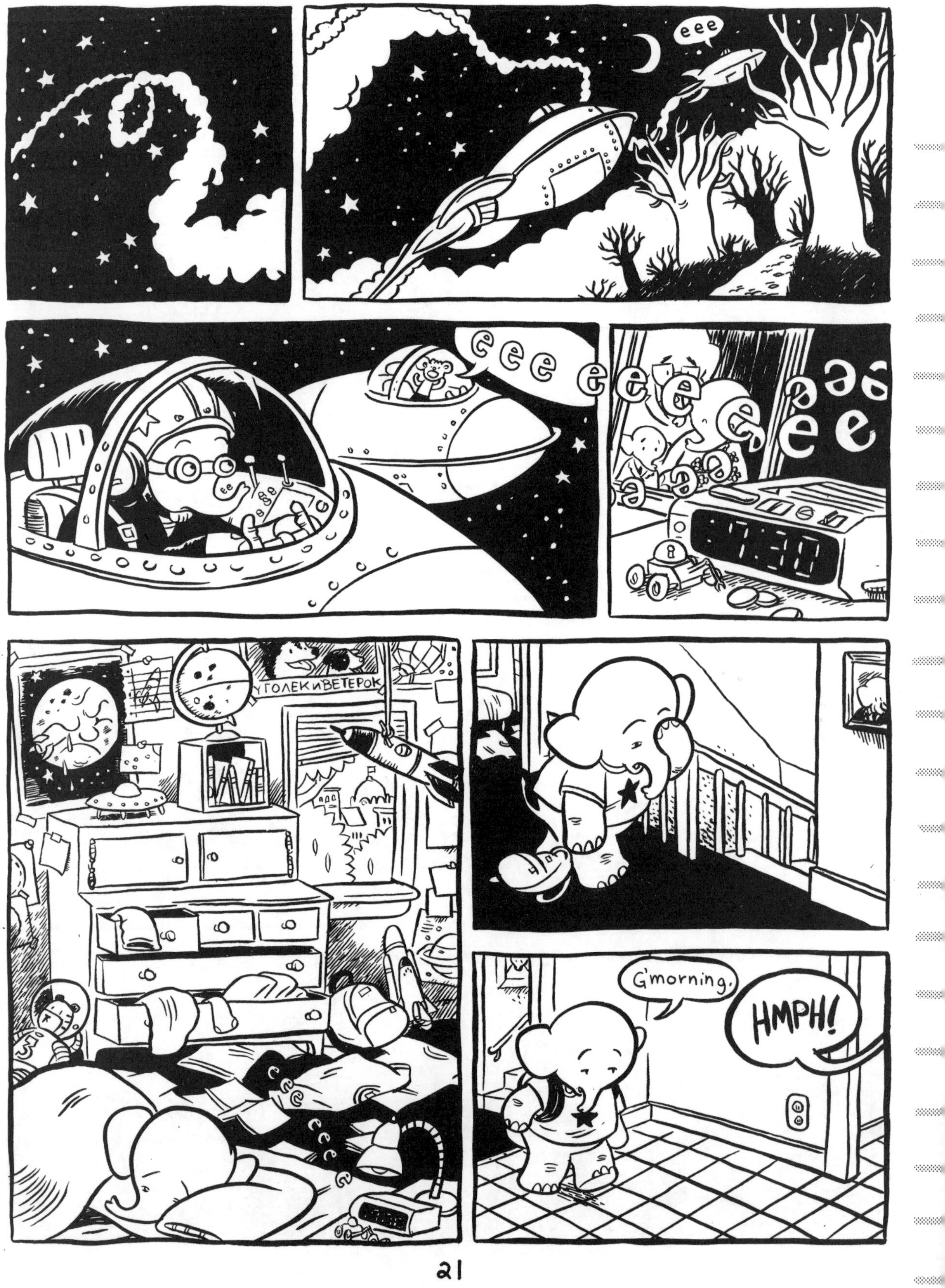
eee
eee
УГОЛЕКиВЕТЕРОК
G'morning.
HMPH!

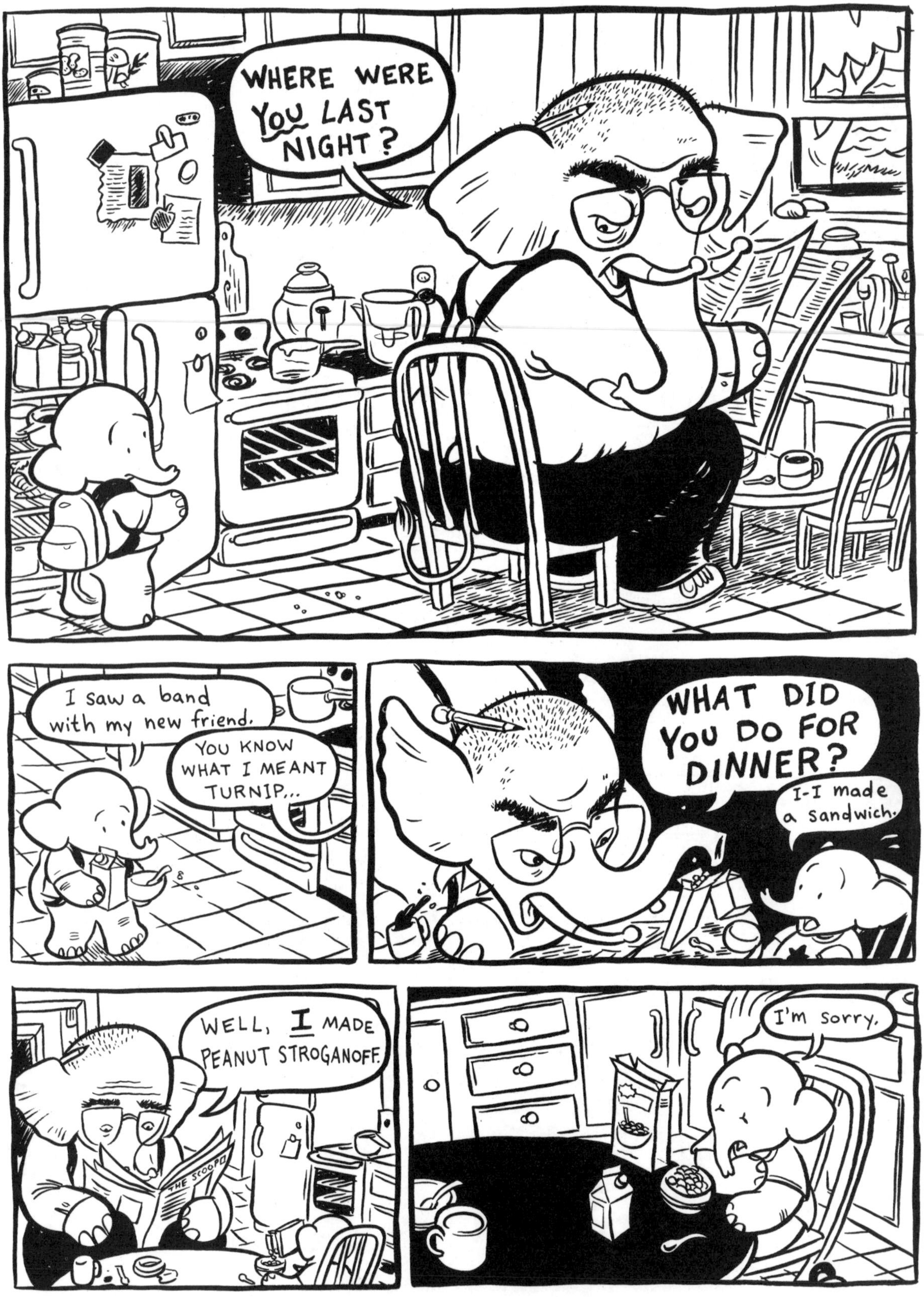
WHERE WERE YOU LAST NIGHT?
I saw a band with my new friend.
YOU KNOW WHAT I MEANT TURNIP...
WHAT DID YOU DO FOR DINNER?
I-I made a sandwich.
WELL, I MADE PEANUT STROGANOFF.
THE SCOOP
I'm sorry.

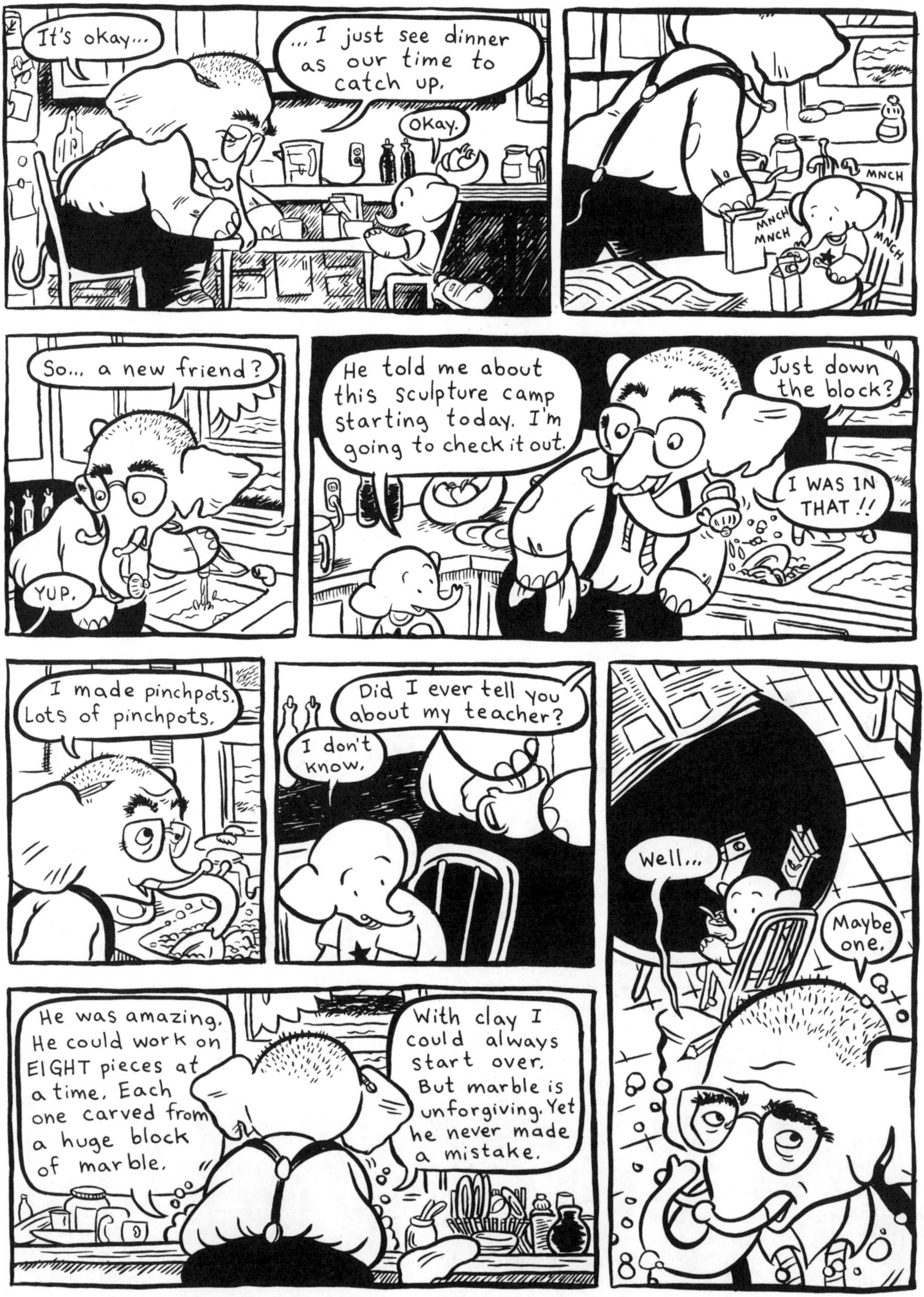
It's okay...
...I just see dinner as our time to catch up.
Okay.
MNCH
MNCH MNCH
MNCH
So... a new friend?
YUP.
He told me about this sculpture camp starting today. I'm going to check it out.
Just down the block?
I WAS IN THAT!!
I made pinchpots. Lots of pinchpots.
Did I ever tell you about my teacher?
I don't know.
Well...
Maybe one.
He was amazing. He could work on EIGHT pieces at a time. Each one carved from a huge block of marble.
With clay I could always start over. But marble is unforgiving. Yet he never made a mistake.

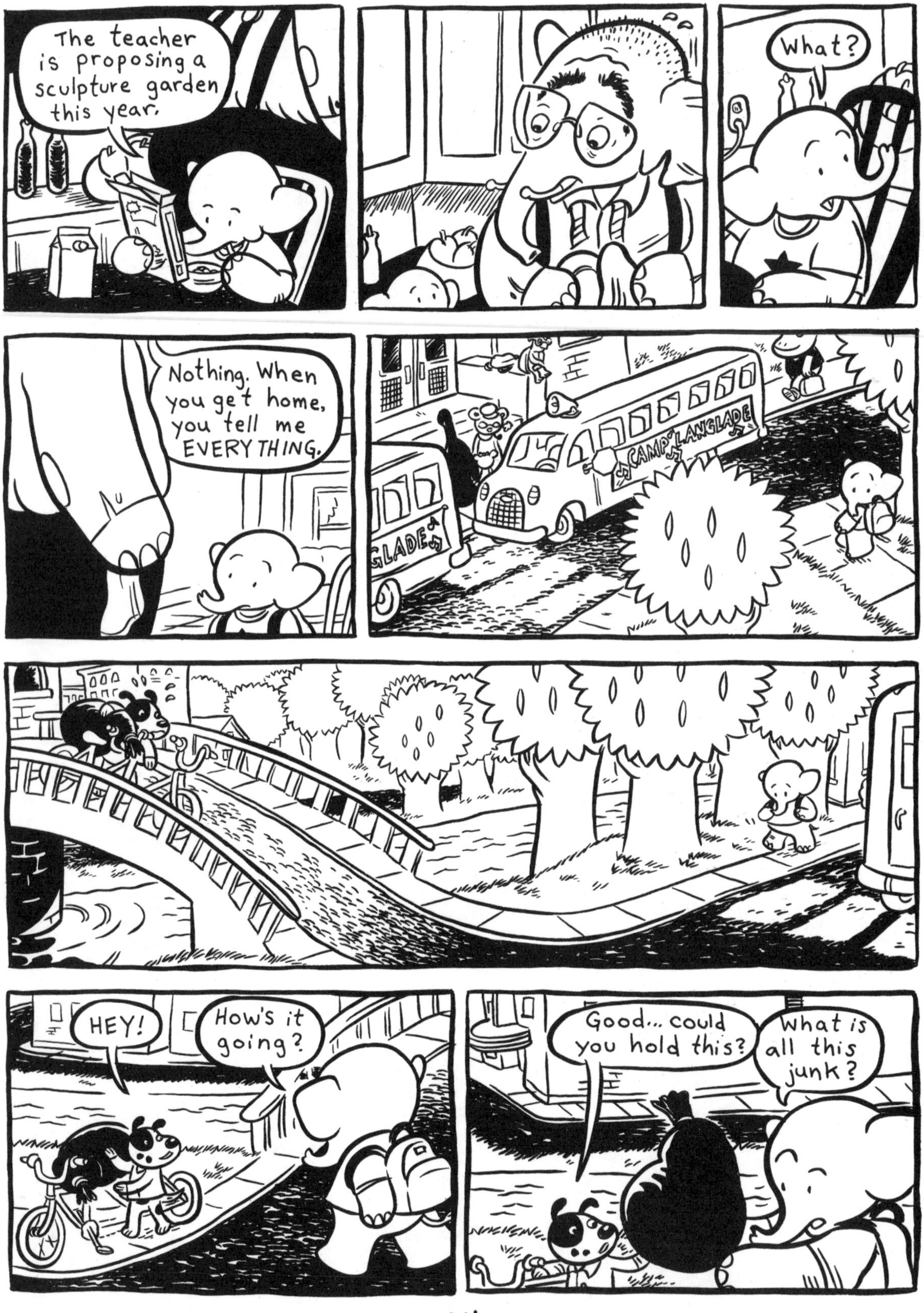
The teacher is proposing a sculpture garden this year.
What?
Nothing. When you get home, you tell me EVERYTHING.
CAMP LANGLADE
GLADE
HEY!
How's it going?
Good... could you hold this?
What is all this junk?

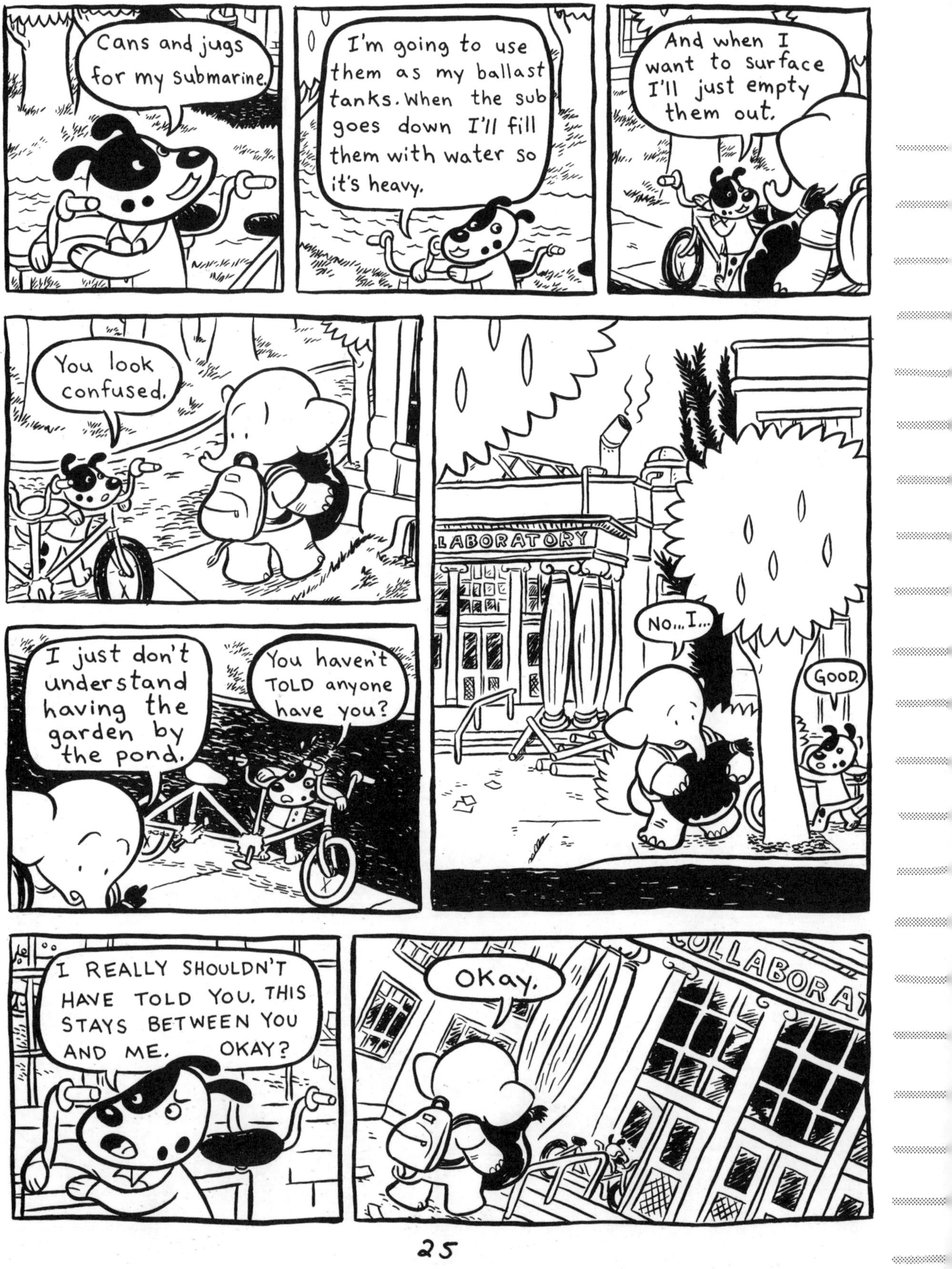
Cans and jugs for my submarine.
I'm going to use them as my ballast tanks. When the sub goes down I'll fill them with water so it's heavy.
And when I want to surface I'll just empty them out.
You look confused.
LABORATORY
No... I...
GOOD.
I just don't understand having the garden by the pond.
You haven't TOLD anyone have you?
I REALLY SHOULDN'T HAVE TOLD YOU. THIS STAYS BETWEEN YOU AND ME. OKAY?
Okay.
COLLABORAT

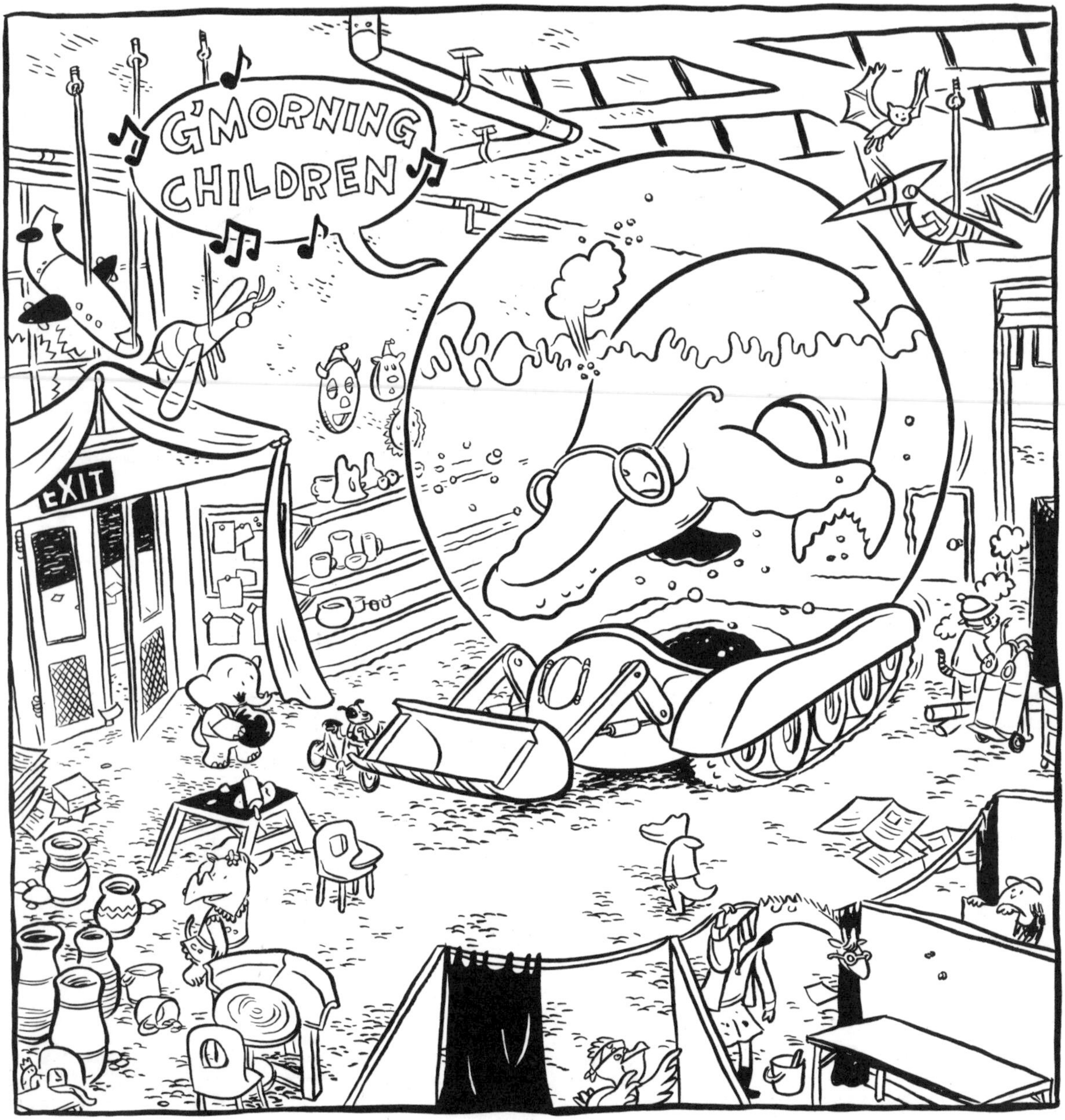
G'MORNING CHILDREN
EXIT

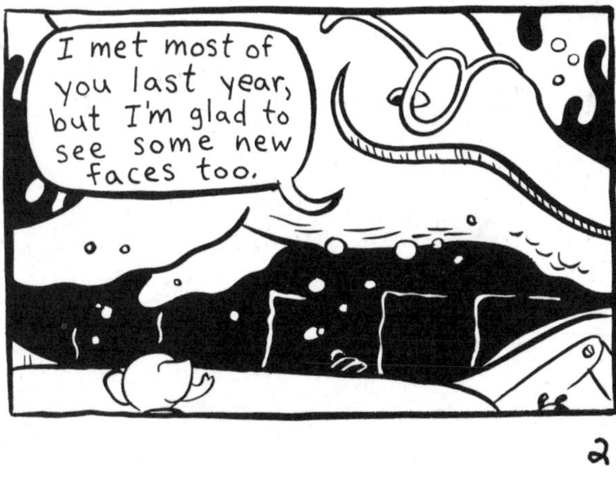
I met most of you last year, but I'm glad to see some new faces too.

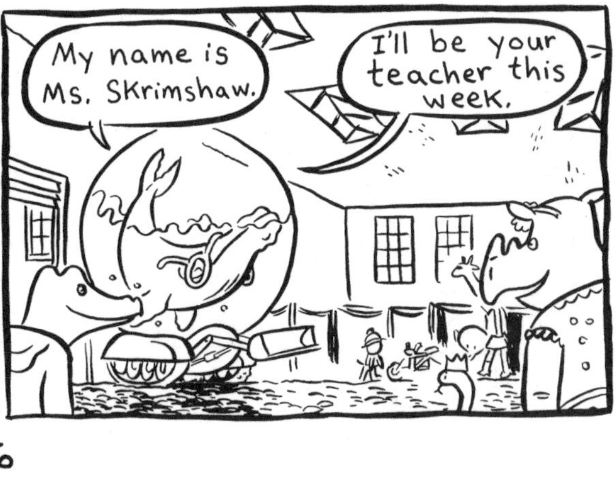
My name is Ms. Skrimshaw.
I'll be your teacher this week.

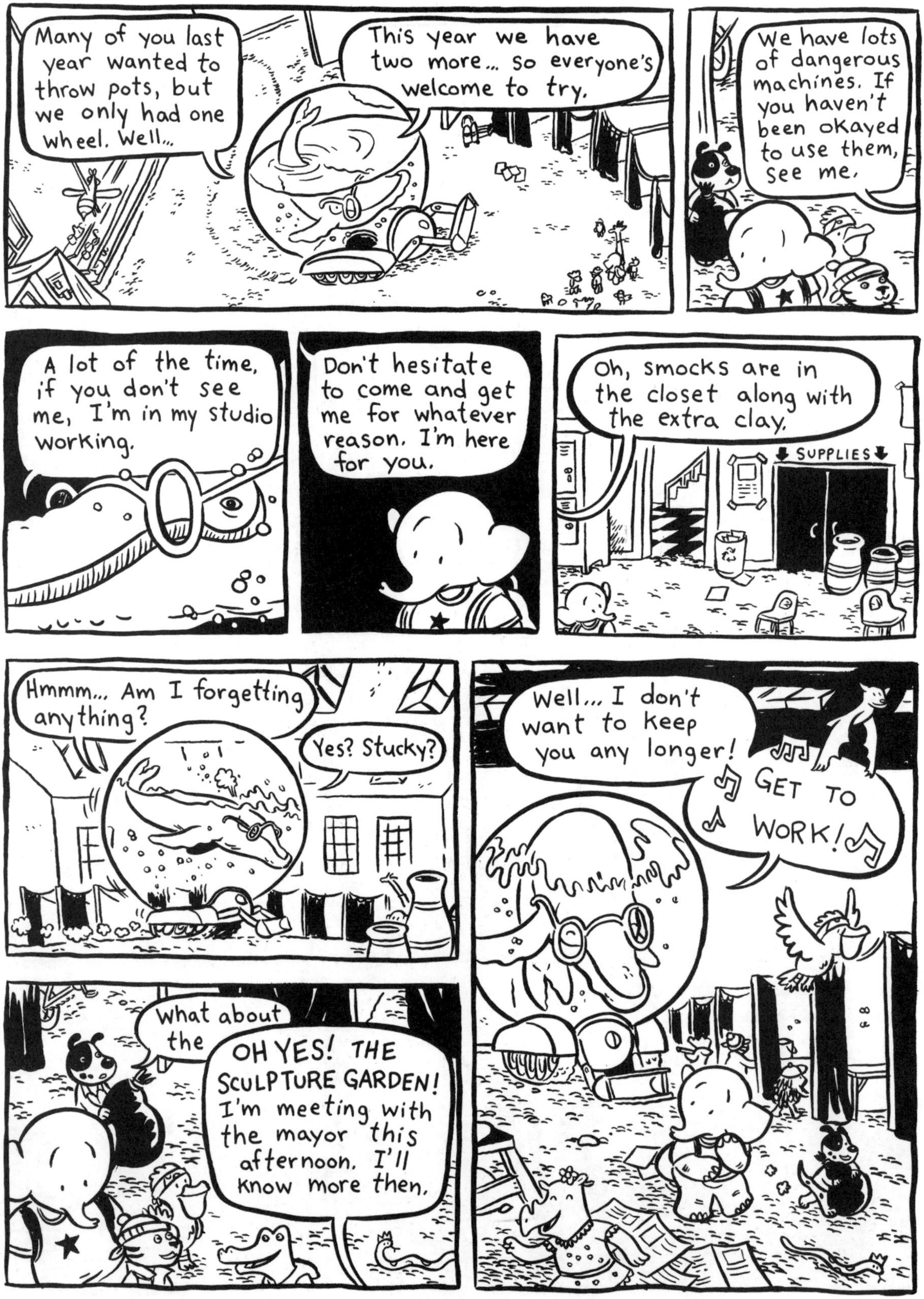
Many of you last year wanted to throw pots, but we only had one wheel. Well...
This year we have two more... so everyone's welcome to try.
We have lots of dangerous machines. If you haven't been okayed to use them, see me.
A lot of the time, if you don't see me, I'm in my studio working.
Don't hesitate to come and get me for whatever reason. I'm here for you.
Oh, smocks are in the closet along with the extra clay.
SUPPLIES
Hmmm... Am I forgetting anything?
Yes? Stucky?
What about the
OH YES! THE SCULPTURE GARDEN! I'm meeting with the mayor this afternoon. I'll know more then.
Well... I don't want to keep you any longer!
GET TO WORK!

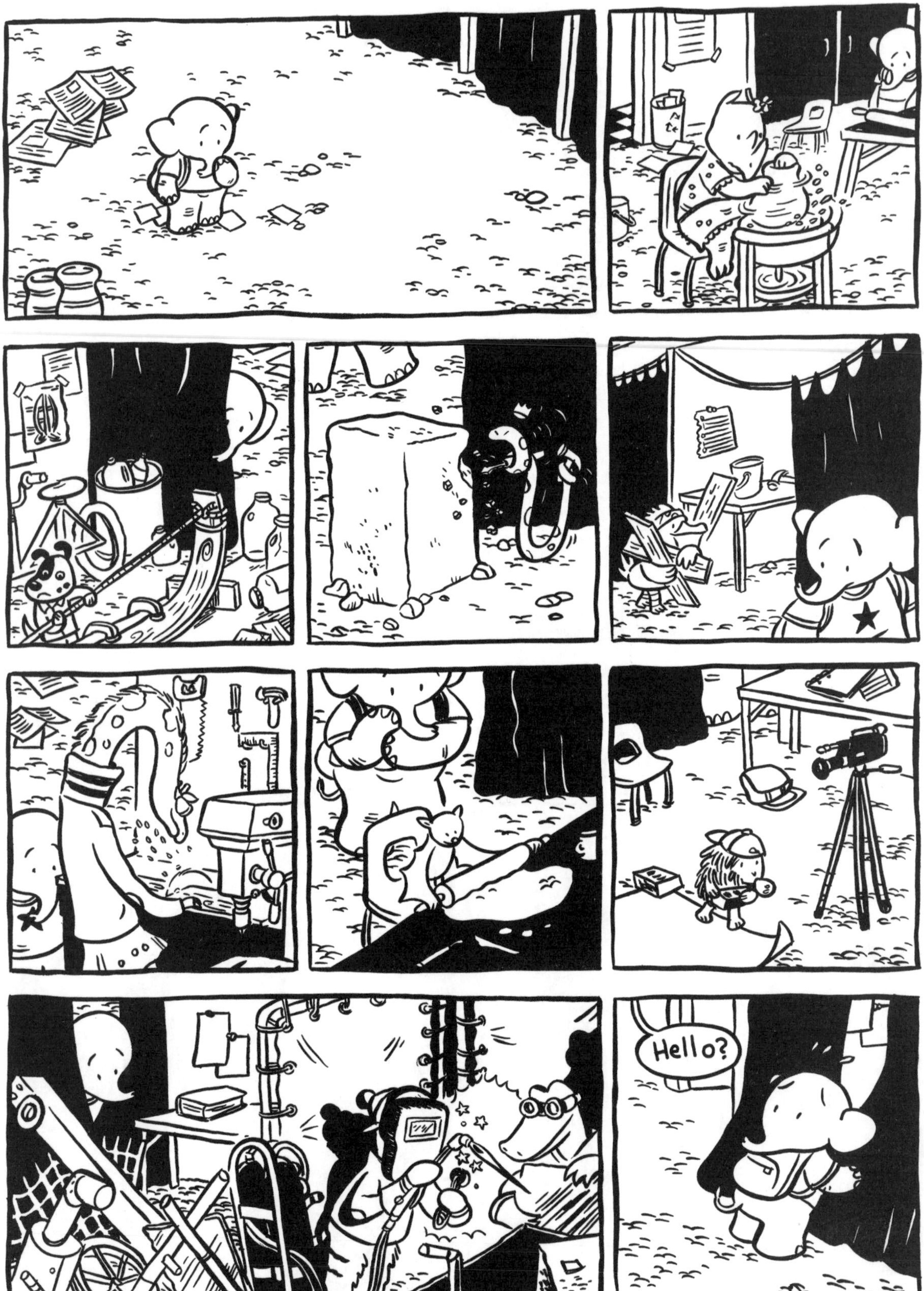
Hello?

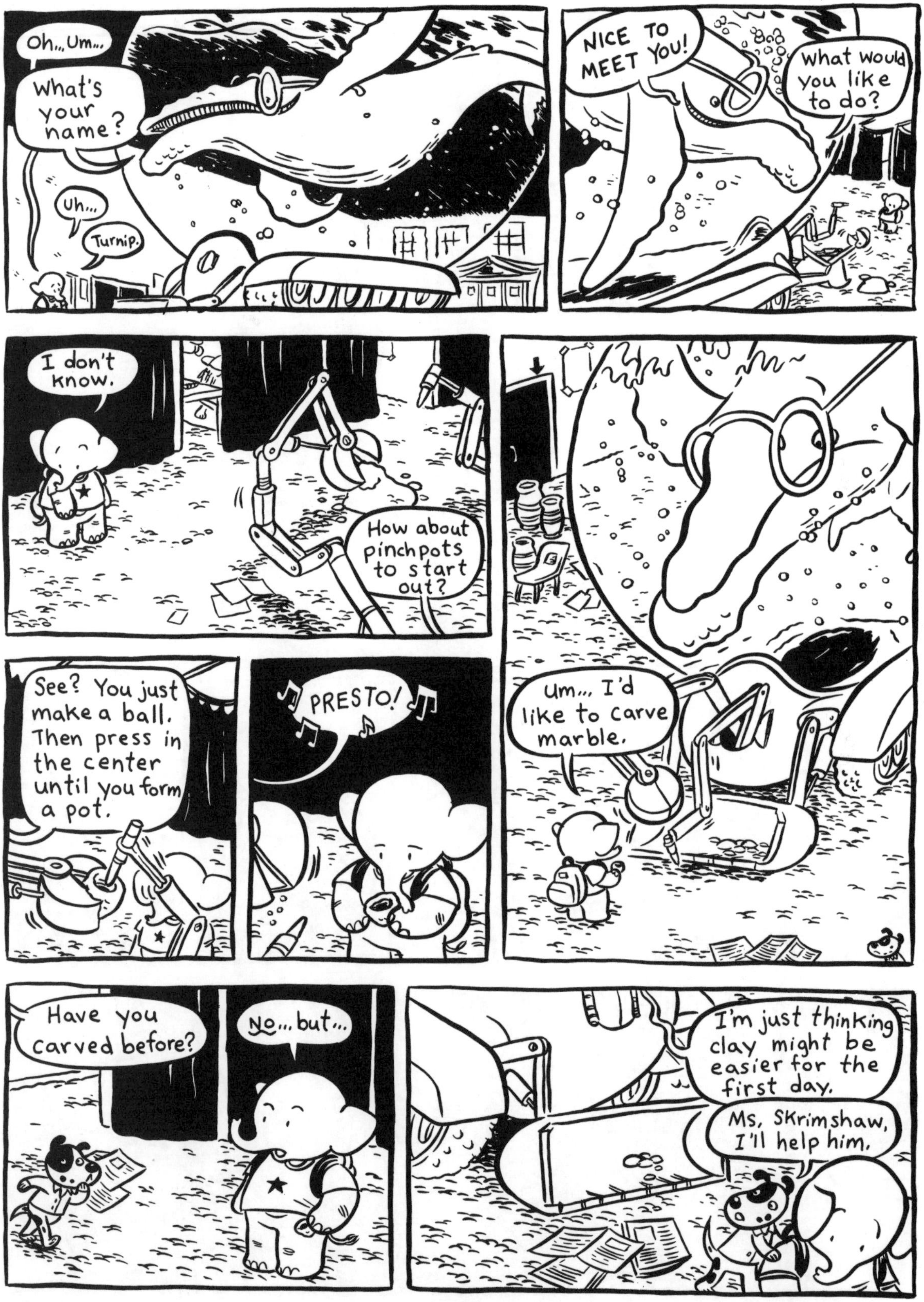

Oh... Um...
What's your name?
Uh...
Turnip.
NICE TO MEET YOU!
What would you like to do?
I don't know.
How about pinchpots to start out?
Um... I'd like to carve marble.
See? You just make a ball. Then press in the center until you form a pot.
PRESTO!
Have you carved before?
No... but...
I'm just thinking clay might be easier for the first day.
Ms. Skrimshaw, I'll help him.

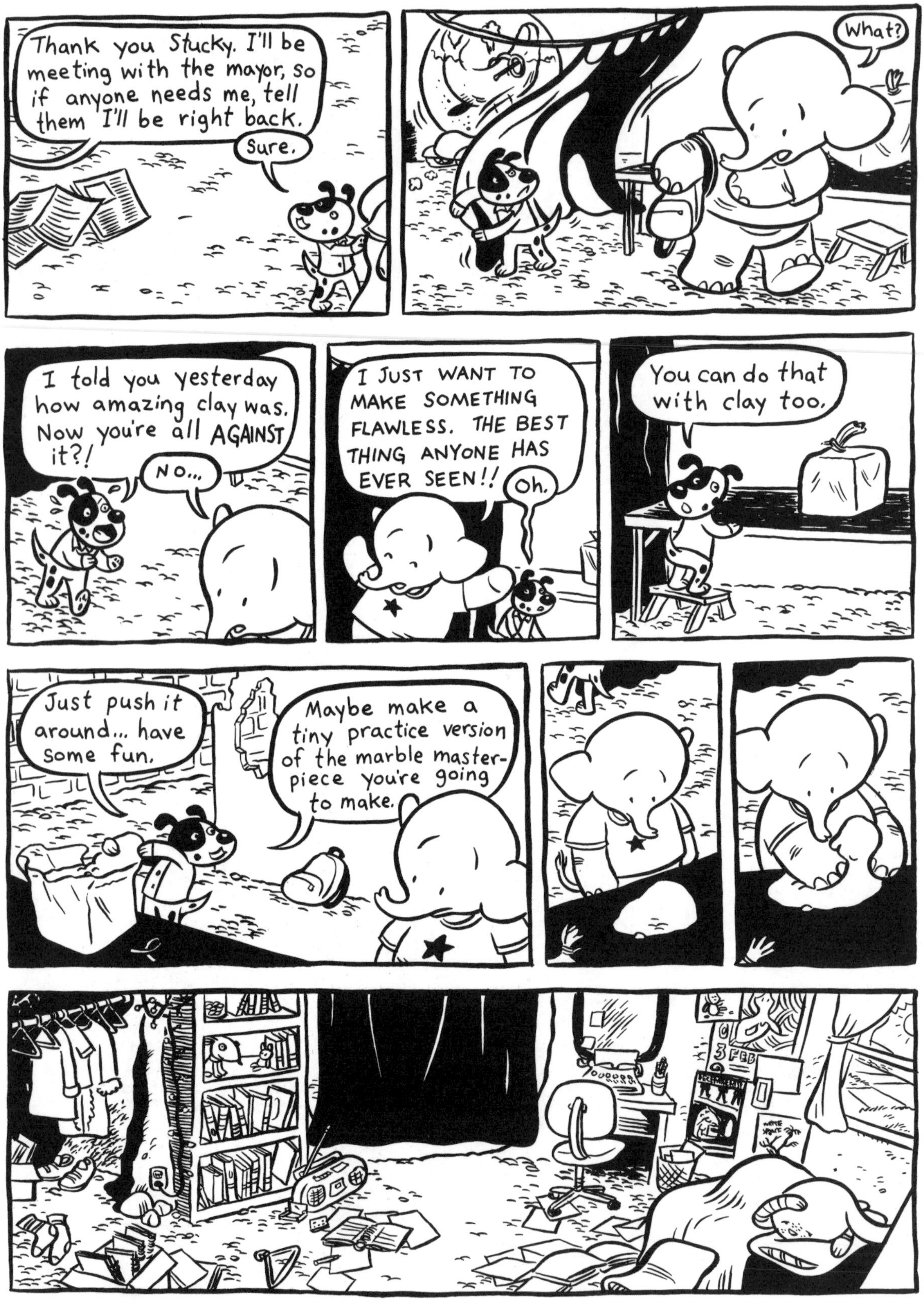

Thank you Stucky. I'll be meeting with the mayor, so if anyone needs me, tell them I'll be right back.
Sure.
What?
I told you yesterday how amazing clay was. Now you're all AGAINST it?!
NO...
I JUST WANT TO MAKE SOMETHING FLAWLESS. THE BEST THING ANYONE HAS EVER SEEN!!
Oh.
You can do that with clay too.
Just push it around... have some fun.
Maybe make a tiny practice version of the marble masterpiece you're going to make.

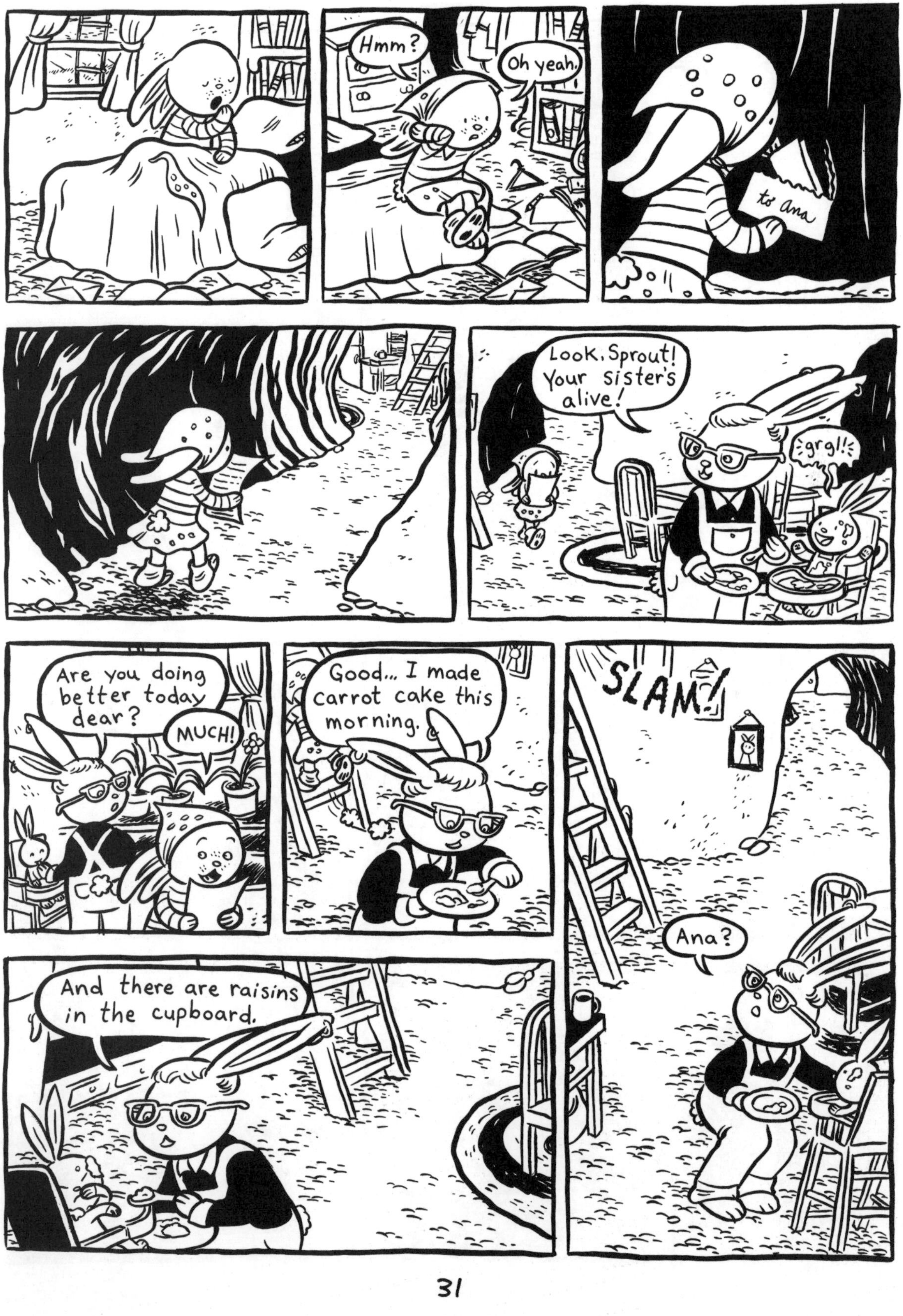
Hmm?
Oh yeah.
to Ana
Look, Sprout! Your sister's alive!
grgl!
Are you doing better today dear?
MUCH!
Good... I made carrot cake this morning.
SLAM!
And there are raisins in the cupboard.
Ana?

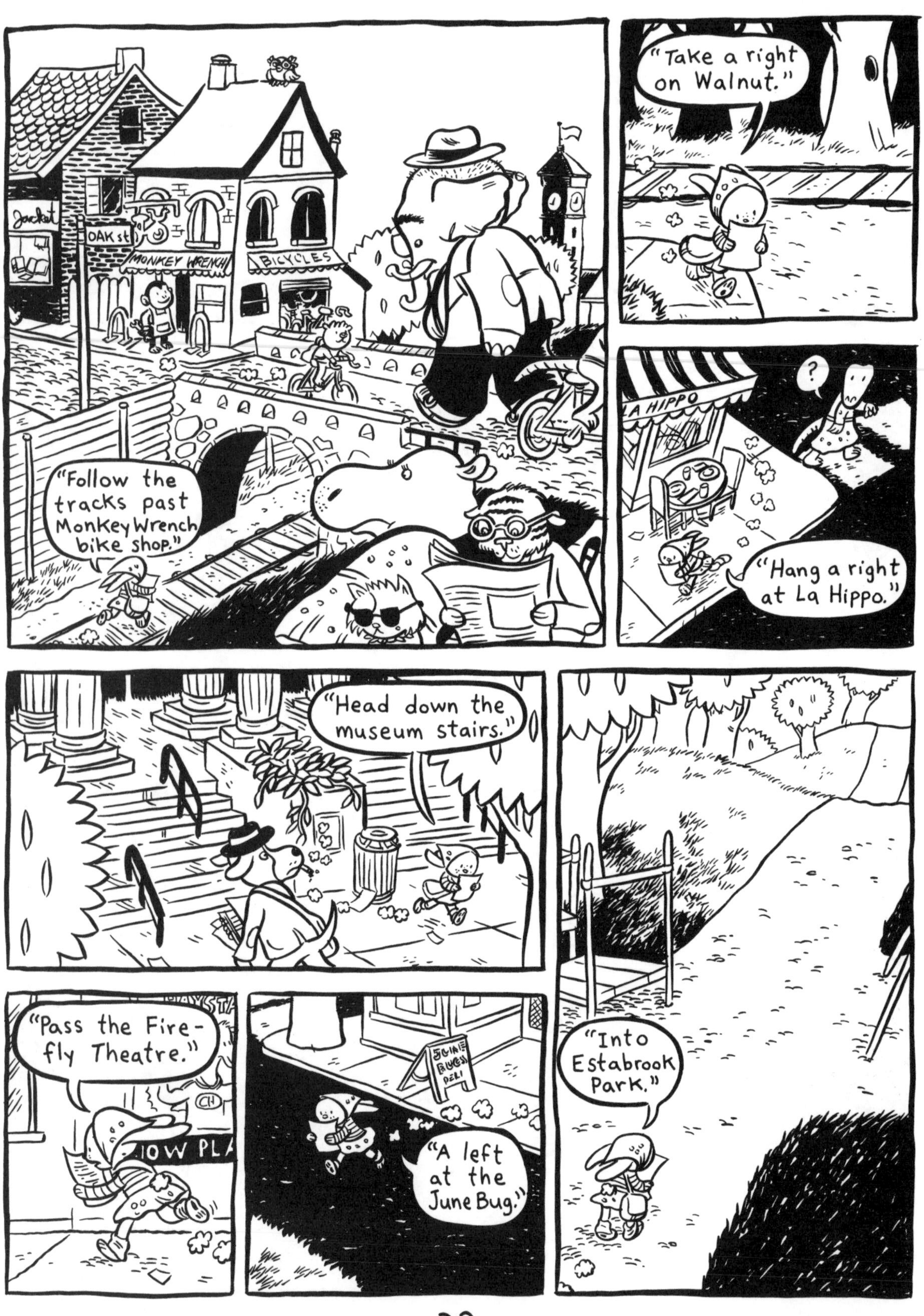
Jacket
OAK st
MONKEY WRENCH
BICYCLES
"Follow the tracks past MonkeyWrench bike shop."
"Take a right on Walnut."
LA HIPPO
?
"Hang a right at La Hippo."
"Head down the museum stairs."
"Pass the Fire-fly Theatre."
"A left at the June Bug."
"Into Estabrook Park."

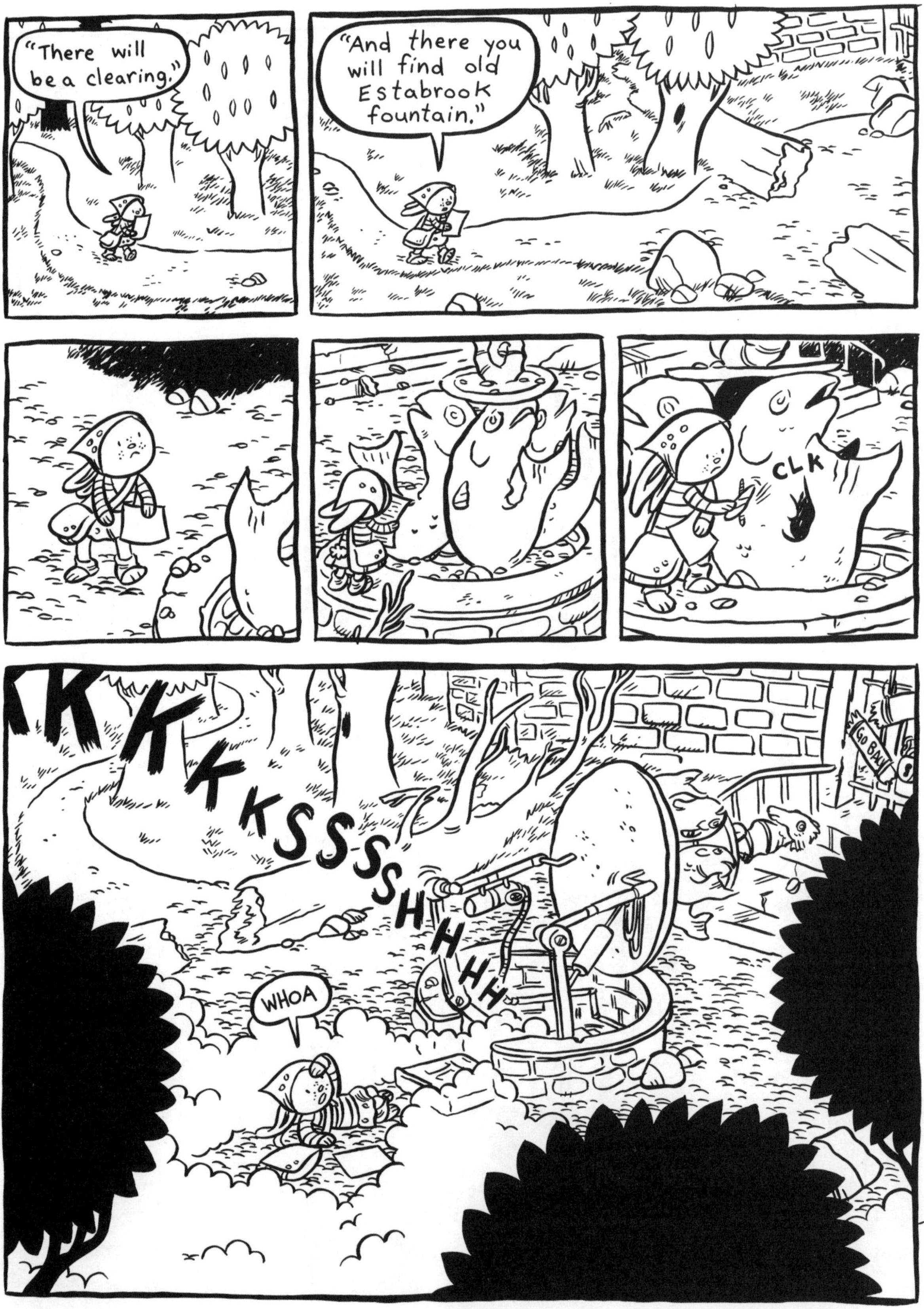
"There will be a clearing."
"And there you will find old Estabrook fountain."
CLK
KKKKKSSSSHHHH
WHOA

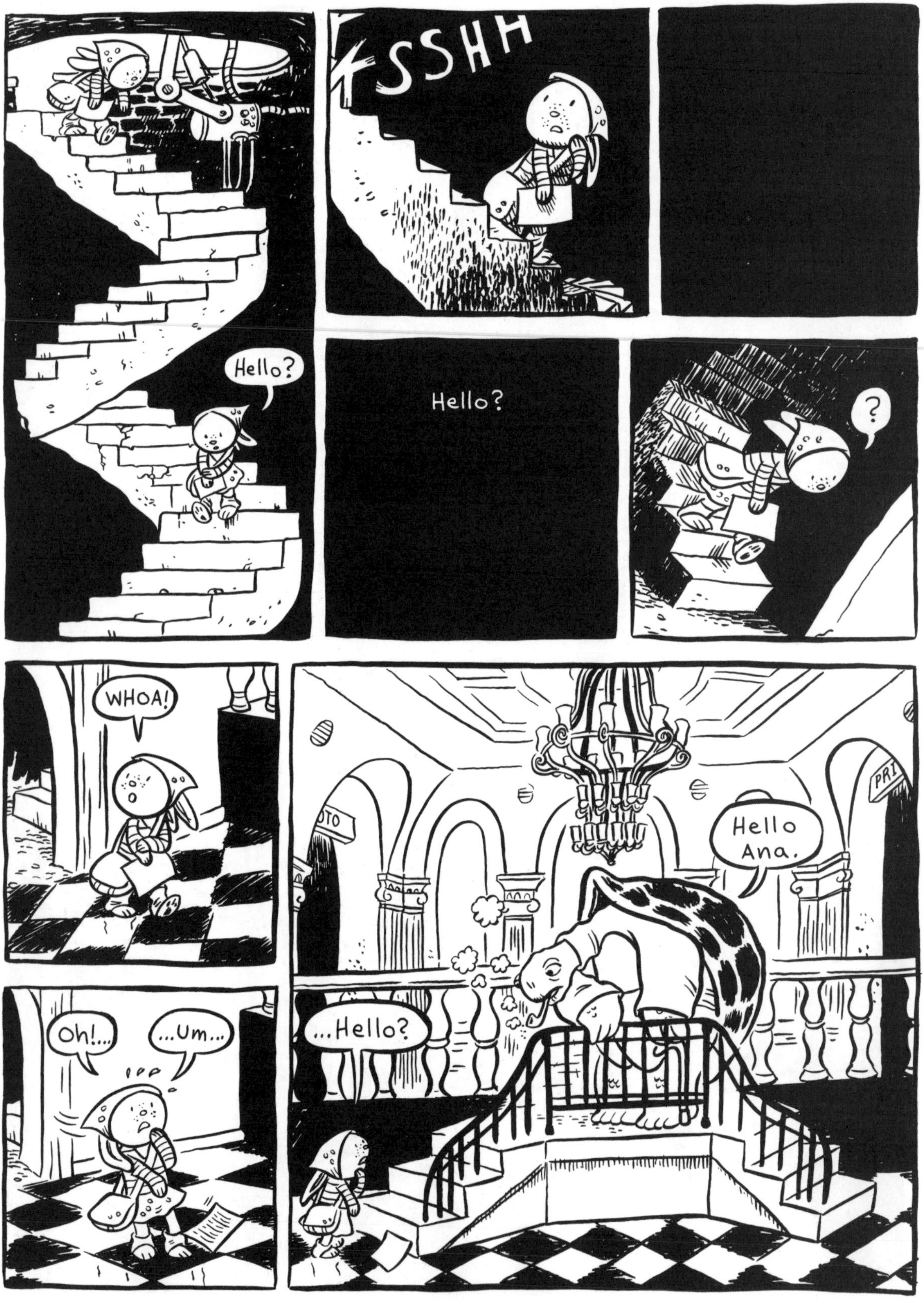
SSHH
Hello?
Hello?
?
WHOA!
Oh!...
...Um...
Hello Ana.
...Hello?

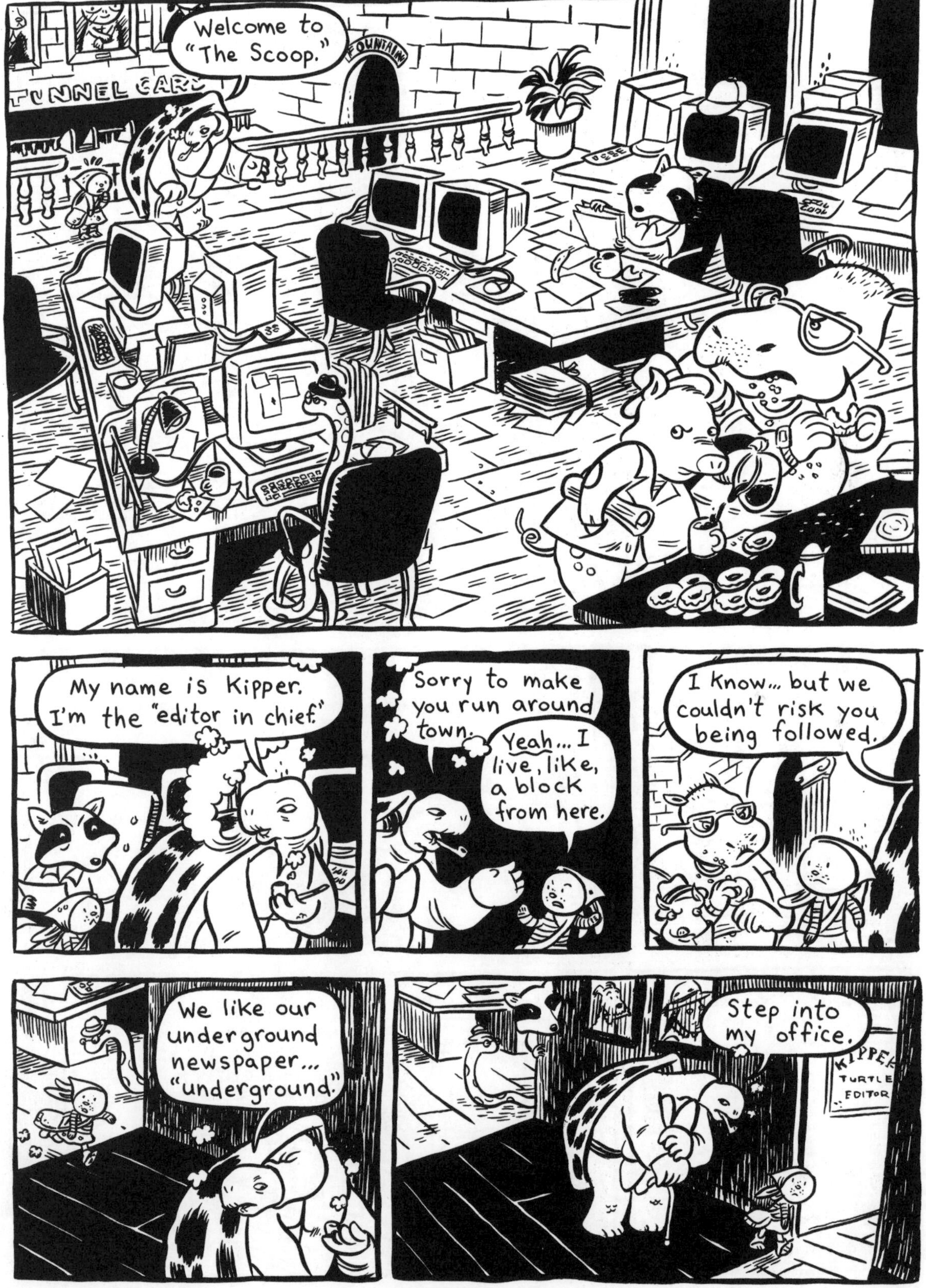
Welcome to "The Scoop."
My name is Kipper. I'm the "editor in chief."
Sorry to make you run around town.
Yeah... I live, like, a block from here.
I know... but we couldn't risk you being followed.
We like our underground newspaper... "underground."
Step into my office.
TURTLE EDITOR

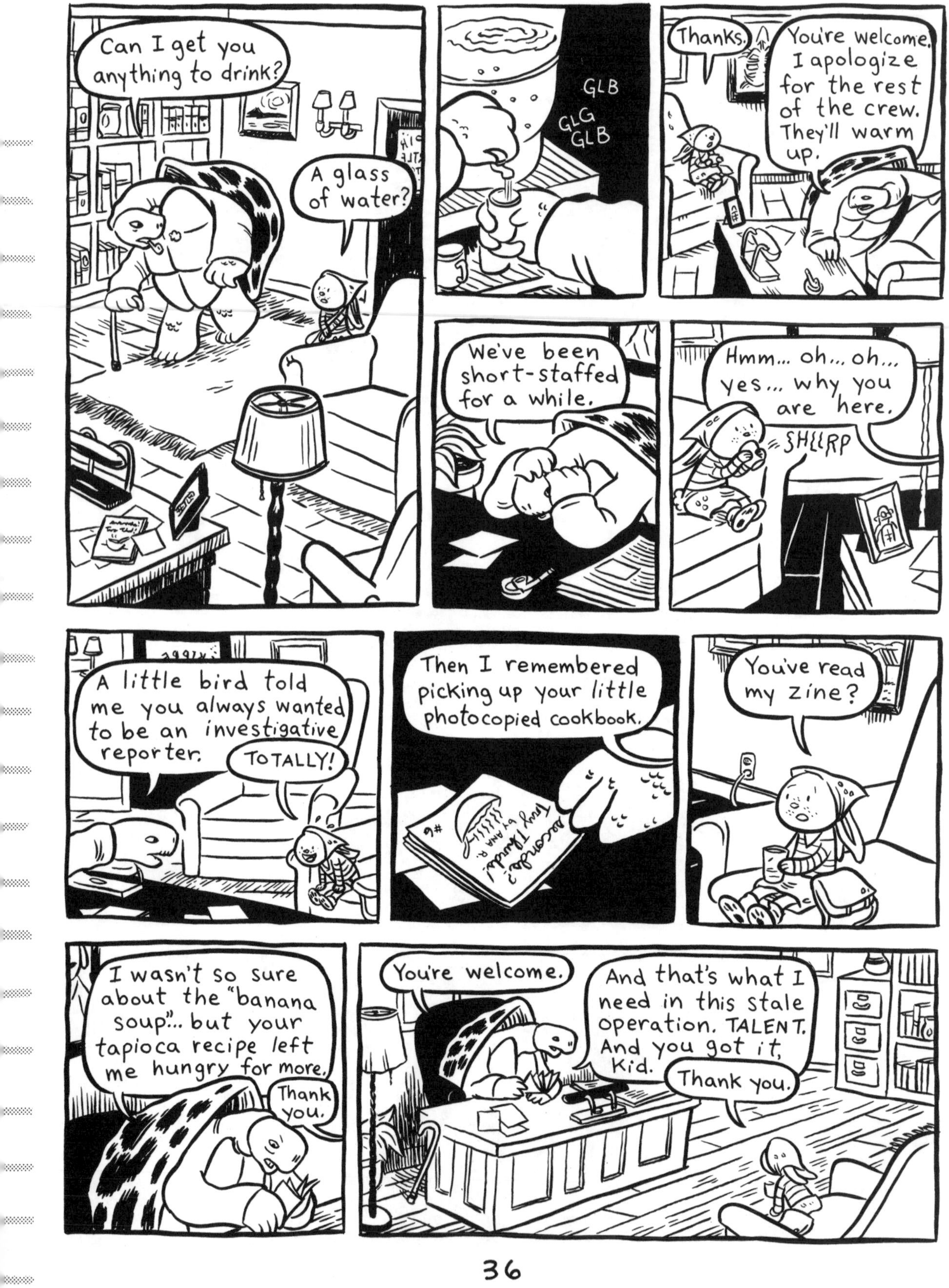
Can I get you anything to drink?
A glass of water?
GLB
GLG
GLB
Thanks.
You're welcome. I apologize for the rest of the crew. They'll warm up.
We've been short-staffed for a while.
Hmm... oh... oh... yes... why you are here.
SHLLRP
A little bird told me you always wanted to be an investigative reporter.
TOTALLY!
Then I remembered picking up your little photocopied cookbook.
You've read my zine?
I wasn't so sure about the "banana soup"... but your tapioca recipe left me hungry for more.
Thank you.
You're welcome.
And that's what I need in this stale operation. TALENT. And you got it, kid.
Thank you.

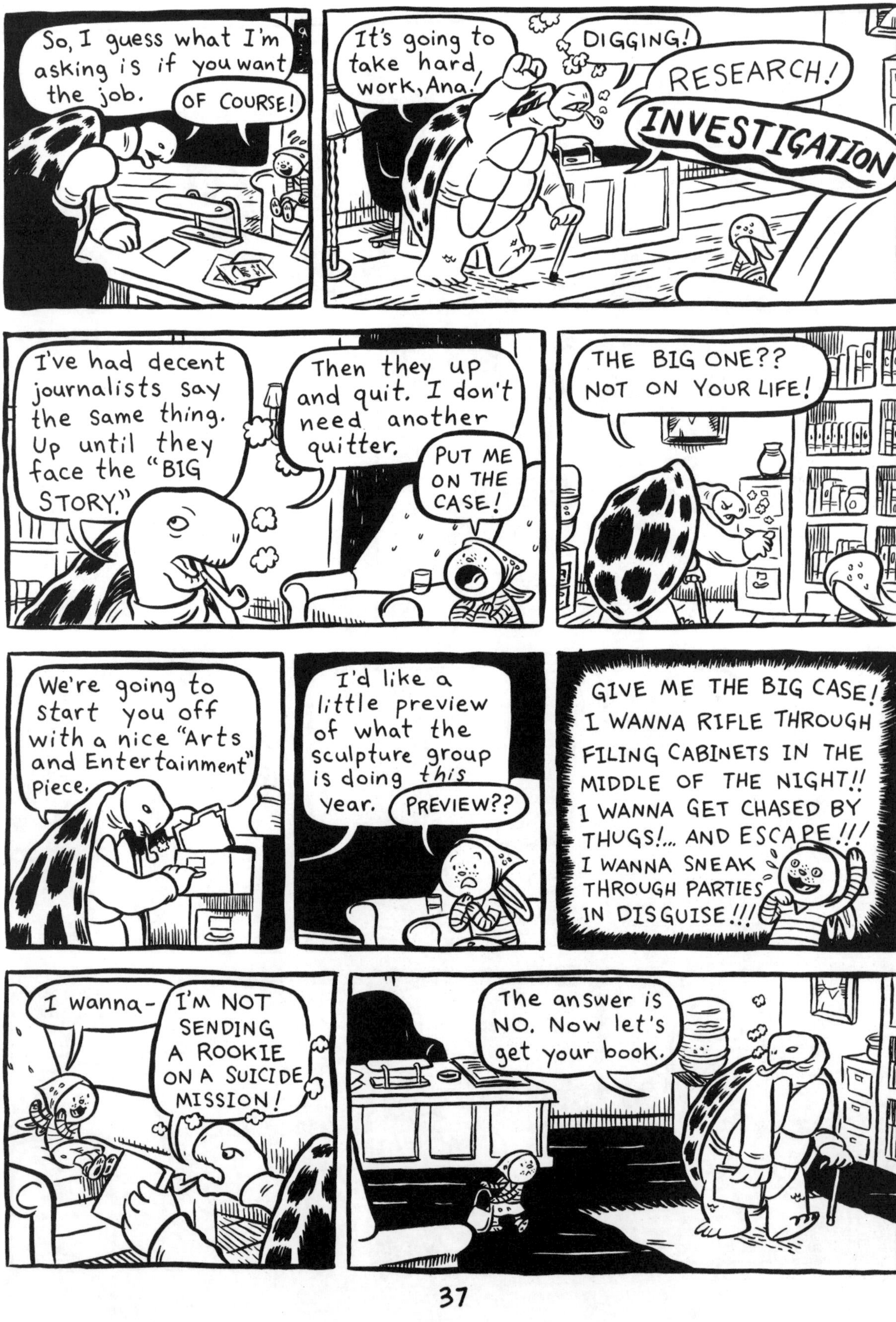
So, I guess what I'm asking is if you want the job.
OF COURSE!
It's going to take hard work, Ana!
DIGGING!
RESEARCH!
INVESTIGATION
I've had decent journalists say the same thing. Up until they face the "BIG STORY."
Then they up and quit. I don't need another quitter.
PUT ME ON THE CASE!
THE BIG ONE?? NOT ON YOUR LIFE!
We're going to start you off with a nice "Arts and Entertainment" piece.
I'd like a little preview of what the sculpture group is doing this year.
PREVIEW??
GIVE ME THE BIG CASE! I WANNA RIFLE THROUGH FILING CABINETS IN THE MIDDLE OF THE NIGHT!! I WANNA GET CHASED BY THUGS!... AND ESCAPE!!! I WANNA SNEAK THROUGH PARTIES IN DISGUISE!!!
I wanna-
I'M NOT SENDING A ROOKIE ON A SUICIDE MISSION!
The answer is NO. Now let's get your book.

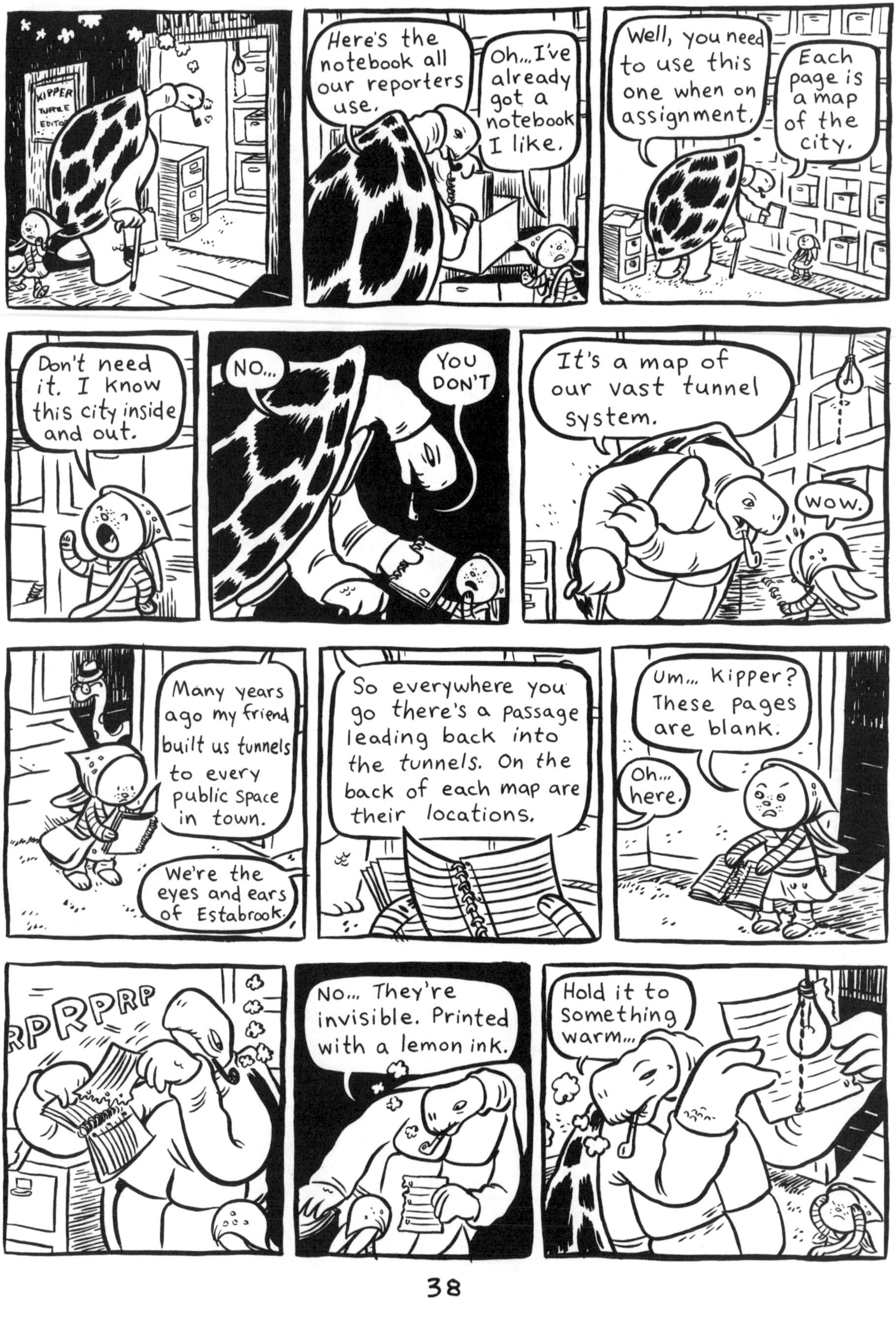
KIPPER TURTLE EDITOR
Here's the notebook all our reporters use.
Oh... I've already got a notebook I like.
Well, you need to use this one when on assignment.
Each page is a map of the city.
Don't need it. I know this city inside and out.
NO...
YOU DON'T
It's a map of our vast tunnel system.
WOW.
Many years ago my friend built us tunnels to every public space in town.
We're the eyes and ears of Estabrook.
So everywhere you go there's a passage leading back into the tunnels. On the back of each map are their locations.
Um... Kipper? These pages are blank.
Oh... here.
RPRPRP
No... They're invisible. Printed with a lemon ink.
Hold it to something warm...

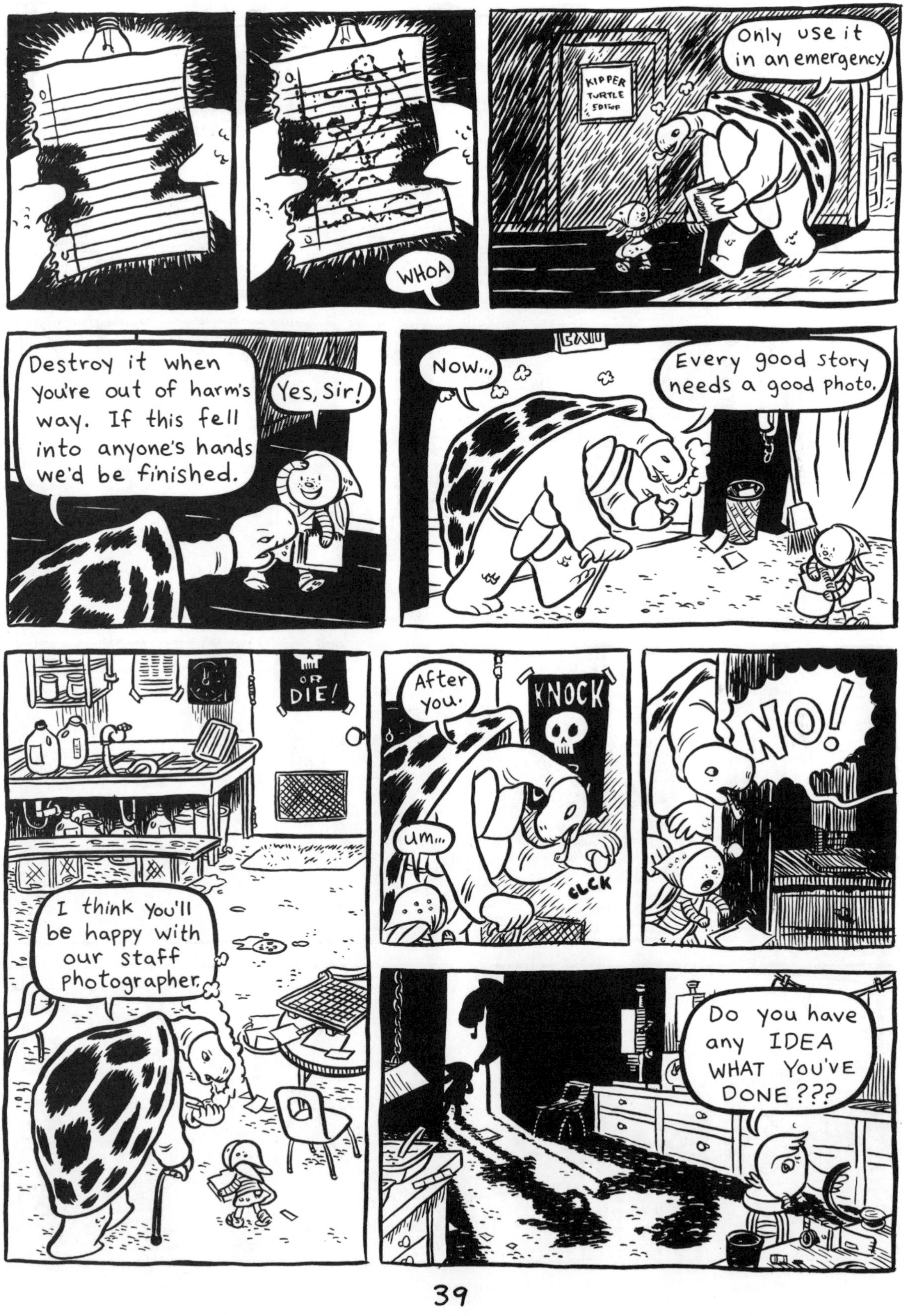
WHOA
KIPPER TURTLE EDITOR
Only use it in an emergency.
Destroy it when you're out of harm's way. If this fell into anyone's hands we'd be finished.
Yes, Sir!
Now...
Every good story needs a good photo.
OR DIE!
I think you'll be happy with our staff photographer.
After you.
KNOCK
um...
CLCK
NO!
Do you have any IDEA WHAT YOU'VE DONE???

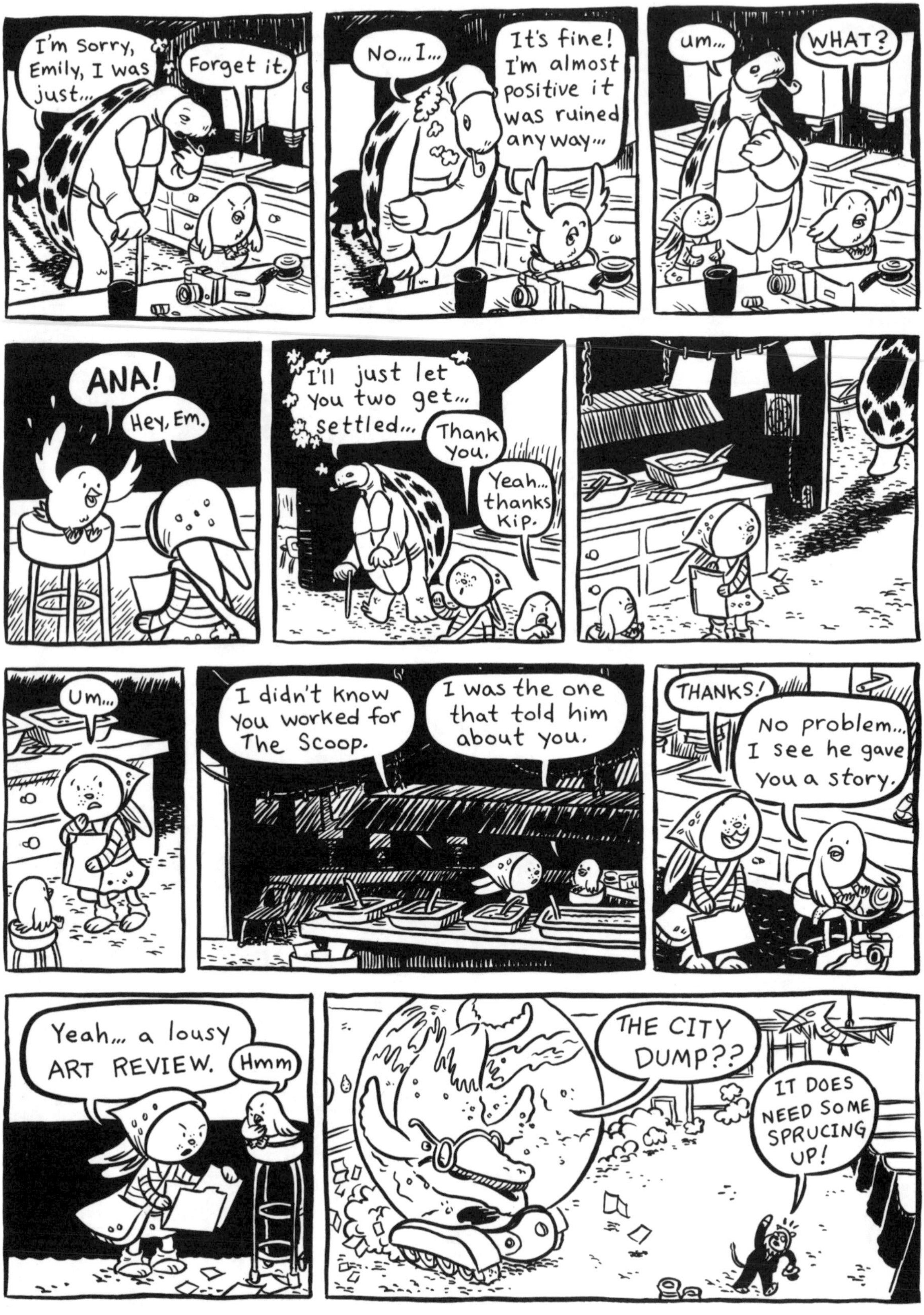
I'm sorry, Emily, I was just...
Forget it.
No... I...
It's fine! I'm almost positive it was ruined anyway...
um...
WHAT?
ANA!
Hey, Em.
I'll just let you two get... settled...
Thank you.
Yeah... thanks Kip.
Um...
I didn't know you worked for The Scoop.
I was the one that told him about you.
THANKS!
No problem... I see he gave you a story.
Yeah... a lousy ART REVIEW.
Hmm
THE CITY DUMP??
IT DOES NEED SOME SPRUCING UP!

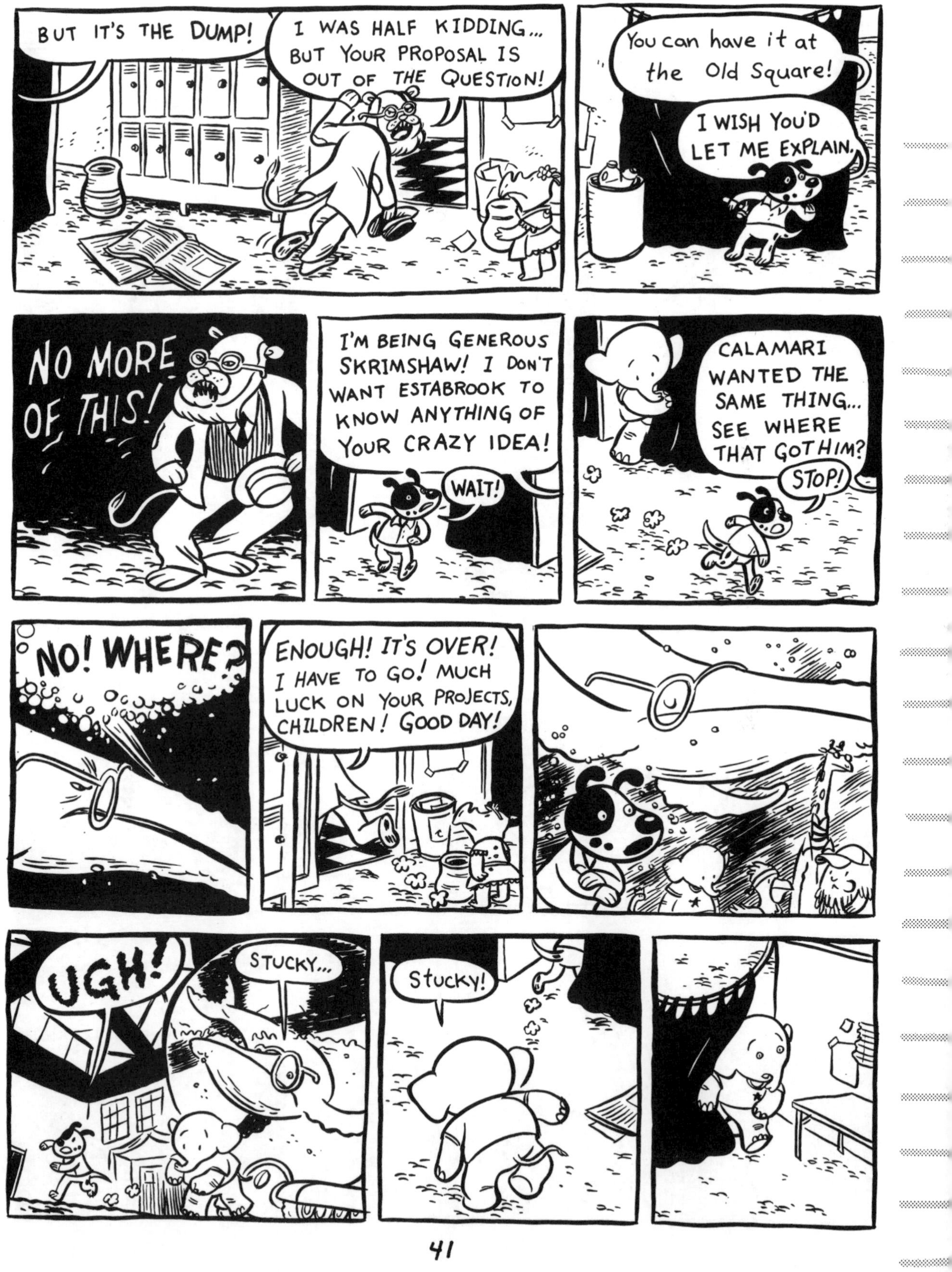

BUT IT'S THE DUMP!
I WAS HALF KIDDING... BUT YOUR PROPOSAL IS OUT OF THE QUESTION!
You can have it at the Old Square!
I WISH YOU'D LET ME EXPLAIN.
NO MORE OF THIS!
I'M BEING GENEROUS SKRIMSHAW! I DON'T WANT ESTABROOK TO KNOW ANYTHING OF YOUR CRAZY IDEA!
WAIT!
CALAMARI WANTED THE SAME THING... SEE WHERE THAT GOT HIM?
STOP!
NO! WHERE?
ENOUGH! IT'S OVER! I HAVE TO GO! MUCH LUCK ON YOUR PROJECTS, CHILDREN! GOOD DAY!
UGH!
STUCKY...
Stucky!

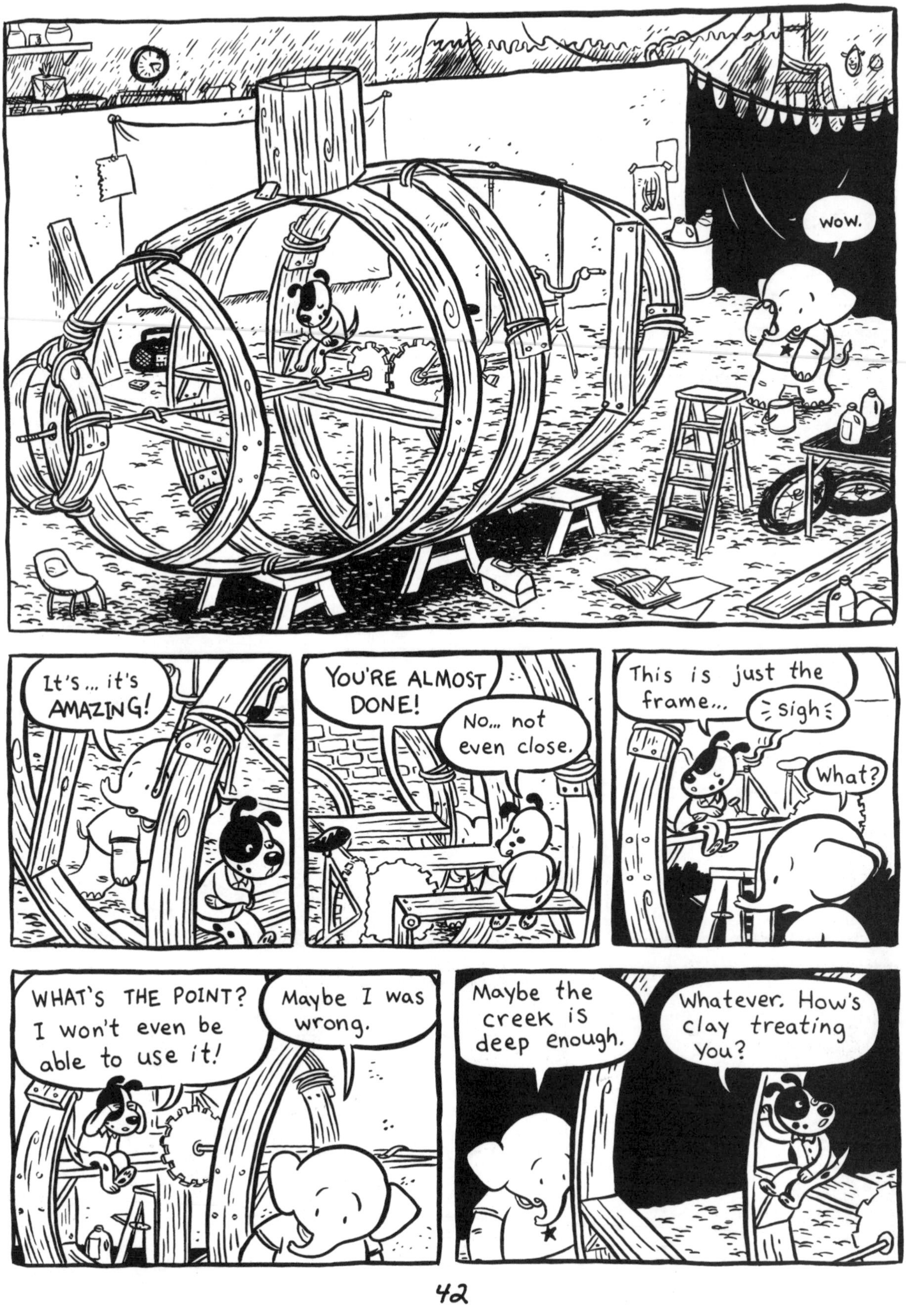
WOW.
It's... it's AMAZING!
YOU'RE ALMOST DONE!
No... not even close.
This is just the frame...
sigh
What?
WHAT'S THE POINT? I won't even be able to use it!
Maybe I was wrong.
Maybe the creek is deep enough.
Whatever. How's clay treating you?

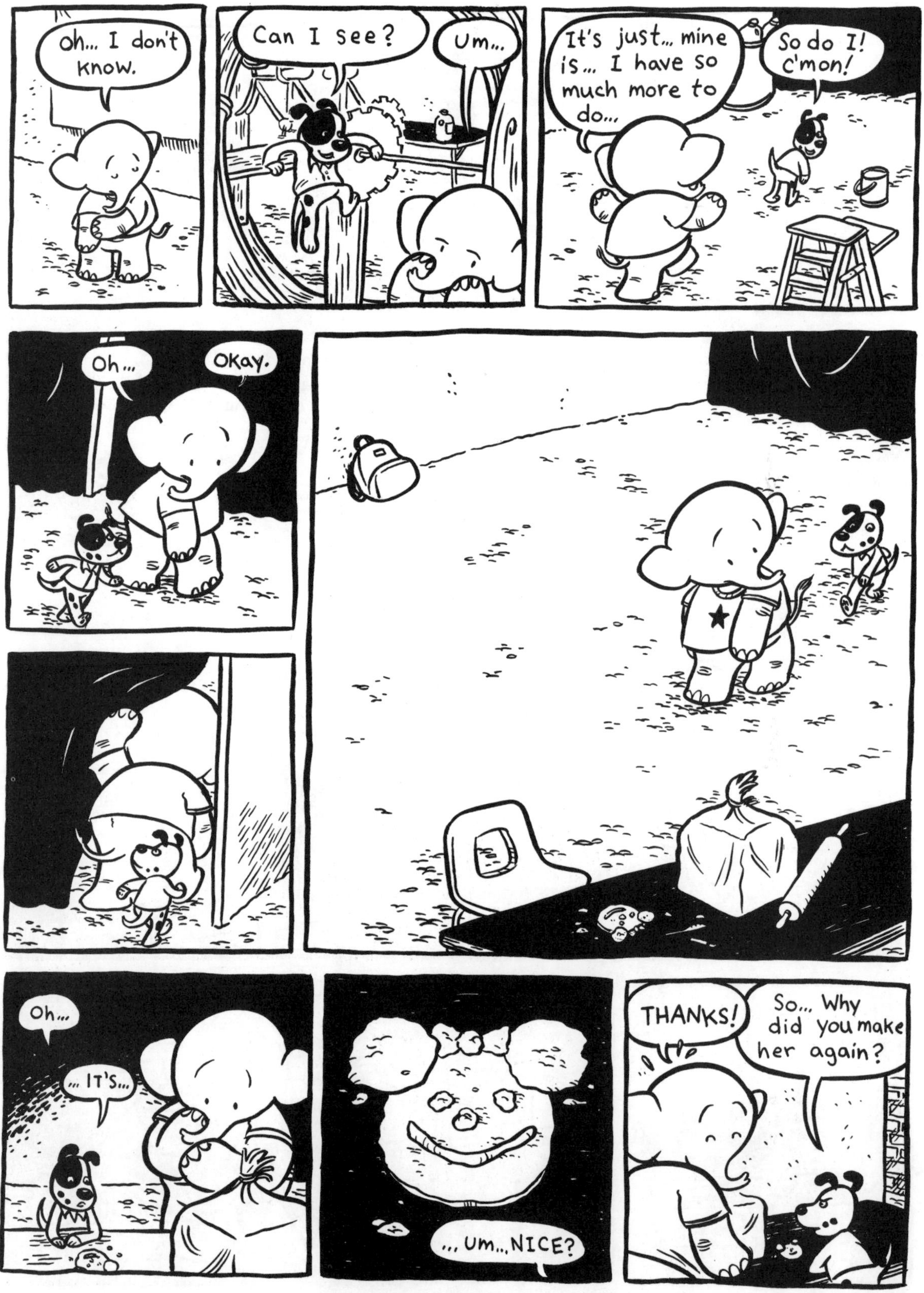
Oh... I don't know.
Can I see?
Um...
It's just... mine is... I have so much more to do...
So do I! c'mon!
Oh...
Okay.
Oh...
... IT'S...
... Um... NICE?
THANKS!
So... Why did you make her again?

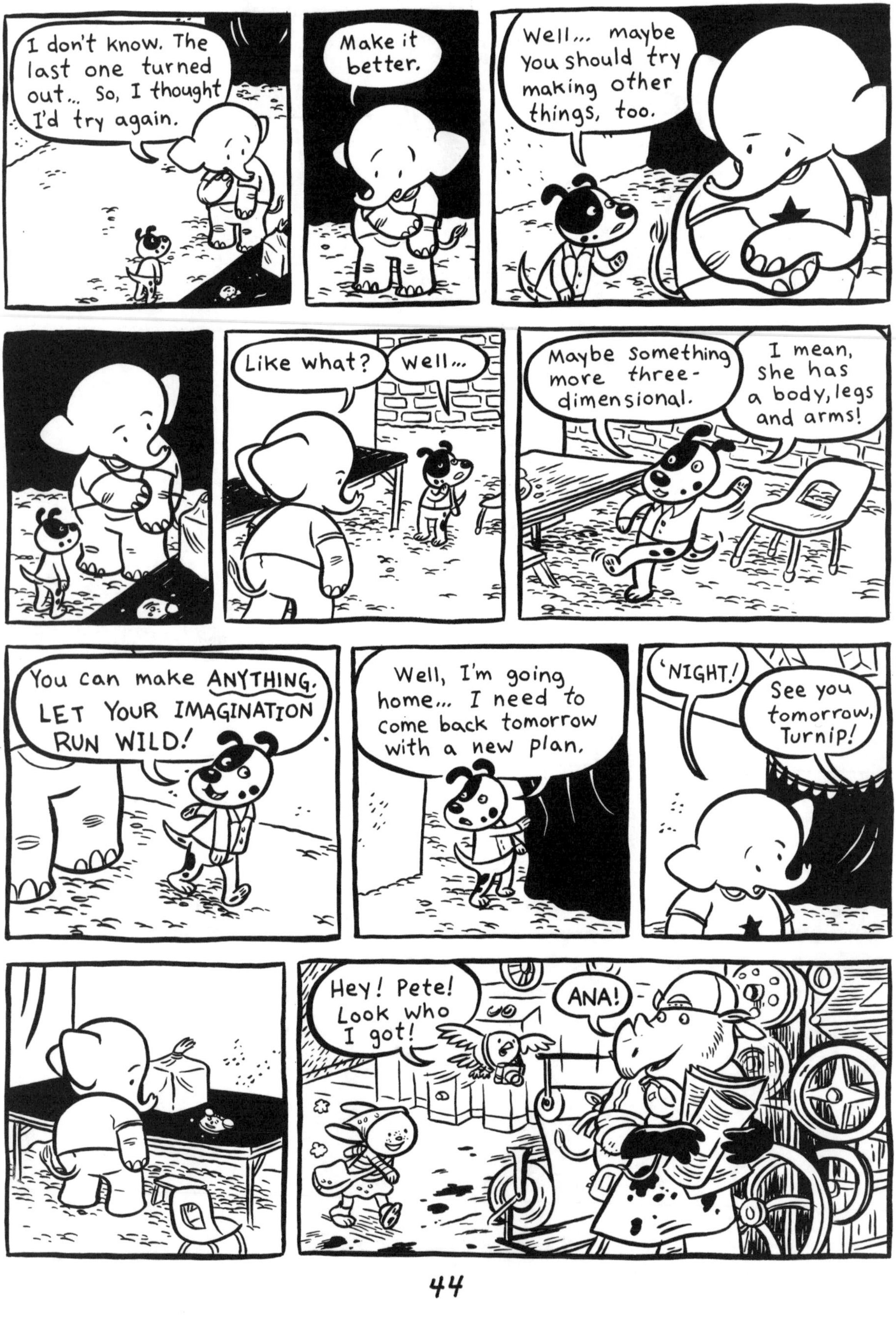
I don't know. The last one turned out... So, I thought I'd try again.
Make it better.
Well... maybe you should try making other things, too.
Like what?
Well...
Maybe something more three-dimensional.
I mean, she has a body, legs and arms!
You can make ANYTHING. LET YOUR IMAGINATION RUN WILD!
Well, I'm going home... I need to come back tomorrow with a new plan.
'NIGHT!
See you tomorrow, Turnip!
Hey! Pete! Look who I got!
ANA!

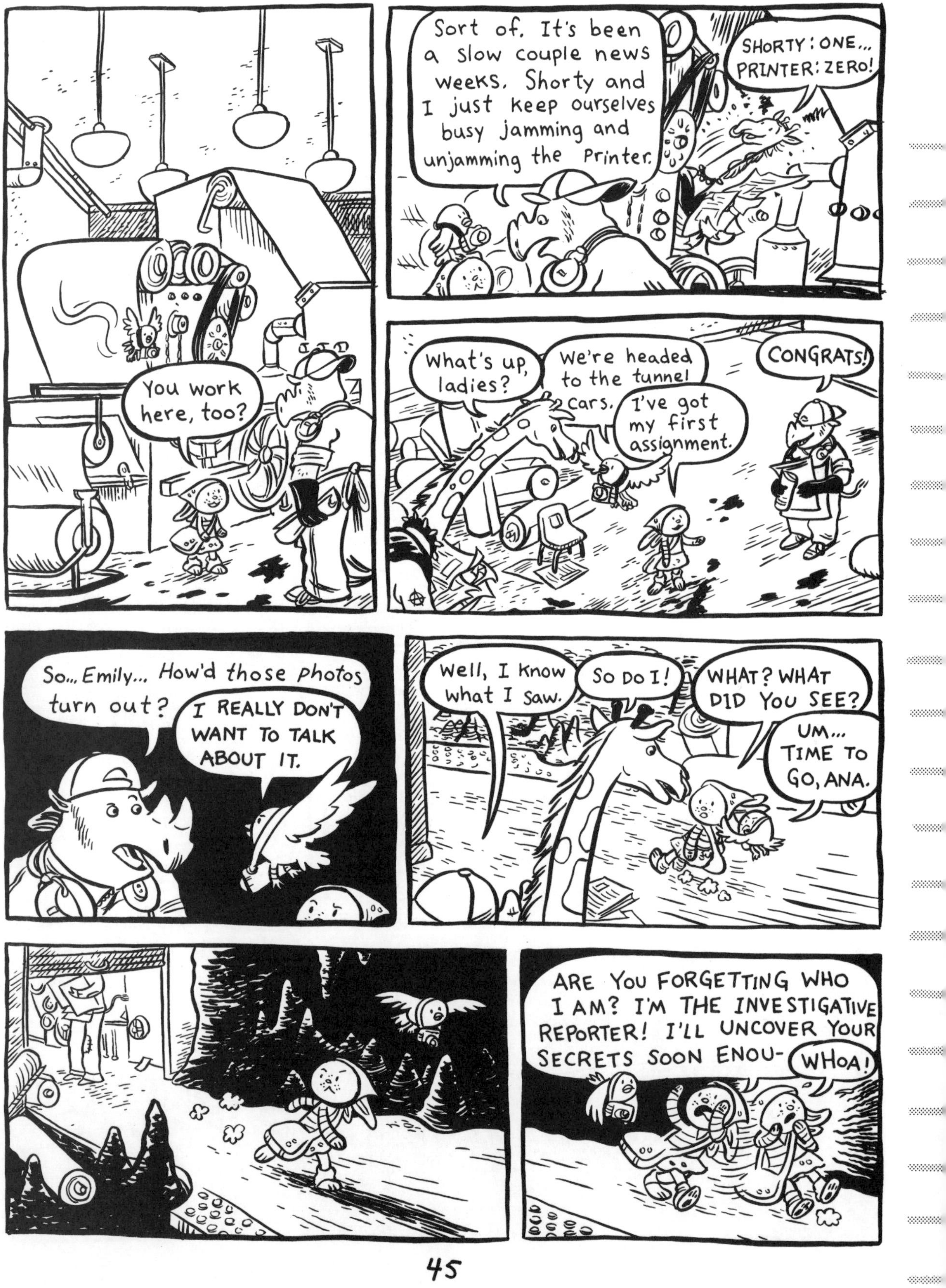
You work here, too?
Sort of. It's been a slow couple news weeks. Shorty and I just keep ourselves busy jamming and unjamming the Printer.
SHORTY: ONE... PRINTER: ZERO!
What's up, ladies?
We're headed to the tunnel cars.
I've got my first assignment.
CONGRATS!
So... Emily... How'd those photos turn out?
I REALLY DON'T WANT TO TALK ABOUT IT.
Well, I know what I saw.
So DO I!
WHAT? WHAT DID YOU SEE?
UM... TIME TO GO, ANA.
ARE YOU FORGETTING WHO I AM? I'M THE INVESTIGATIVE REPORTER! I'LL UNCOVER YOUR SECRETS SOON ENOU-
WHOA!

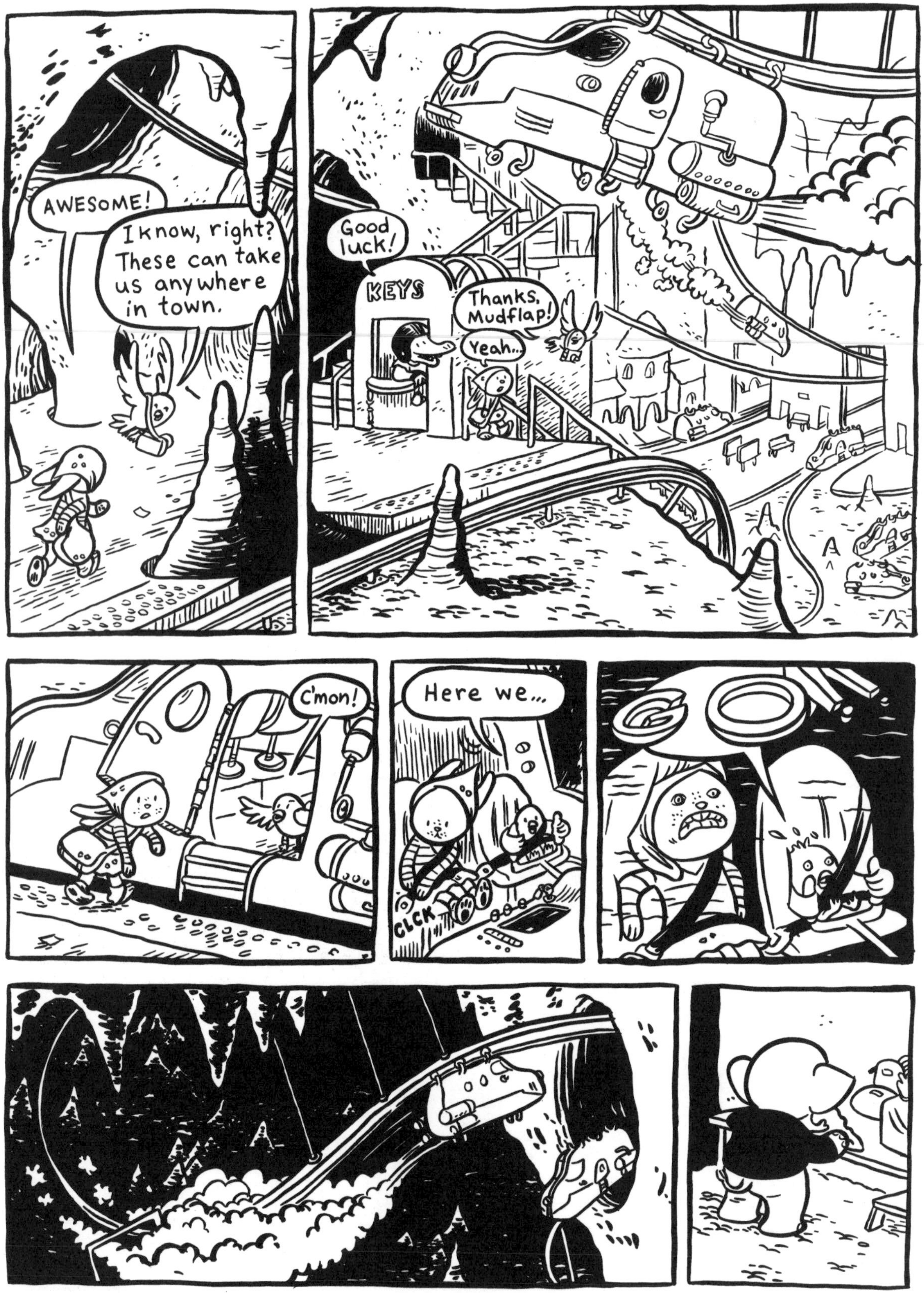

AWESOME!
I know, right? These can take us anywhere in town.
Good luck!
KEYS
Thanks, Mudflap!
Yeah...
C'mon!
Here we...
CLCK

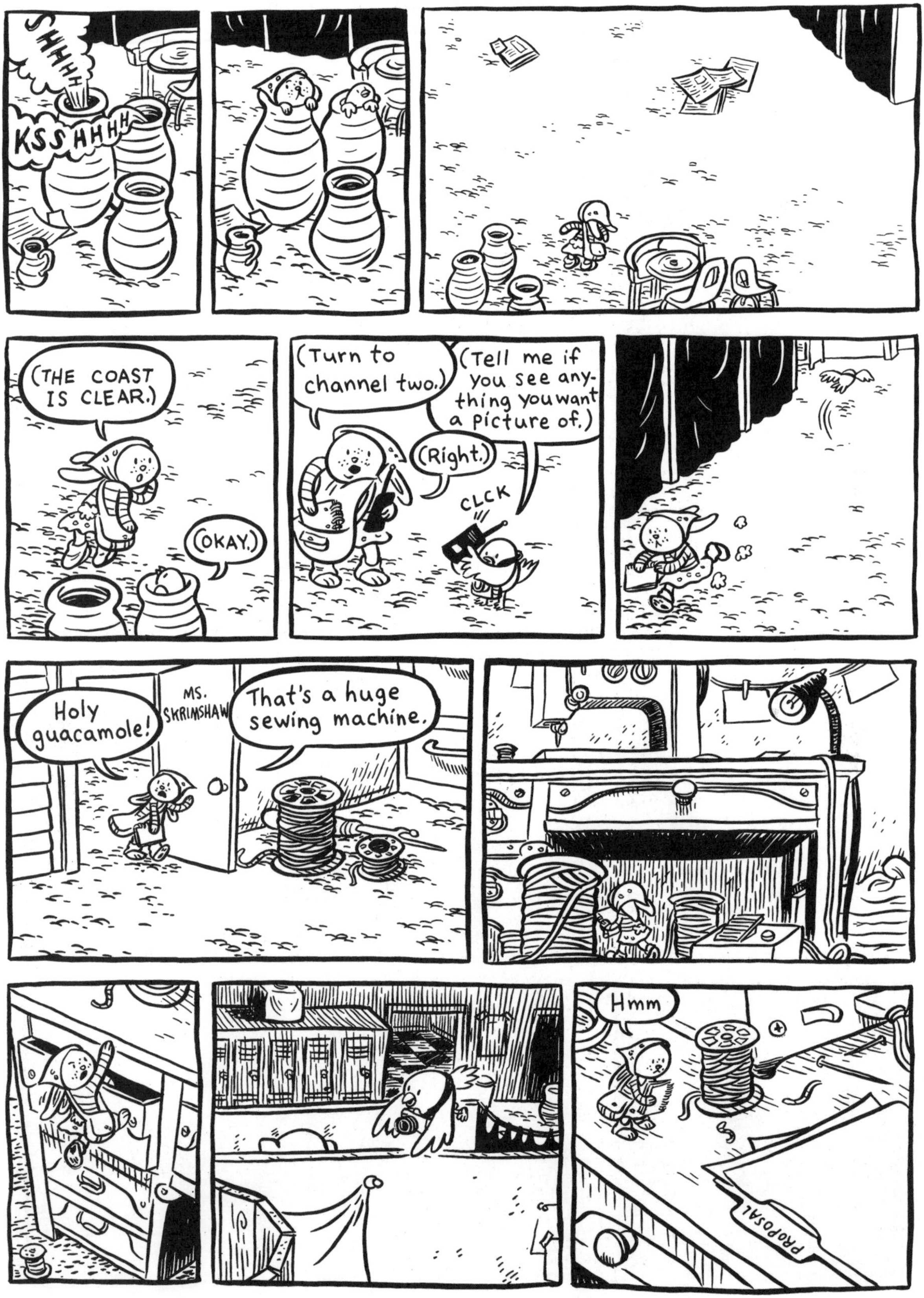
SHHHH
KSSHHHH
(THE COAST IS CLEAR.)
(OKAY.)
(Turn to channel two.)
(Tell me if you see anything you want a picture of.)
(Right.)
CLCK
Holy guacamole!
MS. SKRIMSHAW
That's a huge sewing machine.
Hmm
PROPOSAL

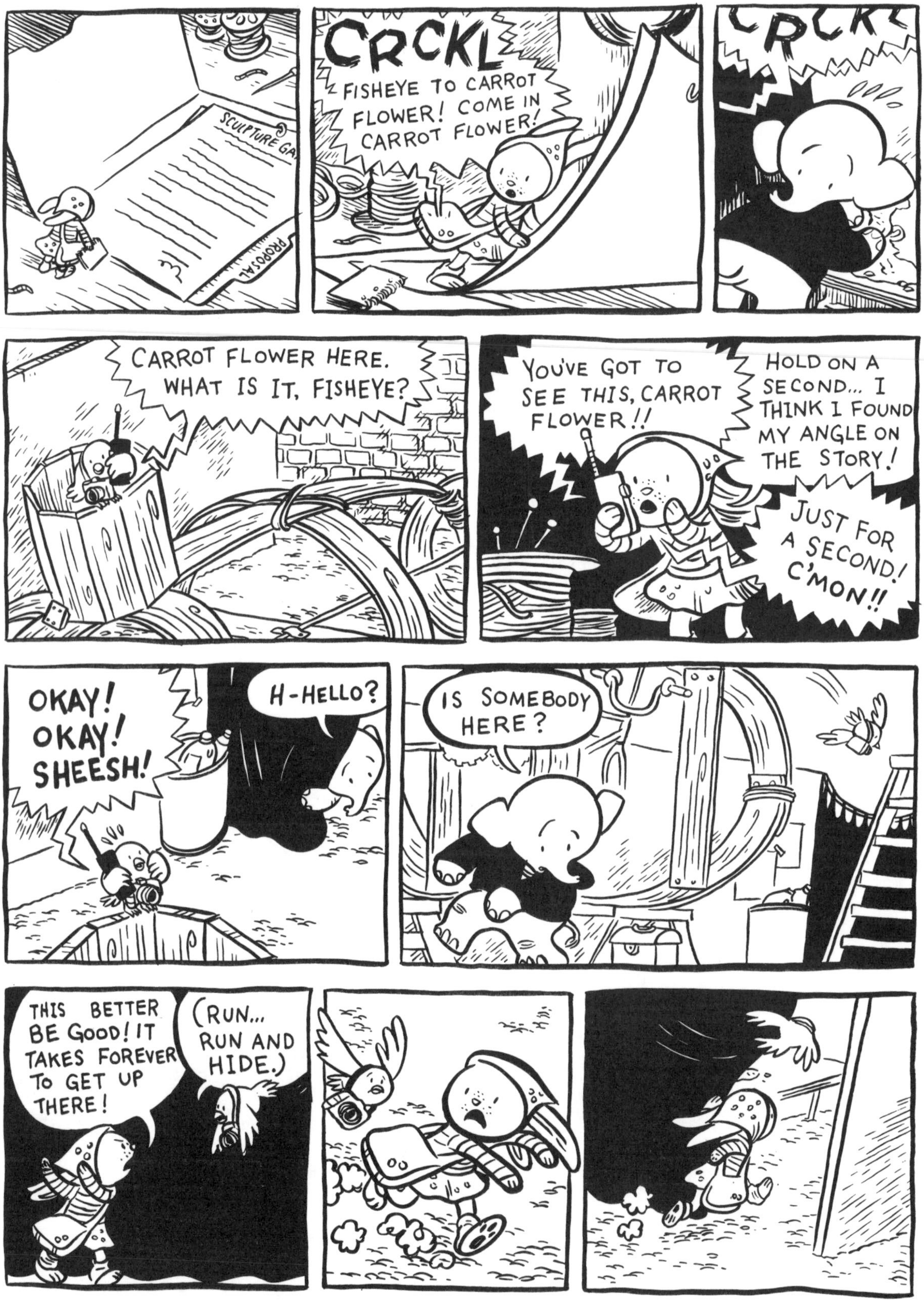

SCULPTURE GA
PROPOSAL
CRCKL
FISHEYE TO CARROT FLOWER! COME IN CARROT FLOWER!
CRCKL
CARROT FLOWER HERE. WHAT IS IT, FISHEYE?
YOU'VE GOT TO SEE THIS, CARROT FLOWER!!
HOLD ON A SECOND... I THINK I FOUND MY ANGLE ON THE STORY!
JUST FOR A SECOND! C'MON!!
OKAY! OKAY! SHEESH!
H-HELLO?
IS SOMEBODY HERE?
THIS BETTER BE GOOD! IT TAKES FOREVER TO GET UP THERE!
(RUN... RUN AND HIDE.)

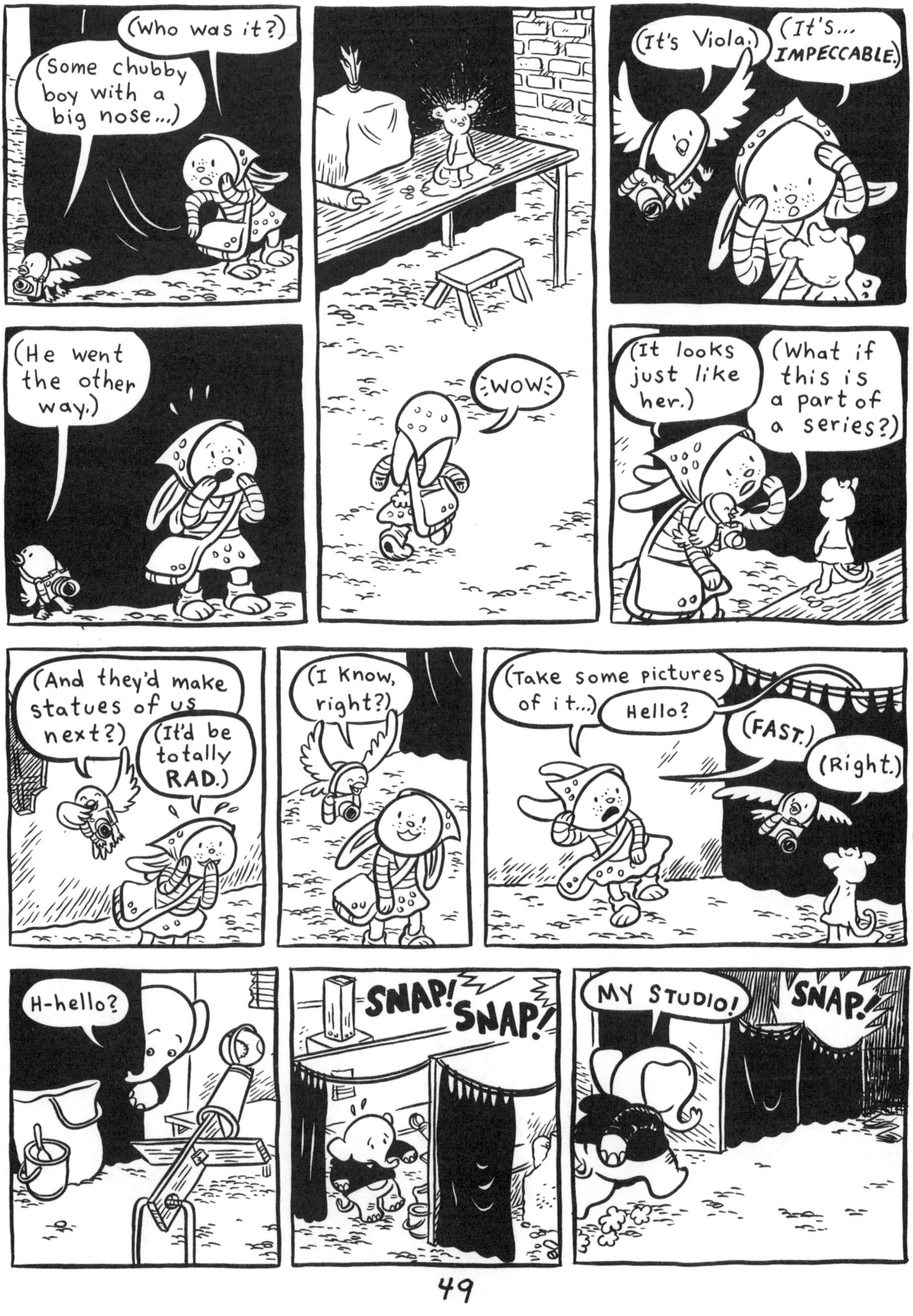
(Who was it?)
(Some chubby boy with a big nose...)
(It's Viola.)
(It's... IMPECCABLE.)
(He went the other way.)
WOW
(It looks just like her.)
(What if this is a part of a series?)
(And they'd make statues of us next?)
(It'd be totally RAD.)
(I know, right?)
(Take some pictures of it...)
Hello?
(FAST.)
(Right.)
H-hello?
SNAP! SNAP!
MY STUDIO!
SNAP!

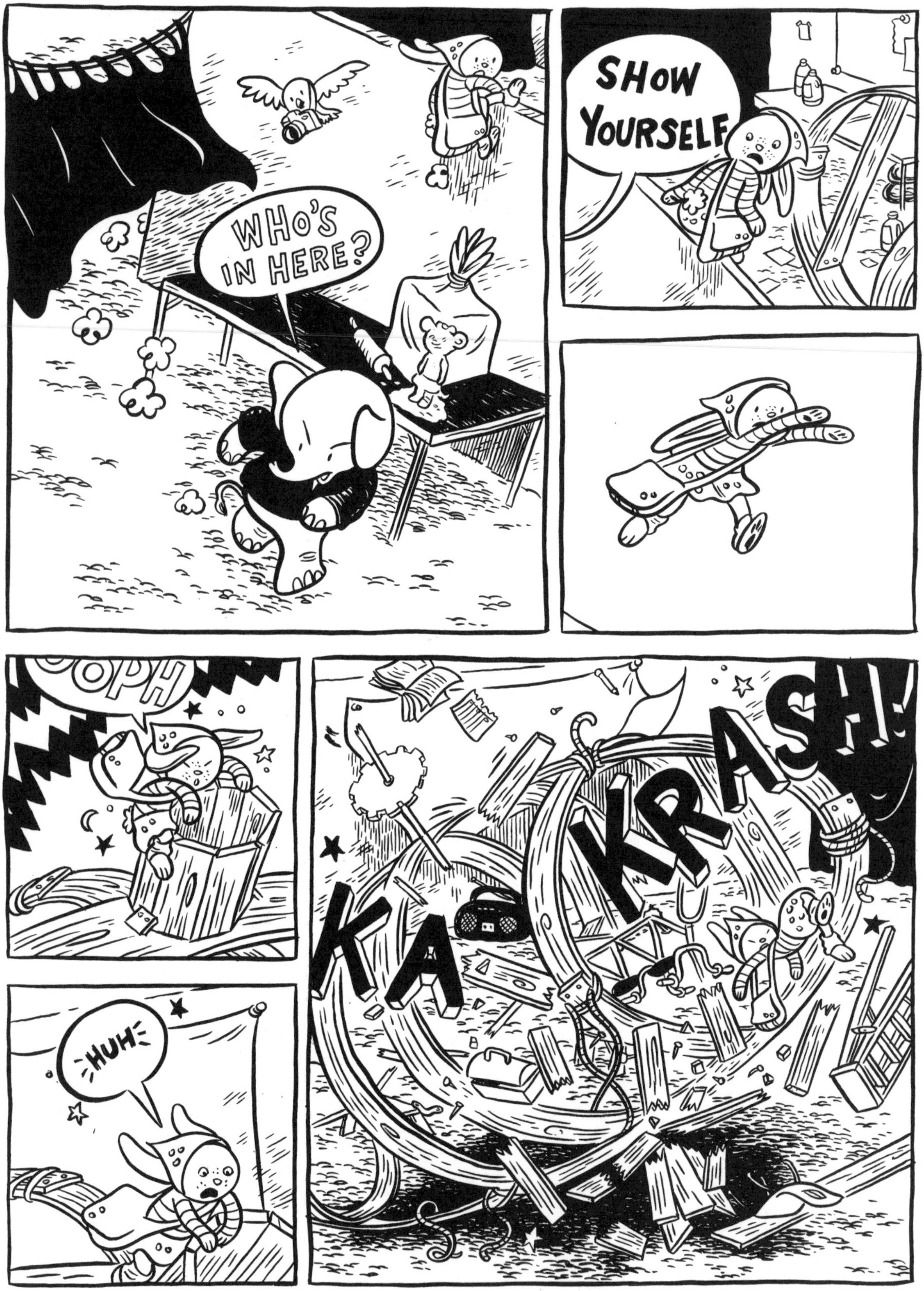
WHO'S IN HERE?
SHOW YOURSELF
OOPH
HUH
KA
KRASH!

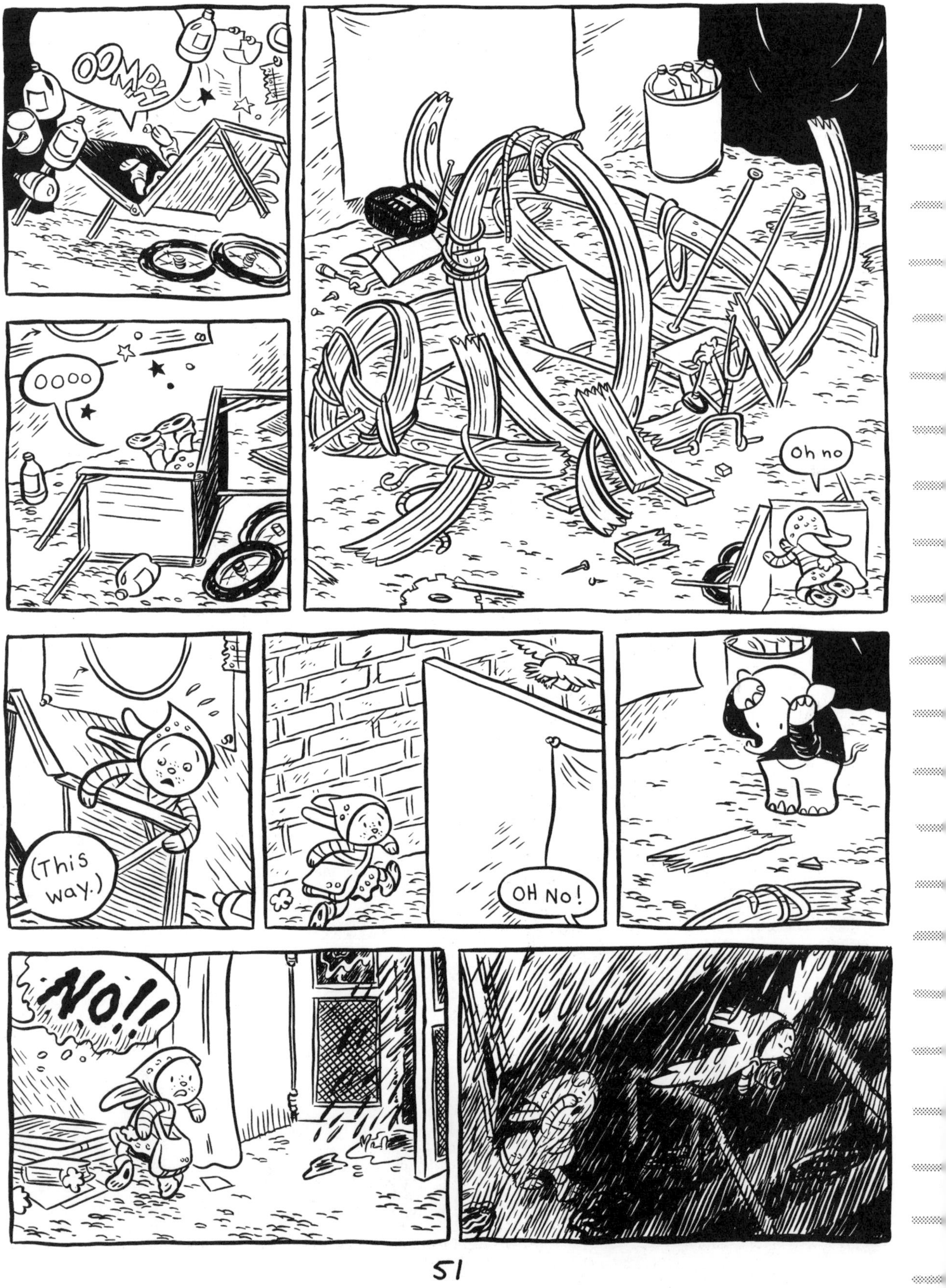
OOMPH
OOOO
Oh no
(This way.)
OH NO!
NO!!

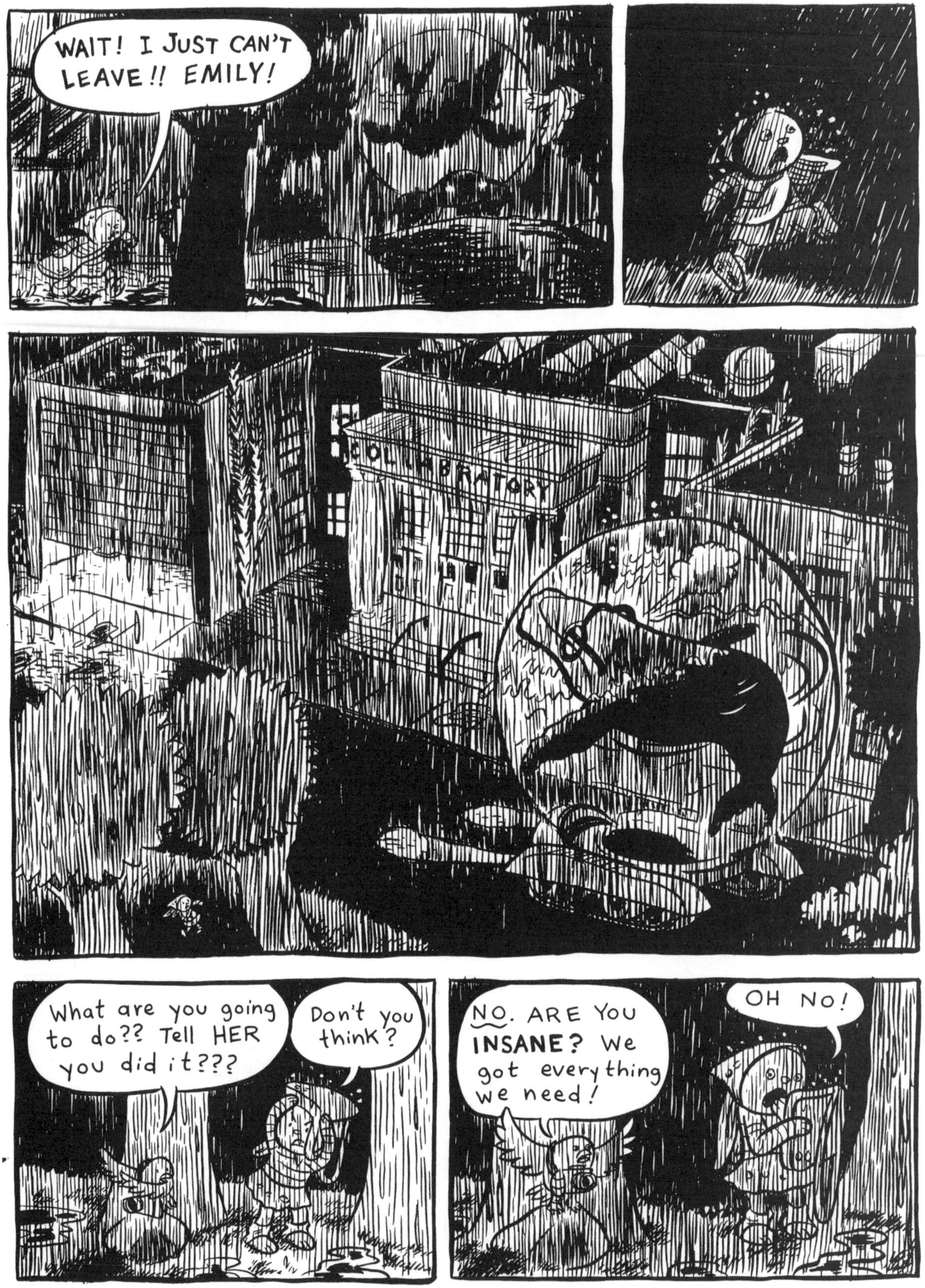
WAIT! I JUST CAN'T LEAVE!! EMILY!
COLLABRATORY
What are you going to do?? Tell HER you did it???
Don't you think?
NO. ARE YOU INSANE? We got everything we need!
OH NO!

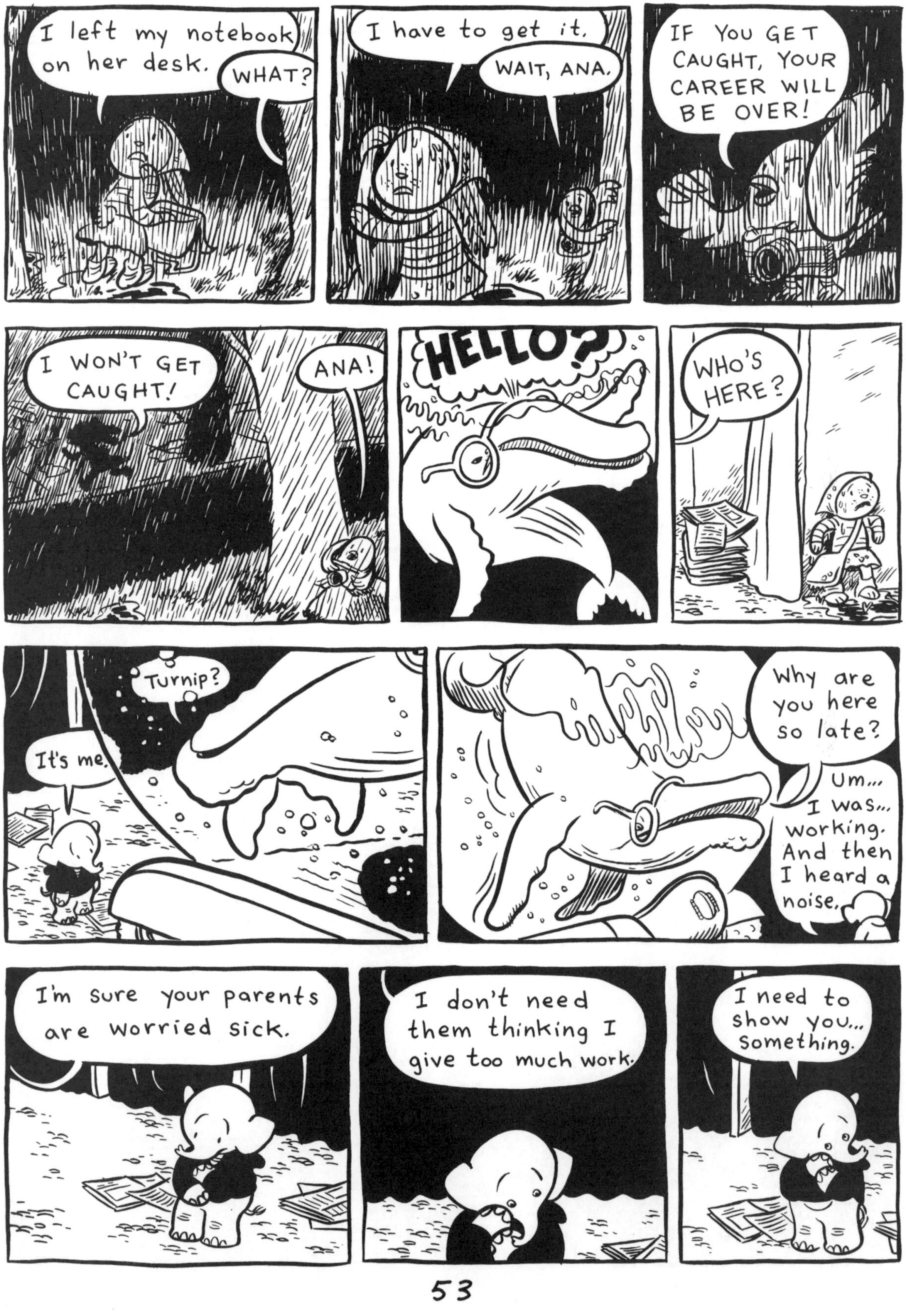
I left my notebook on her desk.
WHAT?
I have to get it.
WAIT, ANA.
IF YOU GET CAUGHT, YOUR CAREER WILL BE OVER!
I WON'T GET CAUGHT!
ANA!
HELLO?
WHO'S HERE?
Turnip?
It's me.
Why are you here so late?
Um... I was... working. And then I heard a noise.
I'm sure your parents are worried sick.
I don't need them thinking I give too much work.
I need to show you... something.

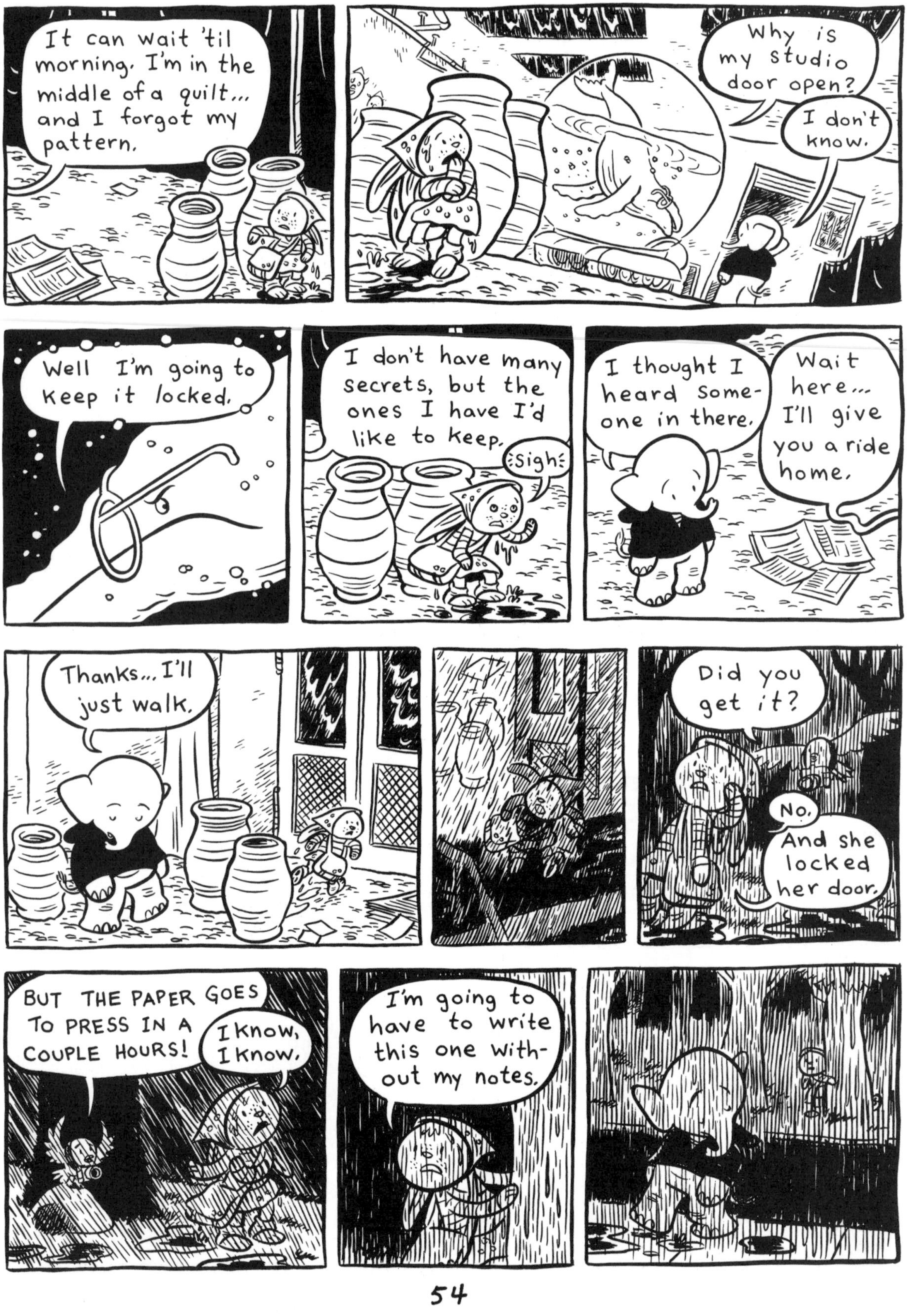
It can wait 'til morning. I'm in the middle of a quilt... and I forgot my pattern.
Why is my studio door open?
I don't know.
Well I'm going to keep it locked.
I don't have many secrets, but the ones I have I'd like to keep.
Sigh
I thought I heard some-one in there.
Wait here... I'll give you a ride home.
Thanks... I'll just walk.
Did you get it?
No.
And she locked her door.
BUT THE PAPER GOES TO PRESS IN A COUPLE HOURS!
I know, I know.
I'm going to have to write this one with-out my notes.

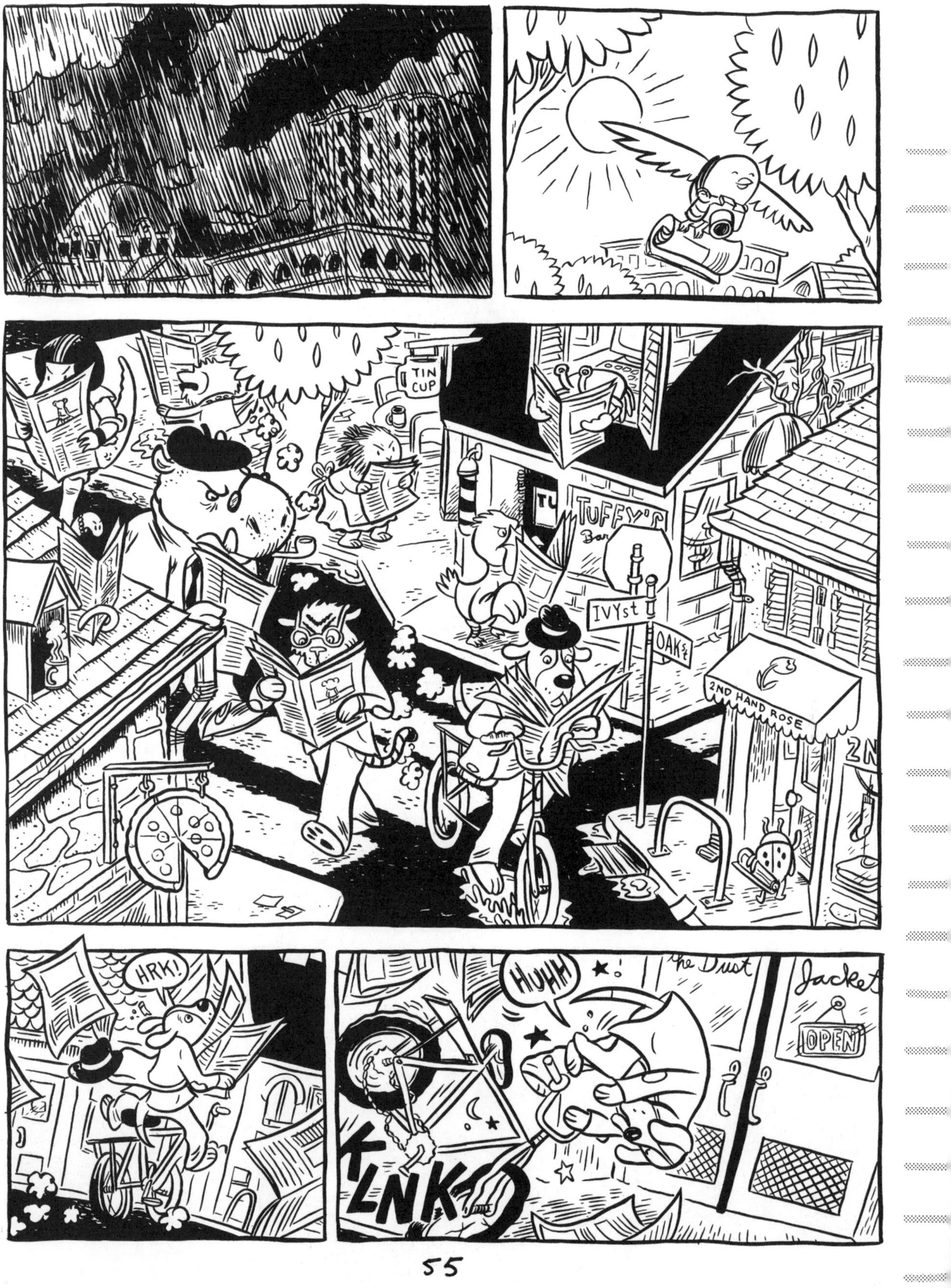
TIN CUP
TUFFY'S
IVY st
OAK st
2ND HAND ROSE
HRK!
HUHH
OPEN
KLNK

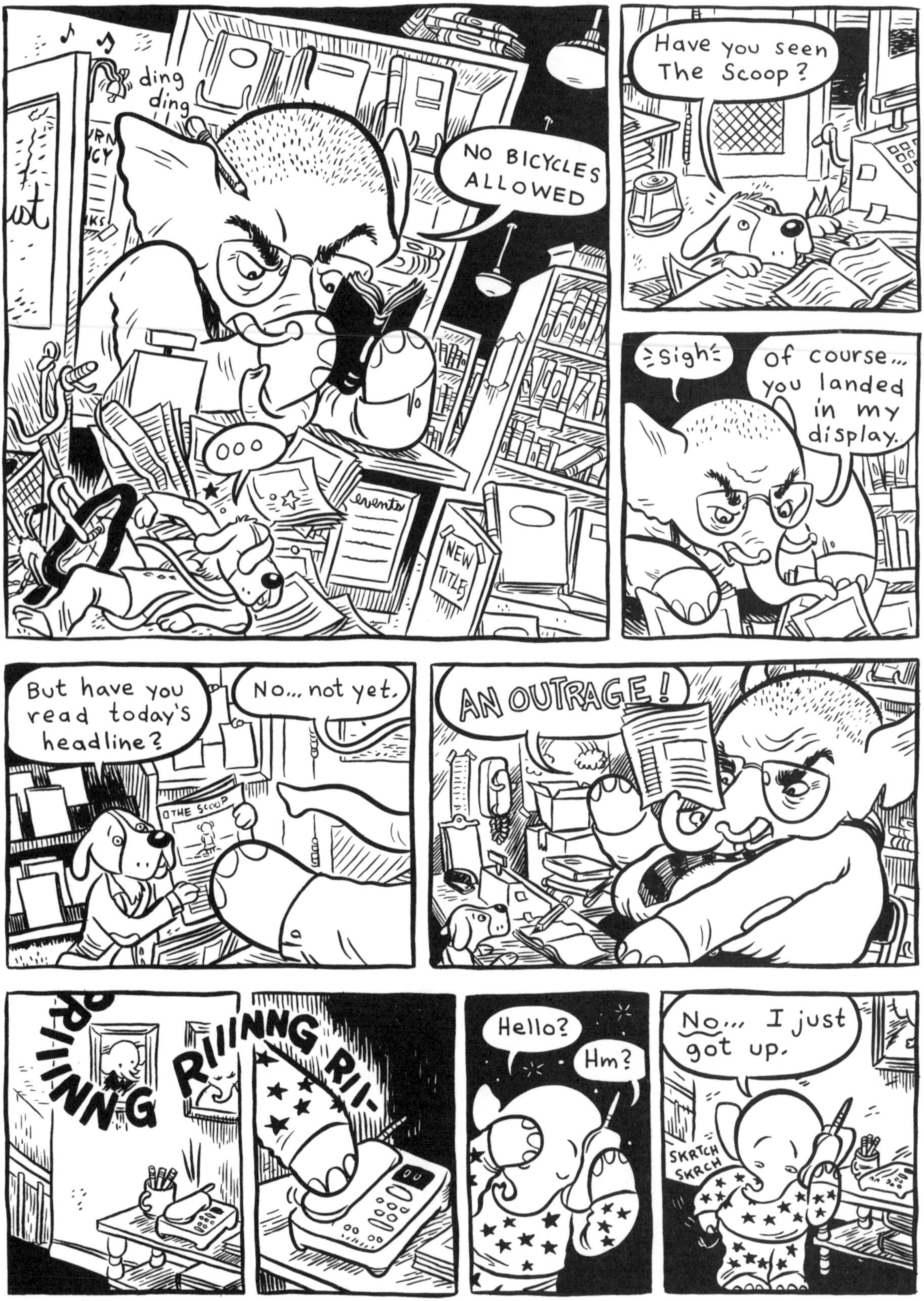
ding
ding
NO BICYCLES ALLOWED
ooo
events
NEW TITLES
Have you seen The Scoop?
Sigh
Of course... you landed in my display.
But have you read today's headline?
No... not yet.
THE SCOOP
AN OUTRAGE!
RIIIING
RIIING
RIIING RII-
Hello?
Hm?
No... I just got up.
SKRTCH
SKRCH

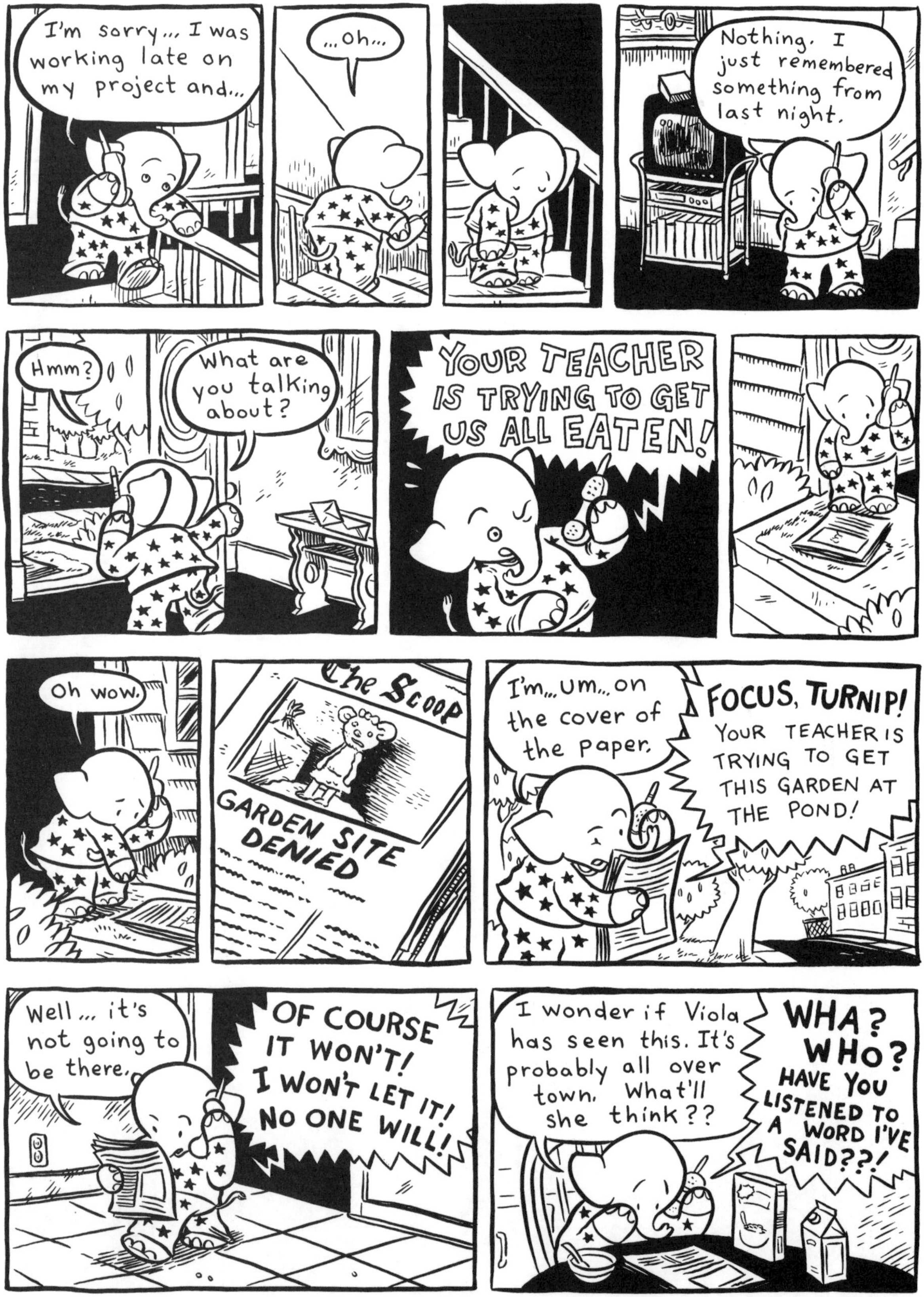
I'm sorry... I was working late on my project and...
...Oh...
Nothing. I just remembered something from last night.
Hmm?
What are you talking about?
YOUR TEACHER IS TRYING TO GET US ALL EATEN!
Oh wow.
The Scoop
GARDEN SITE DENIED
I'm...um...on the cover of the paper.
FOCUS, TURNIP! YOUR TEACHER IS TRYING TO GET THIS GARDEN AT THE POND!
Well... it's not going to be there.
OF COURSE IT WON'T! I WON'T LET IT! NO ONE WILL!
I wonder if Viola has seen this. It's probably all over town. What'll she think??
WHA? WHO? HAVE YOU LISTENED TO A WORD I'VE SAID??!

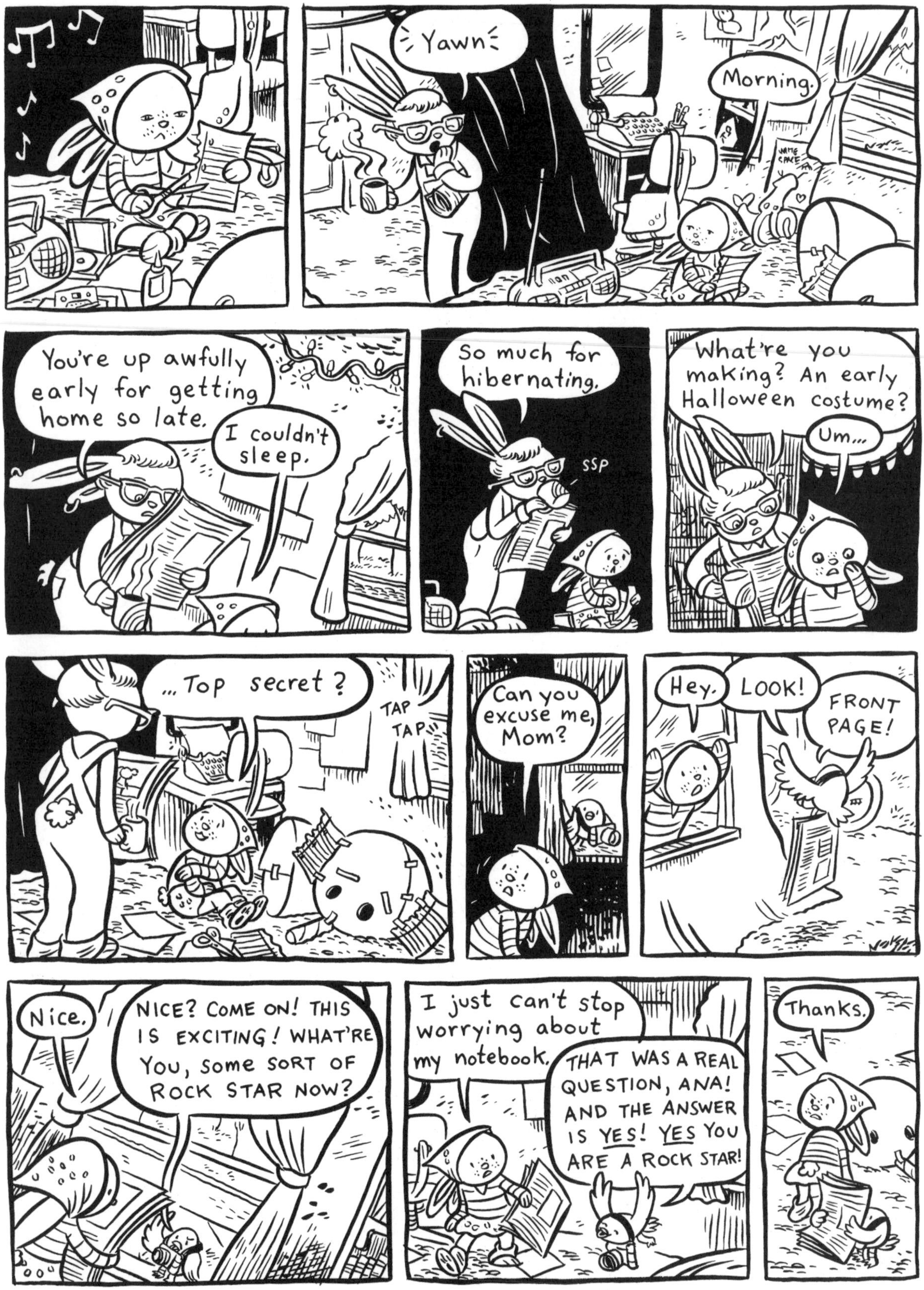
Yawn
Morning.
You're up awfully early for getting home so late.
I couldn't sleep.
So much for hibernating.
SSP
What're you making? An early Halloween costume?
Um...
...Top secret?
TAP TAP
Can you excuse me, Mom?
Hey.
LOOK!
FRONT PAGE!
Nice.
NICE? COME ON! THIS IS EXCITING! WHAT'RE YOU, SOME SORT OF ROCK STAR NOW?
I just can't stop worrying about my notebook.
THAT WAS A REAL QUESTION, ANA! AND THE ANSWER IS YES! YES YOU ARE A ROCK STAR!
Thanks.

I'm totally going to frame this!
First things first, Em.
Hey
Hey
Listen, last night I... I didn't...
I'm sure it was an accident. Don't worry.
Why are you so late?
I over-slept...
And then I saw this!
Yeah.
Do you know who wrote it?
Mm-hmm
No... but did you see the picture?
Do you think she'll be flattered or embarrassed?
Who? Oh, I don't know.
Ms. Skrimshaw is looking for you.

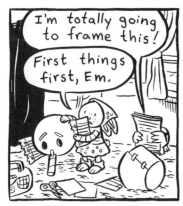

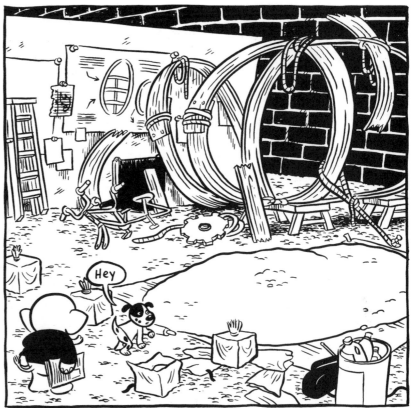

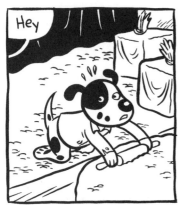

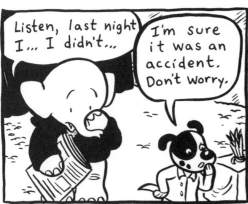

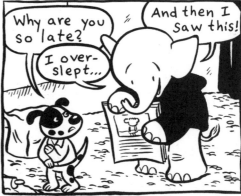

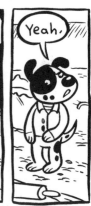

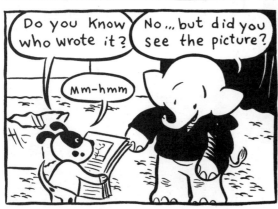

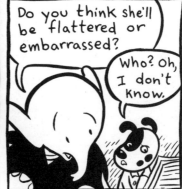

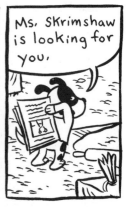

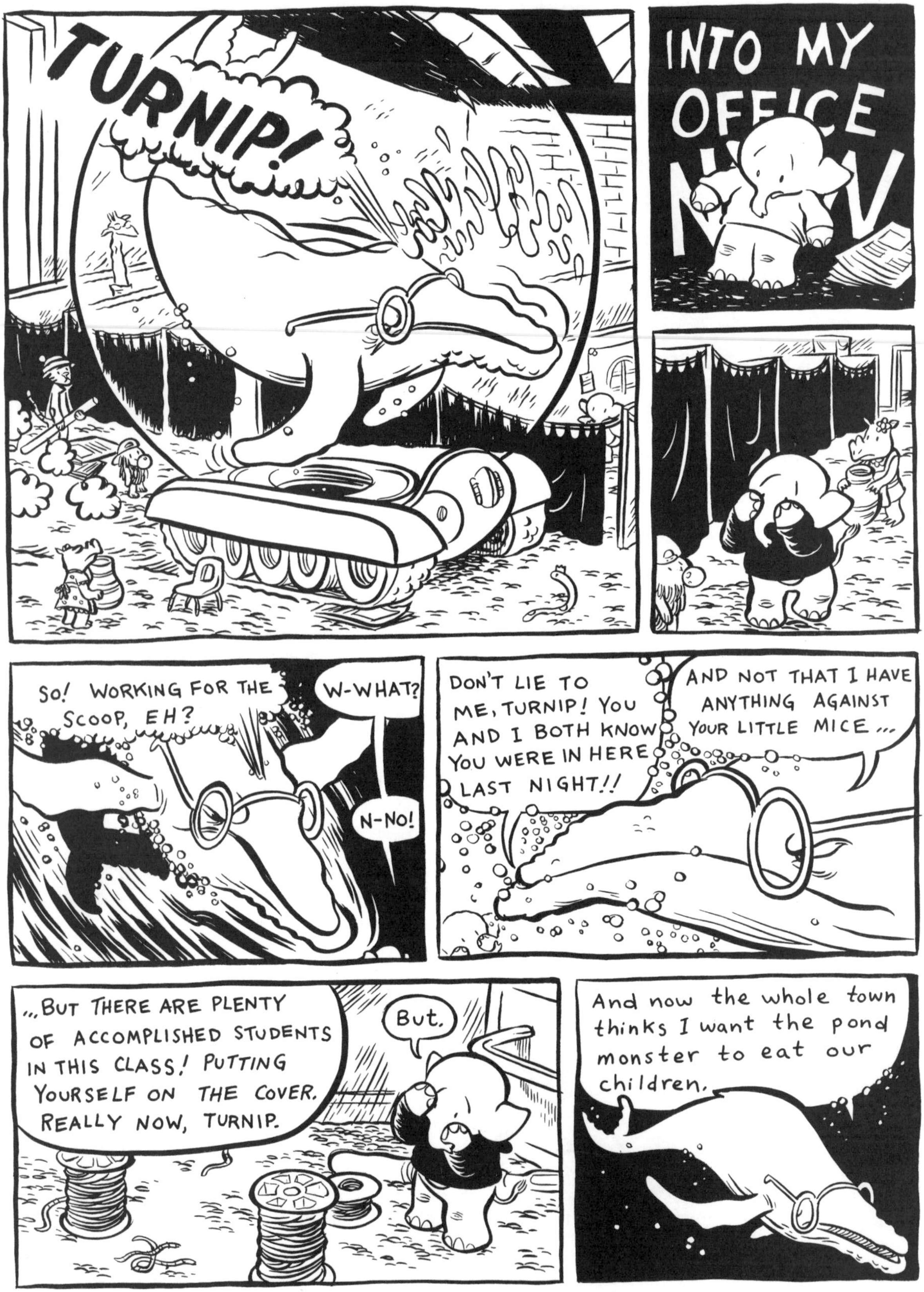

TURNIP!
INTO MY OFFICE NOW
So! WORKING FOR THE SCOOP, EH?
W-WHAT?
N-NO!
DON'T LIE TO ME, TURNIP! YOU AND I BOTH KNOW YOU WERE IN HERE LAST NIGHT!!
AND NOT THAT I HAVE ANYTHING AGAINST YOUR LITTLE MICE ...
... BUT THERE ARE PLENTY OF ACCOMPLISHED STUDENTS IN THIS CLASS! PUTTING YOURSELF ON THE COVER. REALLY NOW, TURNIP.
But.
And now the whole town thinks I want the pond monster to eat our children.

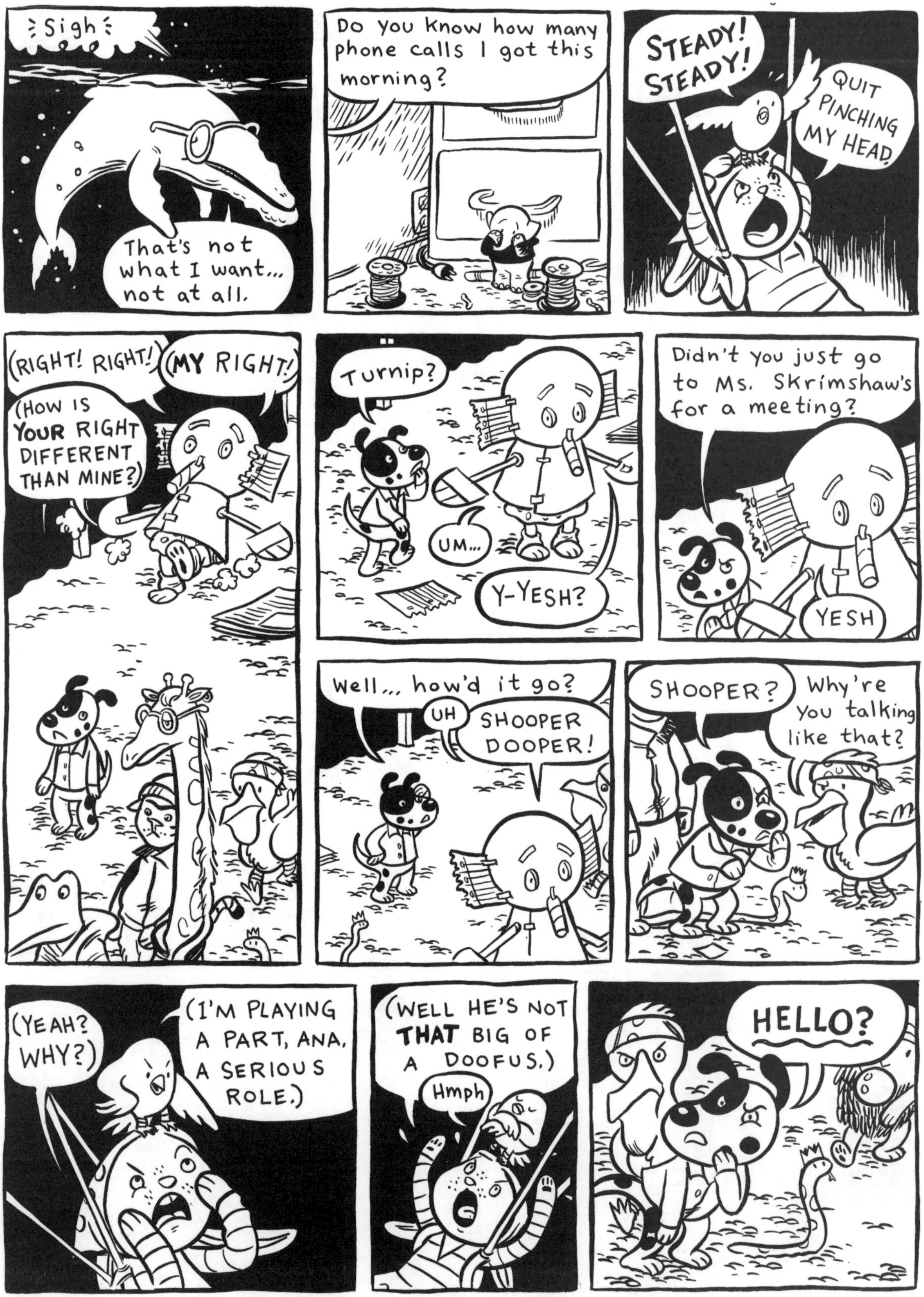
Sigh
That's not what I want... not at all.
Do you know how many phone calls I got this morning?
STEADY! STEADY!
QUIT PINCHING MY HEAD
(RIGHT! RIGHT!)
(MY RIGHT!)
(HOW IS YOUR RIGHT DIFFERENT THAN MINE?)
Turnip?
UM...
Y-YESH?
Didn't you just go to Ms. Skrimshaw's for a meeting?
YESH
Well... how'd it go?
UH
SHOOPER DOOPER!
SHOOPER?
Why're you talking like that?
(YEAH? WHY?)
(I'M PLAYING A PART, ANA. A SERIOUS ROLE.)
(WELL HE'S NOT THAT BIG OF A DOOFUS.)
Hmph
HELLO?

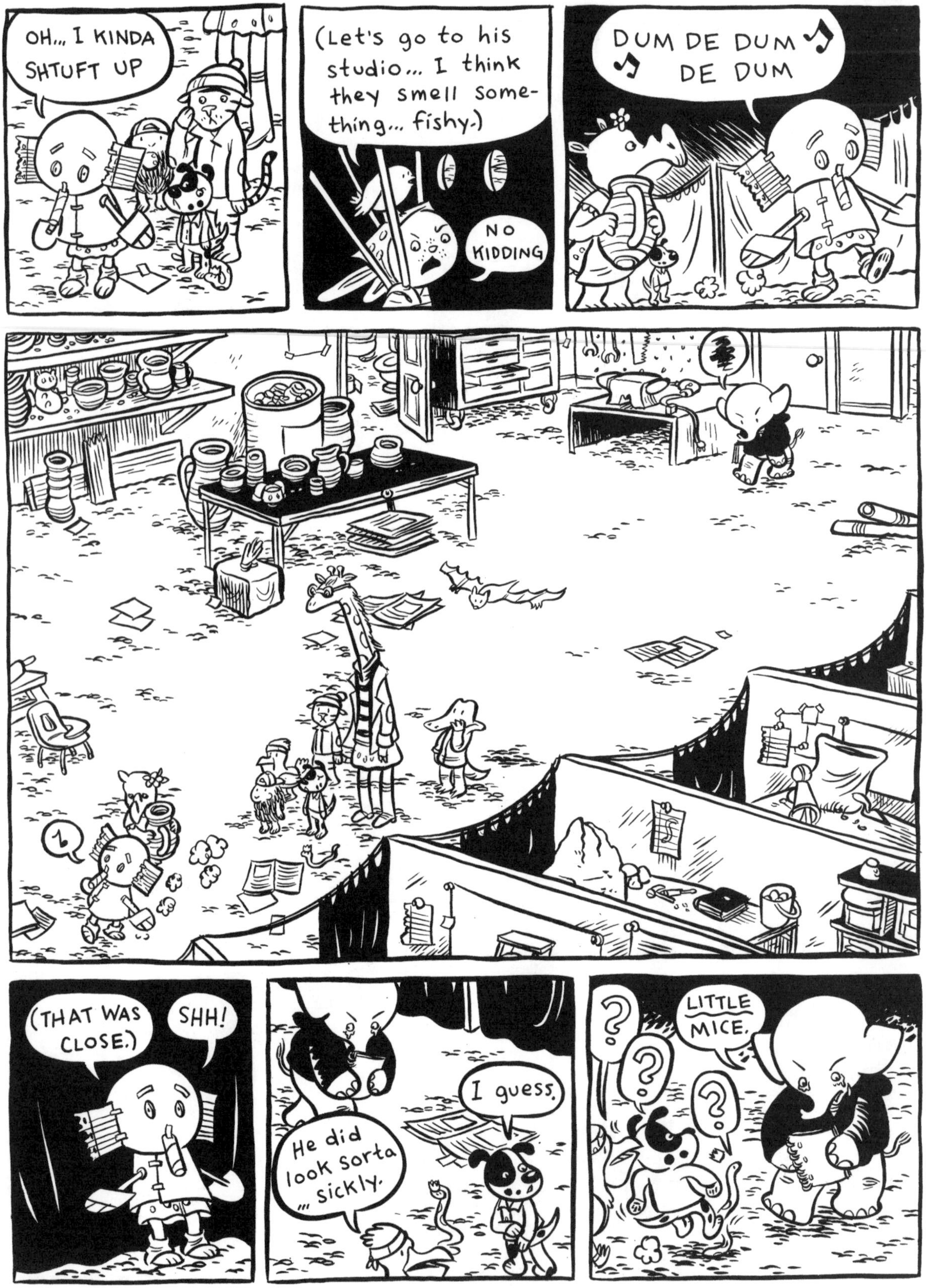
OH... I KINDA SHTUFT UP
(Let's go to his studio... I think they smell something... fishy.)
NO KIDDING
DUM DE DUM DE DUM
(THAT WAS CLOSE.)
SHH!
I guess.
He did look sorta ... sickly.
LITTLE MICE.

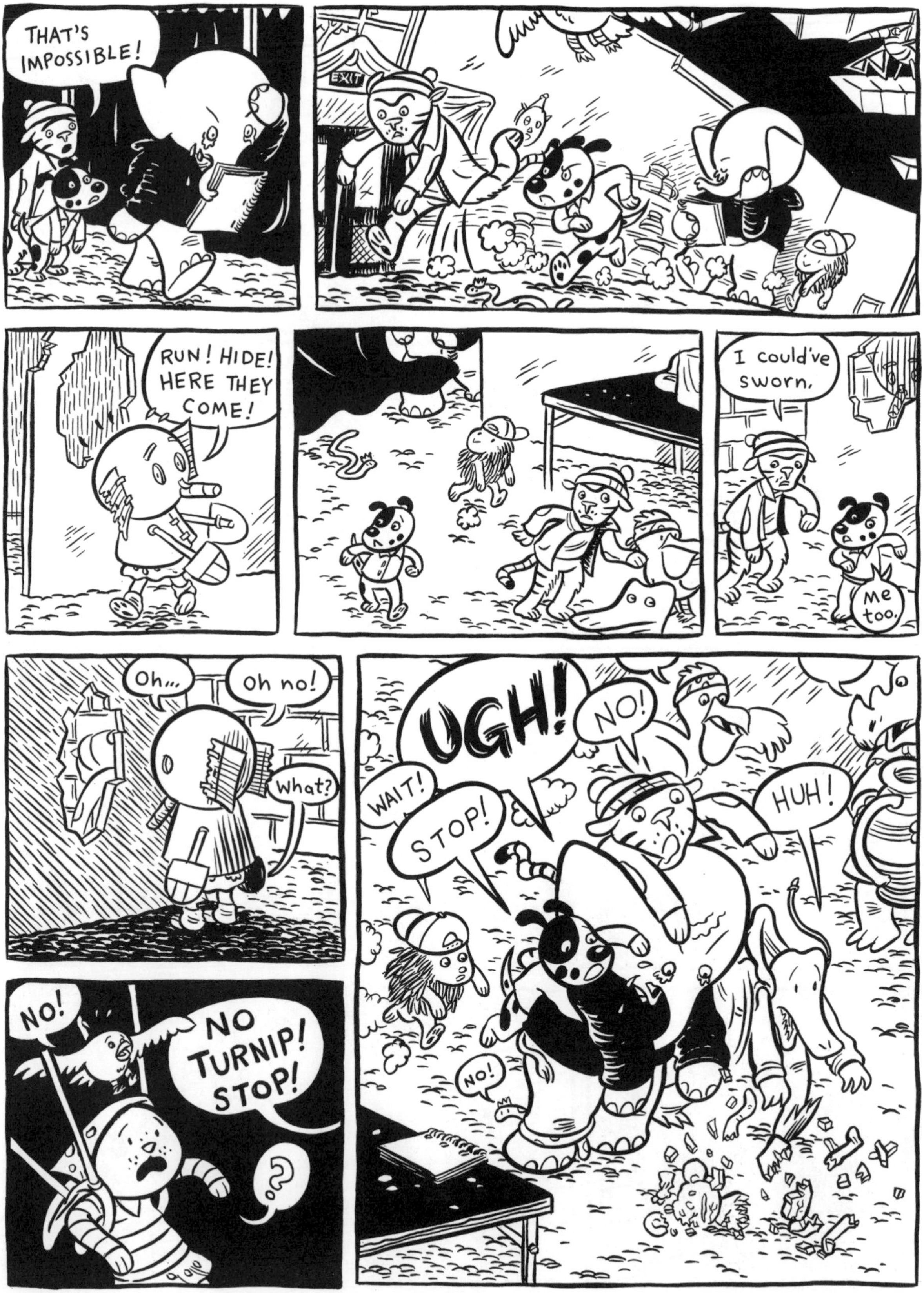
THAT'S IMPOSSIBLE!
RUN! HIDE! HERE THEY COME!
I could've sworn.
Me too.
Oh...
Oh no!
What?
UGH!
NO!
WAIT!
STOP!
HUH!
NO!
NO!
NO TURNIP! STOP!
?

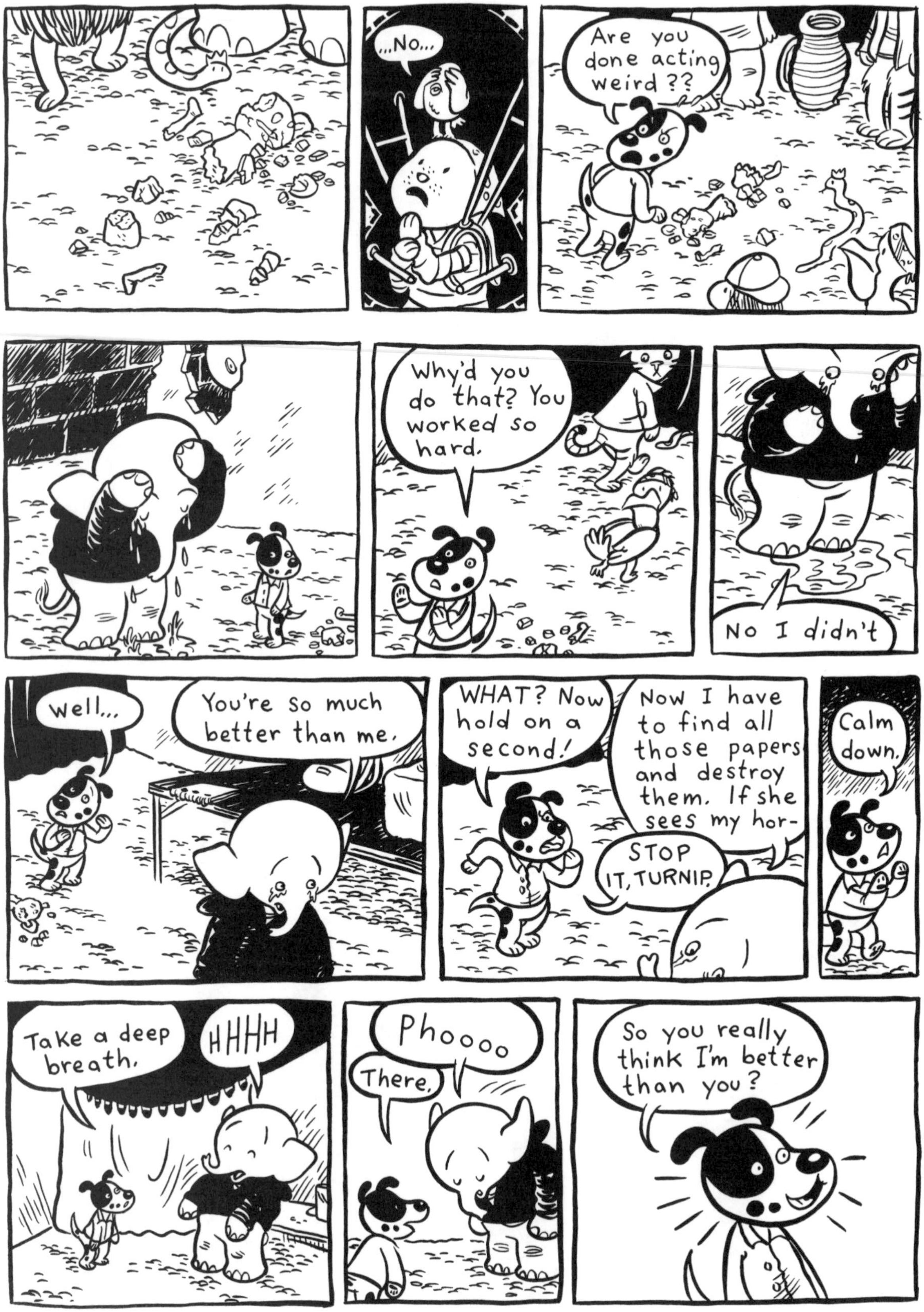
...No...
Are you done acting weird ??
Why'd you do that? You worked so hard.
No I didn't
Well...
You're so much better than me.
WHAT? Now hold on a second!
Now I have to find all those papers and destroy them. If she sees my hor-
STOP IT, TURNIP.
Calm down.
Take a deep breath.
HHHH
Phoooo
There.
So you really think I'm better than you?

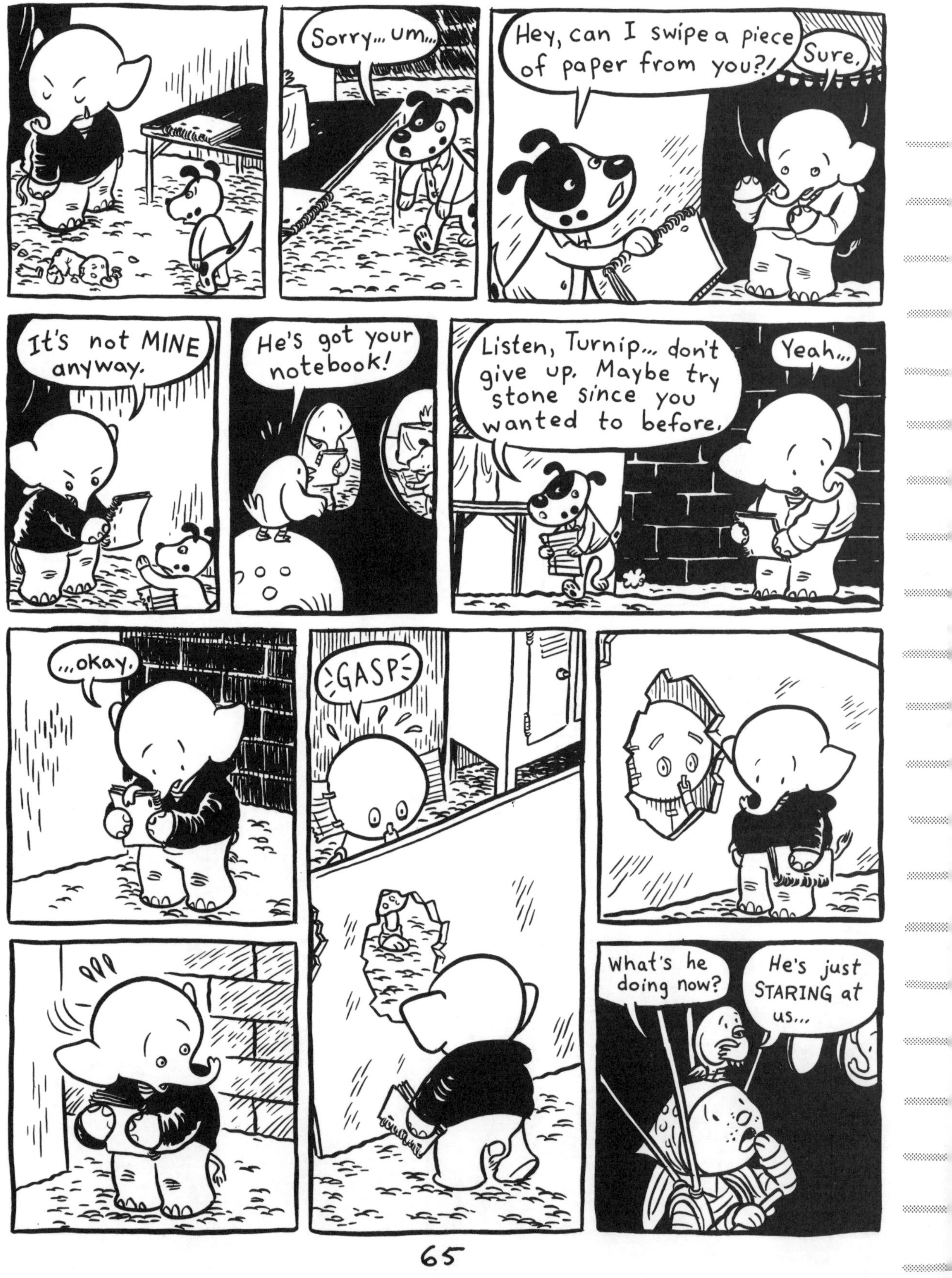
Sorry... um...
Hey, can I swipe a piece of paper from you?!
Sure,
It's not MINE anyway.
He's got your notebook!
Listen, Turnip... don't give up. Maybe try stone since you wanted to before.
Yeah...
...okay.
GASP
What's he doing now?
He's just STARING at us...

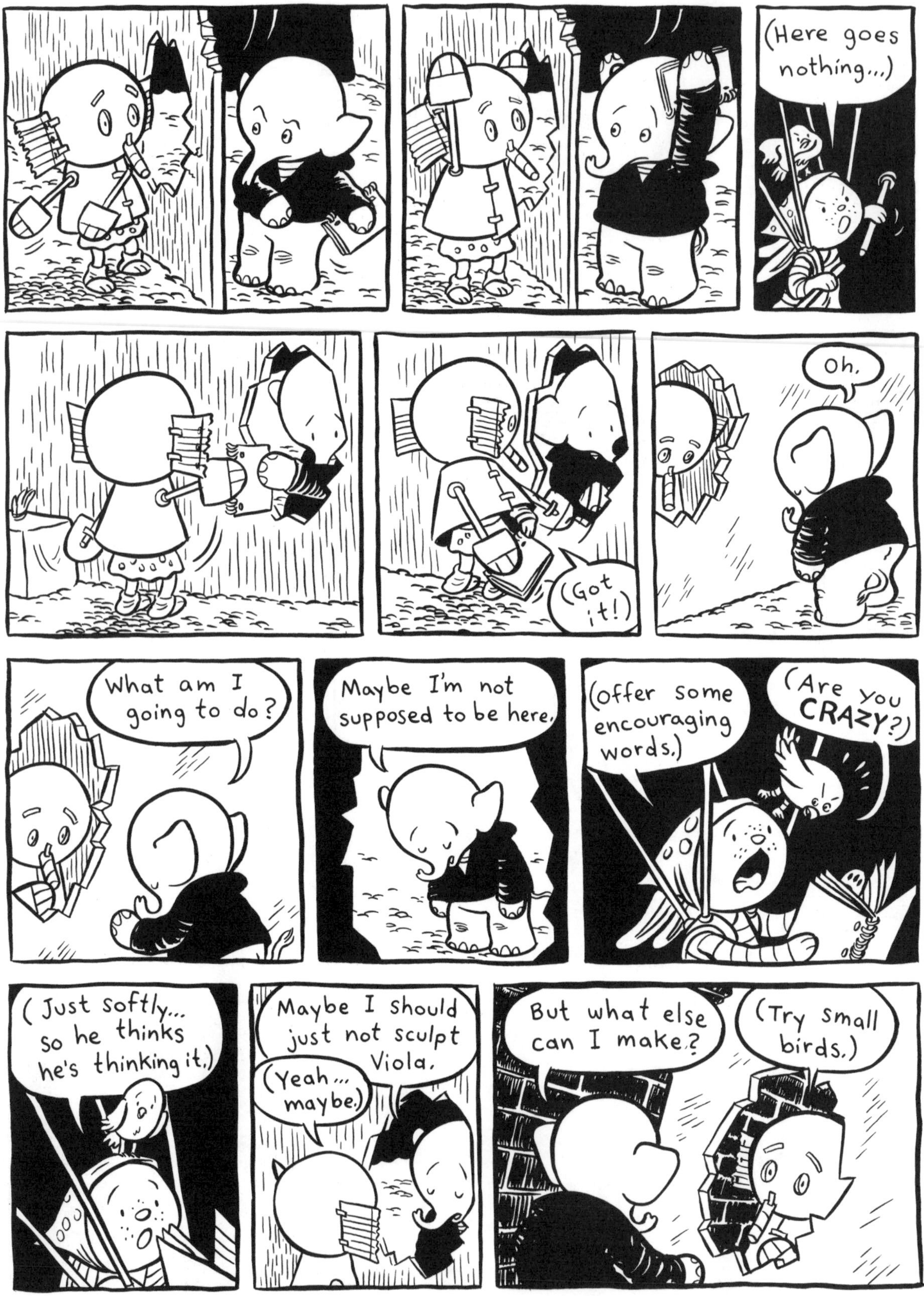
(Here goes nothing...)
Oh.
(Got it!)
What am I going to do?
Maybe I'm not supposed to be here.
(Offer some encouraging words.)
(Are you CRAZY?)
(Just softly... so he thinks he's thinking it.)
Maybe I should just not sculpt Viola.
(Yeah... maybe.)
But what else can I make?
(Try small birds.)

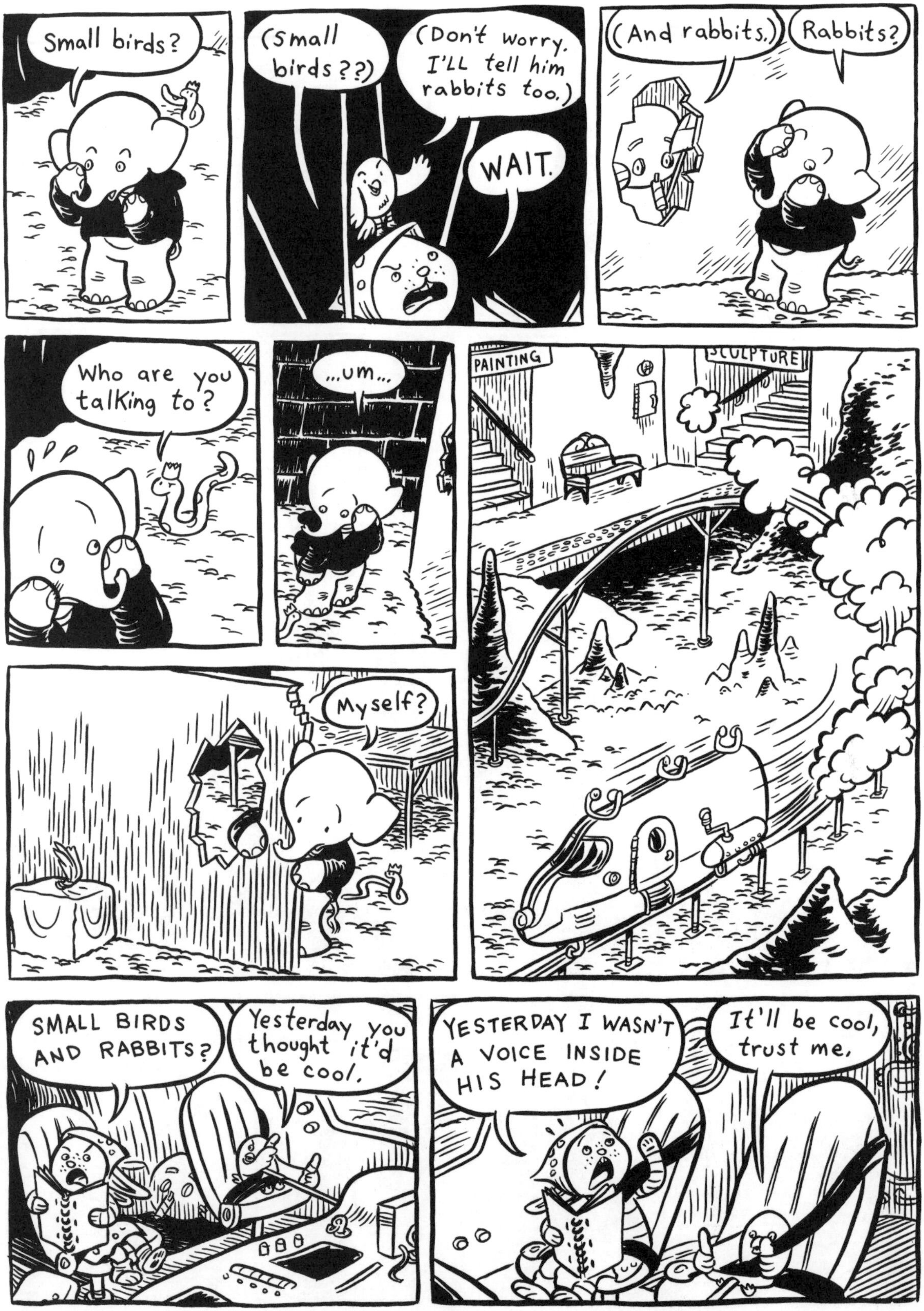

Small birds?
(Small birds??)
(Don't worry. I'LL tell him rabbits too.)
WAIT.
(And rabbits.)
Rabbits?
Who are you talking to?
...um...
PAINTING
SCULPTURE
Myself?
SMALL BIRDS AND RABBITS?
Yesterday you thought it'd be cool.
YESTERDAY I WASN'T A VOICE INSIDE HIS HEAD!
It'll be cool, trust me.

I don't know...

Just be thankful we got your notebook back.

So... you want to go buy the frames now?

Sure... but let's stop at June Bug's first. I'm SUPER hungry.

KKKKSSSSHH

?

OH!... Hey, ladies... You two just sort of popped out of nowhere.

So... what'll it be?

CHERRY PANCAKES!

Sorry, girls. We stopped serving breakfast... seven hours ago.

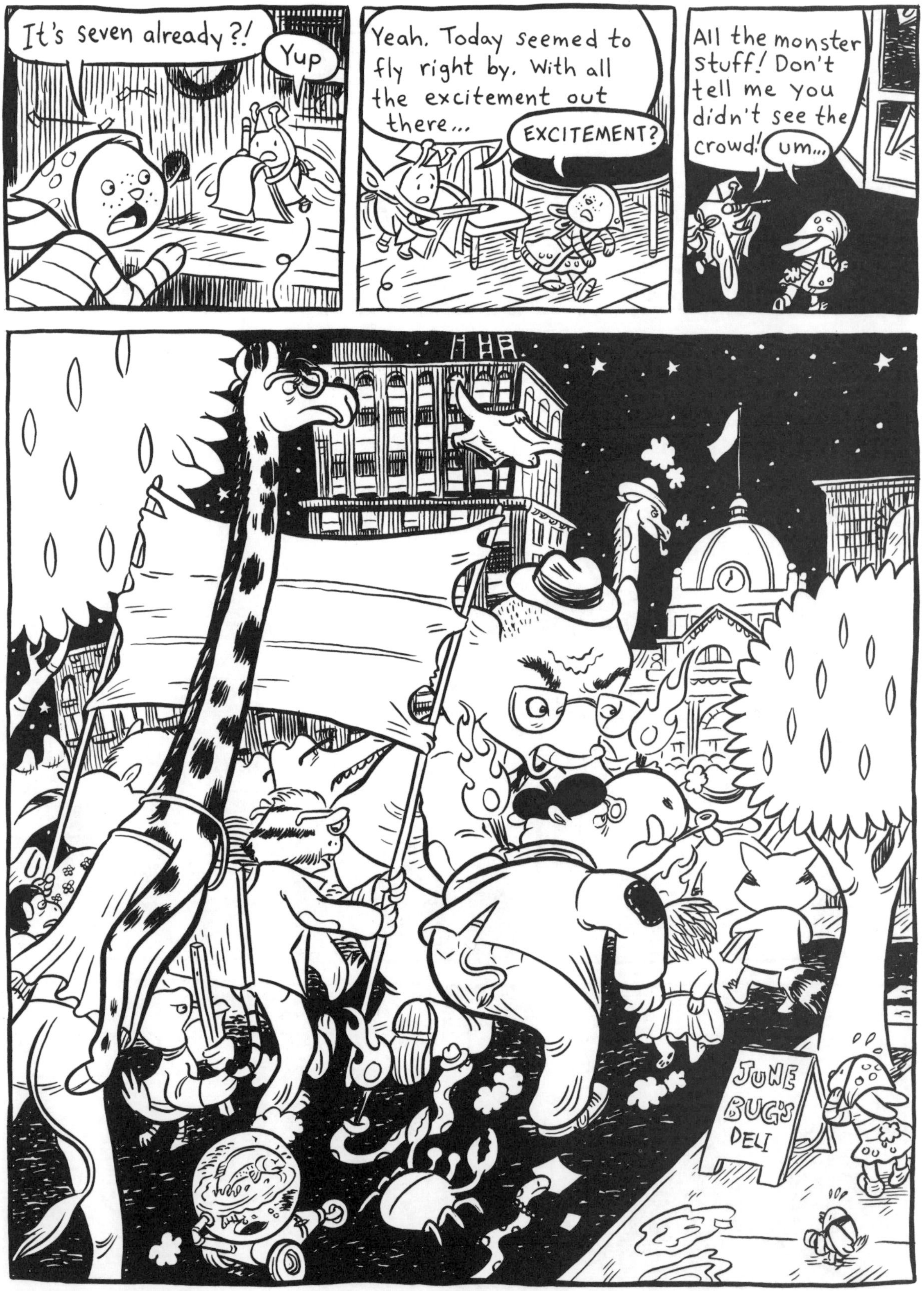
It's seven already?!
Yup
Yeah. Today seemed to fly right by. With all the excitement out there...
EXCITEMENT?
All the monster stuff! Don't tell me you didn't see the crowd!
um...
JUNE BUG'S DELI

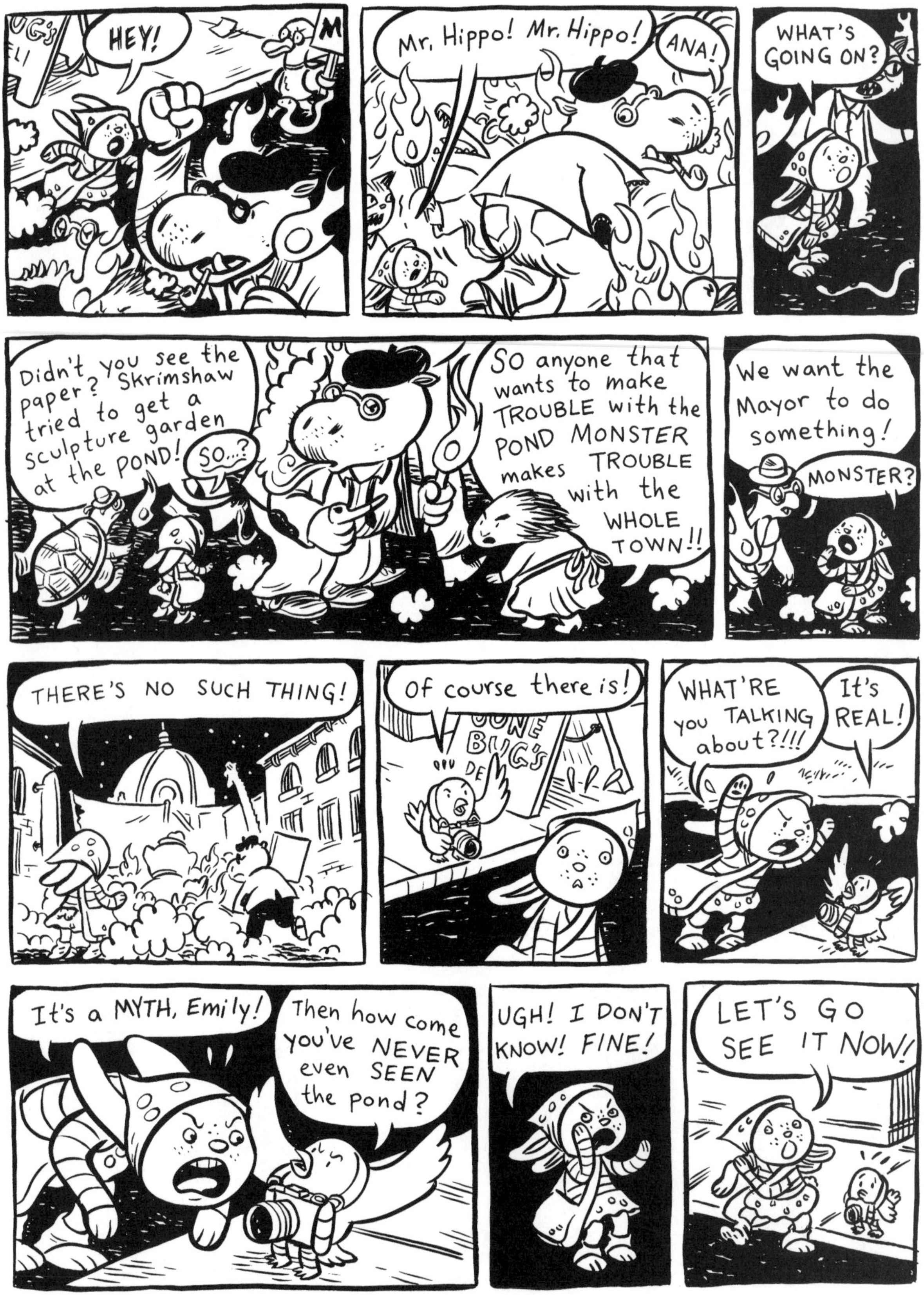
HEY!
Mr. Hippo! Mr. Hippo!
ANA!
WHAT'S GOING ON?
Didn't you see the paper? Skrimshaw tried to get a sculpture garden at the POND!
SO...?
SO anyone that wants to make TROUBLE with the POND MONSTER makes TROUBLE with the WHOLE TOWN!!
We want the Mayor to do something!
MONSTER?
THERE'S NO SUCH THING!
Of course there is!
WHAT'RE you TALKING about?!!!
It's REAL!
It's a MYTH, Emily!
Then how come you've NEVER even SEEN the pond?
UGH! I DON'T KNOW! FINE!
LET'S GO SEE IT NOW!

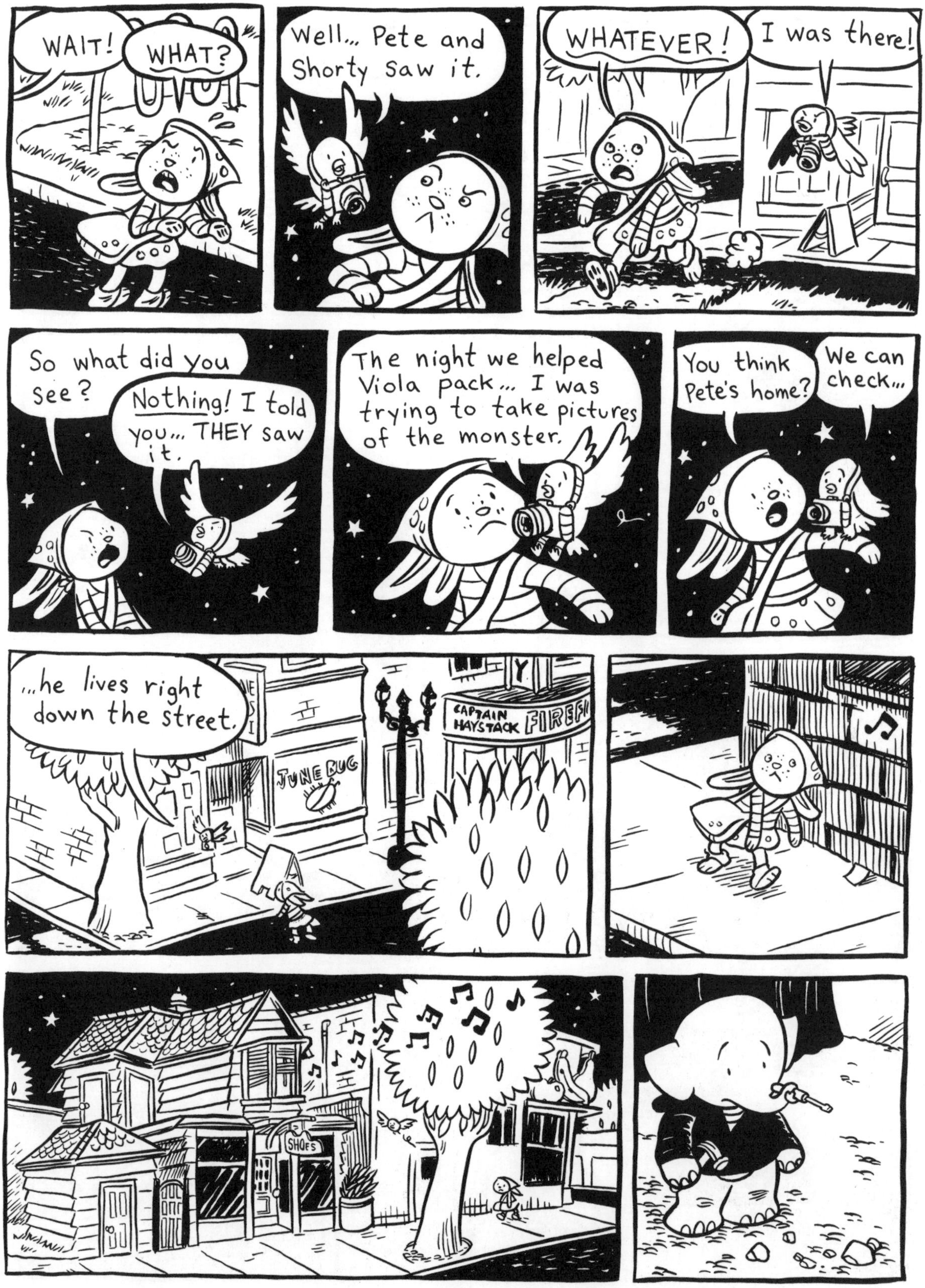
WAIT!
WHAT?
Well... Pete and Shorty saw it.
WHATEVER!
I was there!
So what did you see?
Nothing! I told you... THEY saw it.
The night we helped Viola pack... I was trying to take pictures of the monster.
You think Pete's home?
We can check...
...he lives right down the street.
JUNEBUG
CAPTAIN HAYSTACK
SHOES

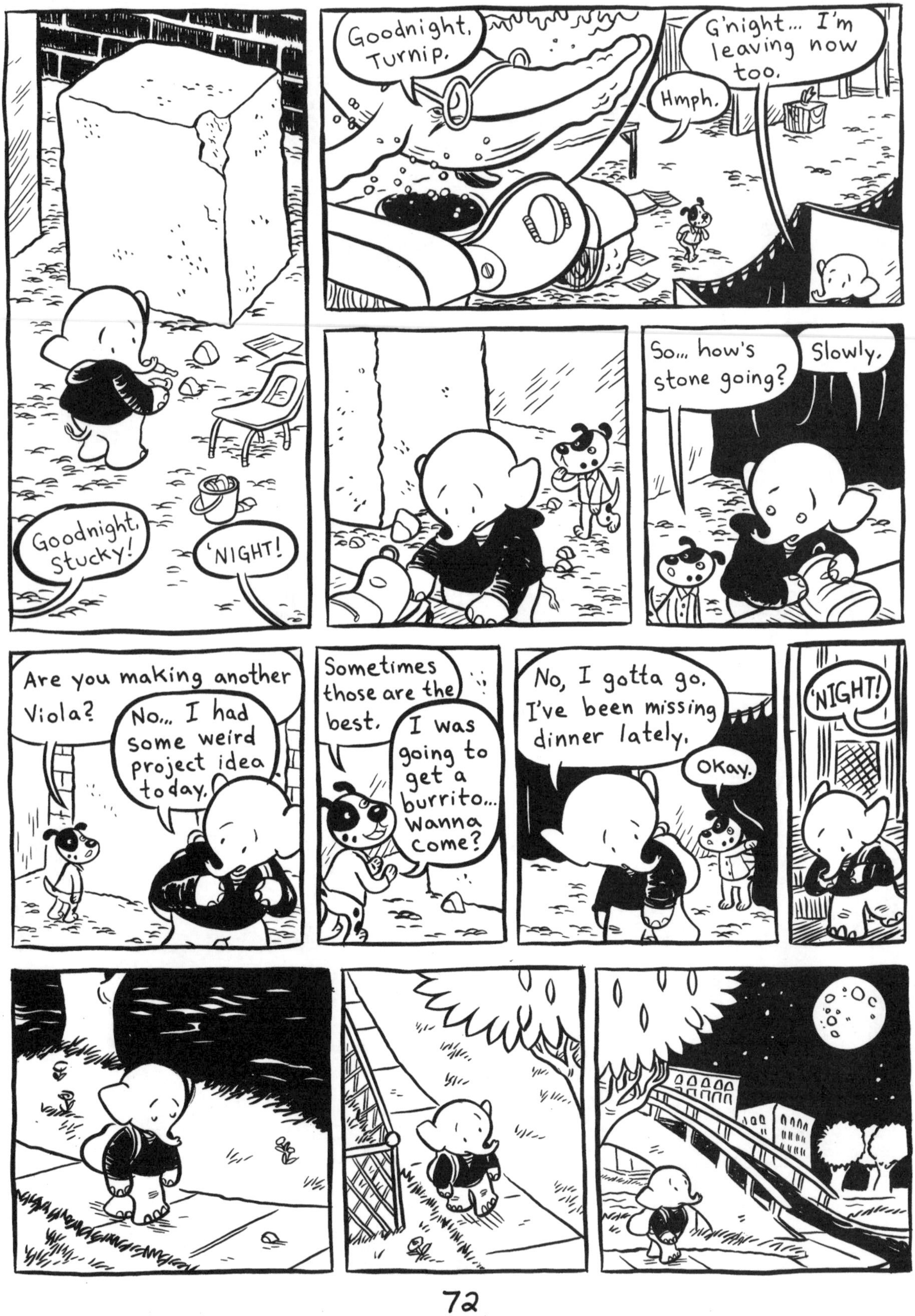
Goodnight, Stucky!
'NIGHT!
Goodnight, Turnip.
Hmph.
G'night... I'm leaving now too.
So... how's stone going?
Slowly.
Are you making another Viola?
No... I had some weird project idea today.
Sometimes those are the best.
I was going to get a burrito... wanna come?
No, I gotta go. I've been missing dinner lately.
Okay.
'NIGHT!

Hello?
Dad?
Sorry to miss dinner. But somebody has to do something about your teacher. I'll be protesting late. Stroganoff leftovers. DAD

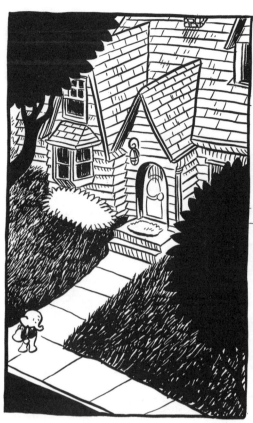

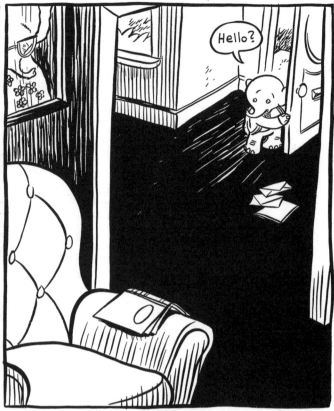

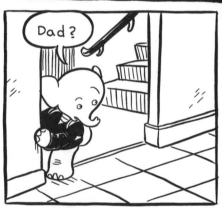

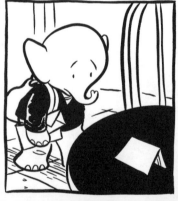

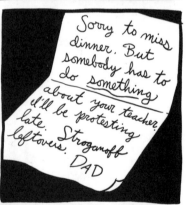

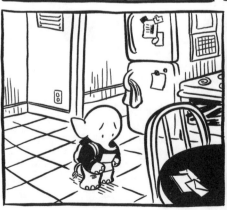

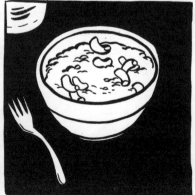

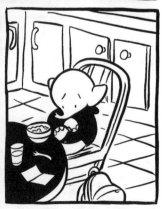

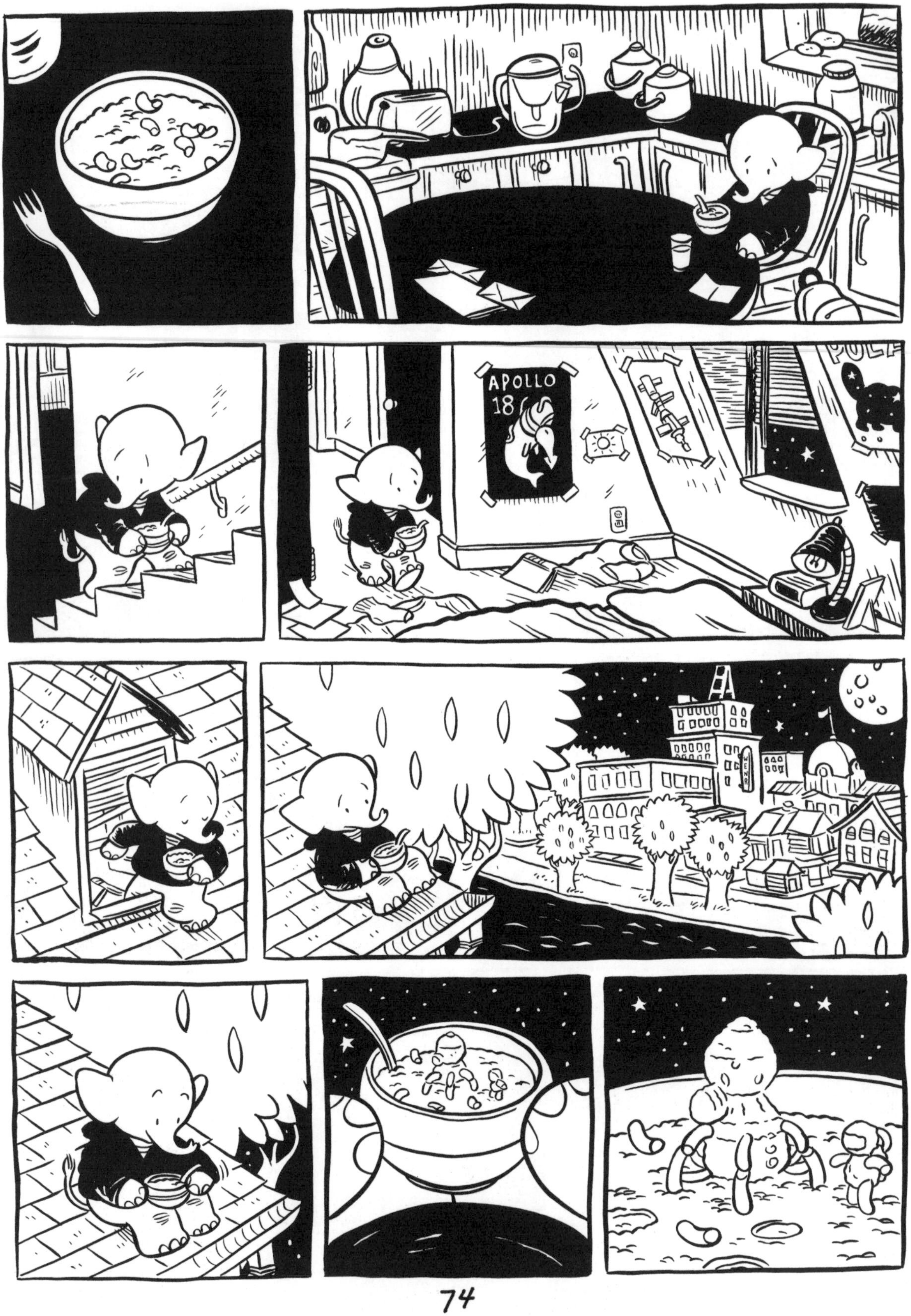
APOLLO

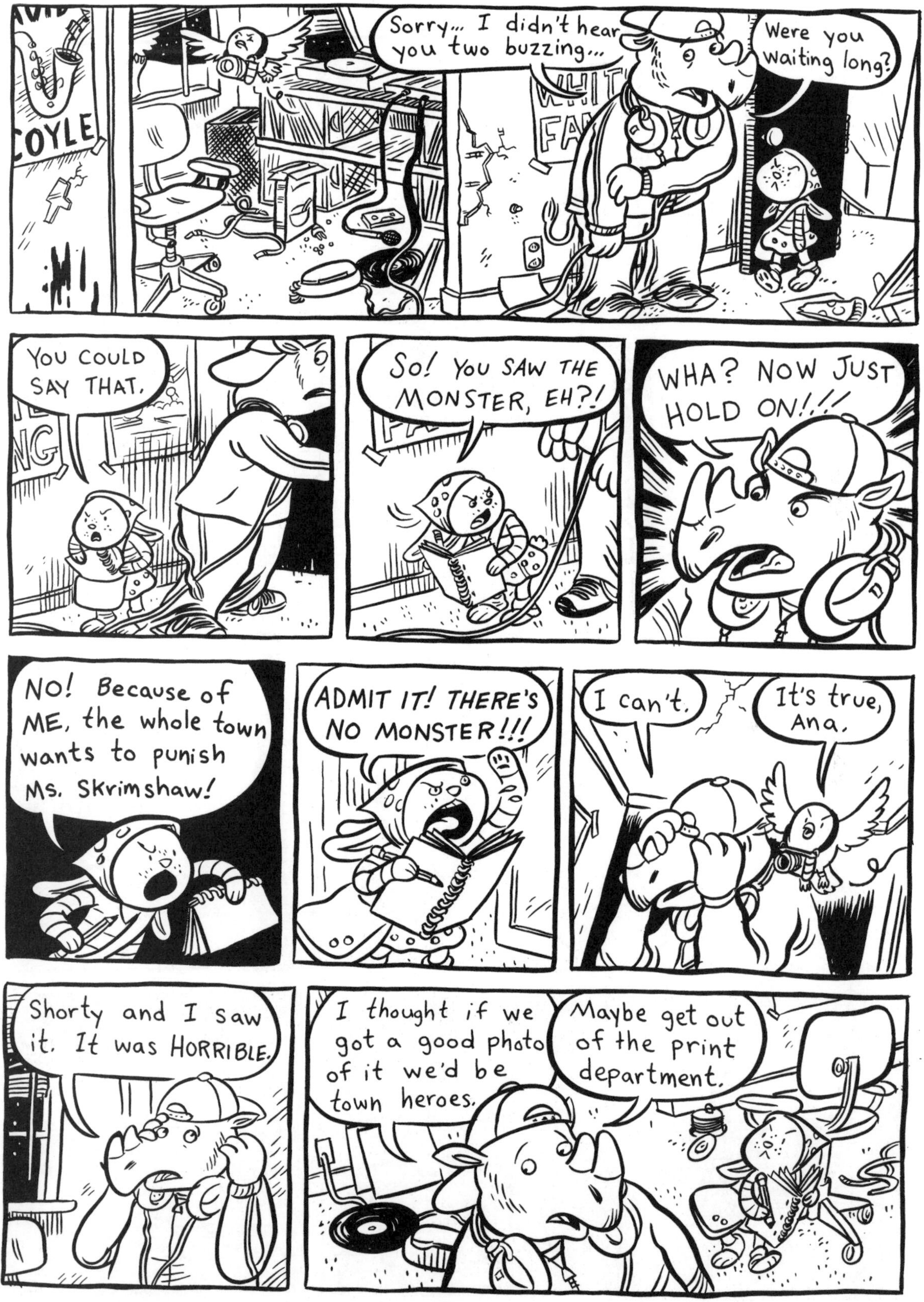
COYLE
Sorry... I didn't hear you two buzzing...
Were you waiting long?
YOU COULD SAY THAT.
So! YOU SAW THE MONSTER, EH?!
WHA? NOW JUST HOLD ON!!!
NO! Because of ME, the whole town wants to punish Ms. Skrimshaw!
ADMIT IT! THERE'S NO MONSTER!!!
I can't.
It's true, Ana.
Shorty and I saw it. It was HORRIBLE.
I thought if we got a good photo of it we'd be town heroes.
Maybe get out of the print department.

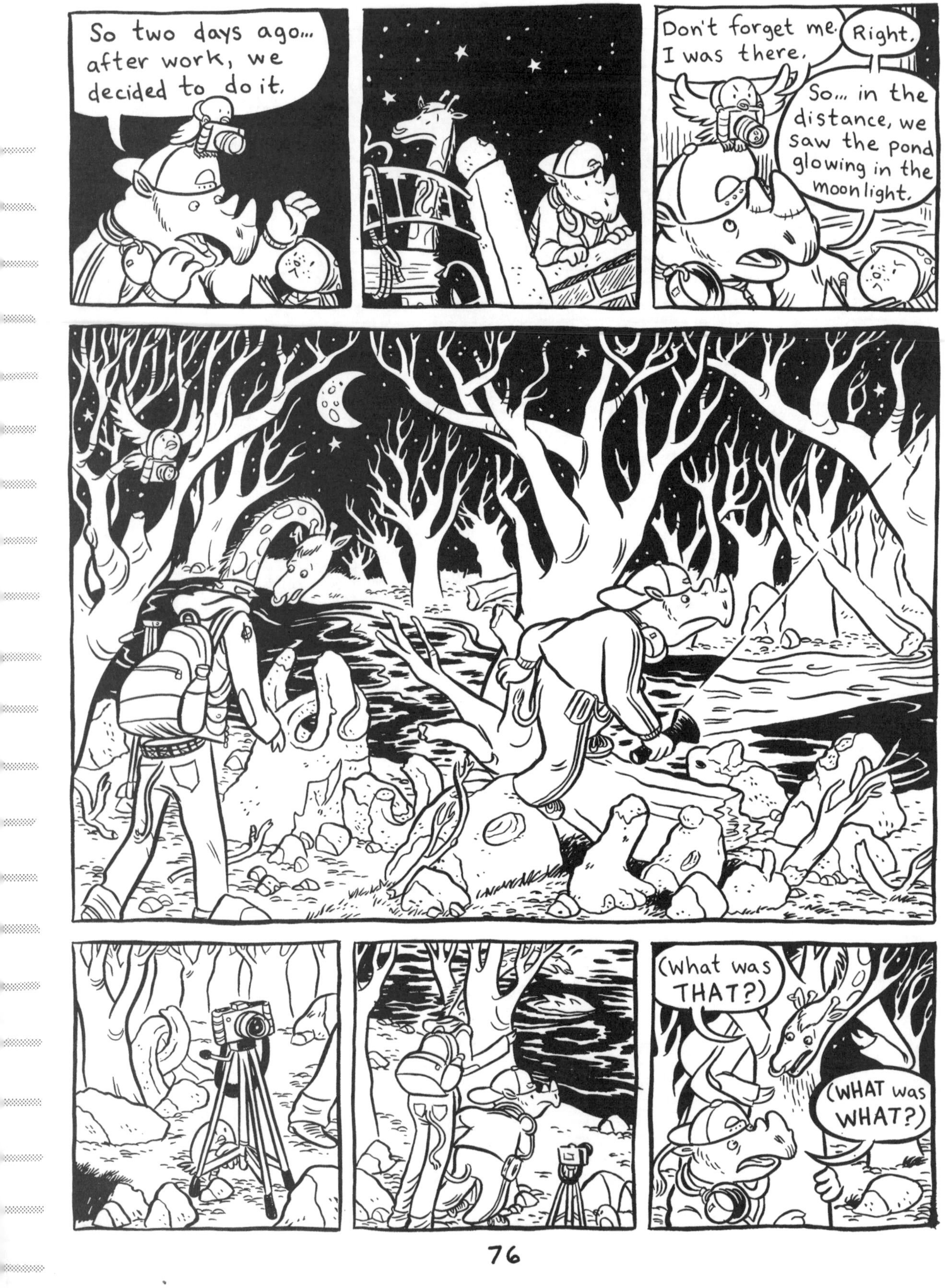
So two days ago... after work, we decided to do it.
Don't forget me. I was there.
Right.
So... in the distance, we saw the pond glowing in the moonlight.
(What was THAT?)
(WHAT was WHAT?)

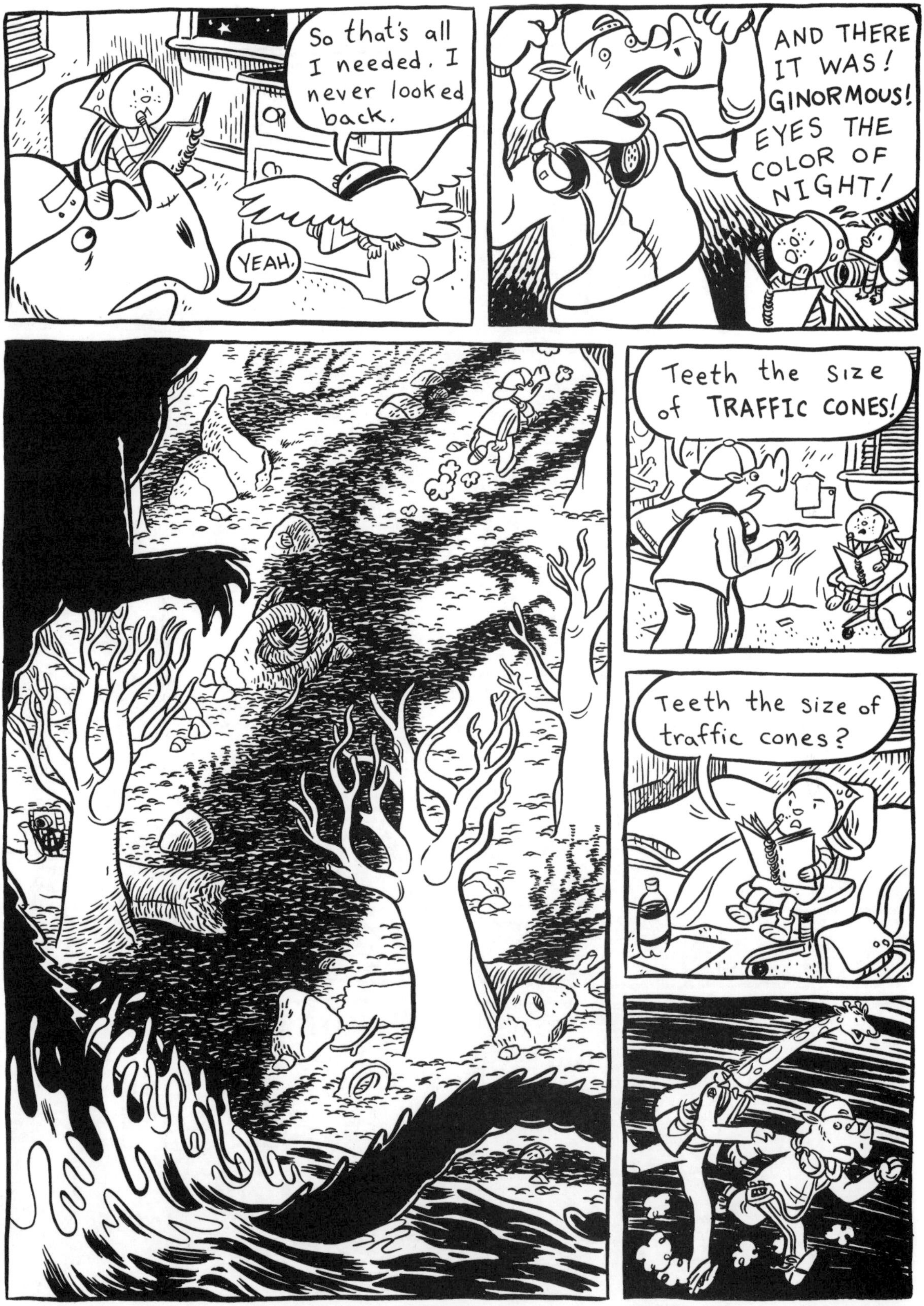
So that's all I needed. I never looked back.
YEAH.
AND THERE IT WAS! GINORMOUS! EYES THE COLOR OF NIGHT!
Teeth the size of TRAFFIC CONES!
Teeth the size of traffic cones?

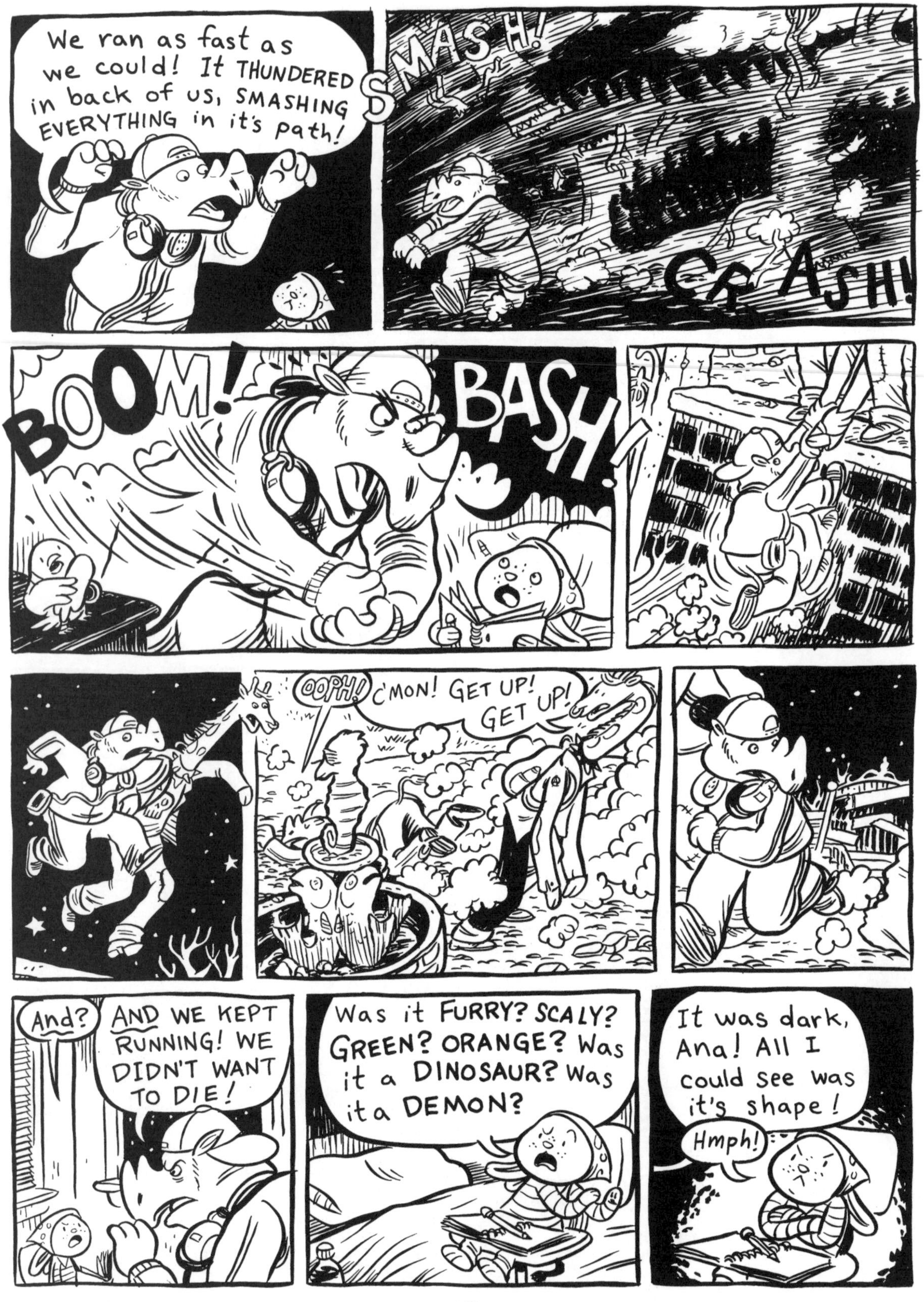
We ran as fast as we could! It THUNDERED in back of us, SMASHING EVERYTHING in it's path!
SMASH!
CRASH!
BOOM!
BASH!
OOPH!
C'MON! GET UP! GET UP!
And?
AND WE KEPT RUNNING! WE DIDN'T WANT TO DIE!
Was it FURRY? SCALY? GREEN? ORANGE? Was it a DINOSAUR? Was it a DEMON?
It was dark, Ana! All I could see was it's shape!
Hmph!

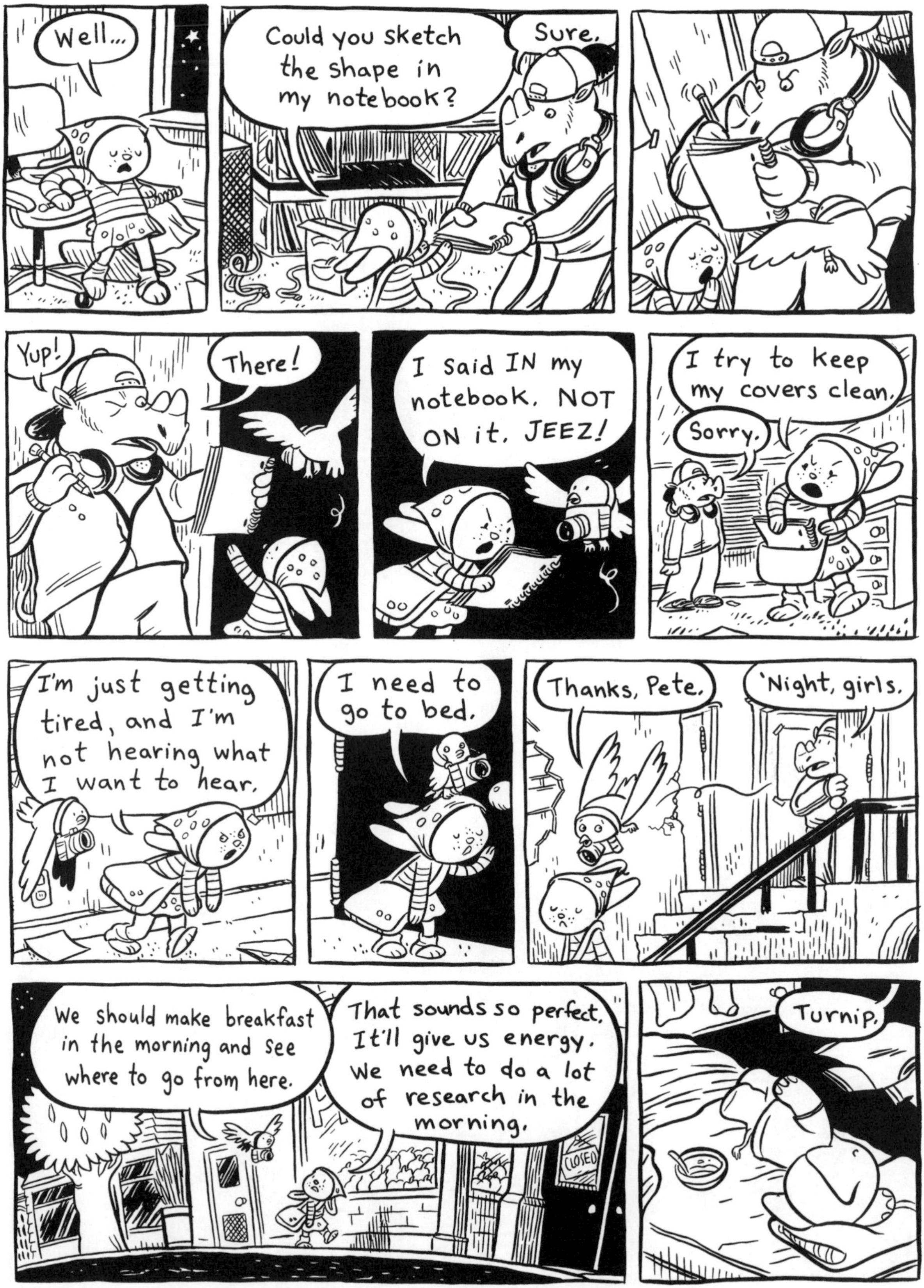
Well...
Could you sketch the shape in my notebook?
Sure.
Yup!
There!
I said IN my notebook. NOT ON it. JEEZ!
I try to keep my covers clean.
Sorry.
I'm just getting tired, and I'm not hearing what I want to hear.
I need to go to bed.
Thanks, Pete.
'Night, girls.
We should make breakfast in the morning and see where to go from here.
That sounds so perfect. It'll give us energy. We need to do a lot of research in the morning.
CLOSED
Turnip.

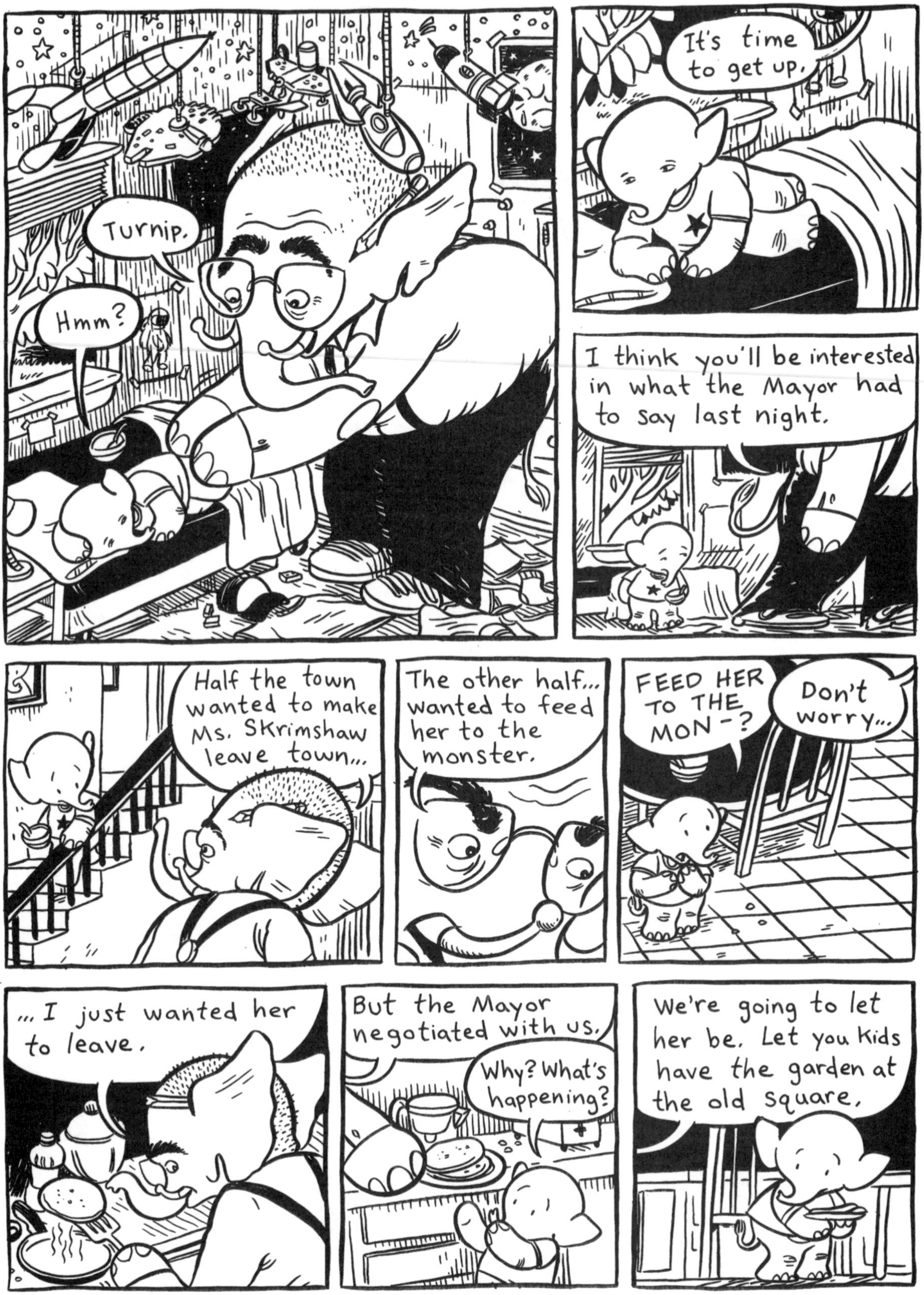
Turnip.
Hmm?
It's time to get up.
I think you'll be interested in what the Mayor had to say last night.
Half the town wanted to make Ms. Skrimshaw leave town...
The other half... wanted to feed her to the monster.
FEED HER TO THE MON-?
Don't worry...
...I just wanted her to leave.
But the Mayor negotiated with us.
Why? What's happening?
We're going to let her be. Let you kids have the garden at the old square.

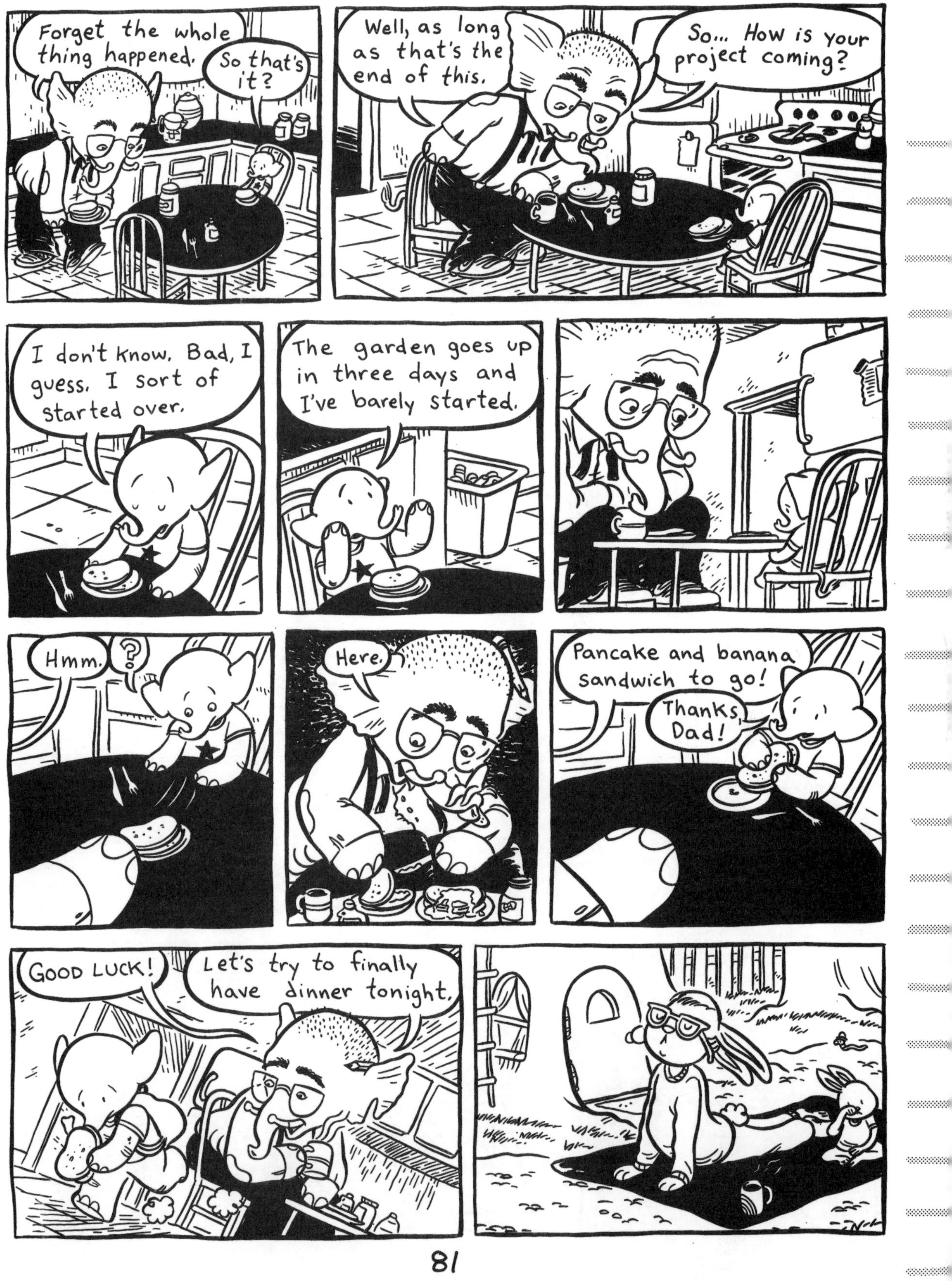
Forget the whole thing happened.
So that's it?
Well, as long as that's the end of this.
So... How is your project coming?
I don't know. Bad, I guess. I sort of started over.
The garden goes up in three days and I've barely started.
Hmm.
?
Here.
Pancake and banana sandwich to go!
Thanks, Dad!
GOOD LUCK!
Let's try to finally have dinner tonight.

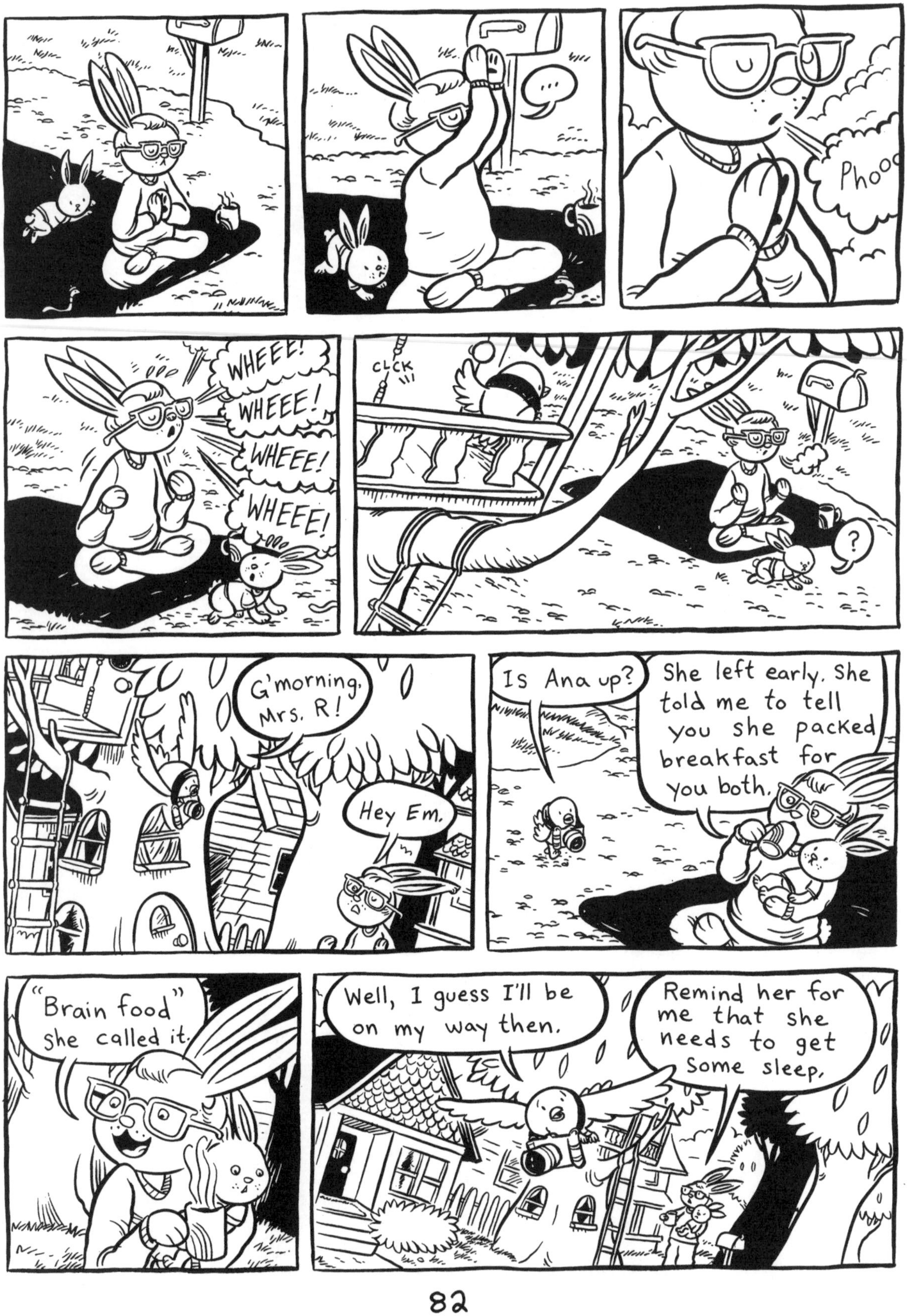
...
Phooo
WHEEE!
WHEEE!
WHEEE!
WHEEE!
CLICK
?
G'morning, Mrs. R!
Hey Em.
Is Ana up?
She left early. She told me to tell you she packed breakfast for you both.
"Brain food" she called it.
Well, I guess I'll be on my way then.
Remind her for me that she needs to get some sleep.

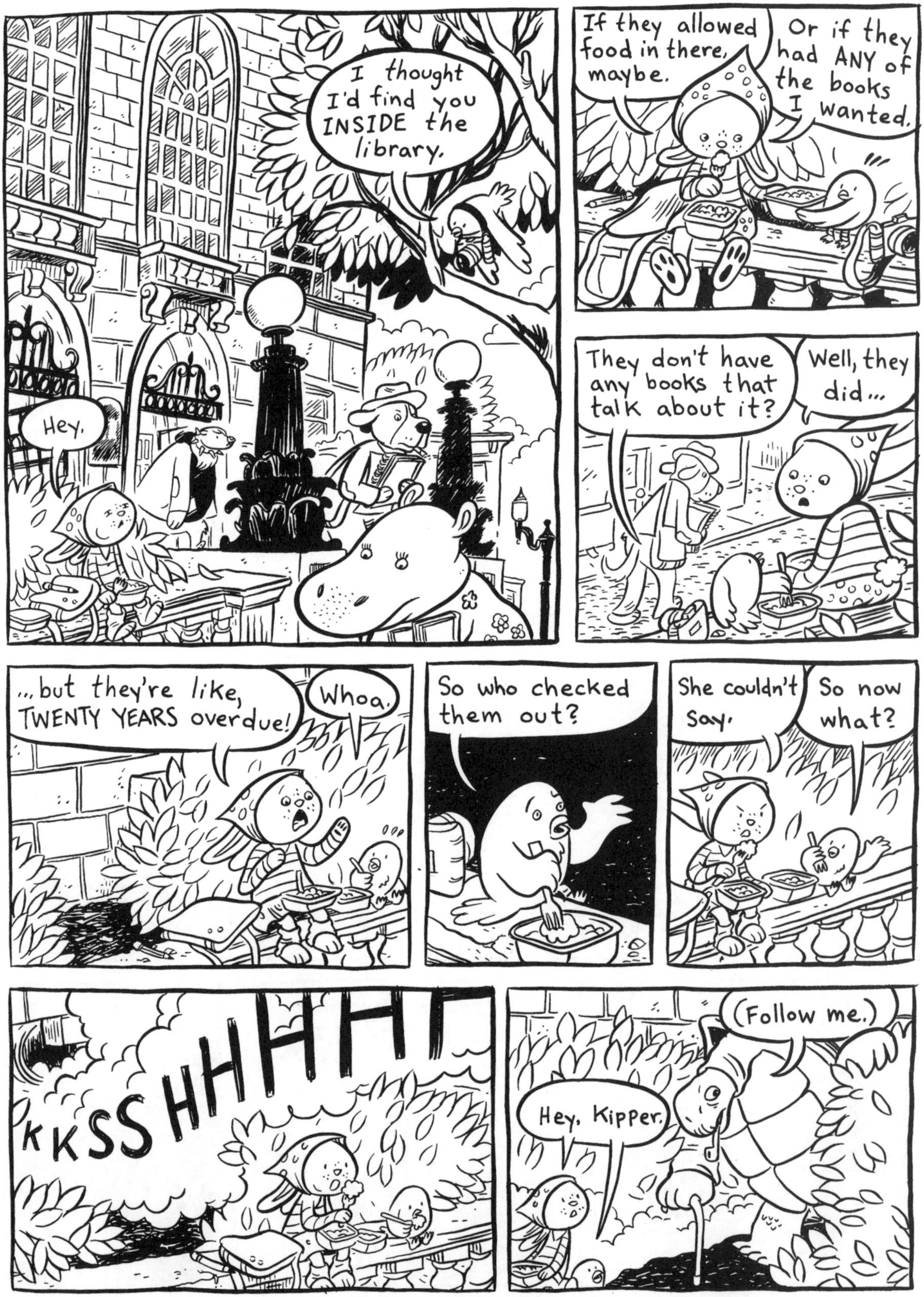
I thought I'd find you INSIDE the library.
Hey.
If they allowed food in there, maybe.
Or if they had ANY of the books I wanted.
They don't have any books that talk about it?
Well, they did...
...but they're like, TWENTY YEARS overdue!
Whoa.
So who checked them out?
She couldn't say.
So now what?
KKSSHHHHH
(Follow me.)
Hey, Kipper.

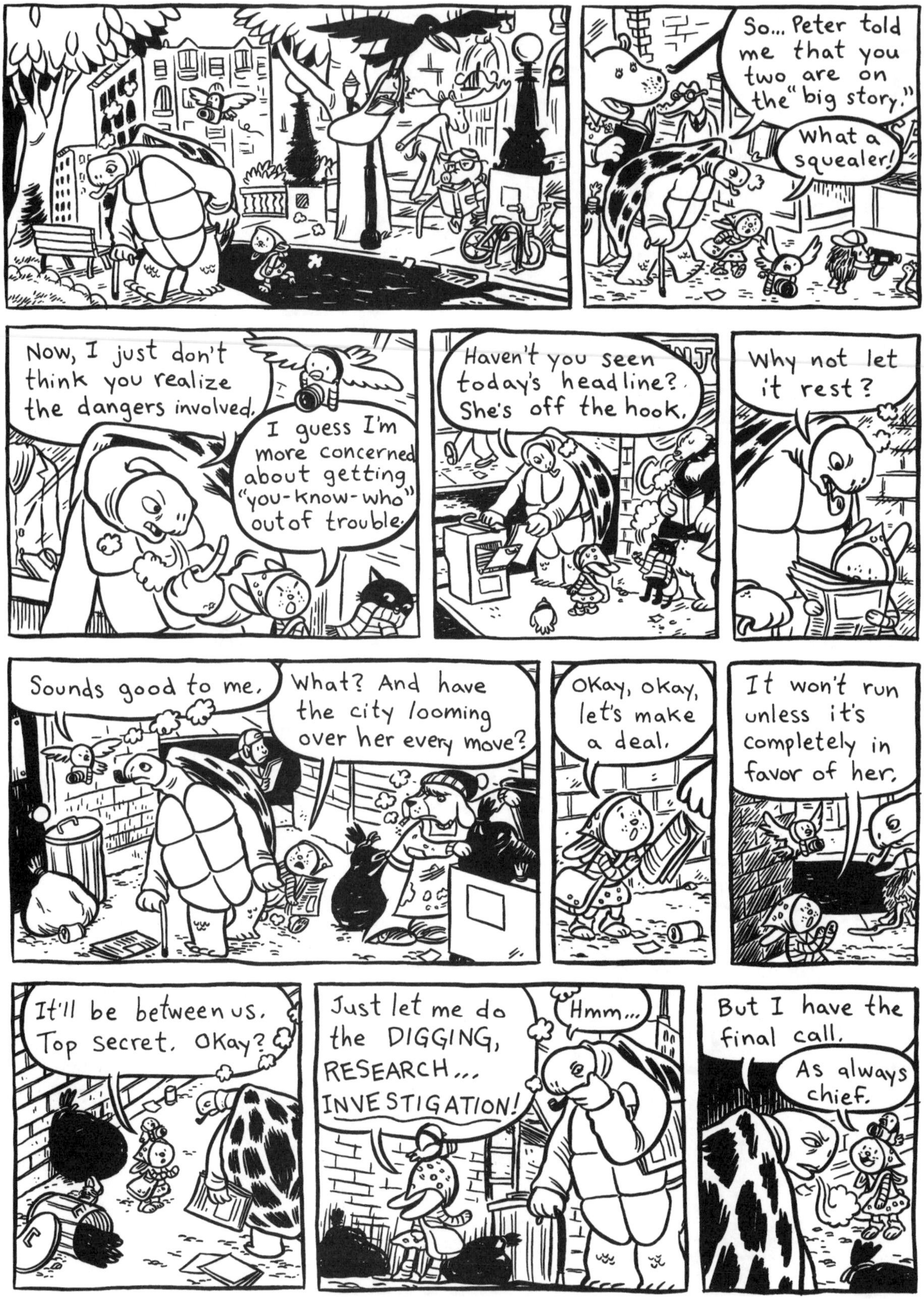
So... Peter told me that you two are on the "big story."
What a squealer!
Now, I just don't think you realize the dangers involved.
I guess I'm more concerned about getting "you-know-who" out of trouble.
Haven't you seen today's headline? She's off the hook.
Why not let it rest?
Sounds good to me.
What? And have the city looming over her every move?
OKay, okay, let's make a deal.
It won't run unless it's completely in favor of her.
It'll be between us. Top secret. OKay?
Just let me do the DIGGING, RESEARCH... INVESTIGATION!
Hmm...
But I have the final call.
As always chief.

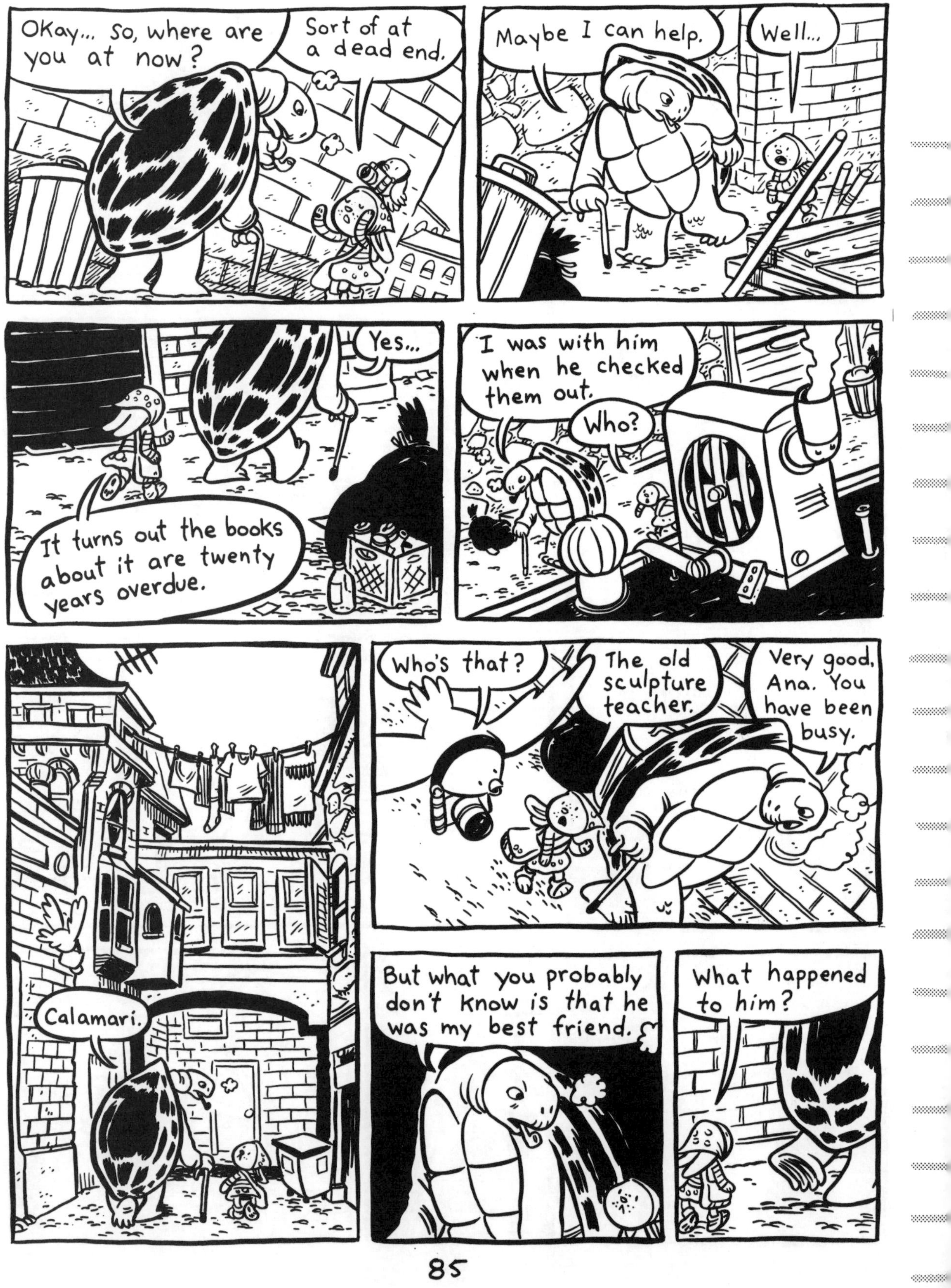

Okay... So, where are you at now?
Sort of at a dead end.
Maybe I can help.
Well...
Yes...
It turns out the books about it are twenty years overdue.
I was with him when he checked them out.
Who?
Calamari.
Who's that?
The old sculpture teacher.
Very good, Ana. You have been busy.
But what you probably don't know is that he was my best friend.
What happened to him?

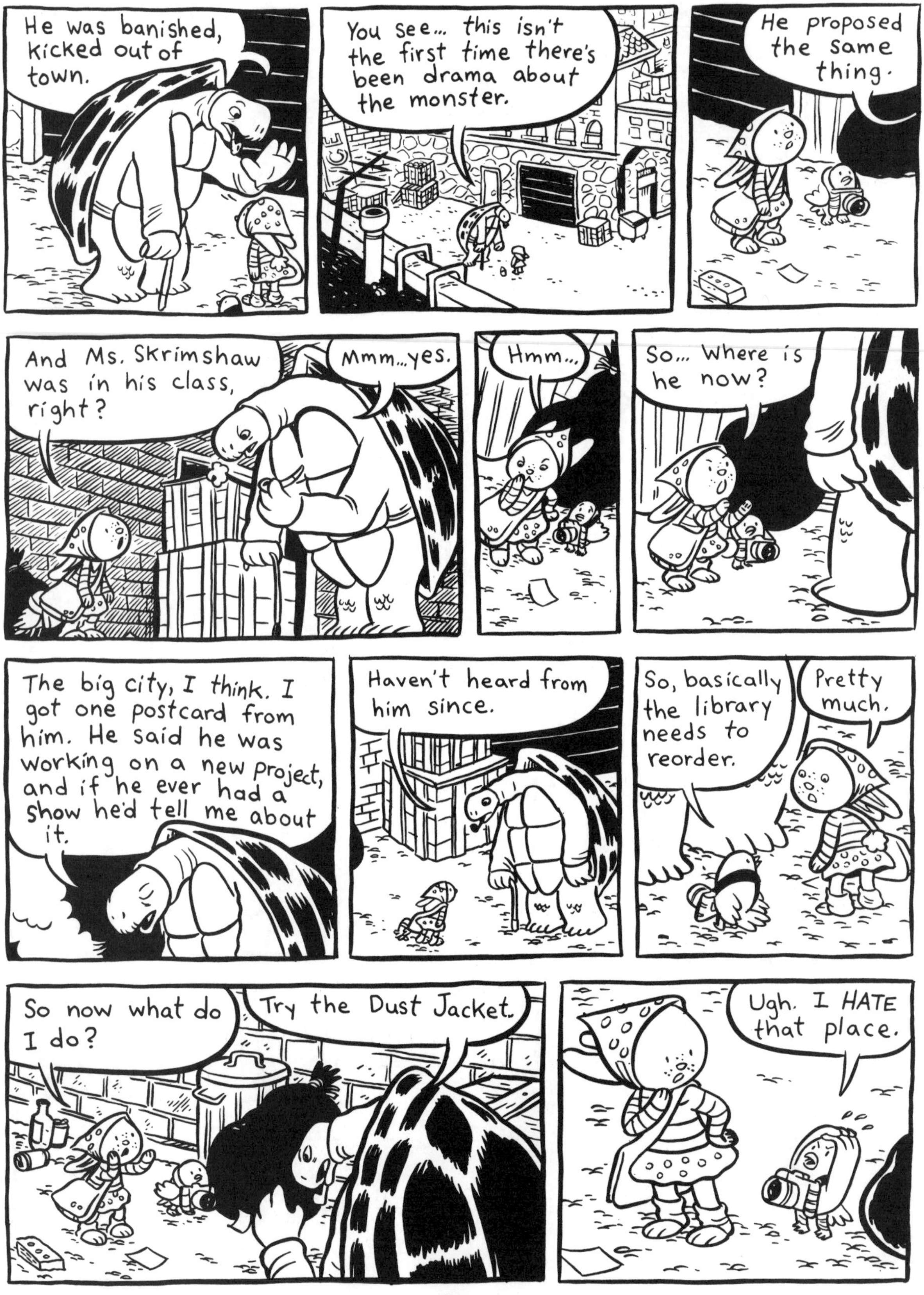
He was banished, kicked out of town.
You see... this isn't the first time there's been drama about the monster.
He proposed the same thing.
And Ms. Skrimshaw was in his class, right?
Mmm...yes.
Hmm...
So... Where is he now?
The big city, I think. I got one postcard from him. He said he was working on a new project, and if he ever had a show he'd tell me about it.
Haven't heard from him since.
So, basically the library needs to reorder.
Pretty much.
So now what do I do?
Try the Dust Jacket.
Ugh. I HATE that place.

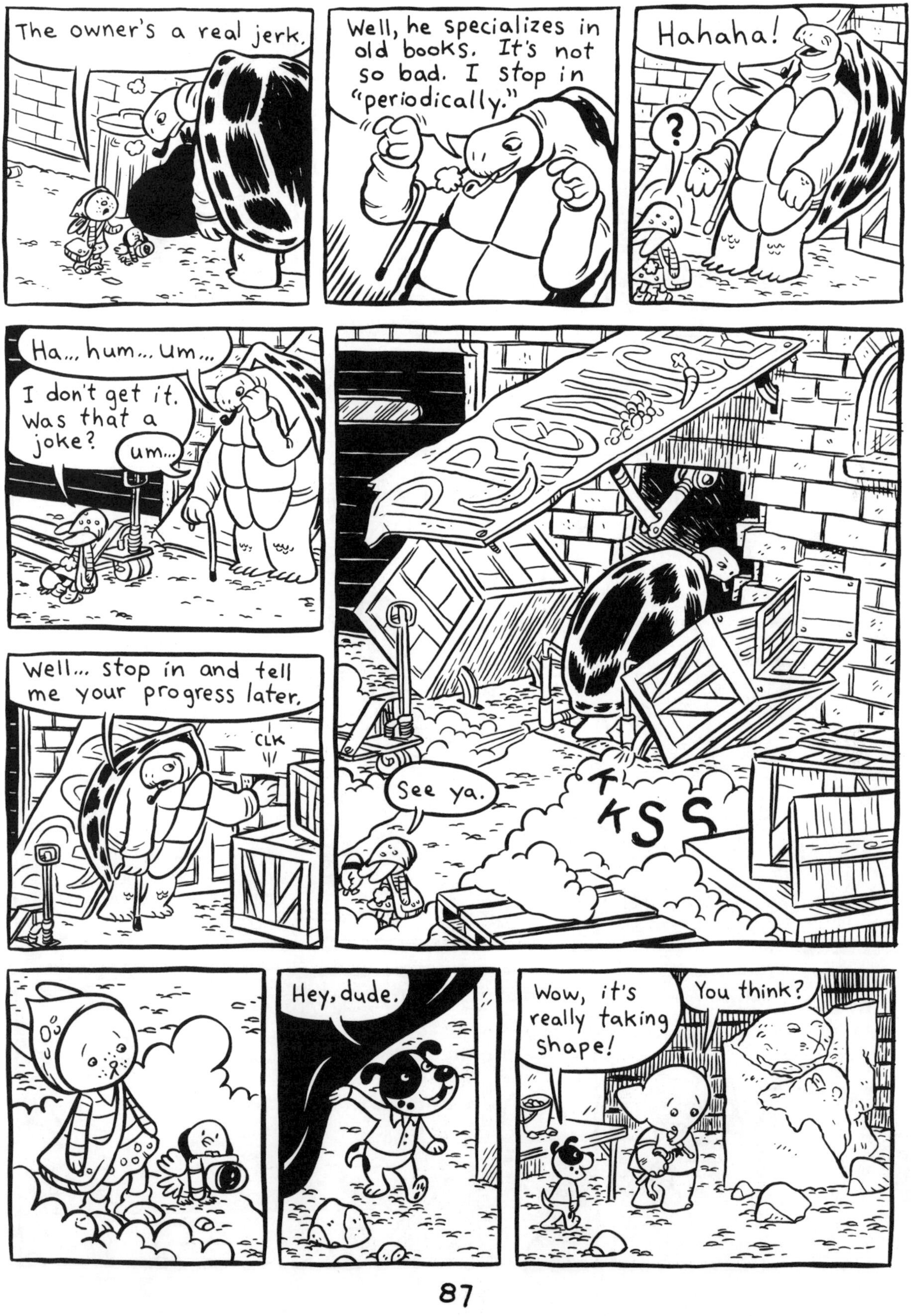
The owner's a real jerk.
Well, he specializes in old books. It's not so bad. I stop in "periodically."
Hahaha!
?
Ha... hum... um...
I don't get it. Was that a joke?
um...
Well... stop in and tell me your progress later.
CLK
See ya.
KKSS
Hey, dude.
Wow, it's really taking shape!
You think?

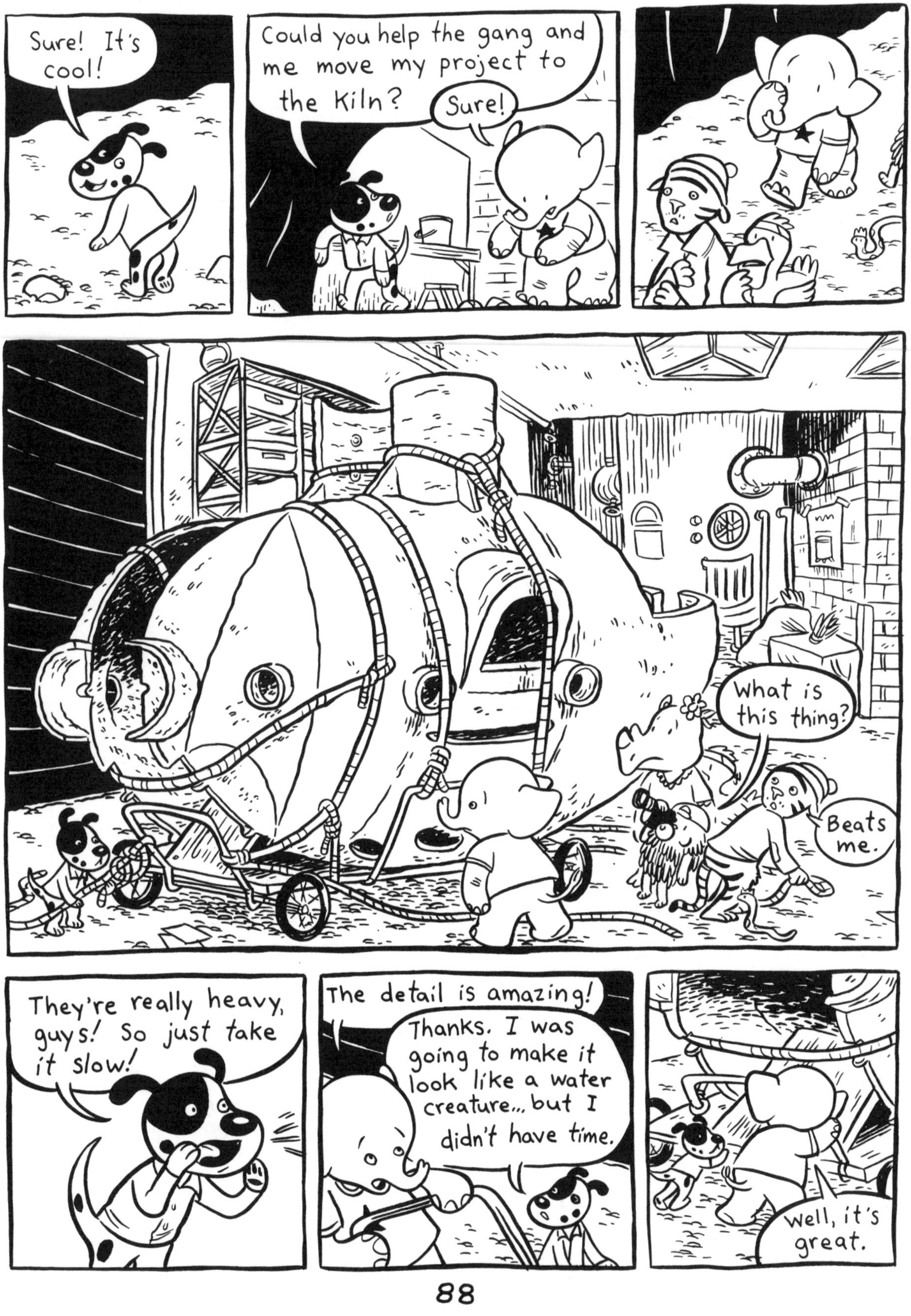
Sure! It's cool!
Could you help the gang and me move my project to the Kiln?
Sure!
What is this thing?
Beats me.
They're really heavy, guys! So just take it slow!
The detail is amazing!
Thanks. I was going to make it look like a water creature... but I didn't have time.
Well, it's great.

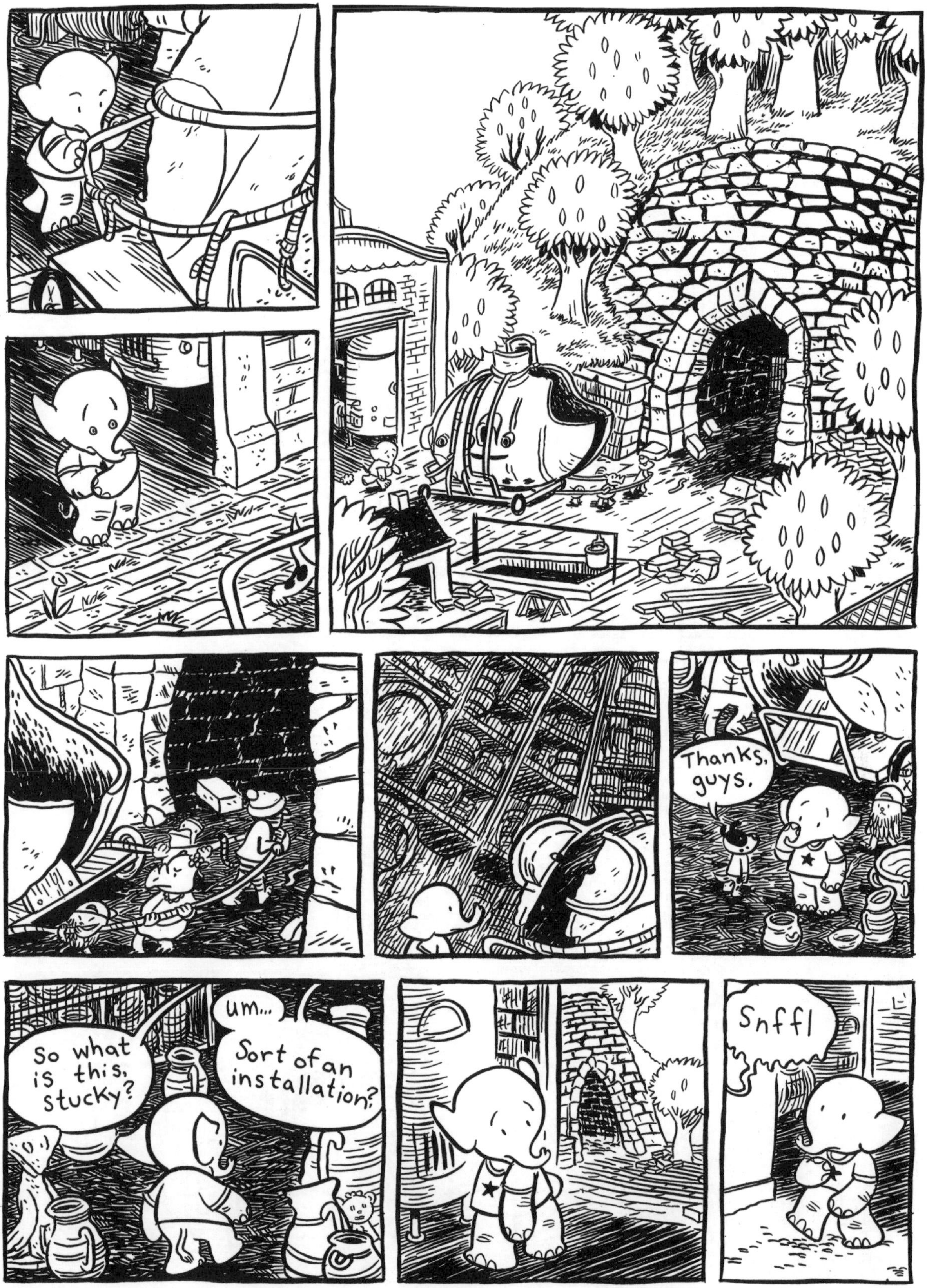
Thanks, guys.
So what is this, stucky?
um...
Sort of an installation?
Snffl

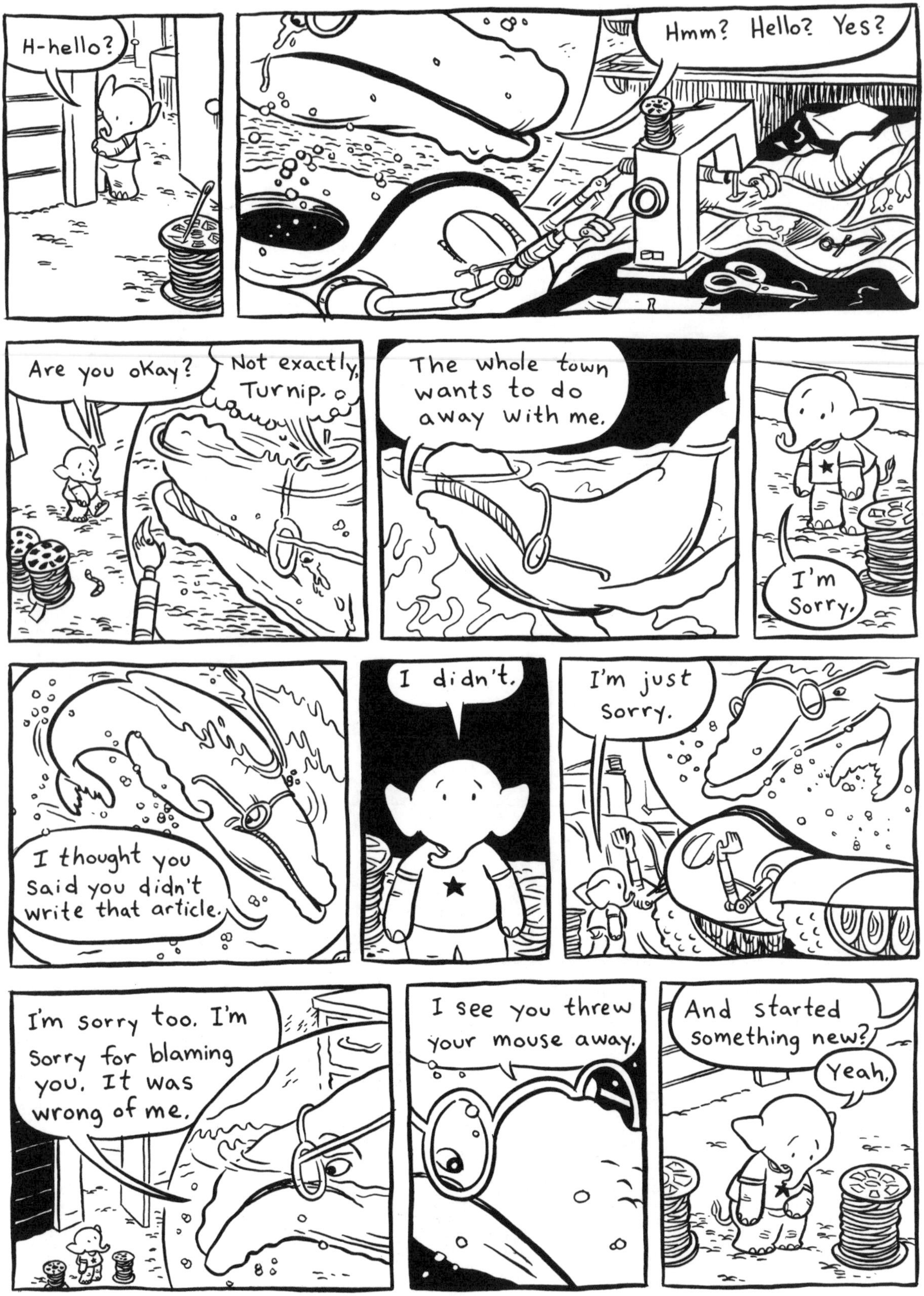
H-hello?
Hmm? Hello? Yes?
Are you okay?
Not exactly, Turnip.
The whole town wants to do away with me.
I'm sorry.
I thought you said you didn't write that article.
I didn't.
I'm just sorry.
I'm sorry too. I'm sorry for blaming you. It was wrong of me.
I see you threw your mouse away.
And started something new?
Yeah.

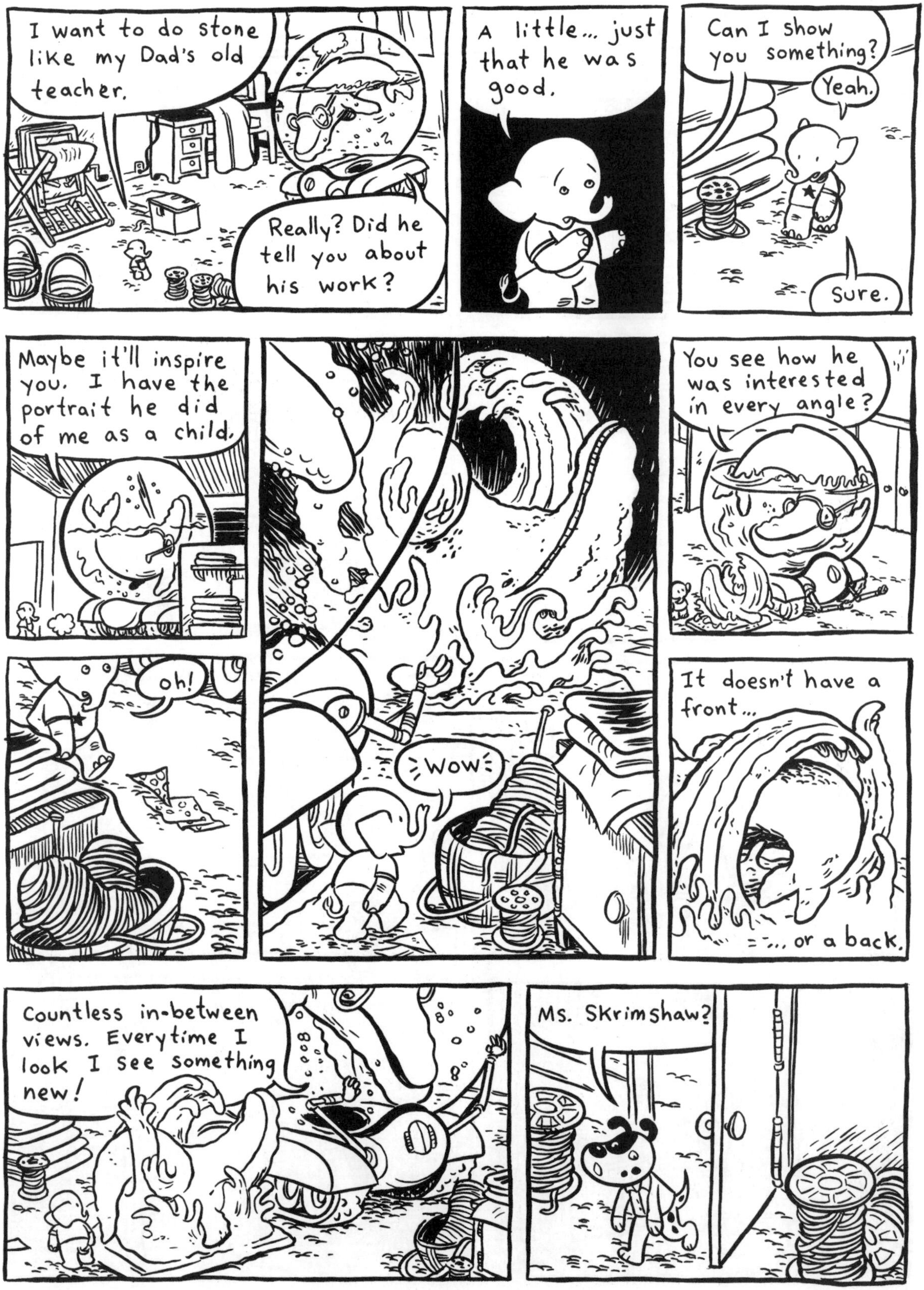
I want to do stone like my Dad's old teacher.
Really? Did he tell you about his work?
A little... just that he was good.
Can I show you something?
Yeah.
Sure.
Maybe it'll inspire you. I have the portrait he did of me as a child.
oh!
WOW
You see how he was interested in every angle?
It doesn't have a front...
... or a back.
Countless in-between views. Everytime I look I see something new!
Ms. Skrimshaw?

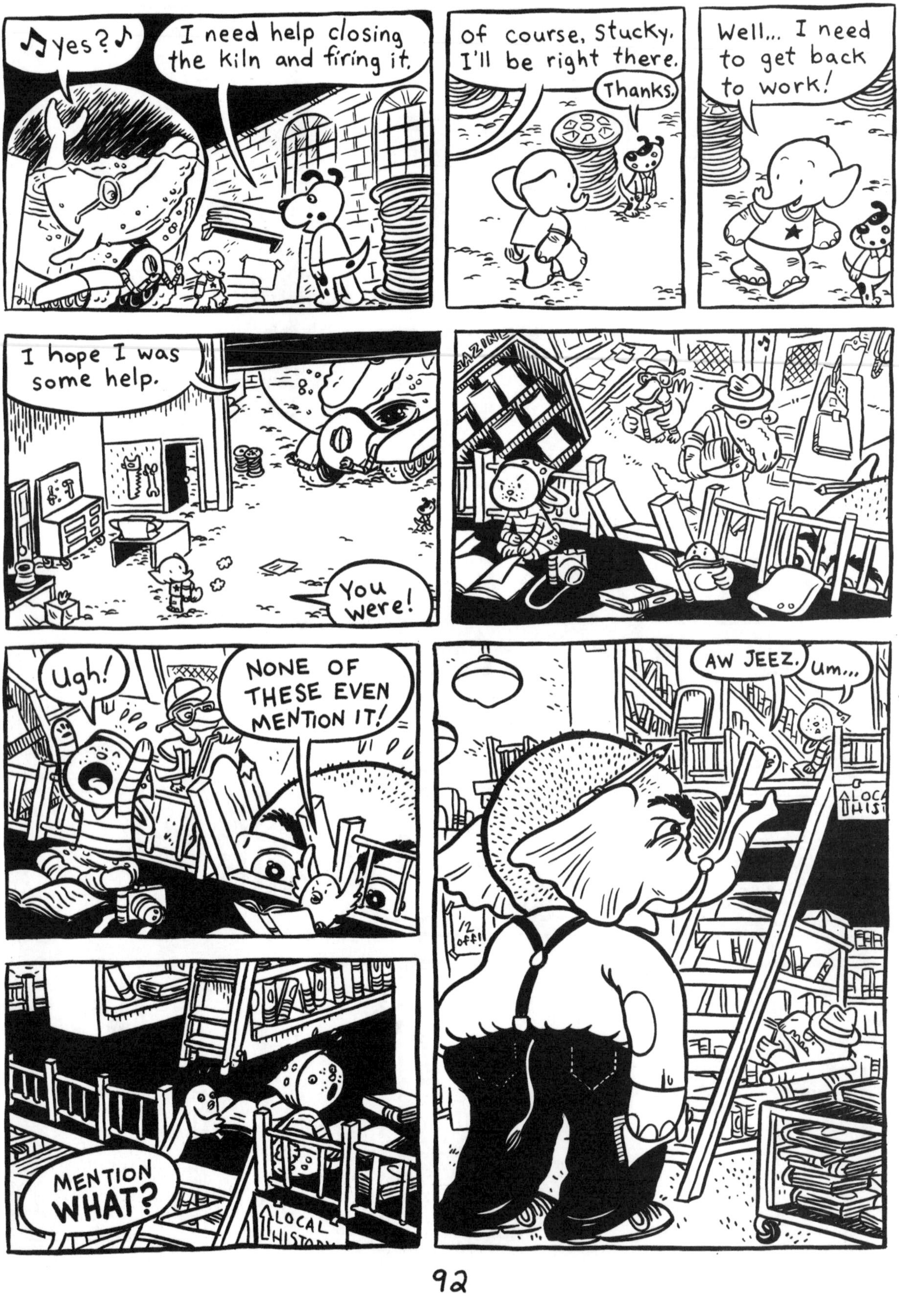
♫ Yes? ♪
I need help closing the kiln and firing it.
Of course, Stucky. I'll be right there.
Thanks.
Well... I need to get back to work!
I hope I was some help.
You were!
Ugh!
NONE OF THESE EVEN MENTION IT!
MENTION WHAT?
LOCAL HISTORY
AW JEEZ.
Um...
LOCAL HIST
1/2 off!

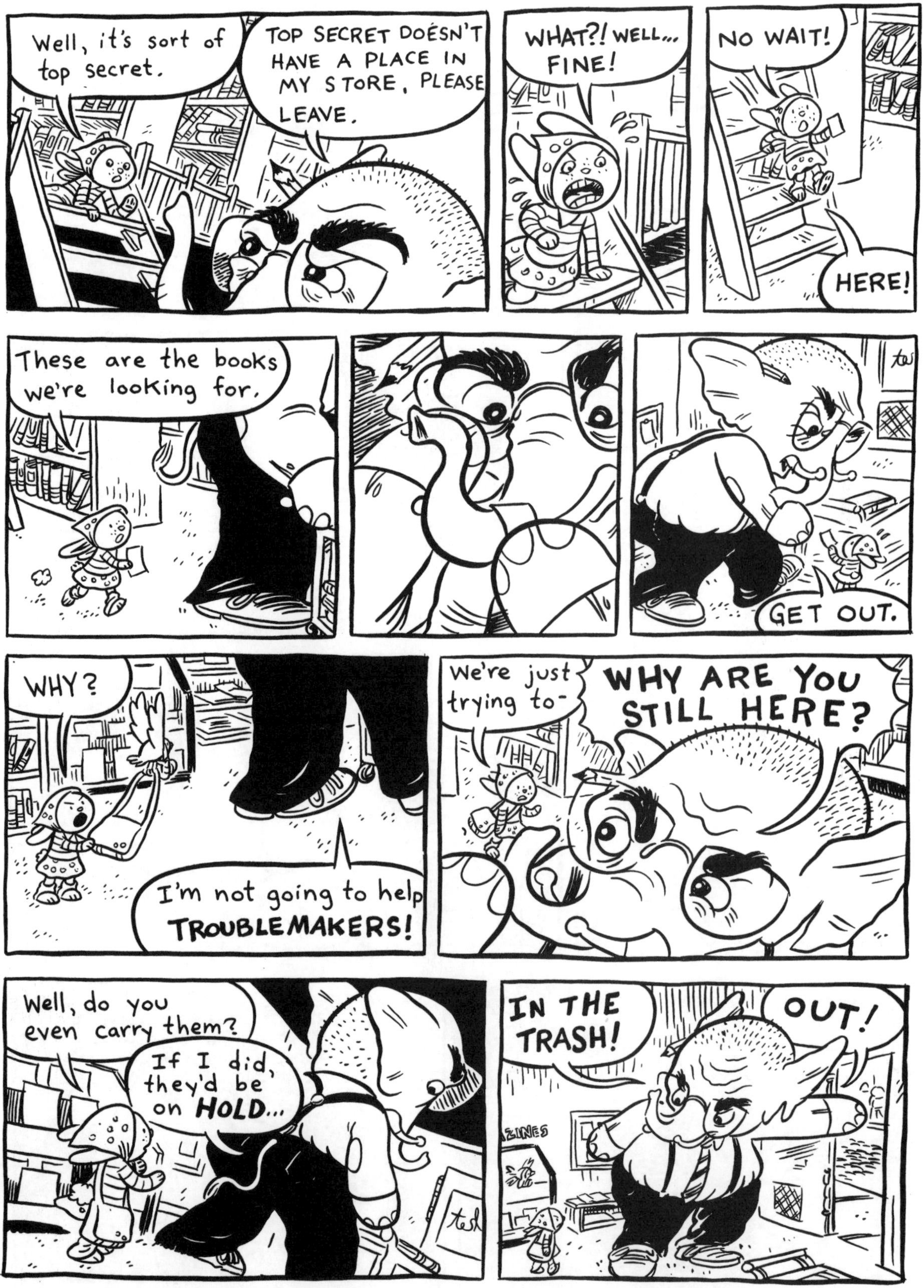
Well, it's sort of top secret.
TOP SECRET DOESN'T HAVE A PLACE IN MY STORE, PLEASE LEAVE.
WHAT?! WELL... FINE!
NO WAIT!
HERE!
These are the books we're looking for.
GET OUT.
WHY?
I'm not going to help TROUBLEMAKERS!
We're just trying to-
WHY ARE YOU STILL HERE?
Well, do you even carry them?
If I did, they'd be on HOLD...
IN THE TRASH!
OUT!
ZINES

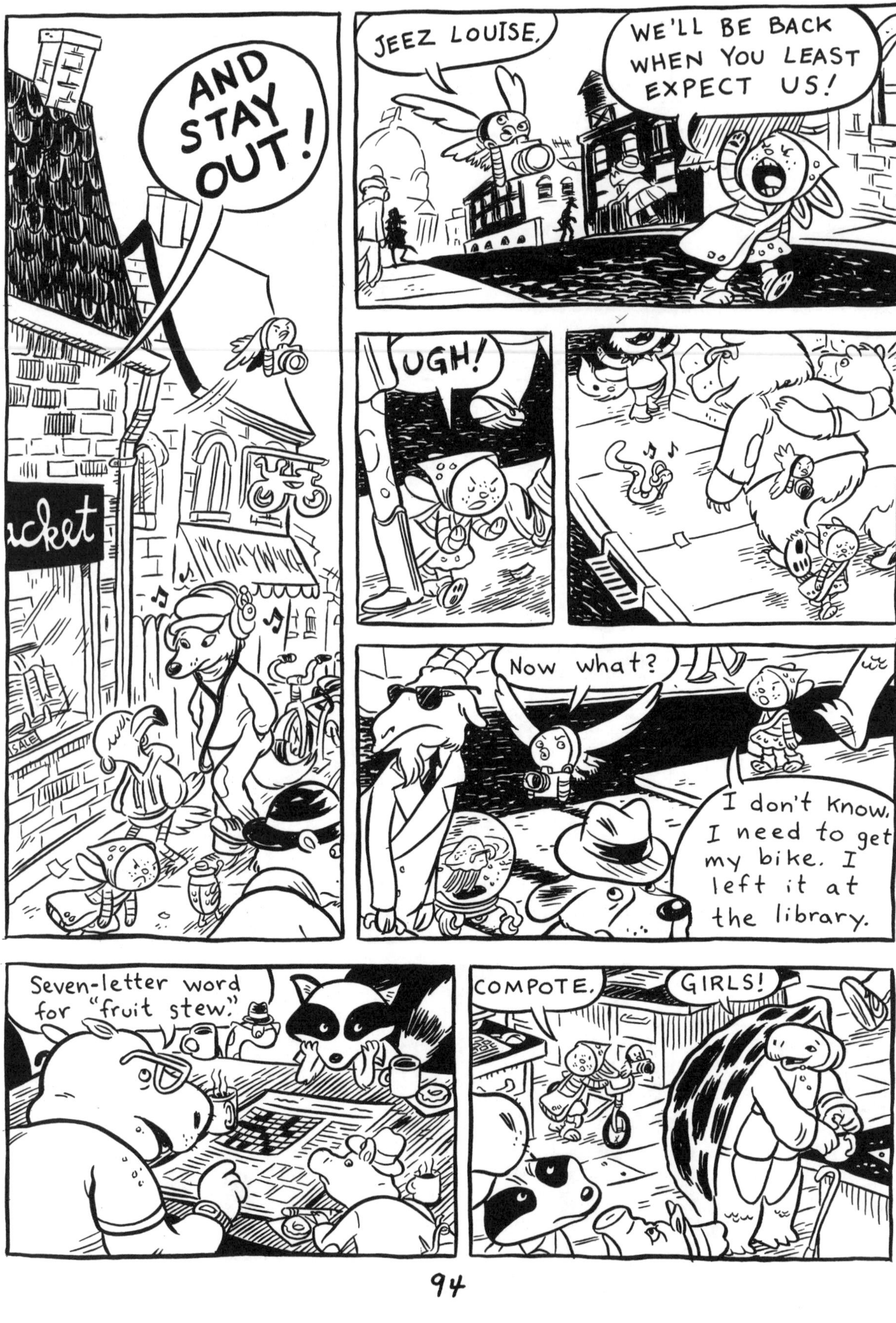
AND STAY OUT!
JEEZ LOUISE.
WE'LL BE BACK WHEN YOU LEAST EXPECT US!
ucket
SALE
UGH!
Now what?
I don't know. I need to get my bike. I left it at the library.
Seven-letter word for "fruit stew."
COMPOTE.
GIRLS!

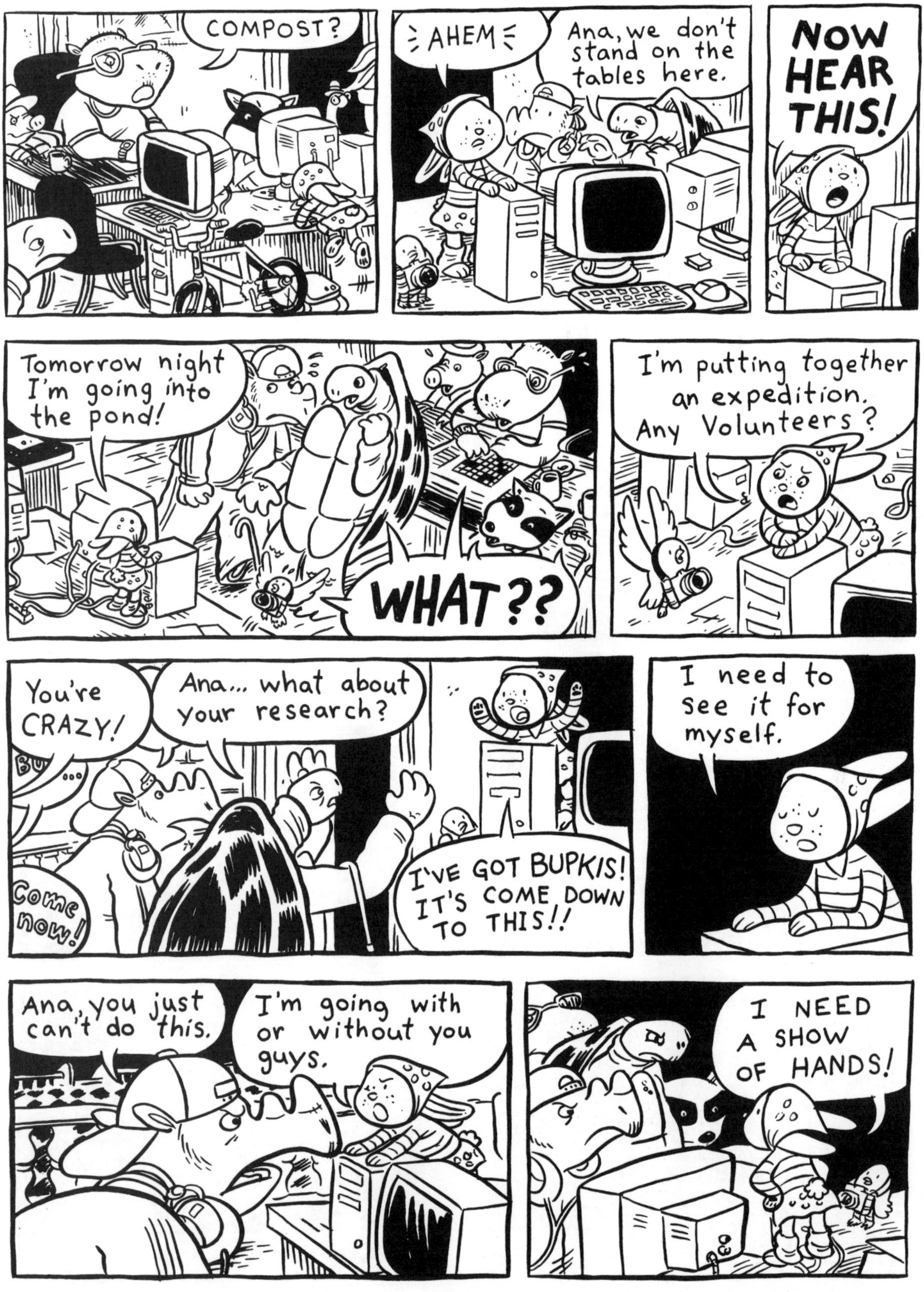
COMPOST?
AHEM
Ana, we don't stand on the tables here.
NOW HEAR THIS!
Tomorrow night I'm going into the pond!
WHAT??
I'm putting together an expedition. Any Volunteers?
You're CRAZY!
Ana... what about your research?
Come now!
I'VE GOT BUPKIS! IT'S COME DOWN TO THIS!!
I need to see it for myself.
Ana, you just can't do this.
I'm going with or without you guys.
I NEED A SHOW OF HANDS!

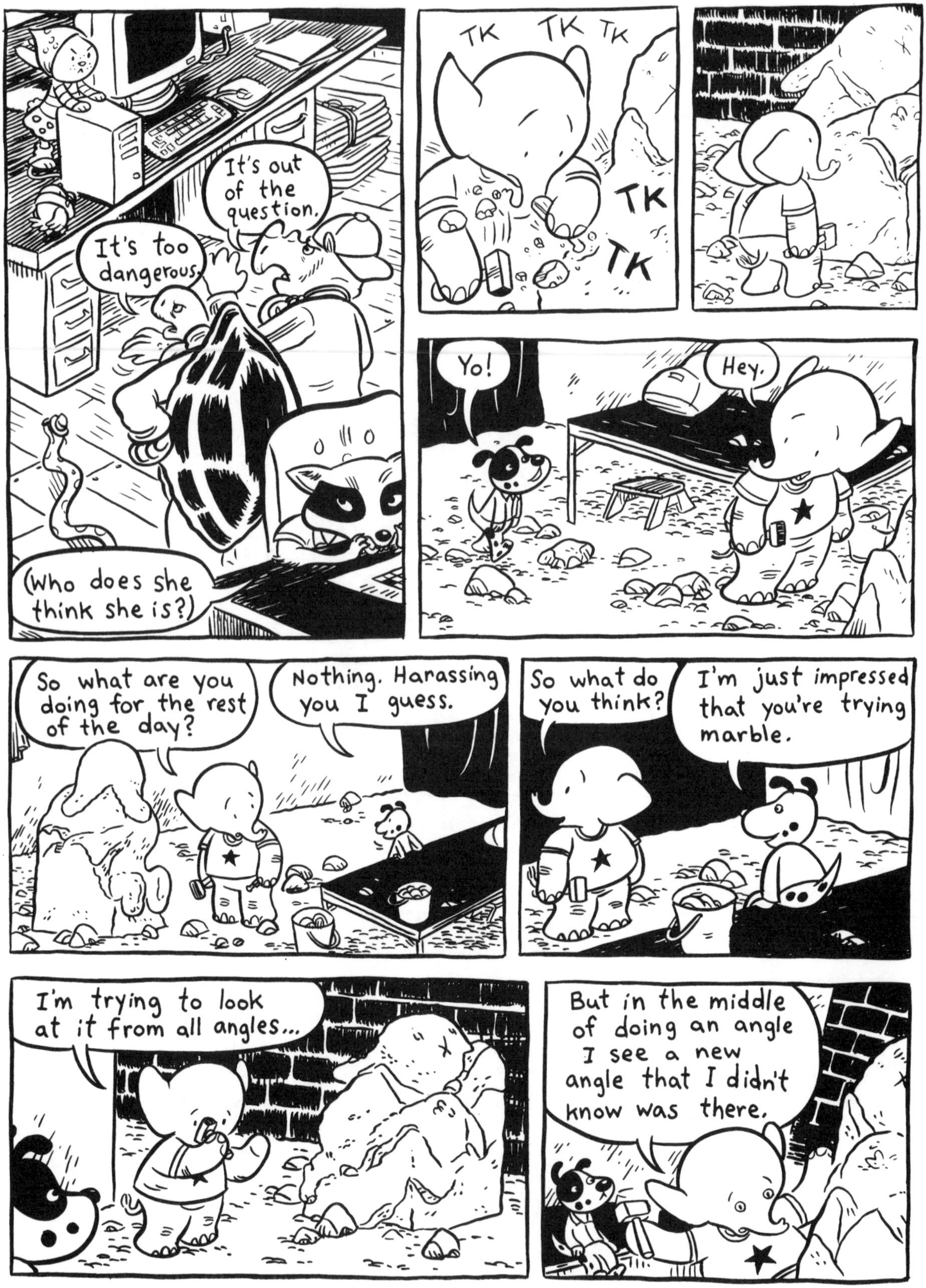
It's out of the question.
It's too dangerous.
(Who does she think she is?)
TK TK TK
TK
TK
Yo!
Hey.
So what are you doing for the rest of the day?
Nothing. Harassing you I guess.
So what do you think?
I'm just impressed that you're trying marble.
I'm trying to look at it from all angles...
But in the middle of doing an angle I see a new angle that I didn't know was there.

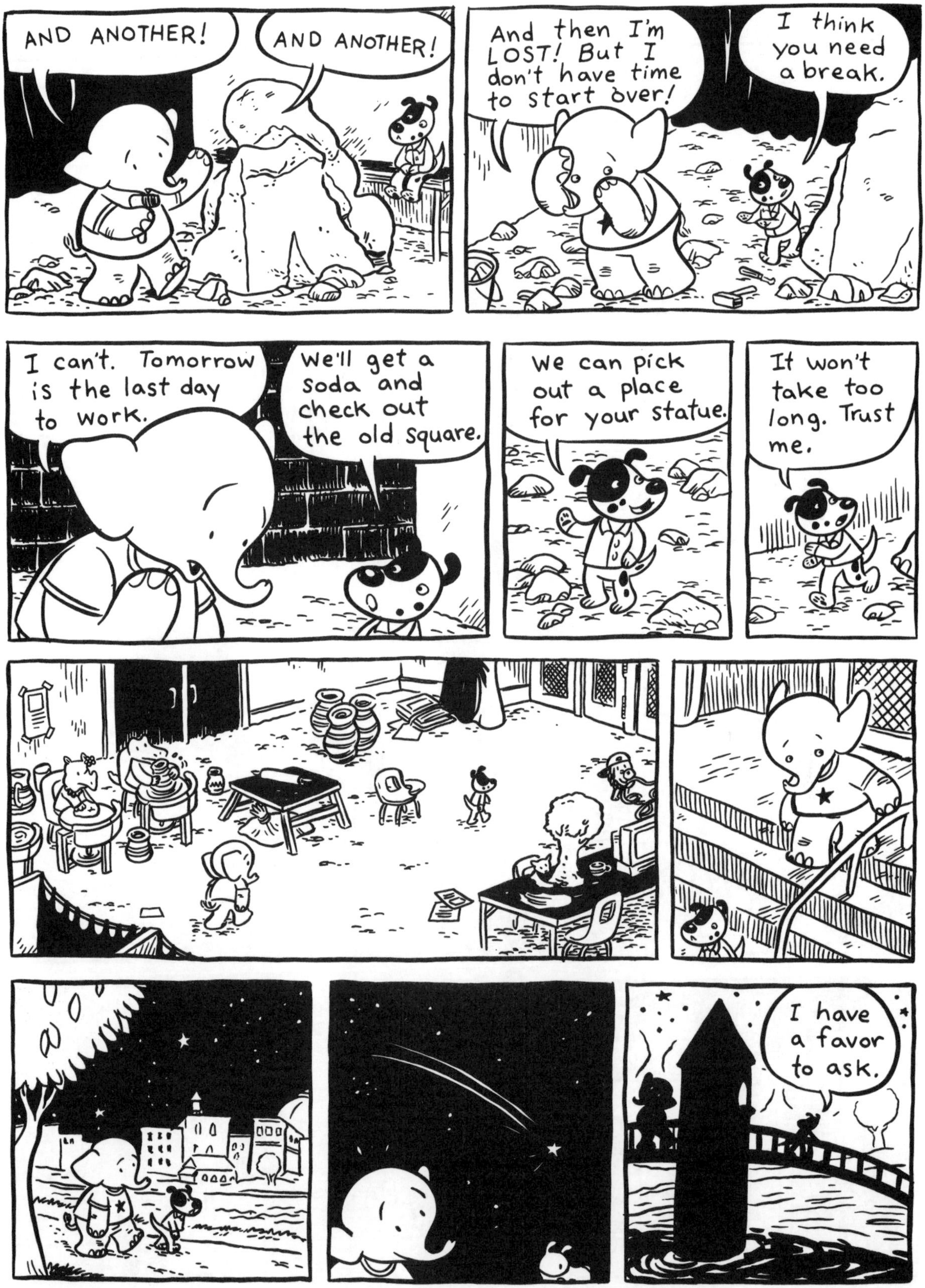
AND ANOTHER!
AND ANOTHER!
And then I'm LOST! But I don't have time to start over!
I think you need a break.
I can't. Tomorrow is the last day to work.
We'll get a soda and check out the old square.
We can pick out a place for your statue.
It won't take too long. Trust me.
I have a favor to ask.

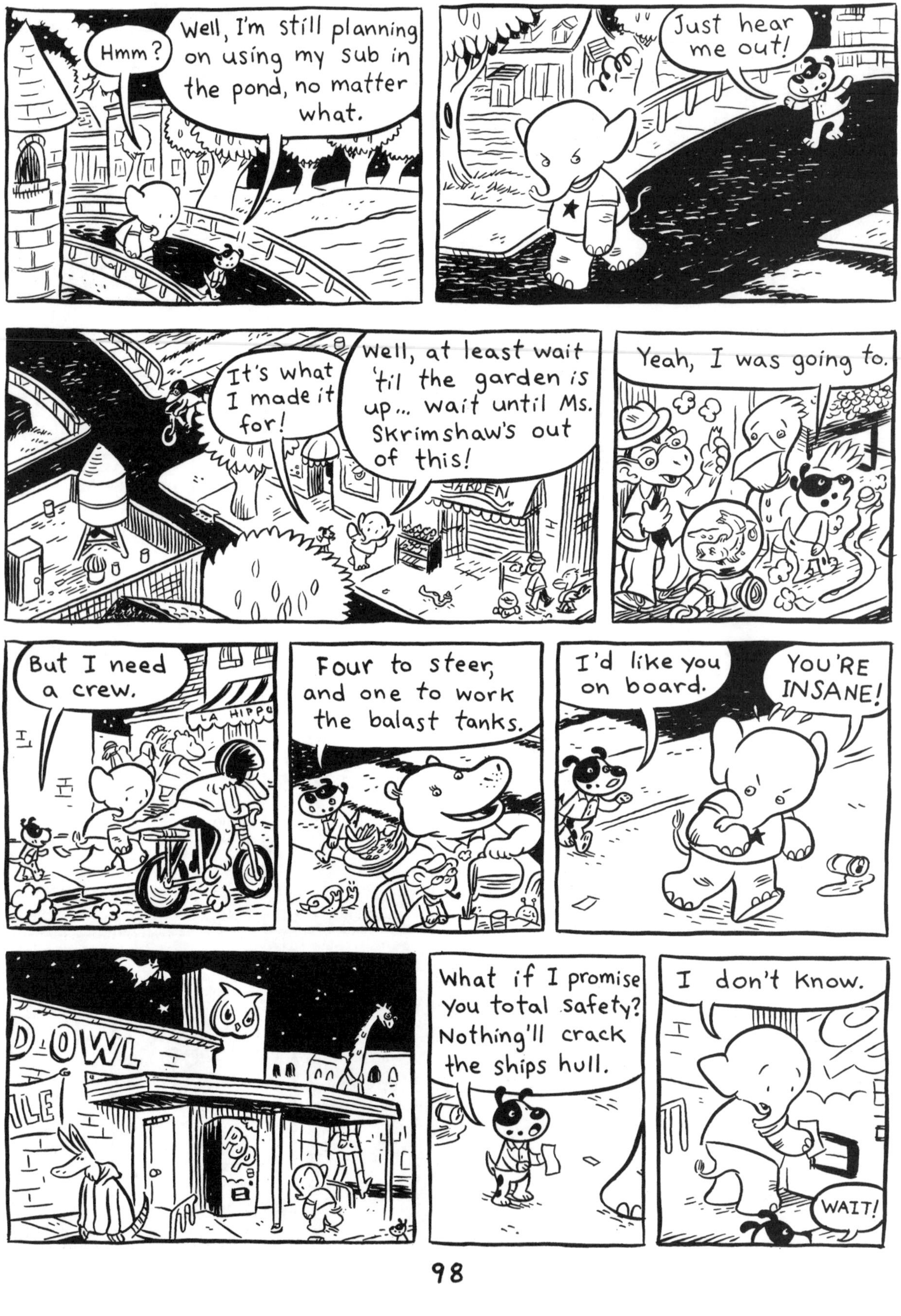
Hmm?
Well, I'm still planning on using my sub in the pond, no matter what.
Just hear me out!
It's what I made it for!
Well, at least wait 'til the garden is up... wait until Ms. Skrimshaw's out of this!
Yeah, I was going to.
But I need a crew.
Four to steer, and one to work the balast tanks.
I'd like you on board.
YOU'RE INSANE!
What if I promise you total safety? Nothing'll crack the ships hull.
I don't know.
WAIT!

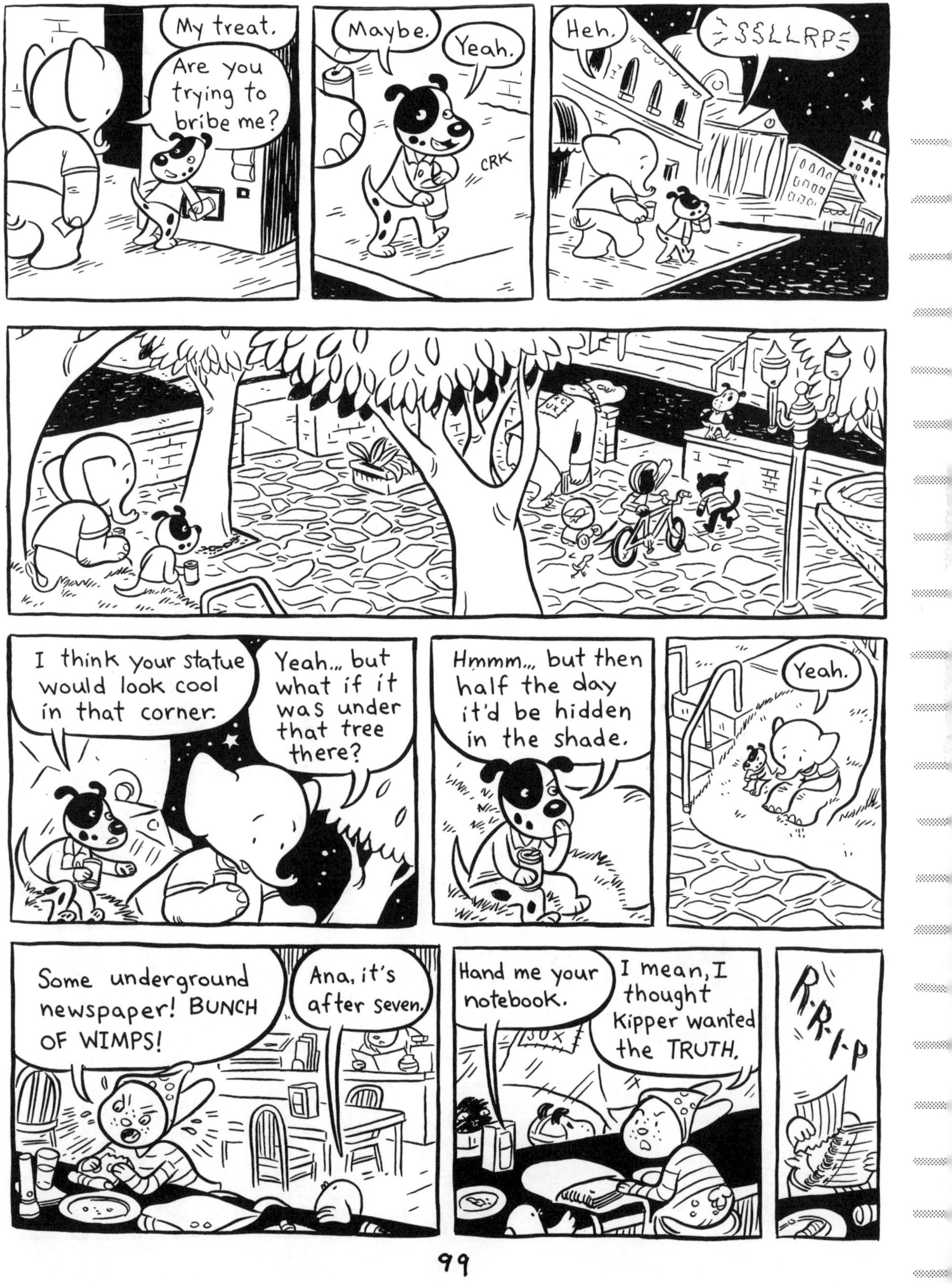
My treat.
Are you trying to bribe me?
Maybe.
Yeah.
CRK
Heh.
SSLLRP
I think your statue would look cool in that corner.
Yeah... but what if it was under that tree there?
Hmmm... but then half the day it'd be hidden in the shade.
Yeah.
Some underground newspaper! BUNCH OF WIMPS!
Ana, it's after seven.
Hand me your notebook.
I mean, I thought Kipper wanted the TRUTH.
R-R-I-P

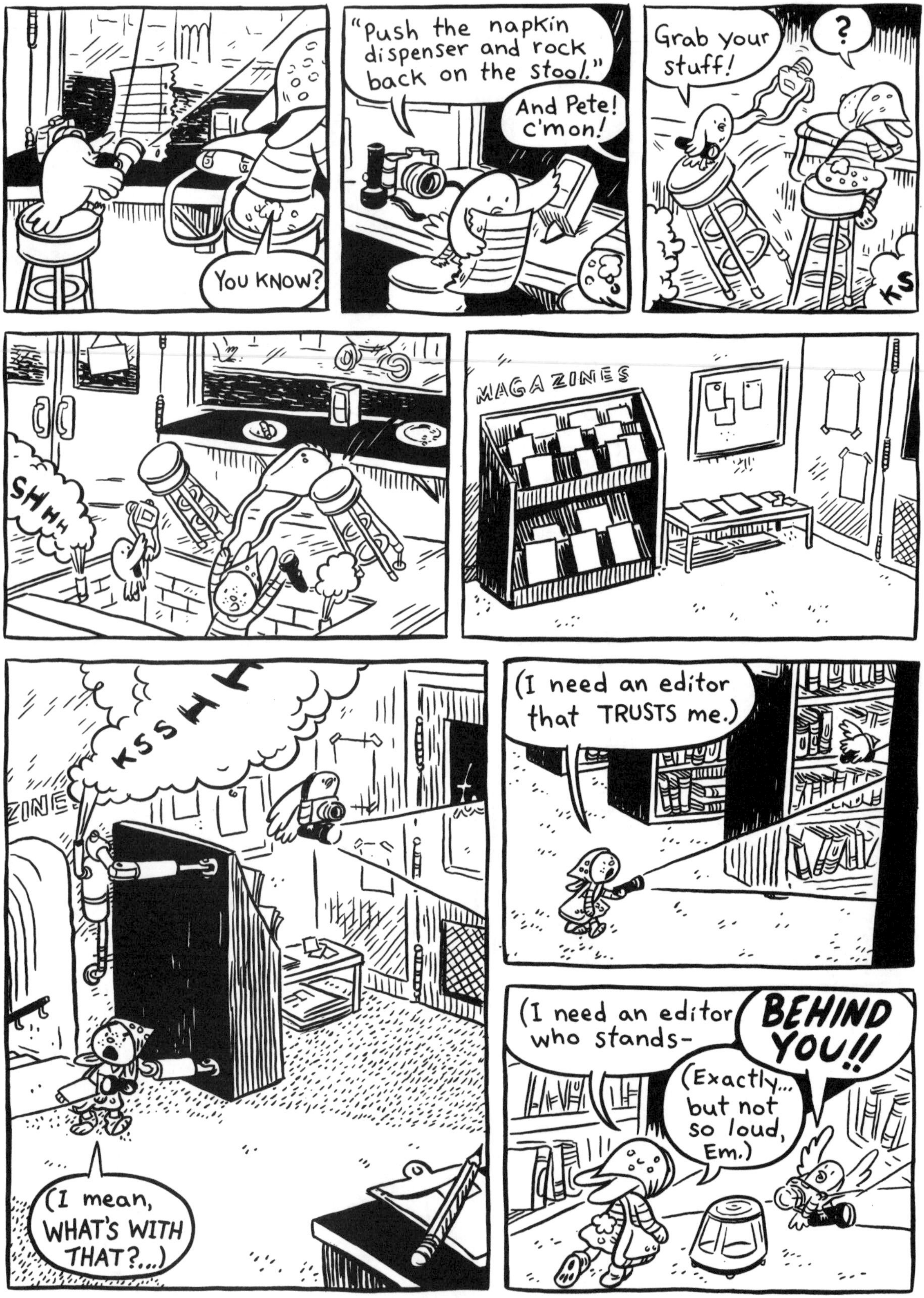

You KNOW?
"Push the napkin dispenser and rock back on the stool."
And Pete! c'mon!
Grab your stuff!
?
KS
SHHH
MAGAZINES
KSSHH
ZINE
(I mean, WHAT'S WITH THAT?...)
(I need an editor that TRUSTS me.)
(I need an editor who stands-
BEHIND YOU!!
(Exactly... but not so loud, Em.)

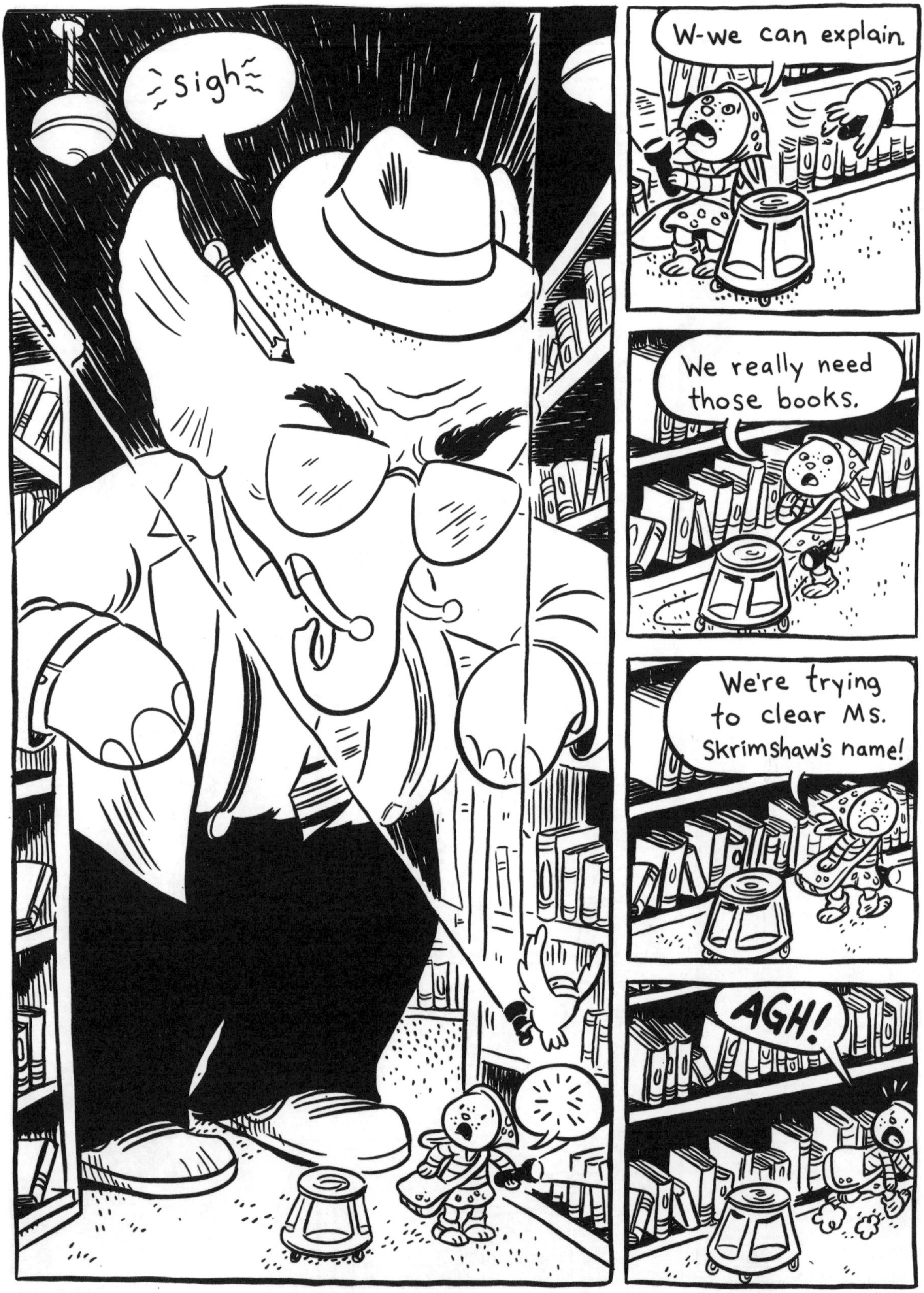
Sigh
W-we can explain.
We really need those books.
We're trying to clear Ms. Skrimshaw's name!
AGH!

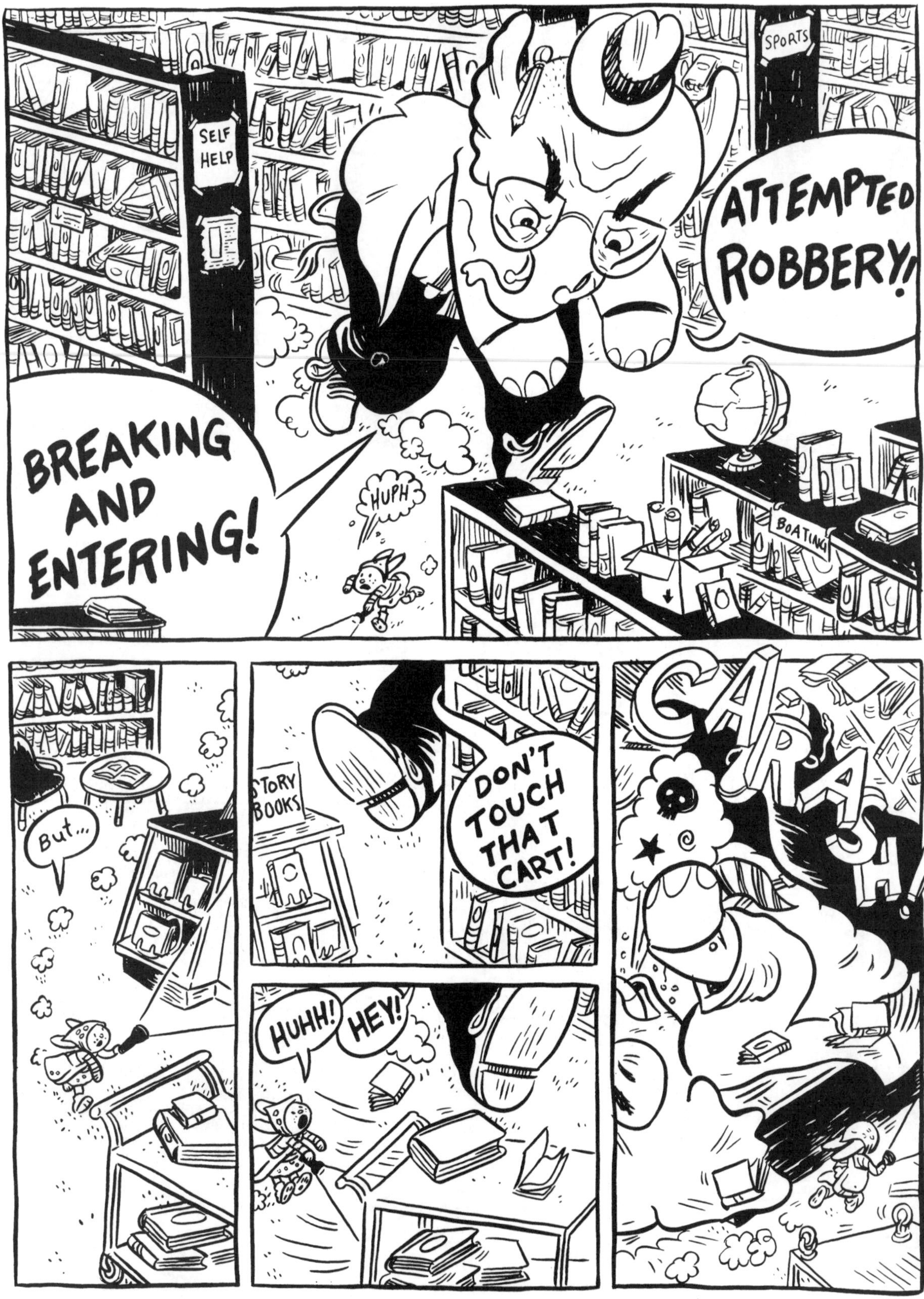
SELF HELP
SPORTS
ATTEMPTED ROBBERY!
BREAKING AND ENTERING!
HUPH
BOATING
But...
STORY BOOKS
DON'T TOUCH THAT CART!
CRASH!
HUHH!
HEY!

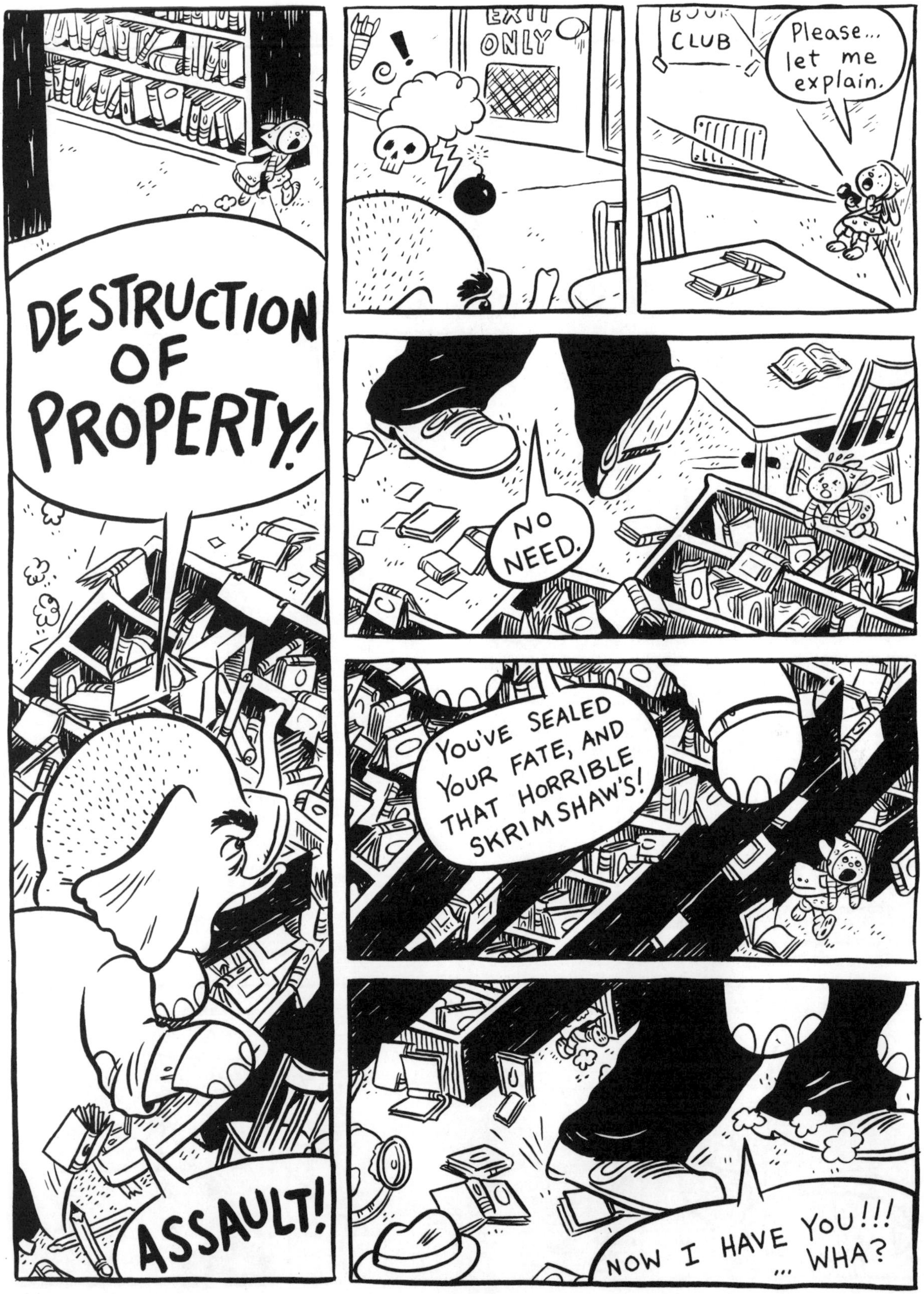
DESTRUCTION OF PROPERTY!
ASSAULT!
EXIT ONLY
BOOK CLUB
Please... let me explain.
NO NEED.
YOU'VE SEALED YOUR FATE, AND THAT HORRIBLE SKRIMSHAW'S!
NOW I HAVE YOU!!! ... WHA?

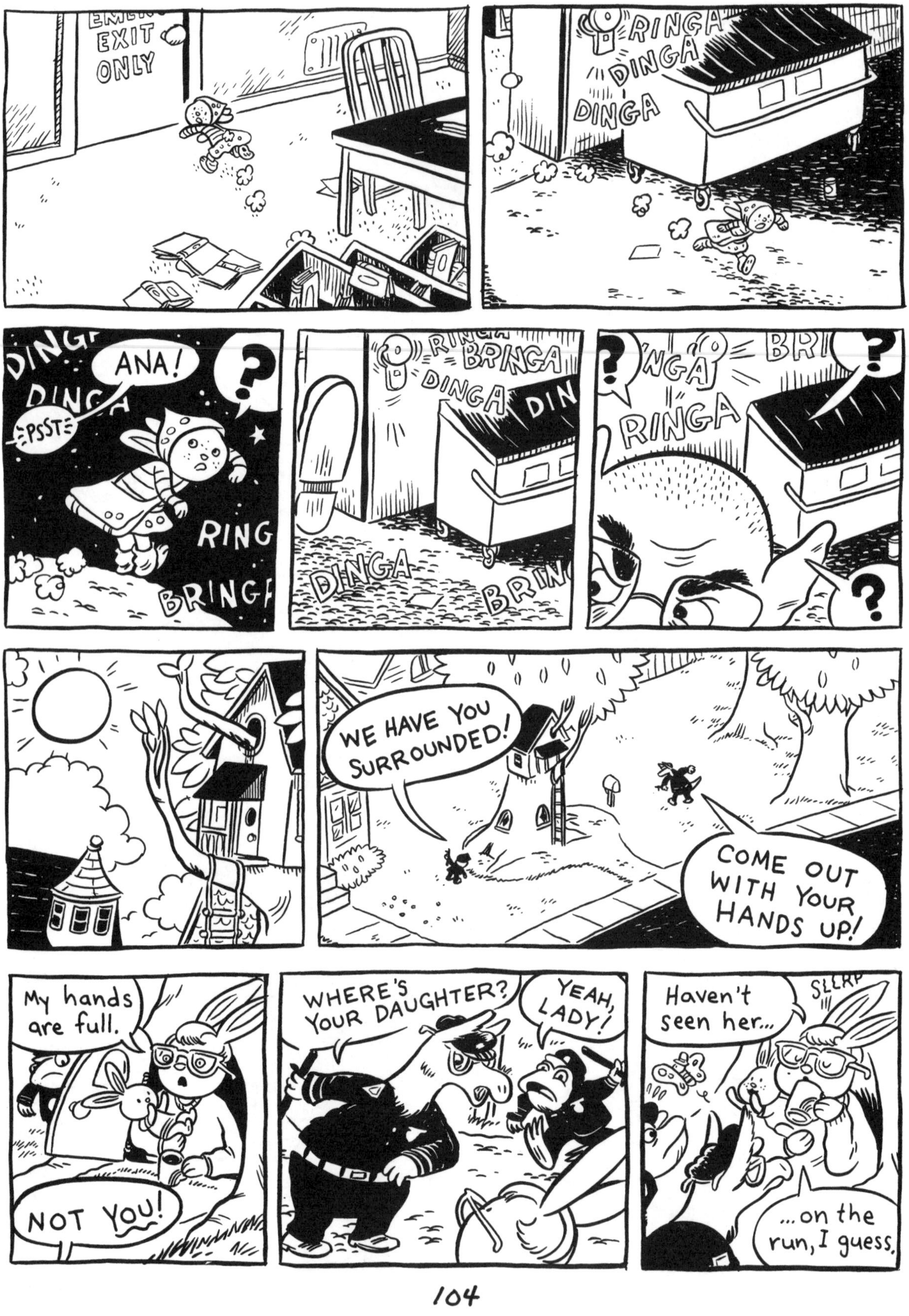
EMERG
EXIT
ONLY
RINGA
DINGA
DINGA
DINGA
DINGA
ANA!
PSSST
?
RING
BRINGA
RINGA
BRINGA
DINGA
DIN
DINGA
BRIN
NGA
BRI
RINGA
?
?
?
WE HAVE YOU SURROUNDED!
COME OUT WITH YOUR HANDS UP!
My hands are full.
NOT YOU!
WHERE'S YOUR DAUGHTER?
YEAH, LADY!
Haven't seen her...
SLURP
...on the run, I guess.

WELL! She's WANTED for BREAKING AND ENTERING, ATTEMPTED ROBBERY, DESTRUCTION OF PROPERTY, and ASSAULT!

≋PSST≋ (Don't forget the doozie she's wanted for.)

(we can't talk about THAT with HER... it's...)

TOP SECRET?

EXCUSE ME! I WASN'T TALKING TO YOU!

(I think she's hiding something.)

UGH!

We'll be back later... with a WARRANT!

I'll be waiting!

Thanks.

That's what mothers are for, Changing diapers and obstructing justice.

≋SNIF≋ ≋SNIF≋

Is that you, Sprout?

≋SNIF≋

≋SNIF≋

NO...

≋SNIF≋

Hmmm...

♪ CARROT FLOWER... ♪

hmm?

I think you need to take a shower.

Oh... I went dumpster diving last night.

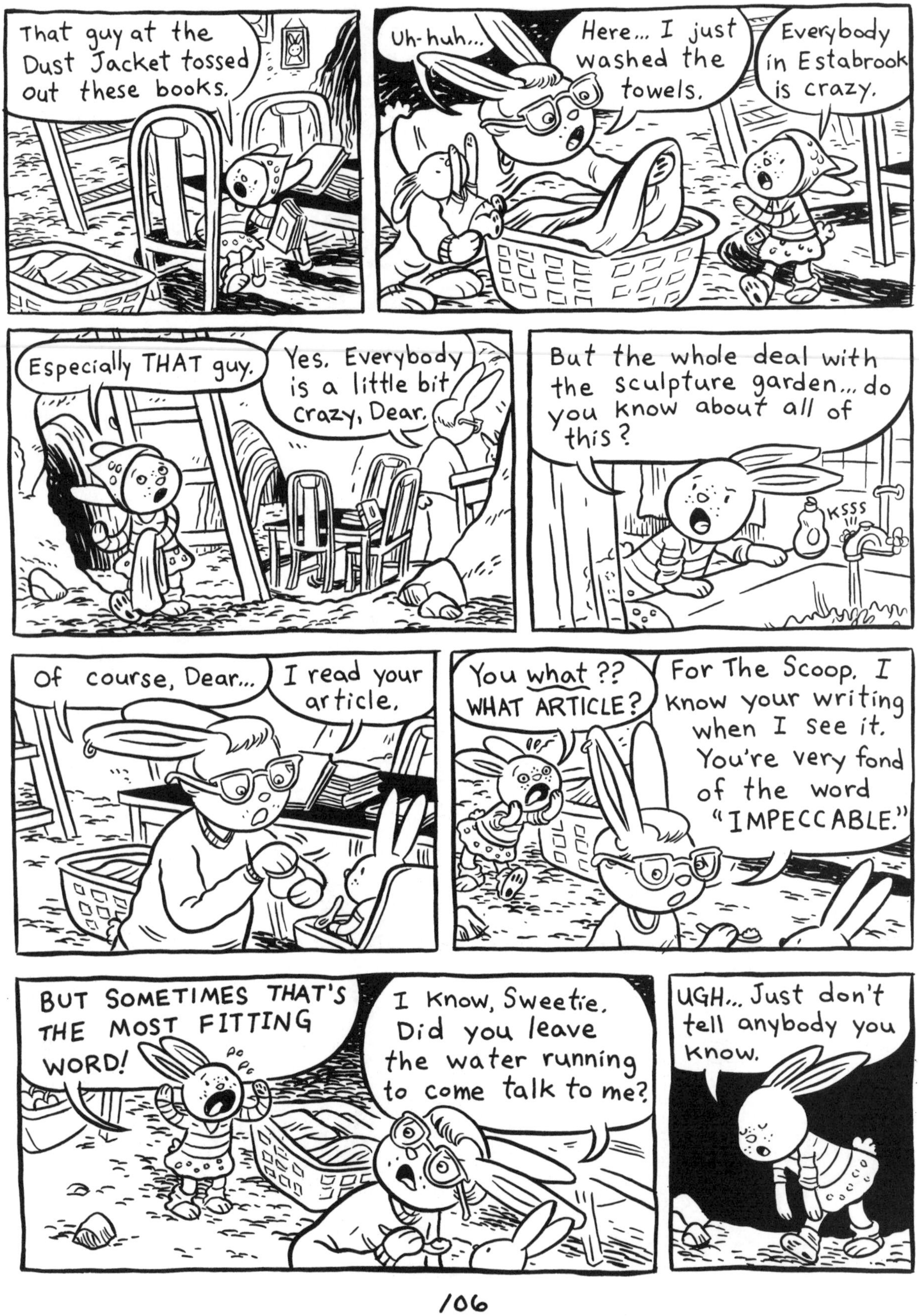
That guy at the Dust Jacket tossed out these books.
Uh-huh...
Here... I just washed the towels.
Everybody in Estabrook is crazy.
Especially THAT guy.
Yes. Everybody is a little bit crazy, Dear.
But the whole deal with the sculpture garden... do you know about all of this?
KSSS
Of course, Dear...
I read your article.
You what?? WHAT ARTICLE?
For The Scoop. I know your writing when I see it. You're very fond of the word "IMPECCABLE."
BUT SOMETIMES THAT'S THE MOST FITTING WORD!
I know, Sweetie. Did you leave the water running to come talk to me?
UGH... Just don't tell anybody you know.

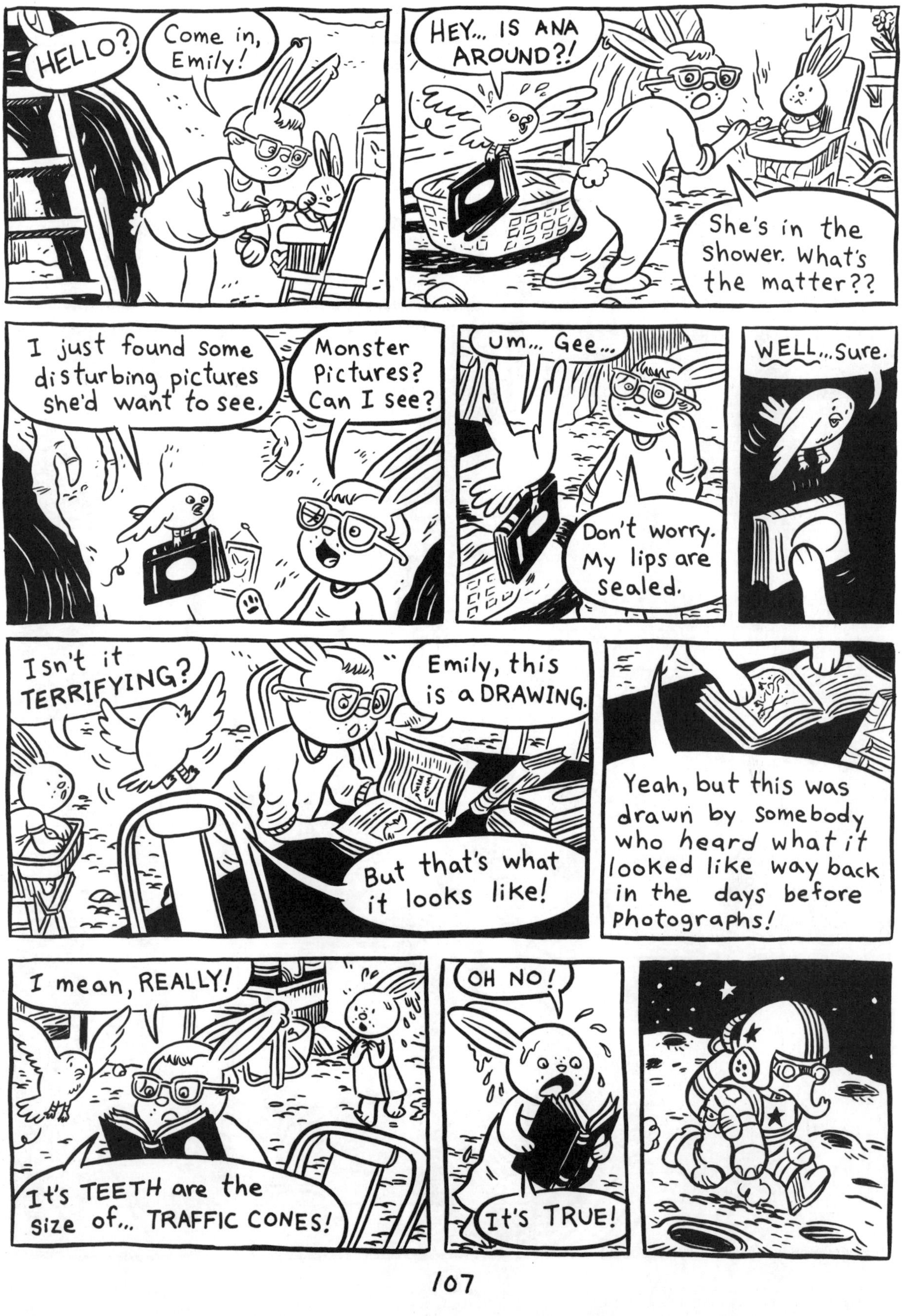
HELLO?
Come in, Emily!
HEY... IS ANA AROUND?!
She's in the shower. What's the matter??
I just found some disturbing pictures she'd want to see.
Monster Pictures? Can I see?
um... Gee...
Don't worry. My lips are sealed.
WELL... Sure.
Isn't it TERRIFYING?
Emily, this is a DRAWING.
But that's what it looks like!
Yeah, but this was drawn by somebody who heard what it looked like way back in the days before photographs!
I mean, REALLY!
It's TEETH are the size of... TRAFFIC CONES!
OH NO!
It's TRUE!

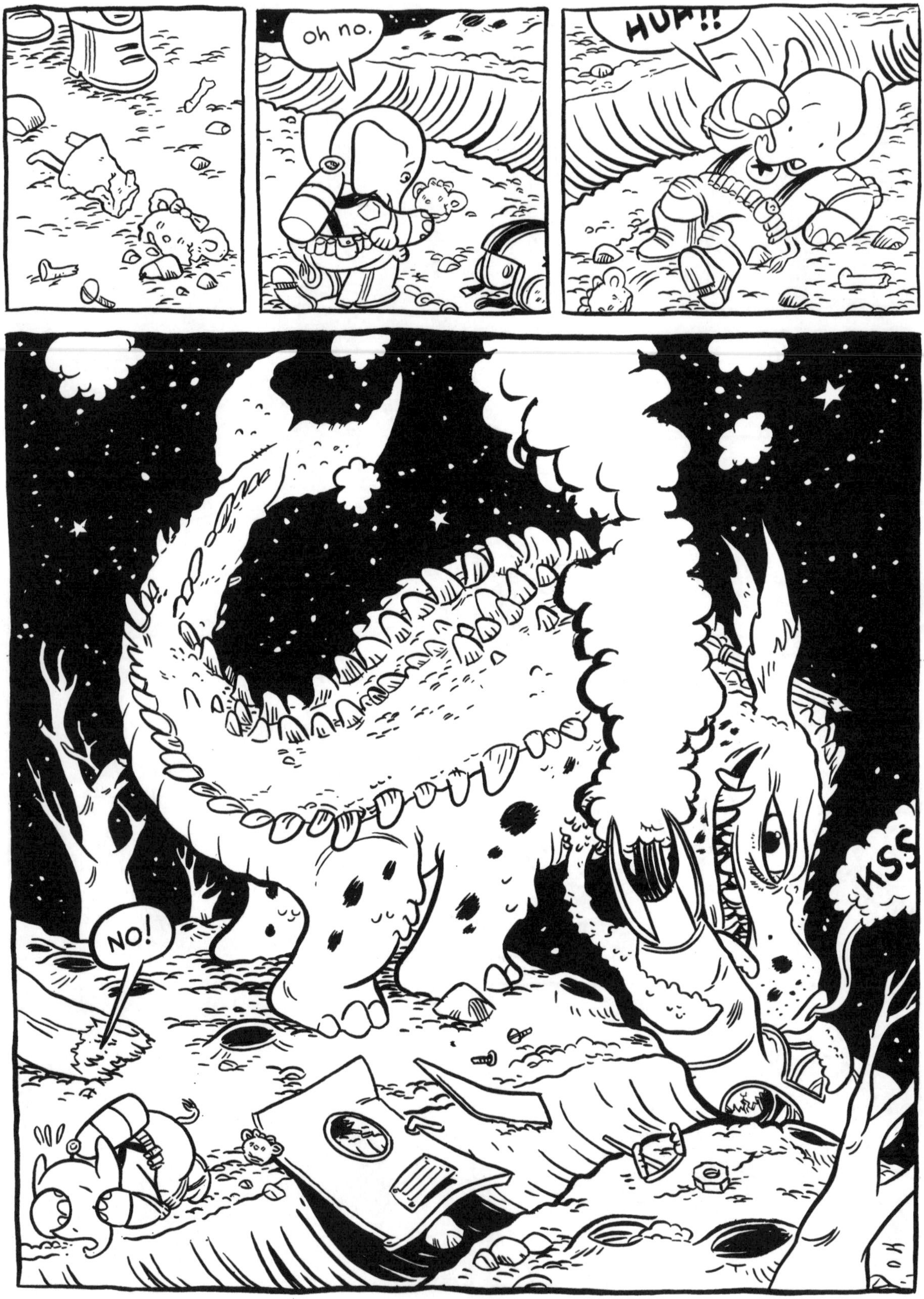
oh no.
HUA!!
NO!
KSS

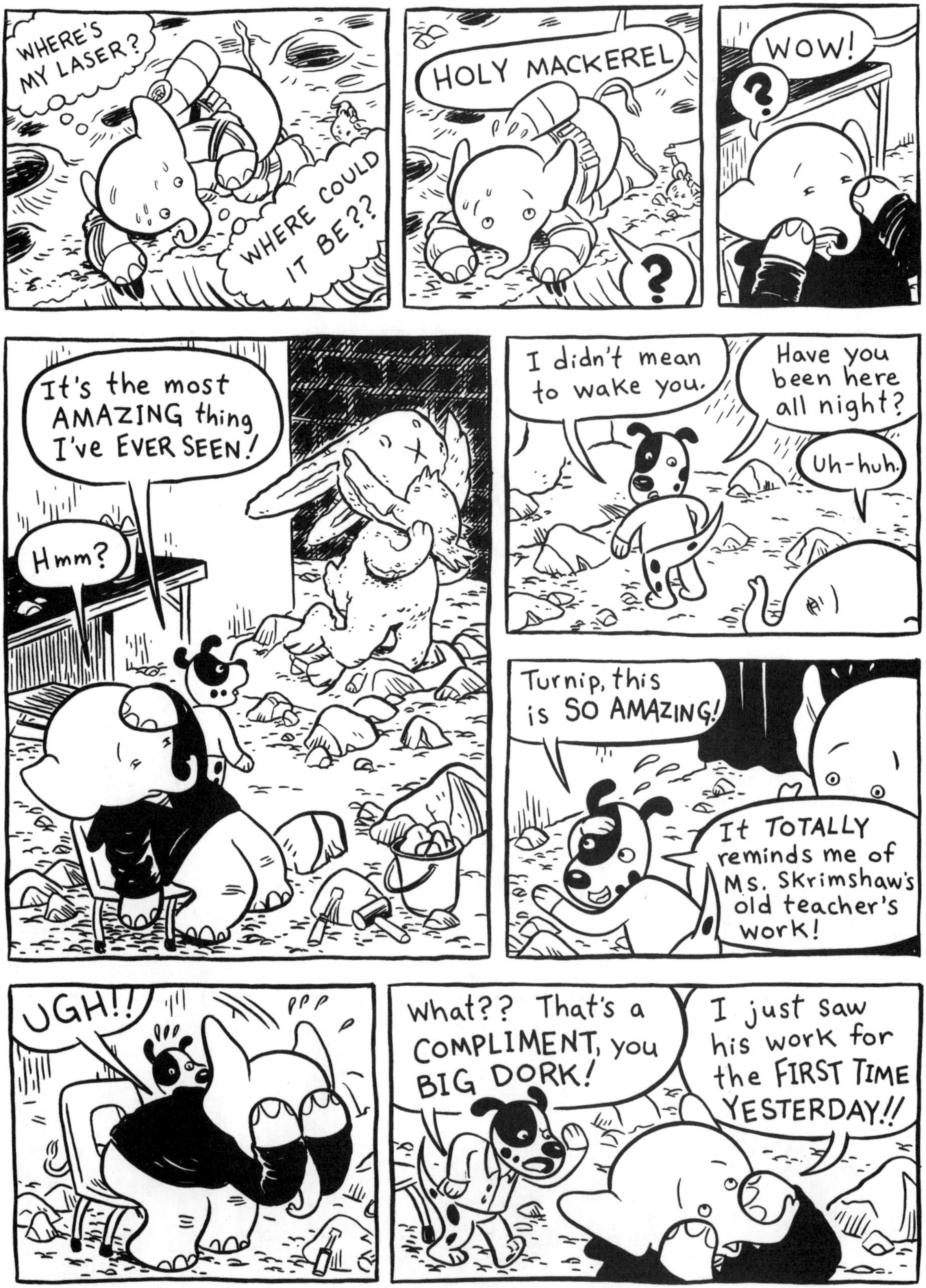
WHERE'S MY LASER?
WHERE COULD IT BE??
HOLY MACKEREL
?
WOW!
?
It's the most AMAZING thing I've EVER SEEN!
Hmm?
I didn't mean to wake you.
Have you been here all night?
Uh-huh.
Turnip, this is SO AMAZING!
It TOTALLY reminds me of Ms. Skrimshaw's old teacher's work!
UGH!!
What?? That's a COMPLIMENT, you BIG DORK!
I just saw his work for the FIRST TIME YESTERDAY!!

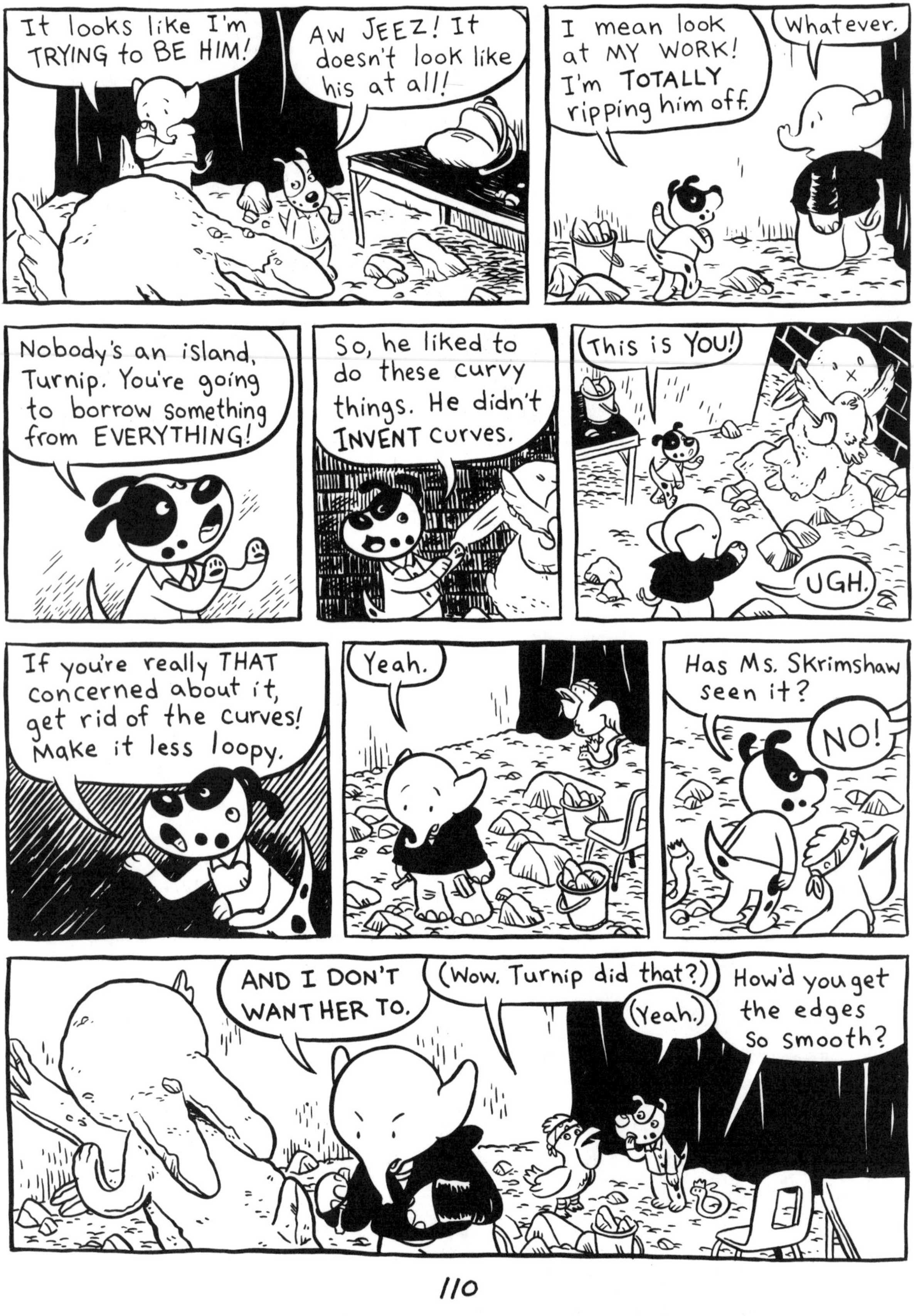

It looks like I'm TRYING to BE HIM!
Aw JEEZ! It doesn't look like his at all!
I mean look at MY WORK! I'm TOTALLY ripping him off.
Whatever.
Nobody's an island, Turnip. You're going to borrow something from EVERYTHING!
So, he liked to do these curvy things. He didn't INVENT curves.
This is YOU!
UGH.
If you're really THAT concerned about it, get rid of the curves! Make it less loopy.
Yeah.
Has Ms. Skrimshaw seen it?
NO!
AND I DON'T WANT HER TO.
(Wow. Turnip did that?)
(Yeah.)
How'd you get the edges so smooth?

I'm BUSY, Max.
Just first show me how you hold your chisel.
Just like THIS!
That's the same way I hold it!
How come yours is so...
UGH!
WHAT?
(I think we should leave him alone.)
How's Turnip coming along?
AMAZINGLY... But I wouldn't go in there yet.
Yeah?
Yeah... could you help me mix my glaze?
What's your first ingredient?
80% Gertsley Borate.
FLINT
RUTILE
20% Synthetic Bone Ash...

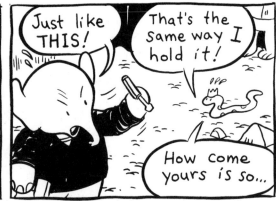

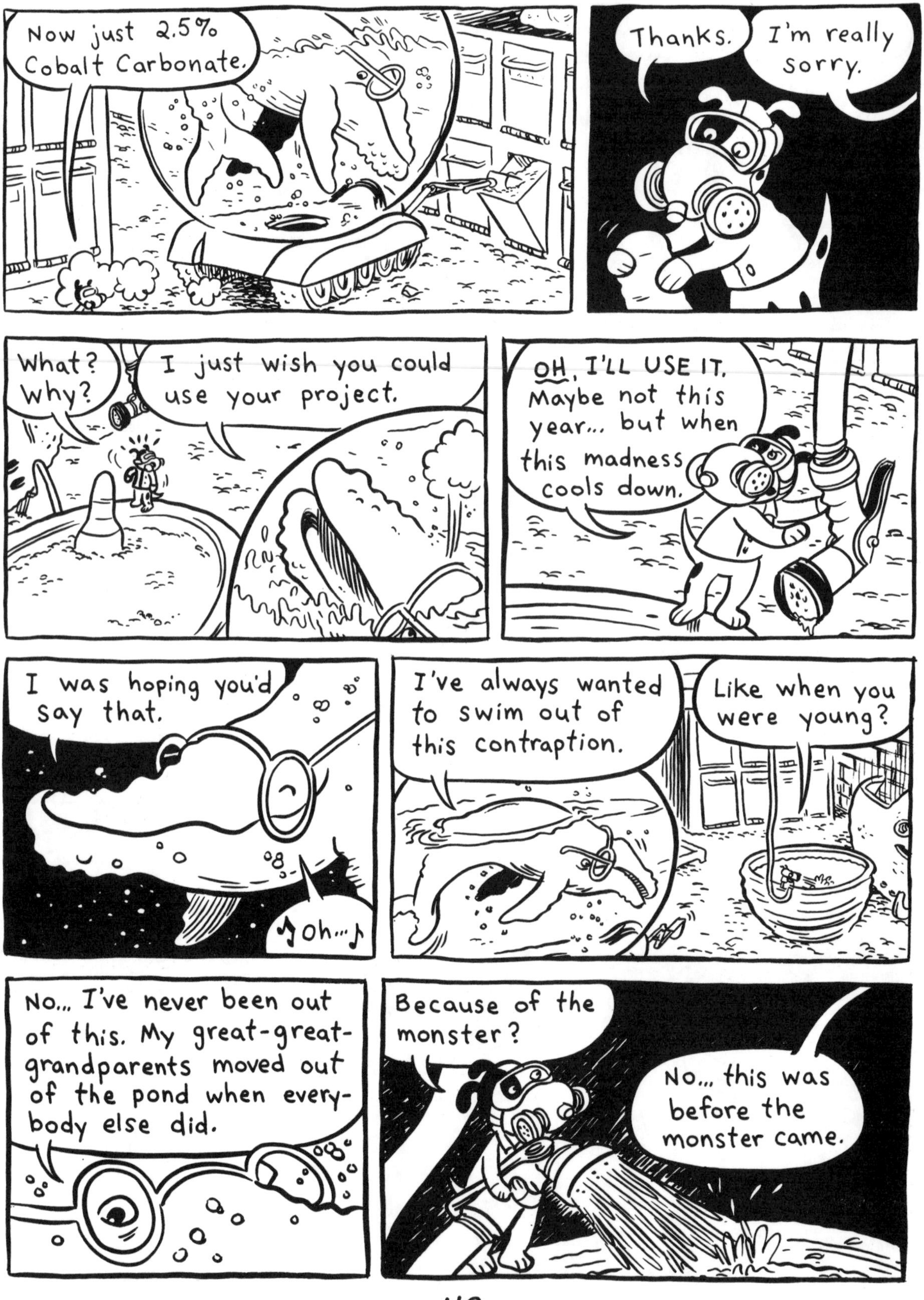
Now just 2.5% Cobalt Carbonate.
Thanks.
I'm really sorry.
What? Why?
I just wish you could use your project.
OH, I'LL USE IT. Maybe not this year... but when this madness cools down.
I was hoping you'd say that.
♪Oh...♪
I've always wanted to swim out of this contraption.
Like when you were young?
No... I've never been out of this. My great-great-grandparents moved out of the pond when everybody else did.
Because of the monster?
No... this was before the monster came.

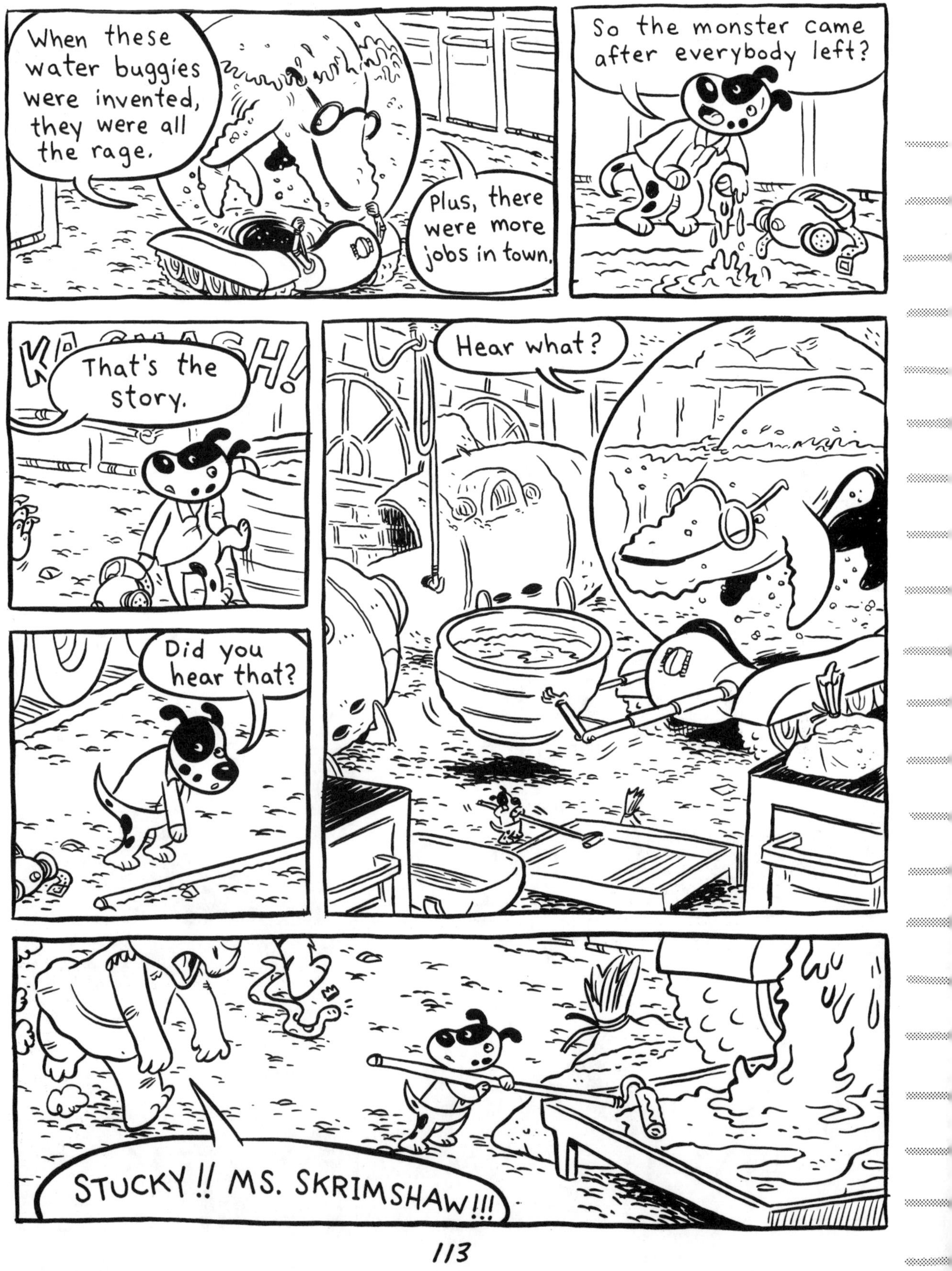
When these water buggies were invented, they were all the rage.
Plus, there were more jobs in town.
So the monster came after everybody left?
KA-SMASH!
That's the story.
Hear what?
Did you hear that?
STUCKY!! MS. SKRIMSHAW!!!

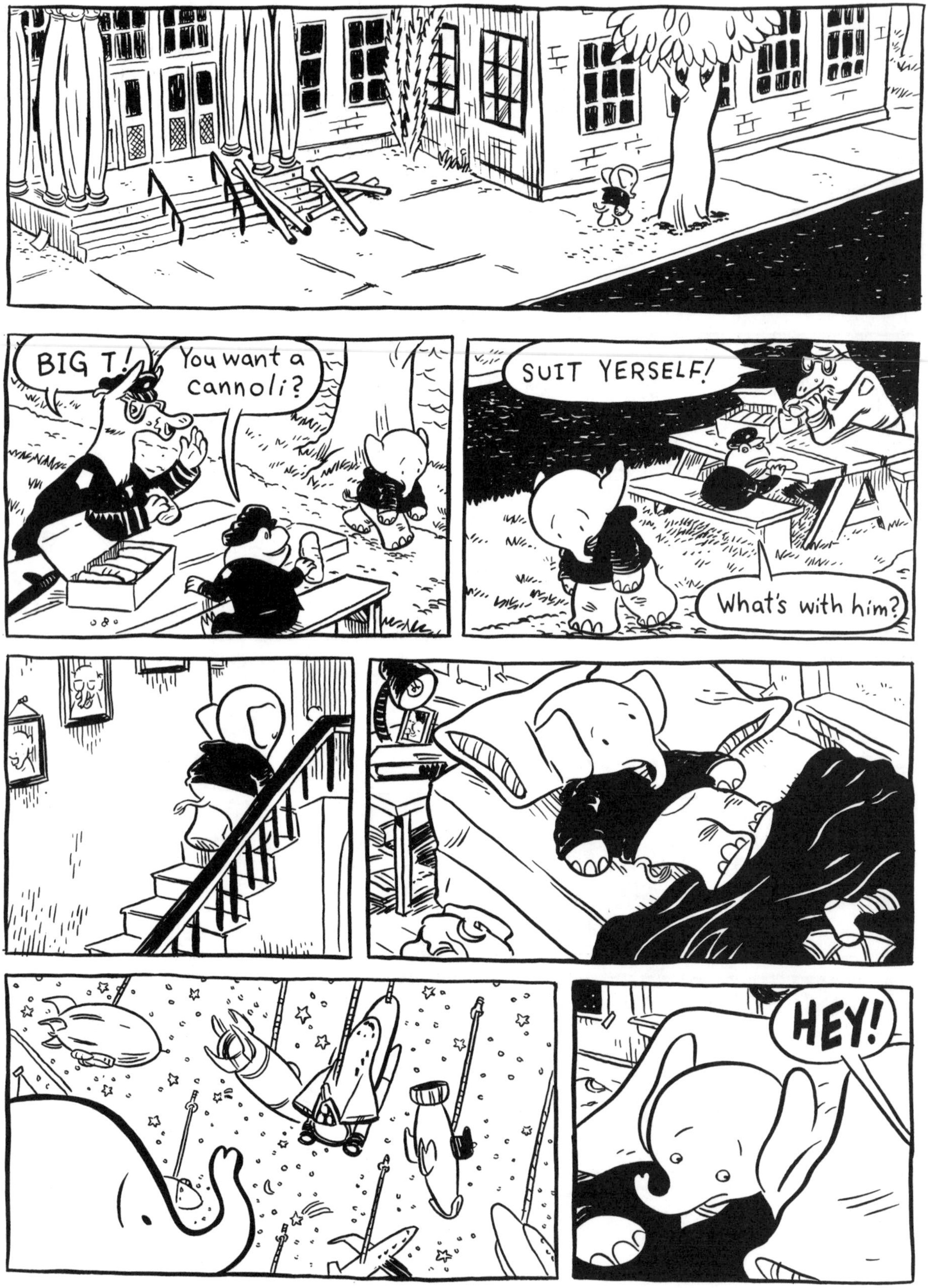
BIG T!
You want a cannoli?
SUIT YERSELF!
What's with him?
HEY!

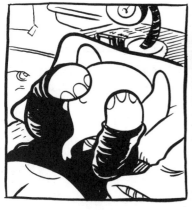

WHY'D YOU DO THAT?!

IT JUST BROKE! I DIDN'T DO IT ON PURPOSE.

WHAT?

THE LOOPS HELD IT TOGETHER!

So you're just giving up?

I LOST, STUCKY!

IT'S OVER!

WOULD YOU QUIT SHOUTING, AND JUST LOOK OUT YOUR WINDOW FOR A SECOND?

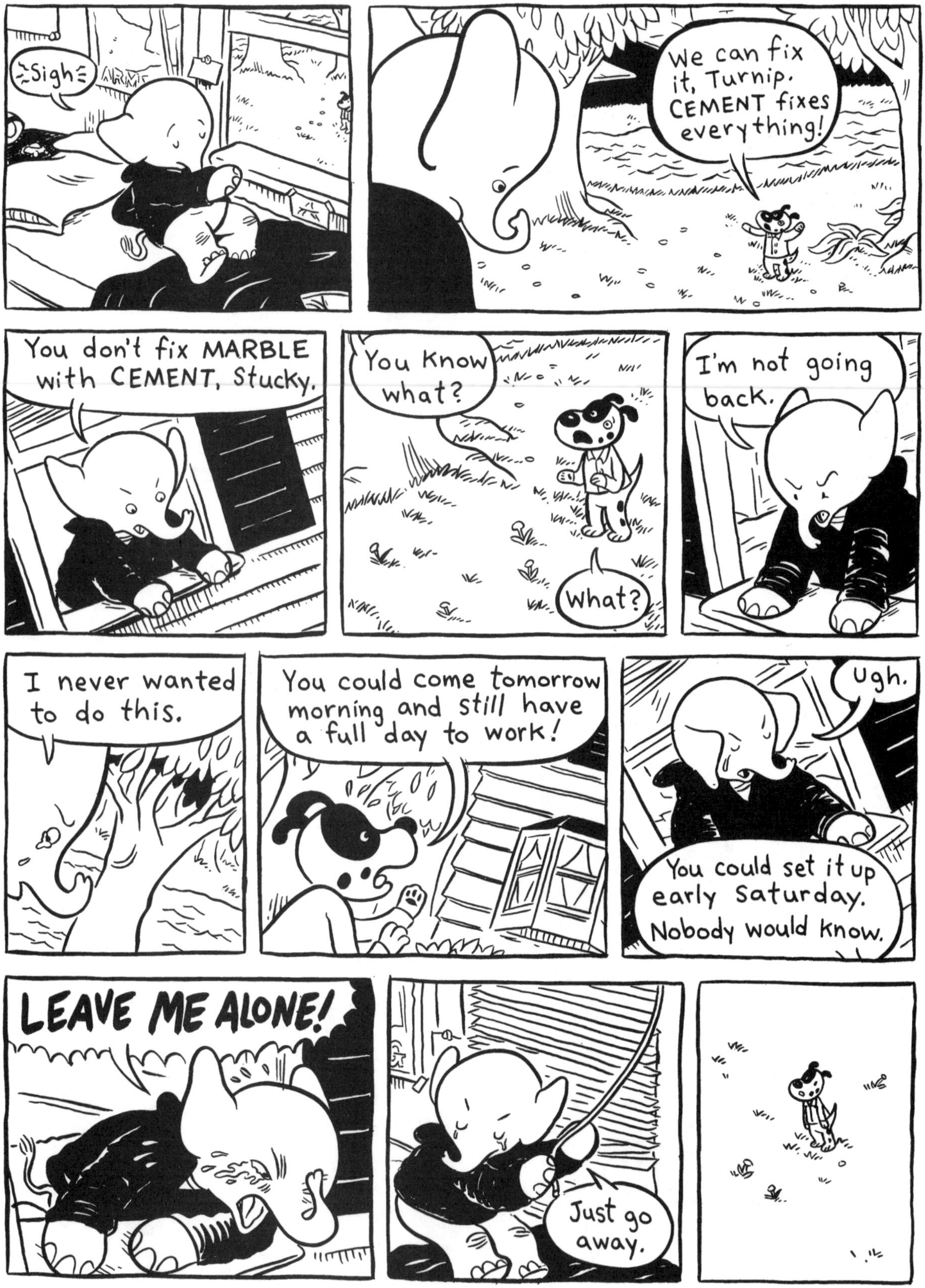
Sigh
We can fix it, Turnip. CEMENT fixes everything!
You don't fix MARBLE with CEMENT, Stucky.
You know what?
What?
I'm not going back.
I never wanted to do this.
You could come tomorrow morning and still have a full day to work!
Ugh.
You could set it up early Saturday. Nobody would know.
LEAVE ME ALONE!
Just go away.

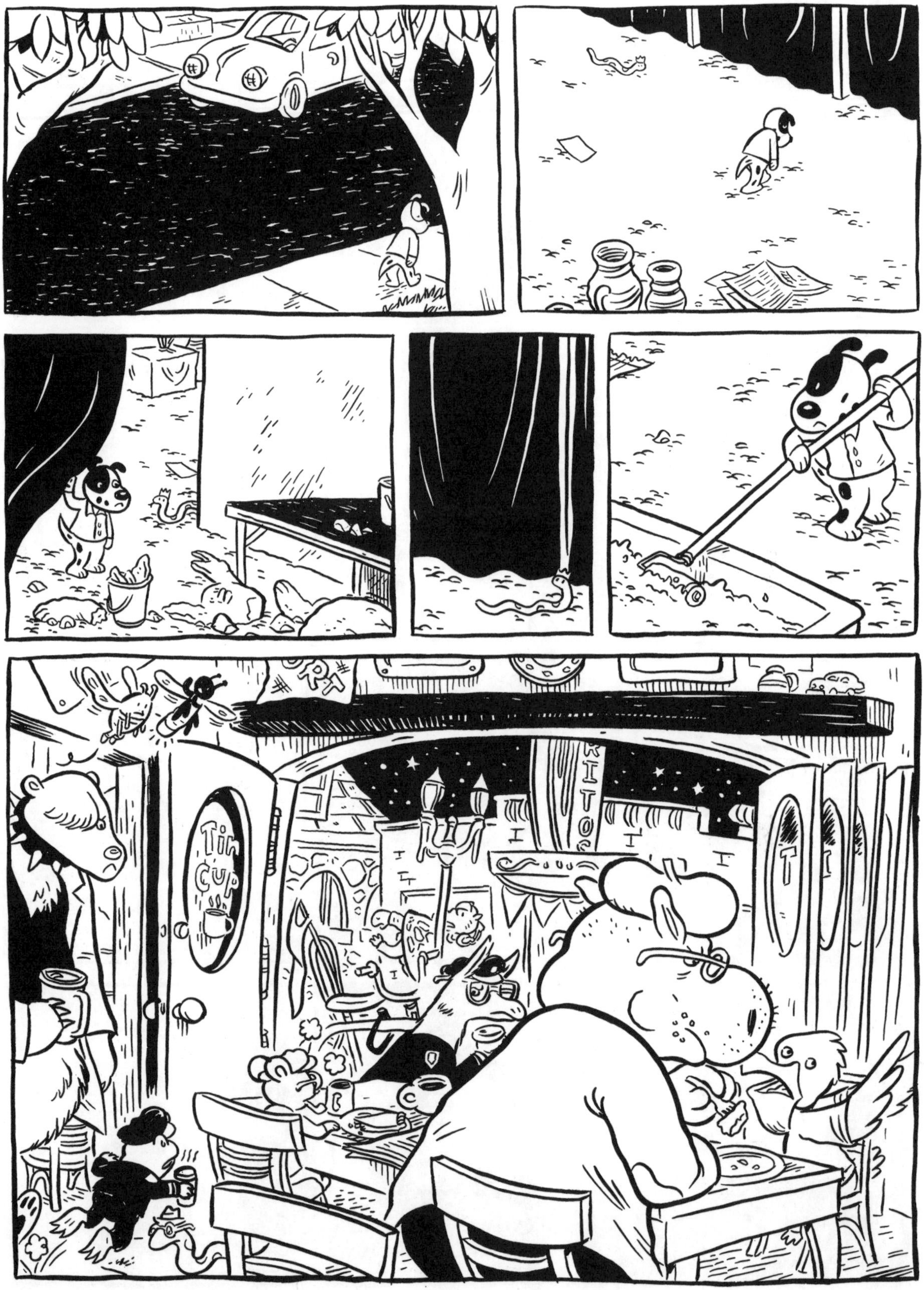
Tin Cup

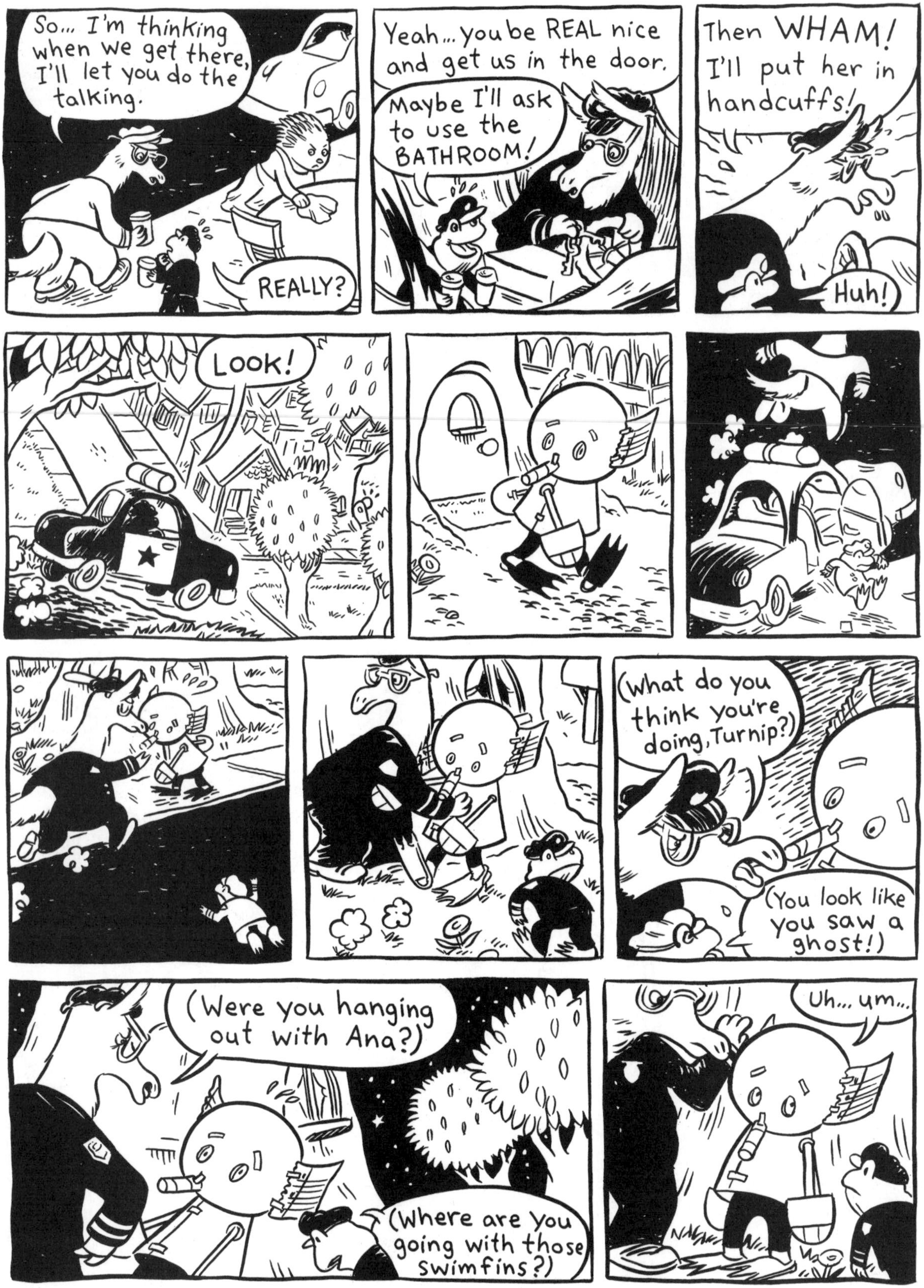
So... I'm thinking when we get there, I'll let you do the talking.
REALLY?
Yeah... you be REAL nice and get us in the door.
Maybe I'll ask to use the BATHROOM!
Then WHAM! I'll put her in handcuffs!
Huh!
Look!
(What do you think you're doing, Turnip?)
(You look like you saw a ghost!)
(Were you hanging out with Ana?)
(Where are you going with those swimfins?)
Uh... um...

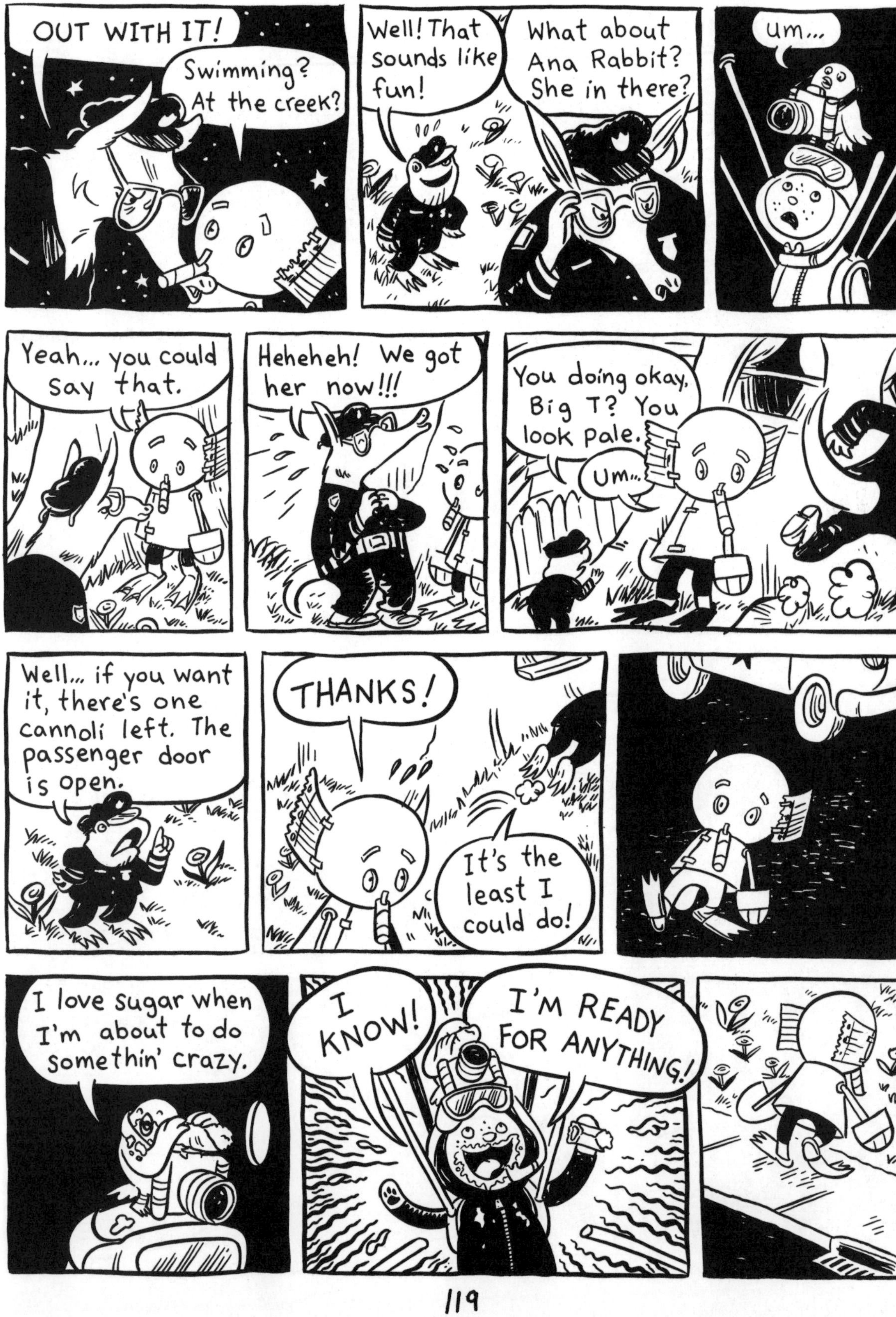
OUT WITH IT!
Swimming? At the creek?
Well! That sounds like fun!
What about Ana Rabbit? She in there?
Um...
Yeah... you could say that.
Heheheh! We got her now!!!
You doing okay, Big T? You look pale.
Um...
Well... if you want it, there's one cannoli left. The passenger door is open.
THANKS!
It's the least I could do!
I love sugar when I'm about to do somethin' crazy.
I KNOW!
I'M READY FOR ANYTHING!

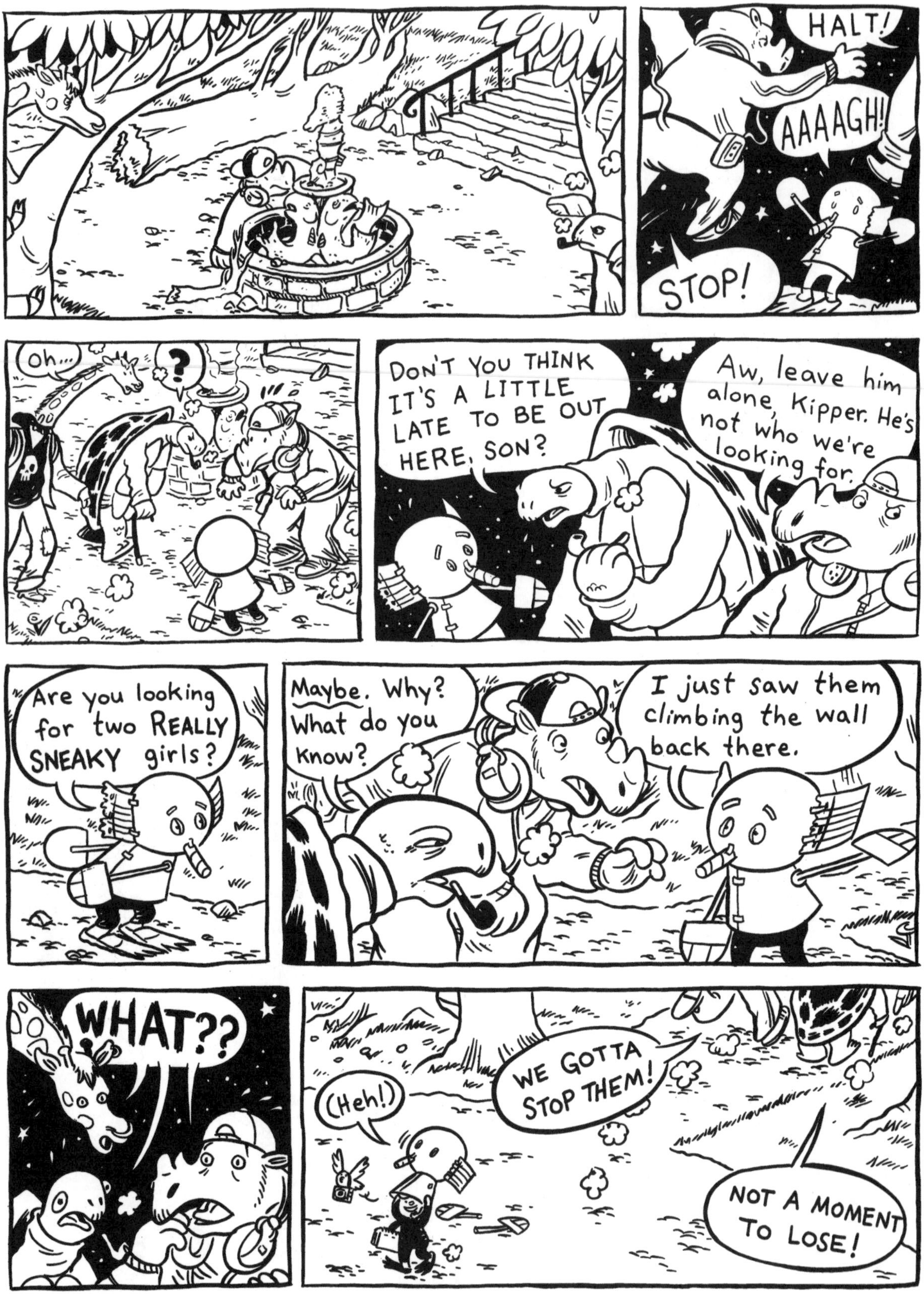
HALT!
AAAAGH!
STOP!
Oh...
?
DON'T YOU THINK IT'S A LITTLE LATE TO BE OUT HERE, SON?
Aw, leave him alone, Kipper. He's not who we're looking for.
Are you looking for two REALLY SNEAKY girls?
Maybe. Why? What do you know?
I just saw them climbing the wall back there.
WHAT??
(Heh!)
WE GOTTA STOP THEM!
NOT A MOMENT TO LOSE!

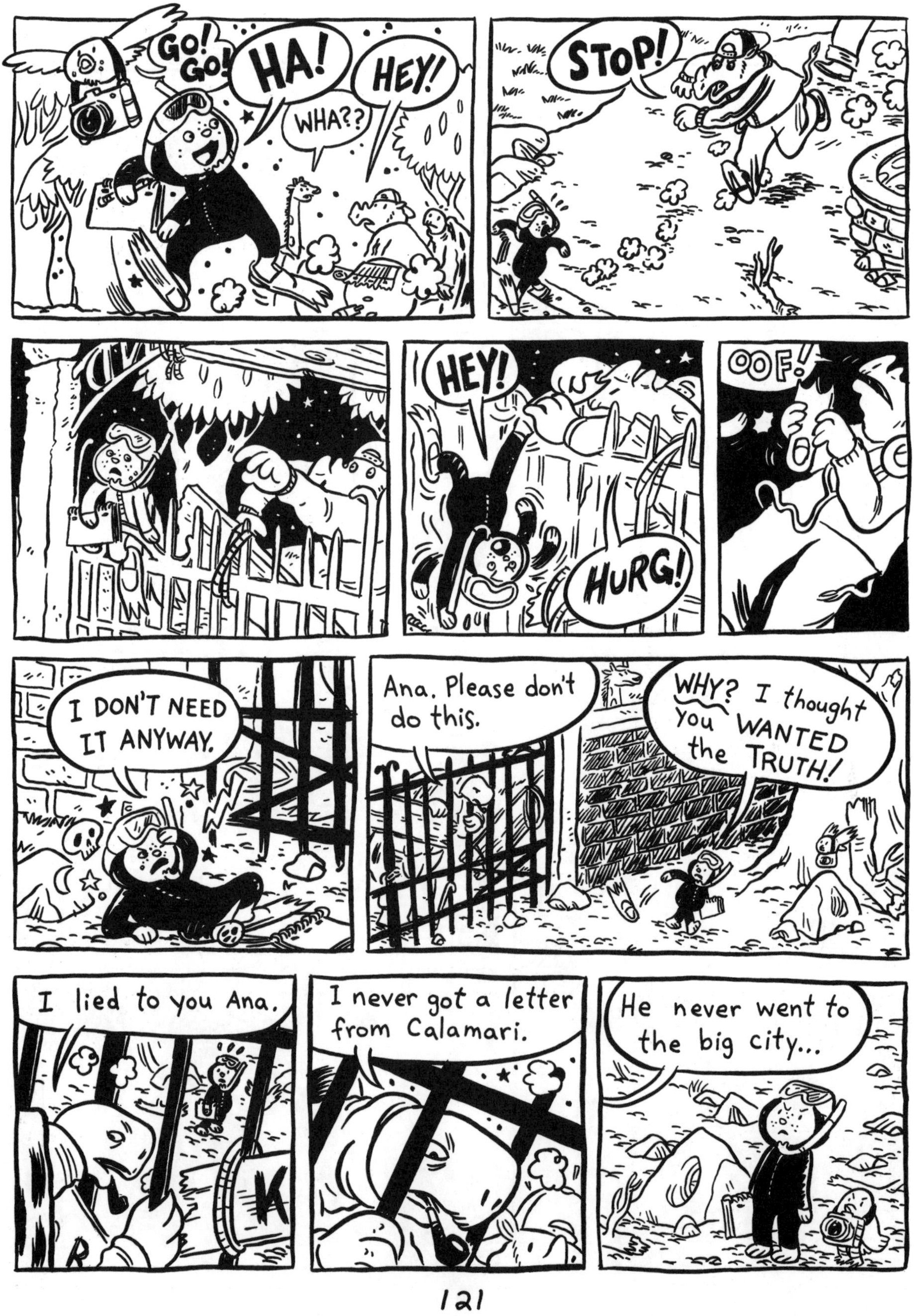
GO! GO!
HA!
WHA??
HEY!
STOP!
HEY!
HURG!
OOF!
I DON'T NEED IT ANYWAY.
Ana. Please don't do this.
WHY? I thought you WANTED the TRUTH!
I lied to you Ana.
I never got a letter from Calamari.
He never went to the big city...

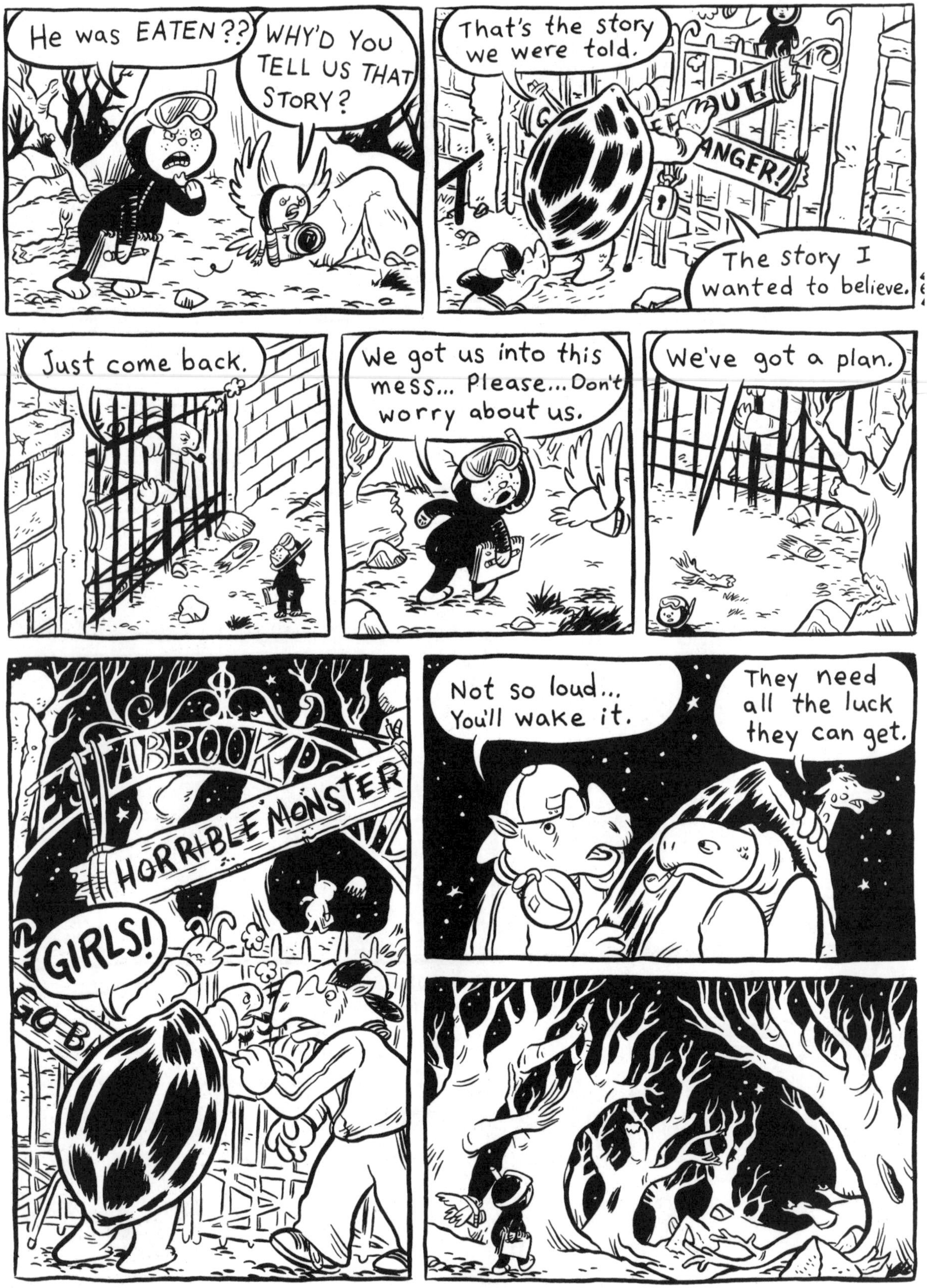
He was EATEN??
WHY'D YOU TELL US THAT STORY?
That's the story we were told.
The story I wanted to believe.
Just come back.
We got us into this mess... Please... Don't worry about us.
We've got a plan.
HORRIBLE MONSTER
GIRLS!
Not so loud... You'll wake it.
They need all the luck they can get.

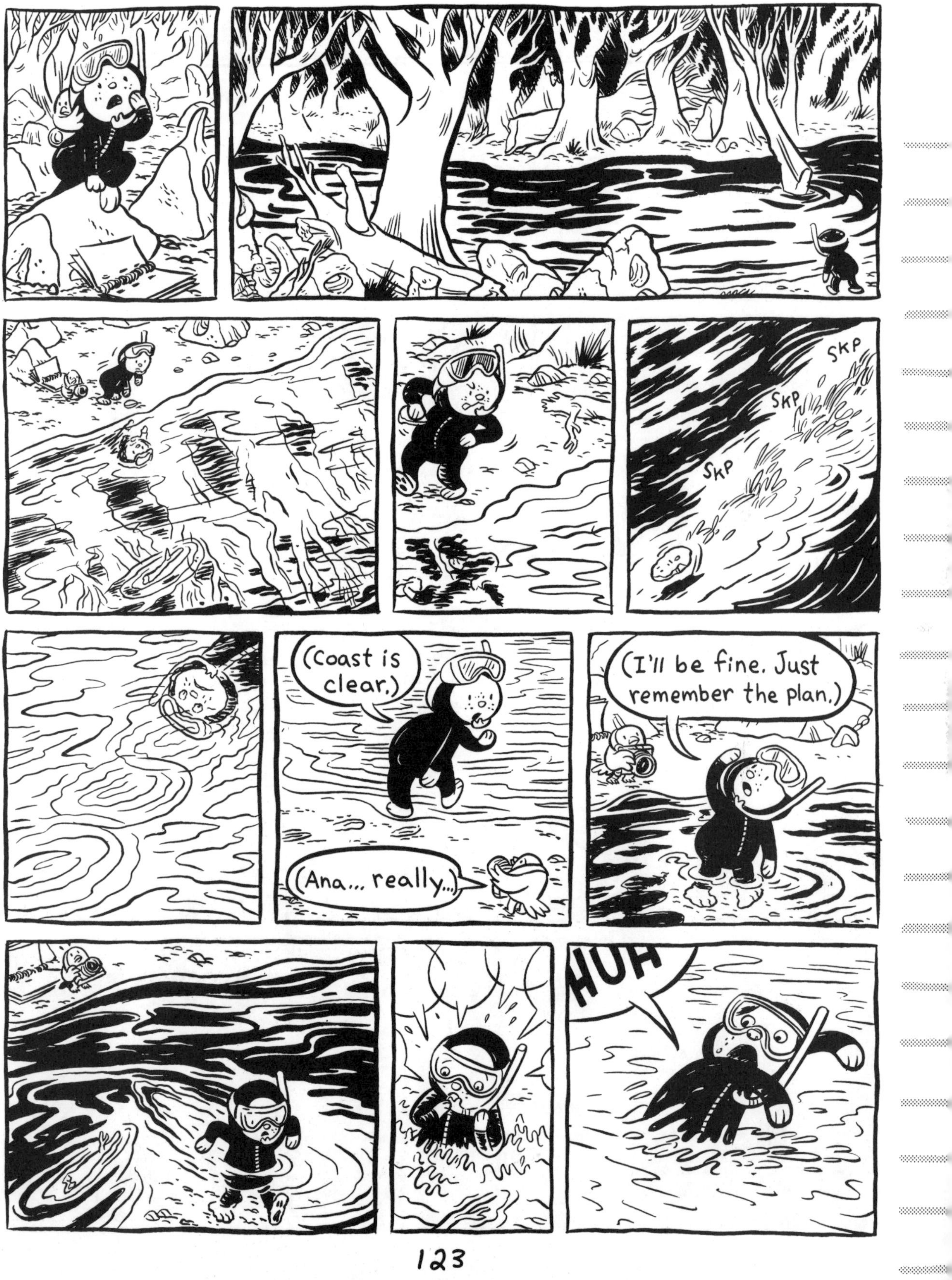
SKP
SKP
SKP
(Coast is clear.)
(Ana... really...)
(I'll be fine. Just remember the plan.)
HUH

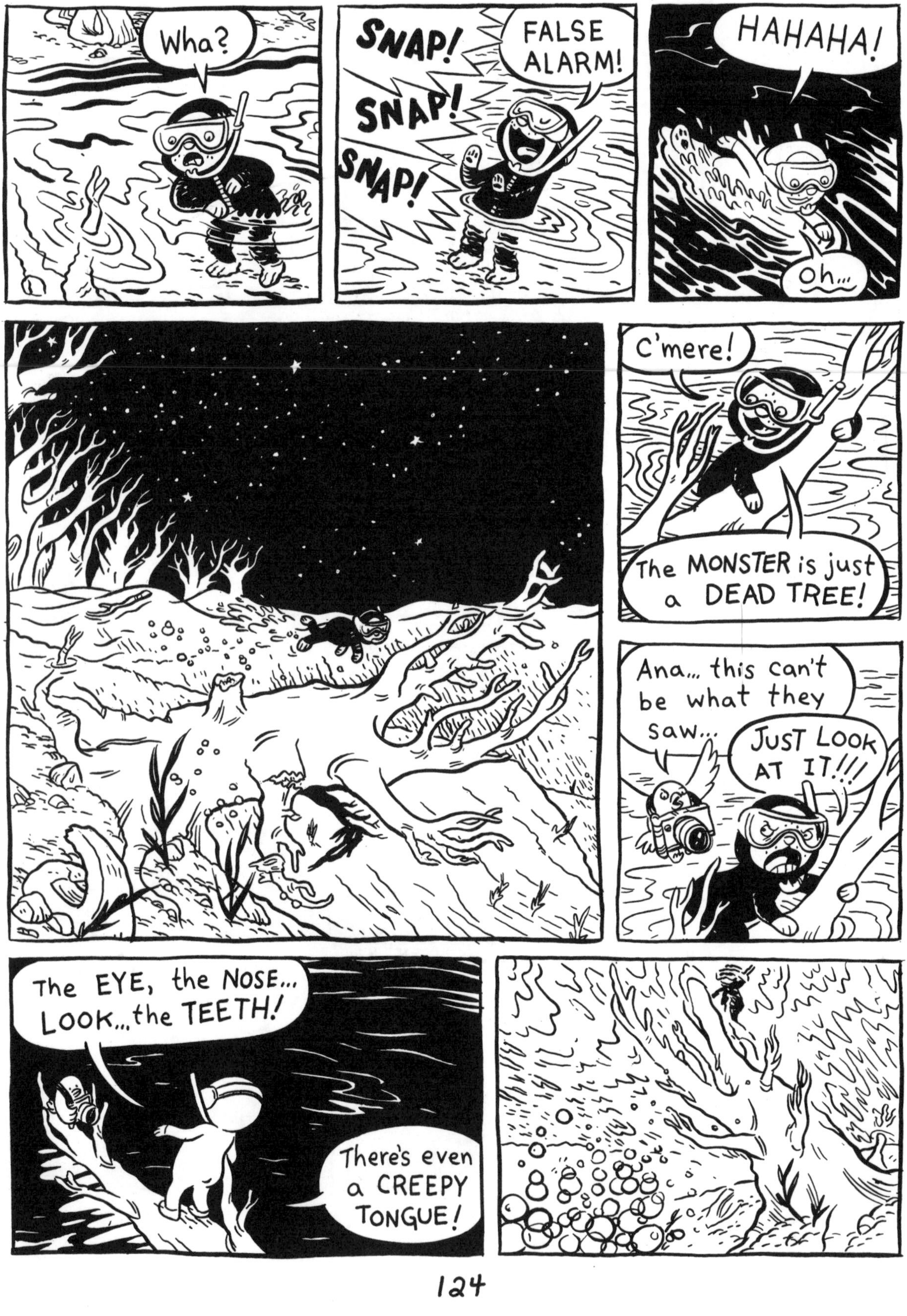
Wha?
SNAP!
SNAP!
SNAP!
FALSE ALARM!
HAHAHA!
Oh...
C'mere!
The MONSTER is just a DEAD TREE!
Ana... this can't be what they saw...
JUST LOOK AT IT!!!
The EYE, the NOSE... LOOK... the TEETH!
There's even a CREEPY TONGUE!

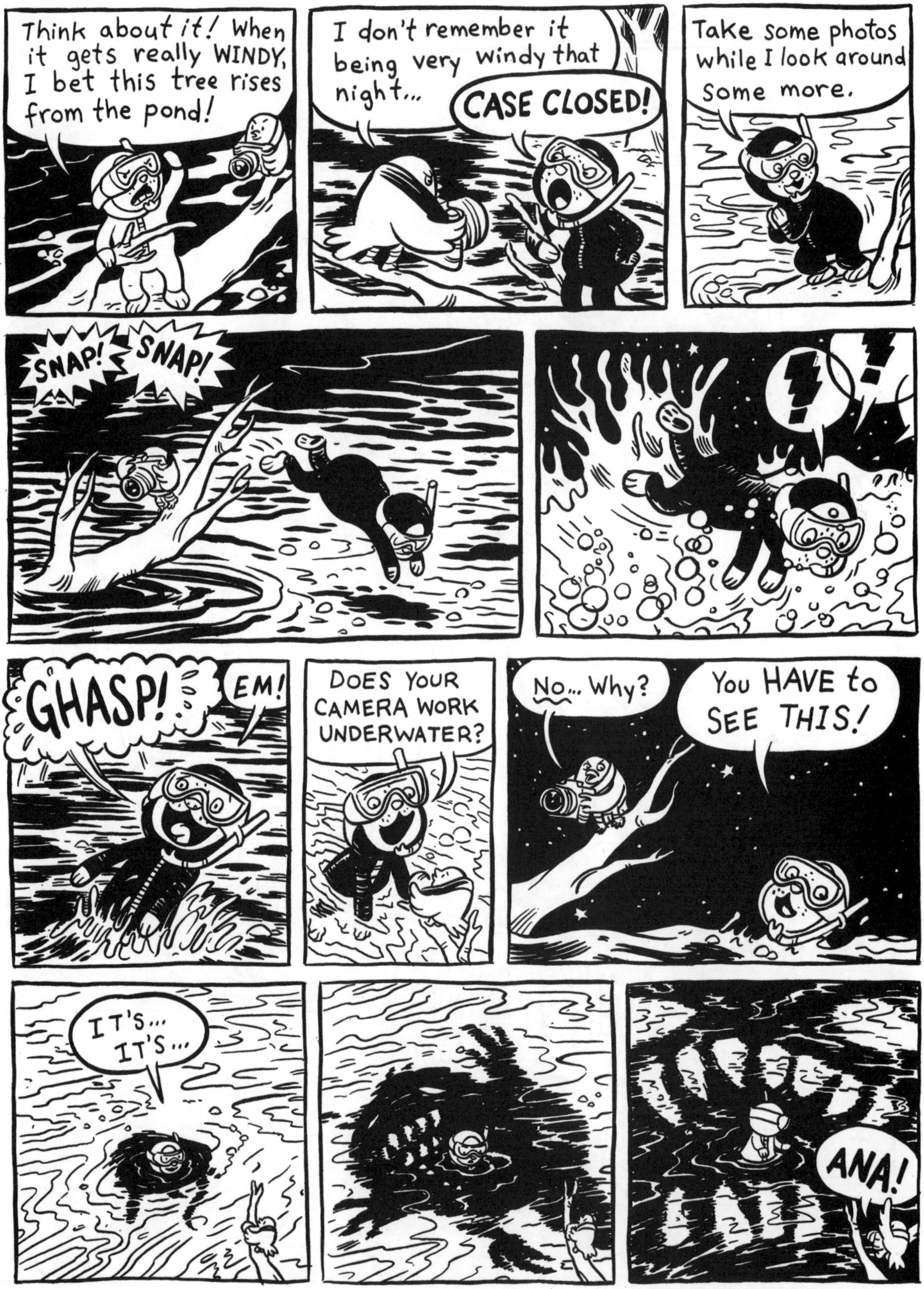

Think about it! When it gets really WINDY, I bet this tree rises from the pond!
I don't remember it being very windy that night...
CASE CLOSED!
Take some photos while I look around some more.
SNAP!
SNAP!
GHASP!
EM!
DOES YOUR CAMERA WORK UNDERWATER?
No... Why?
You HAVE to SEE THIS!
IT'S... IT'S...
ANA!

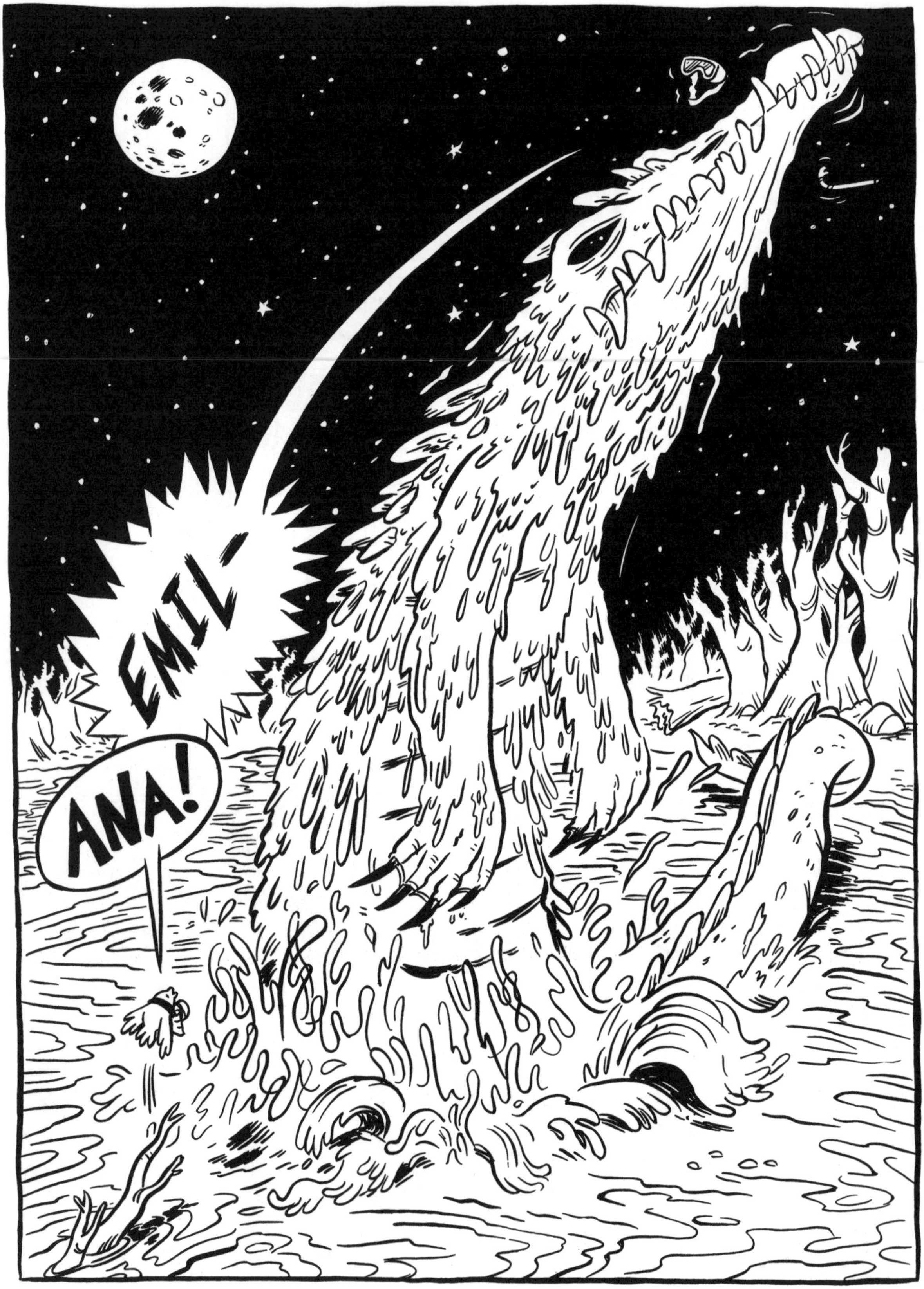
EMIL
ANA!

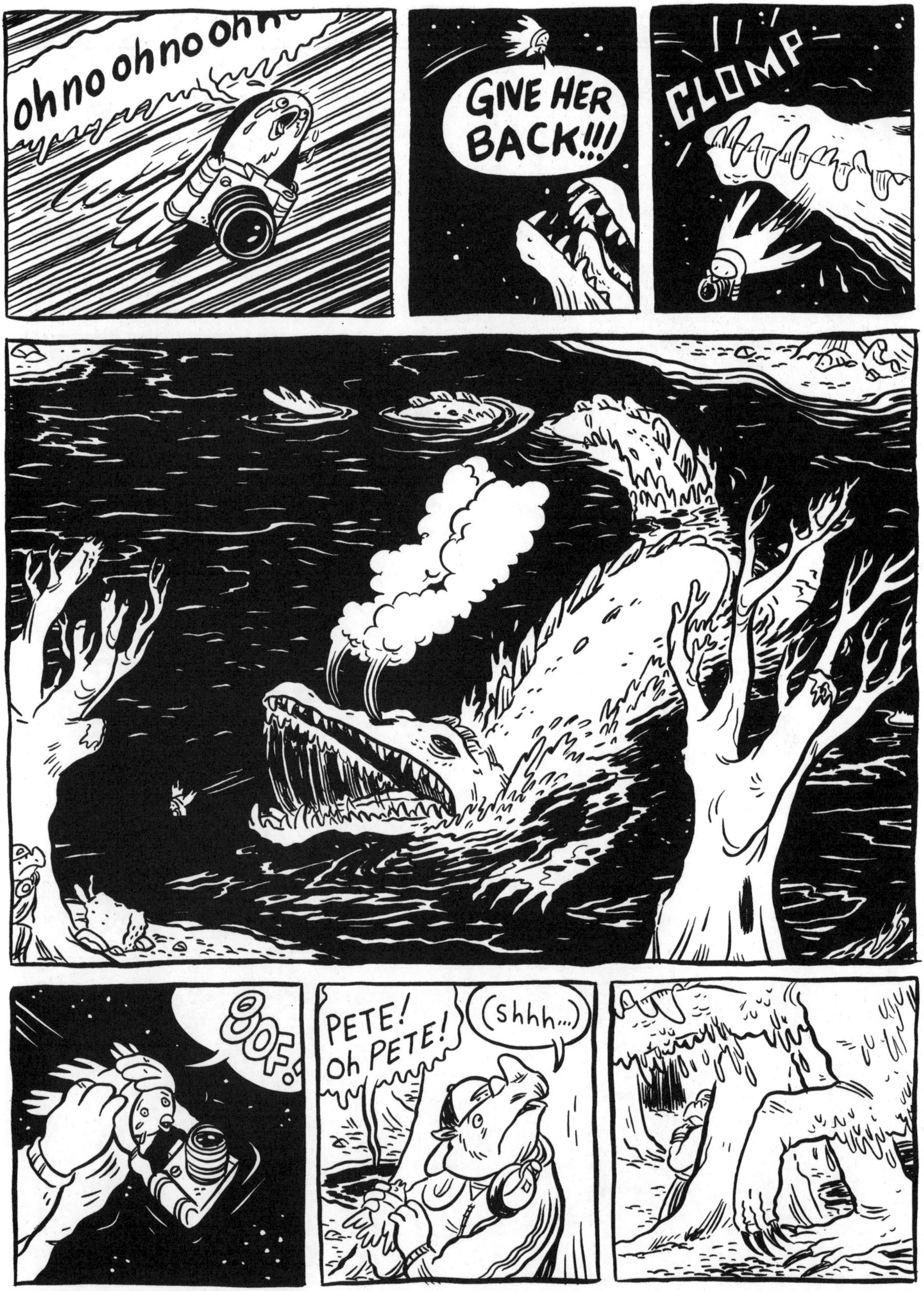
ohnoohnoohnoohno
GIVE HER BACK!!!
CLOMP
OOF.
PETE! oh PETE!
(shhh...)

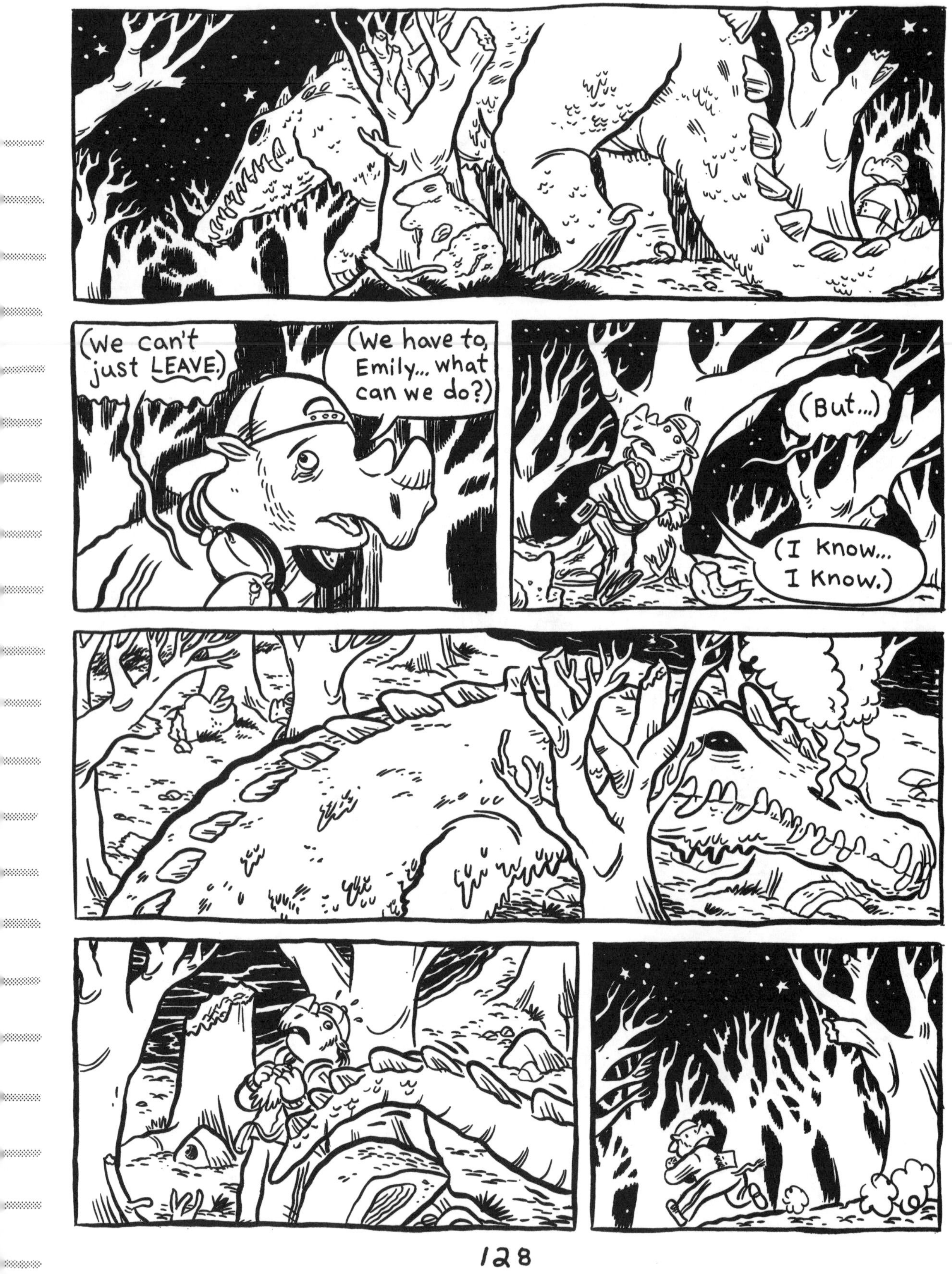
(We can't just LEAVE.)
(We have to, Emily... what can we do?)
(But...)
(I know... I know.)

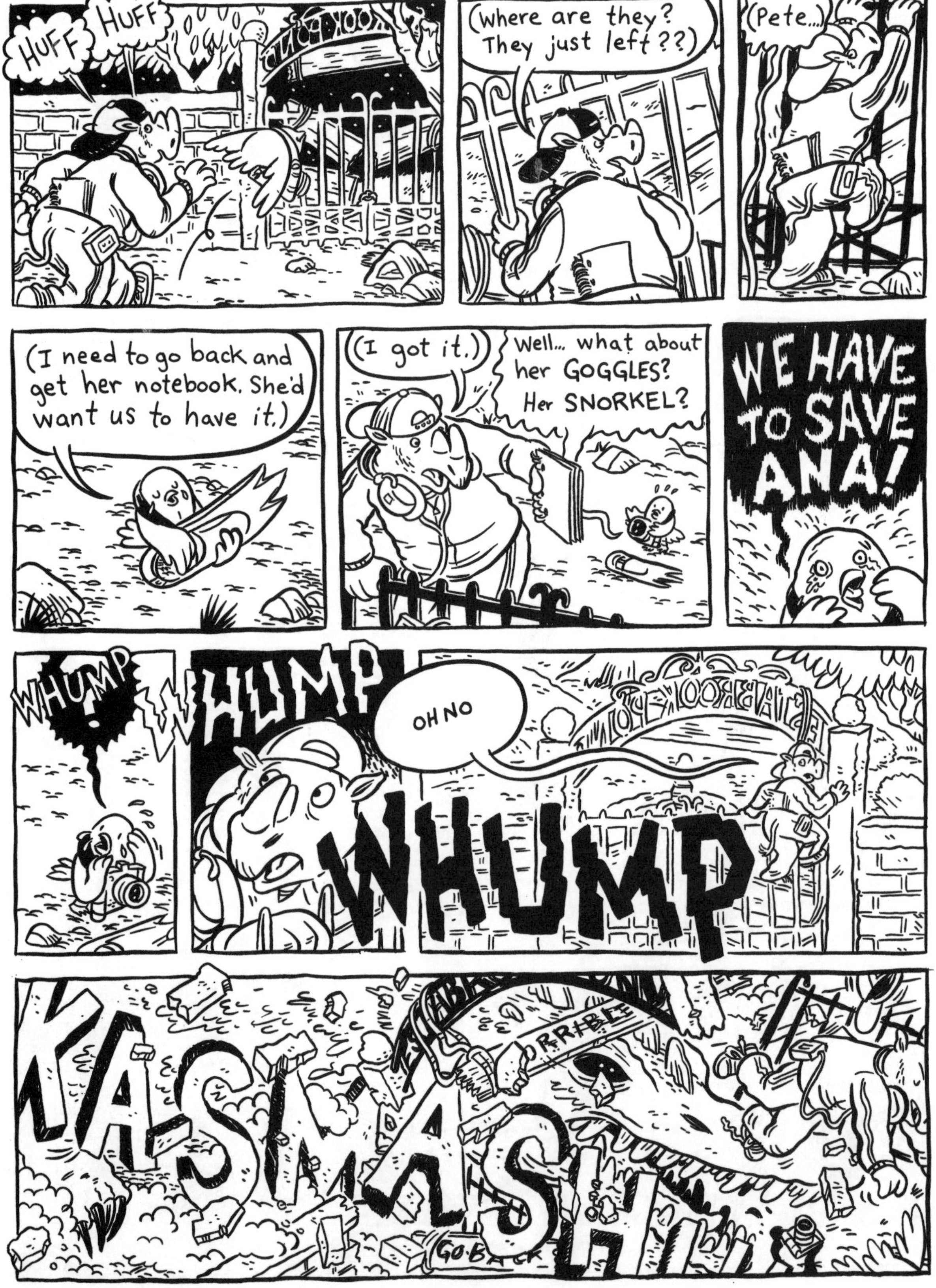
HUFF HUFF
(Where are they? They just left??)
(Pete...)
(I need to go back and get her notebook. She'd want us to have it.)
(I got it.)
Well... what about her GOGGLES? Her SNORKEL?
WE HAVE TO SAVE ANA!
WHUMP
WHUMP
OH NO
WHUMP
KA-SMASH!!
GO BACK

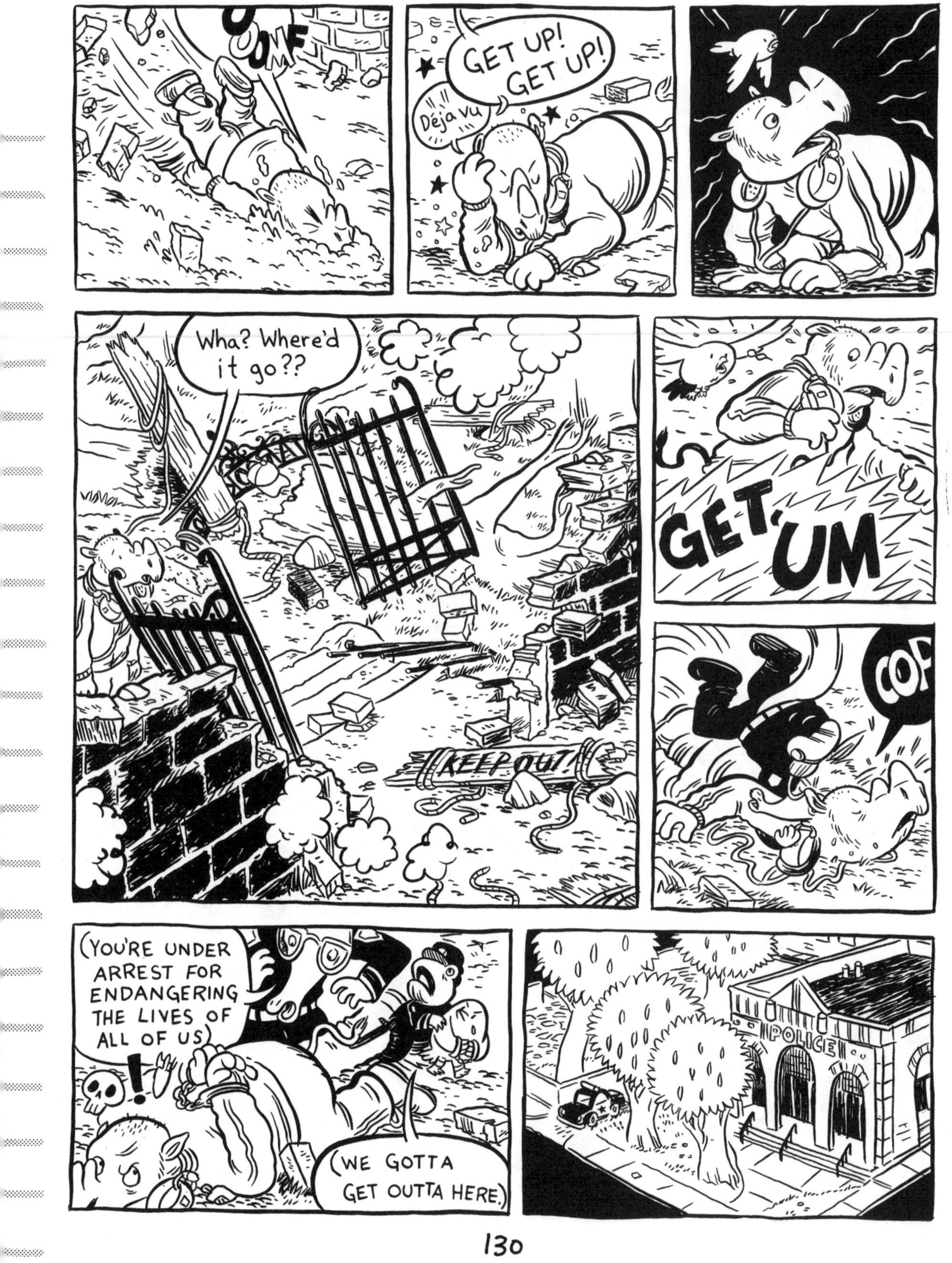
GET UP! GET UP!
Déja vu
Wha? Where'd it go??
KEEP OUT!
GET 'UM
COP
(YOU'RE UNDER ARREST FOR ENDANGERING THE LIVES OF ALL OF US)
(WE GOTTA GET OUTTA HERE)
POLICE

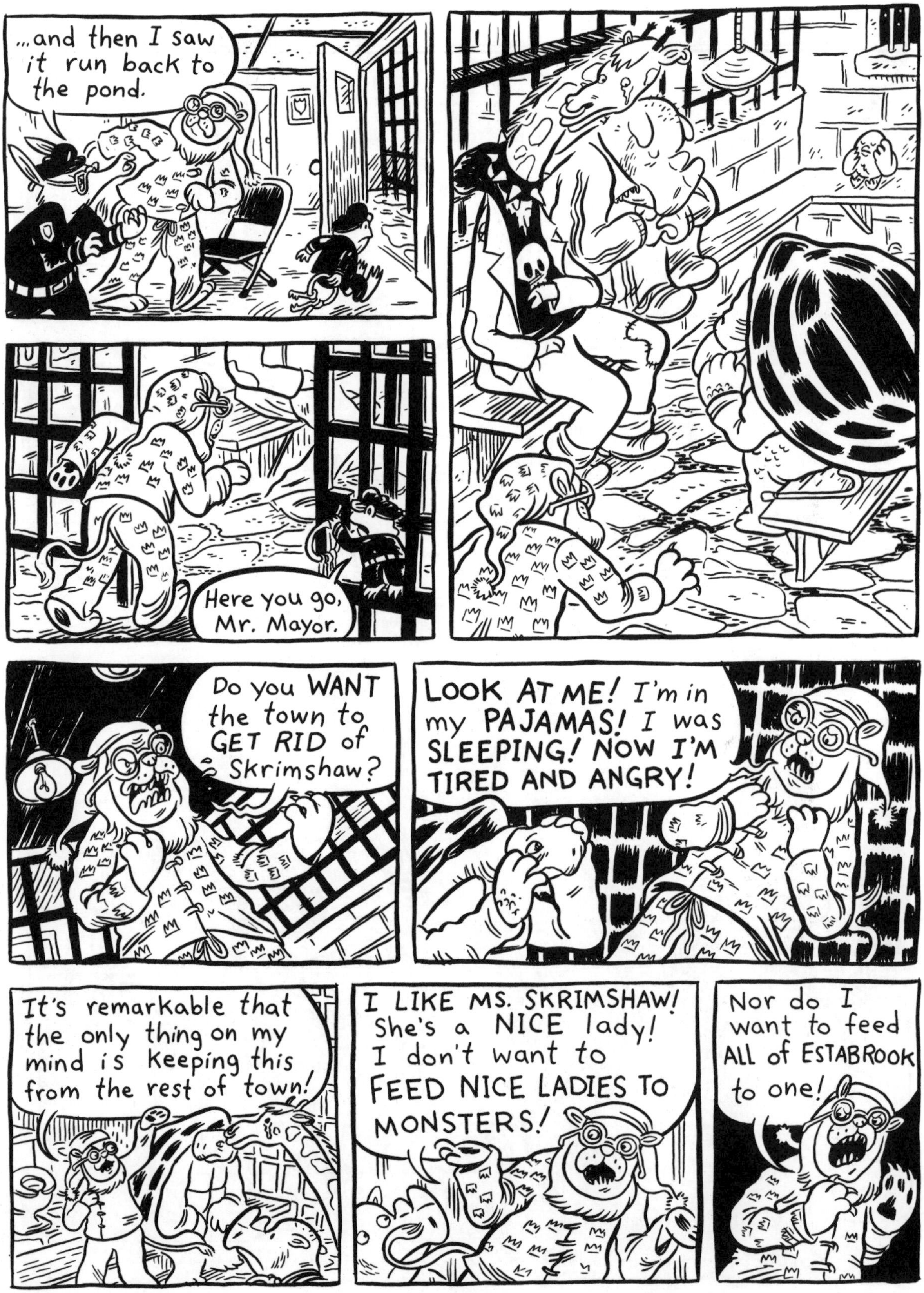
...and then I saw it run back to the pond.
Here you go, Mr. Mayor.
Do you WANT the town to GET RID of Skrimshaw?
LOOK AT ME! I'm in my PAJAMAS! I was SLEEPING! NOW I'M TIRED AND ANGRY!
It's remarkable that the only thing on my mind is keeping this from the rest of town!
I LIKE MS. SKRIMSHAW! She's a NICE lady! I don't want to FEED NICE LADIES TO MONSTERS!
Nor do I want to feed ALL of ESTABROOK to one!

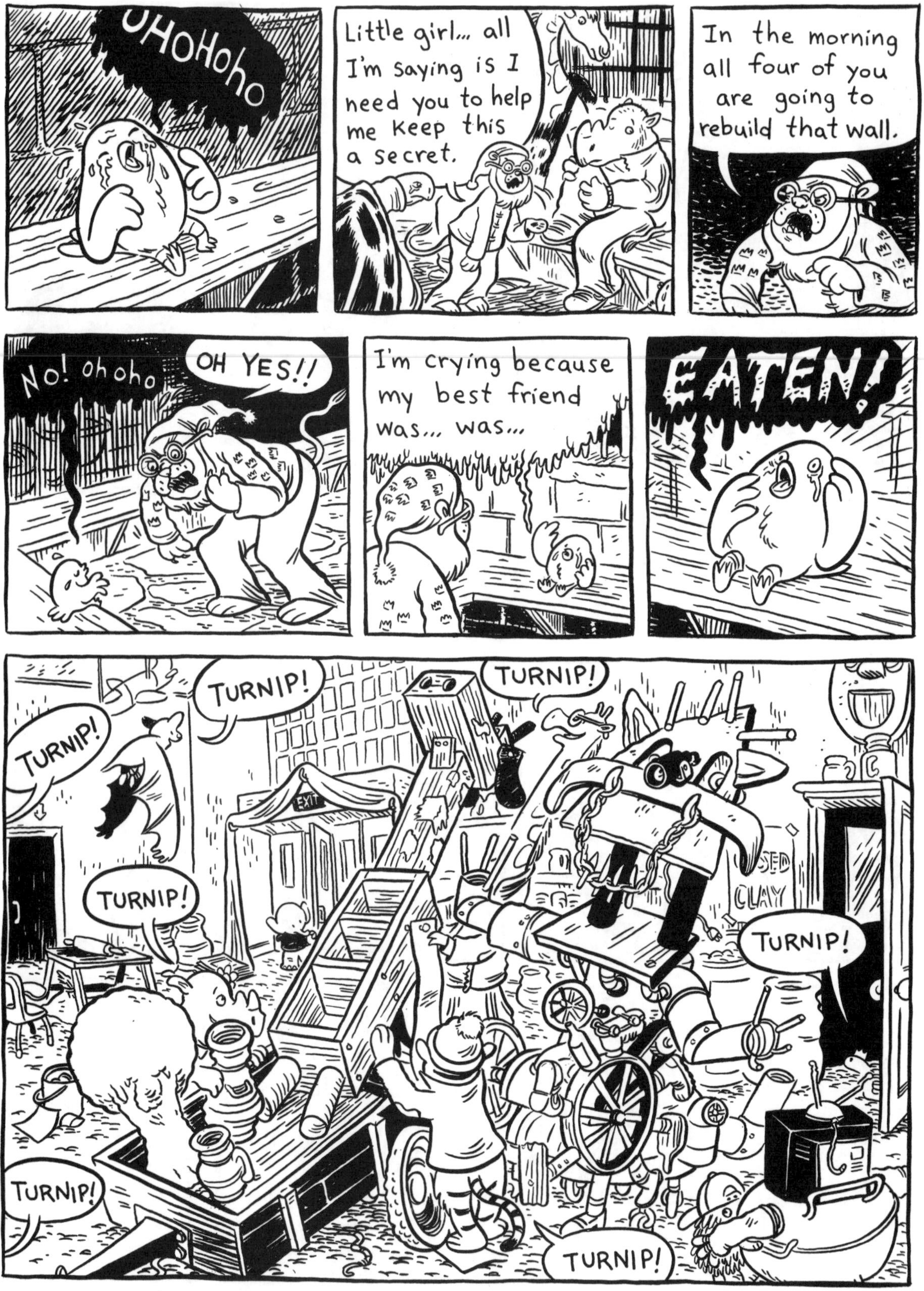
OHOHoho
Little girl... all I'm saying is I need you to help me keep this a secret.
In the morning all four of you are going to rebuild that wall.
No! oh oho
OH YES!!
I'm crying because my best friend was... was...
EATEN!
TURNIP!
TURNIP!
TURNIP!
TURNIP!
TURNIP!
TURNIP!
TURNIP!

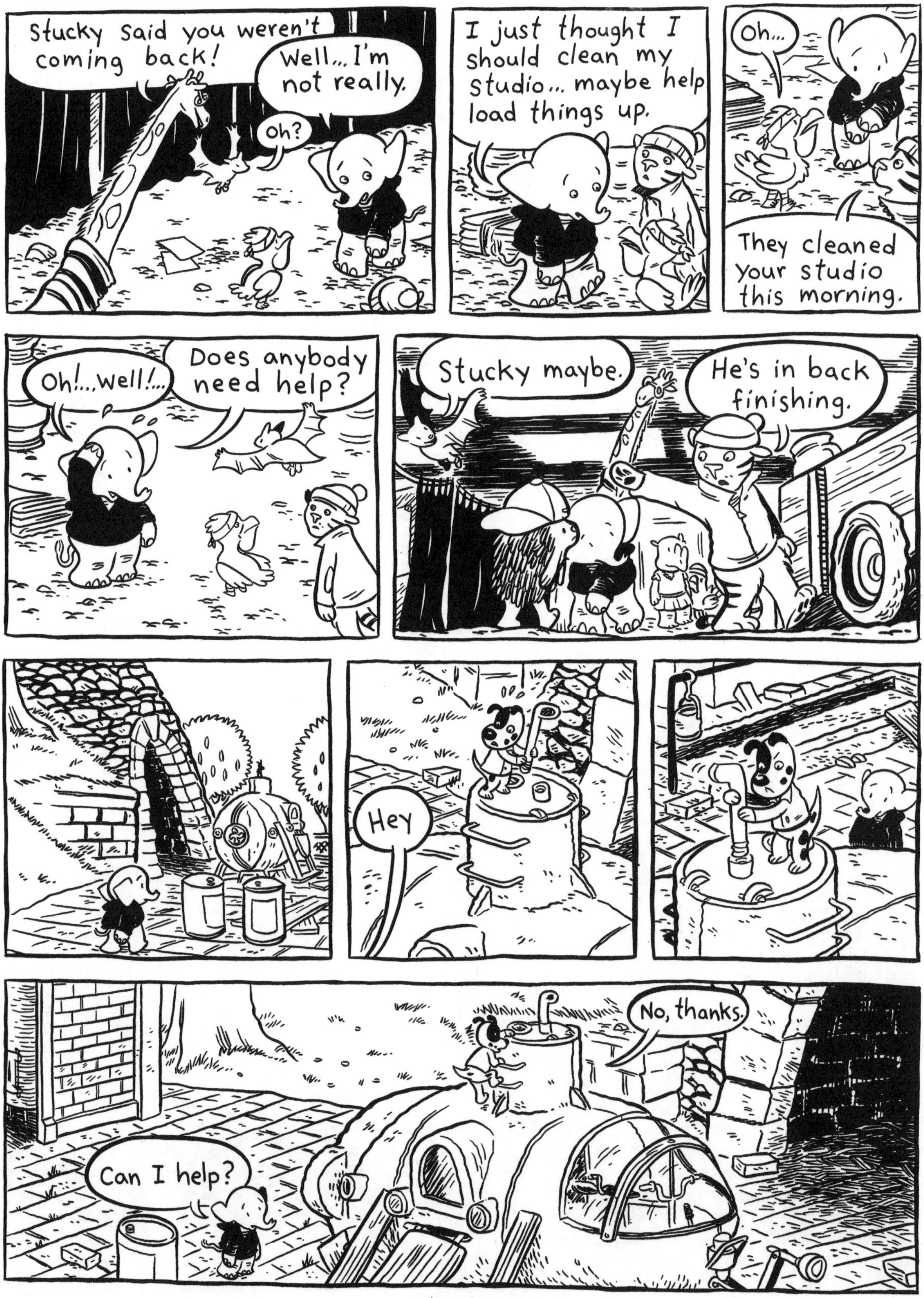
Stucky said you weren't coming back!
Well... I'm not really.
Oh?
I just thought I should clean my studio... maybe help load things up.
Oh...
They cleaned your studio this morning.
Oh!...well!...
Does anybody need help?
Stucky maybe.
He's in back finishing.
Hey
No, thanks.
Can I help?

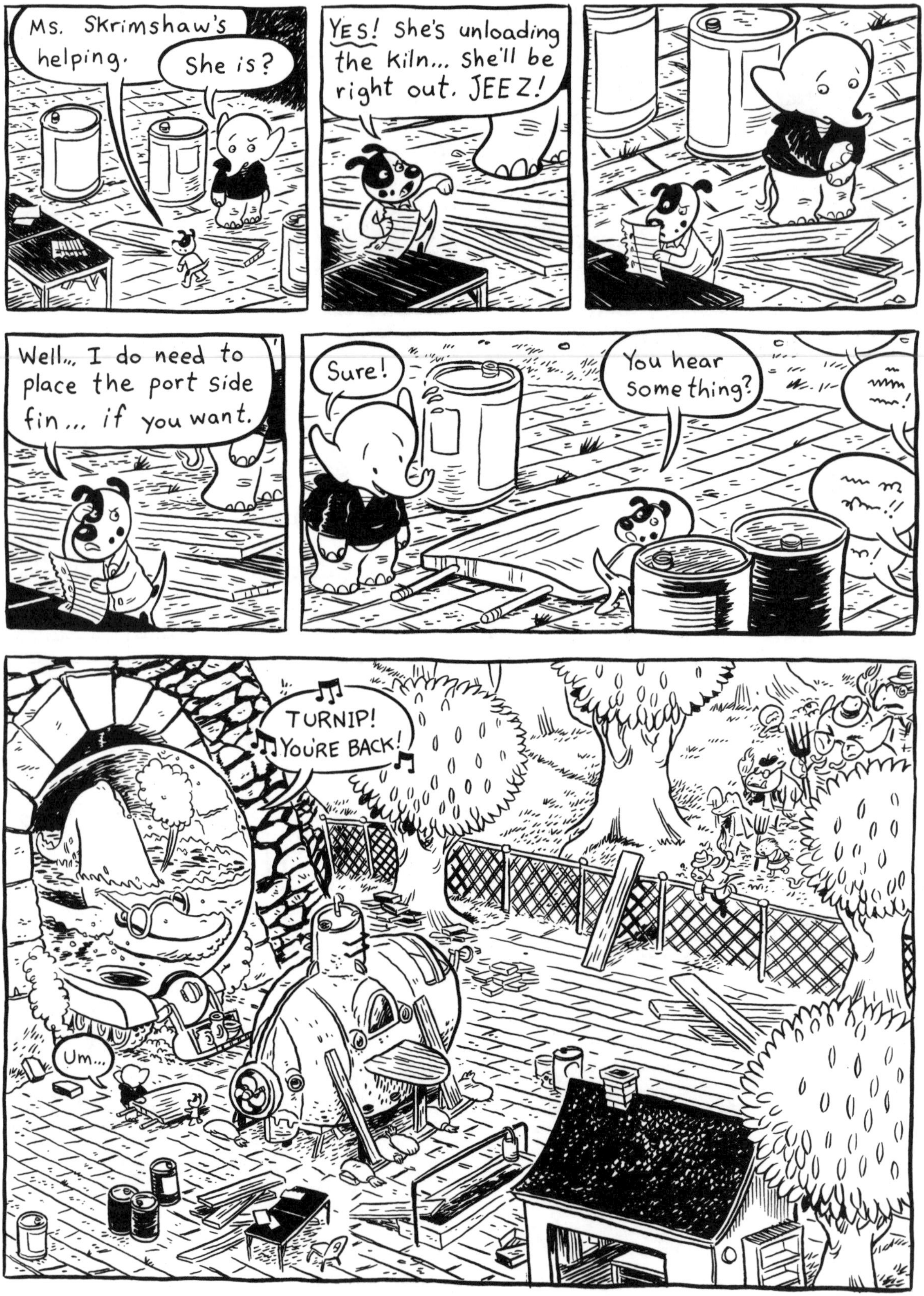

Ms. Skrimshaw's helping.
She is?
YES! She's unloading the kiln... She'll be right out. JEEZ!
Well... I do need to place the port side fin... if you want.
Sure!
You hear something?
TURNIP! YOU'RE BACK!
Um...

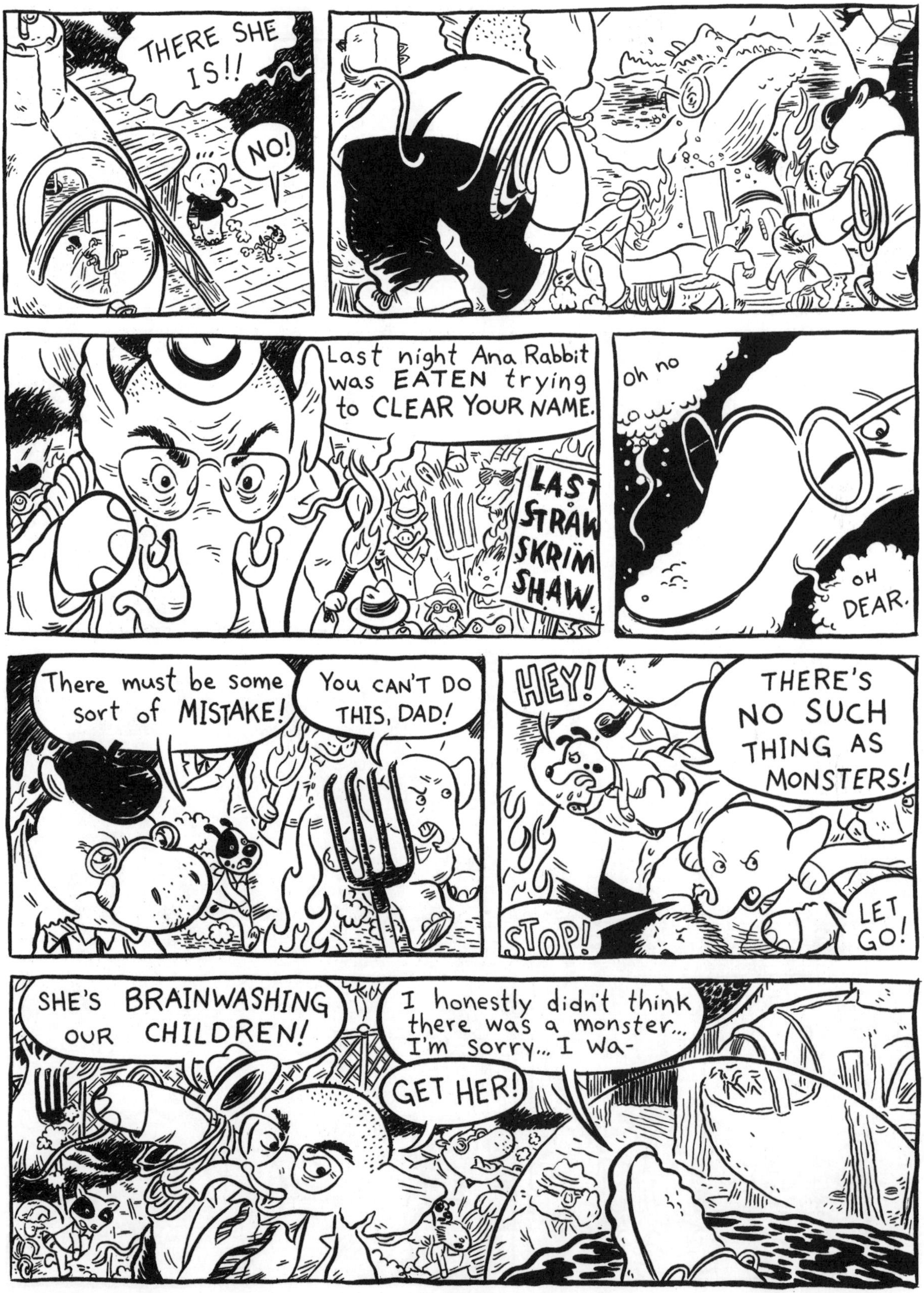
THERE SHE IS!!
NO!
Last night Ana Rabbit was EATEN trying to CLEAR YOUR NAME.
LAST STRAW SKRIMSHAW
oh no
OH DEAR.
There must be some sort of MISTAKE!
You CAN'T DO THIS, DAD!
HEY!
THERE'S NO SUCH THING AS MONSTERS!
STOP!
LET GO!
SHE'S BRAINWASHING OUR CHILDREN!
I honestly didn't think there was a monster... I'm sorry... I Wa-
GET HER!

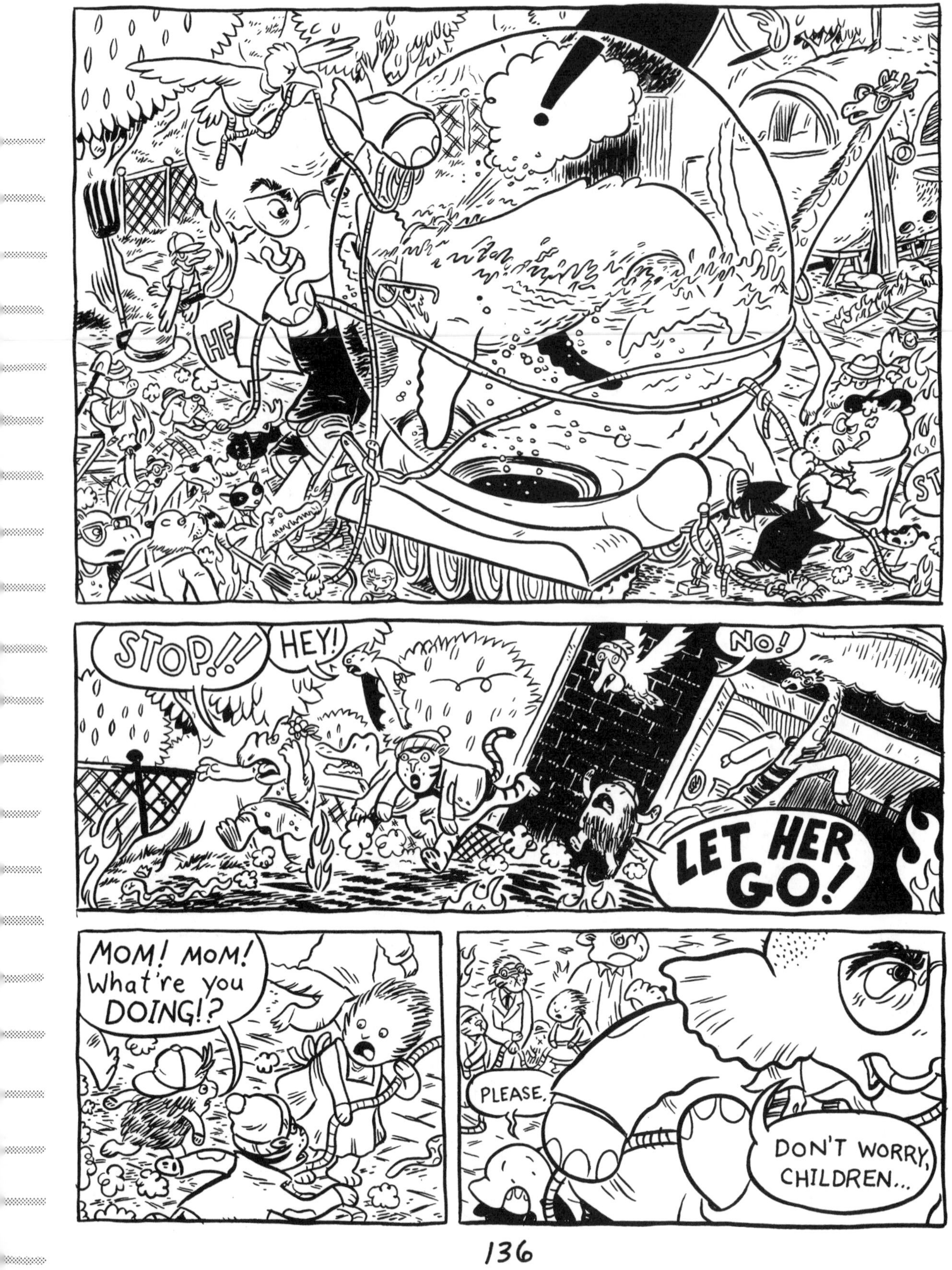
!
STOP!!
HEY!
NO!
LET HER GO!
MOM! MOM! What're you DOING!?
PLEASE.
DON'T WORRY, CHILDREN...

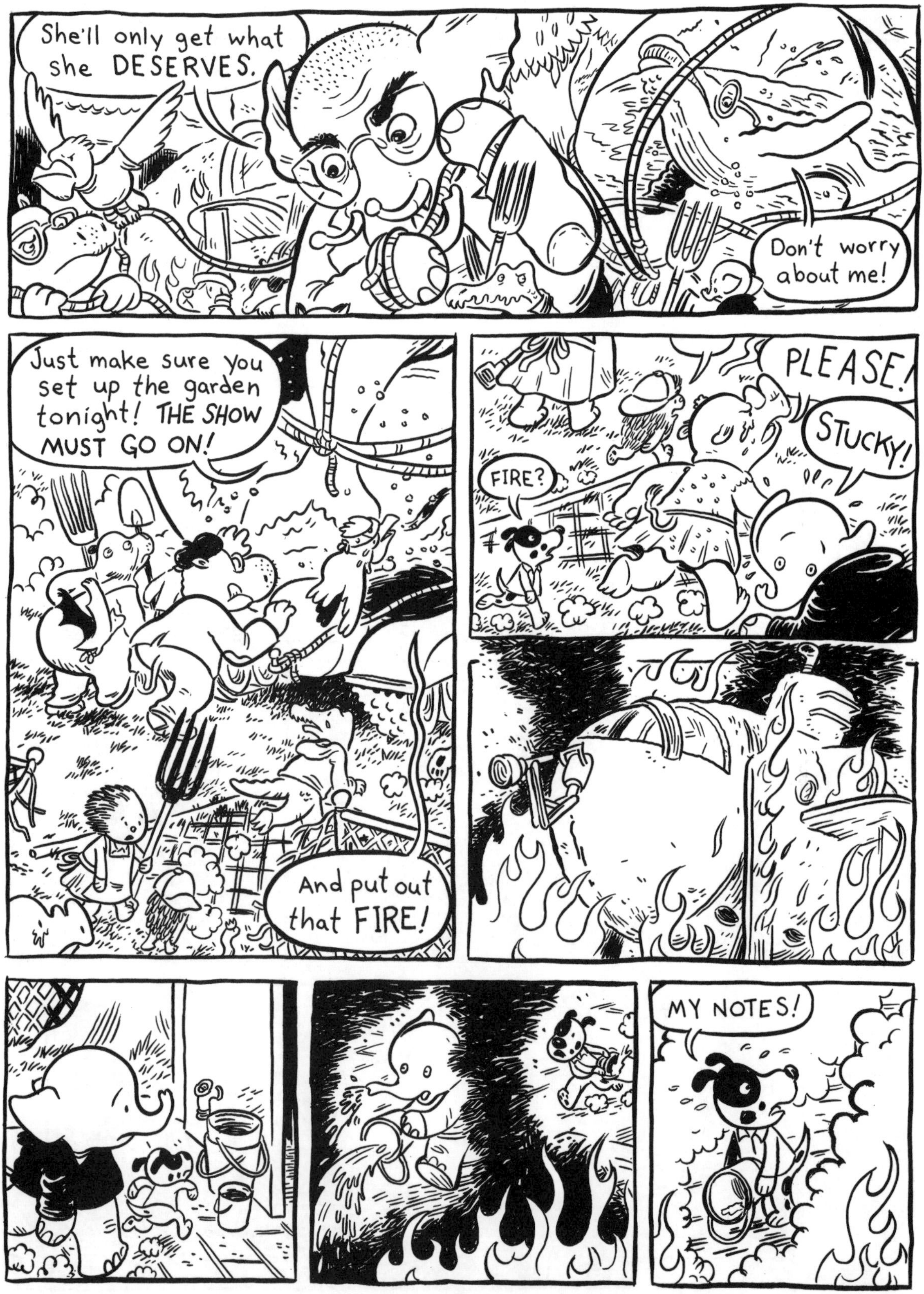
She'll only get what she DESERVES.
Don't worry about me!
Just make sure you set up the garden tonight! THE SHOW MUST GO ON!
And put out that FIRE!
PLEASE!
STUCKY!
FIRE?
MY NOTES!

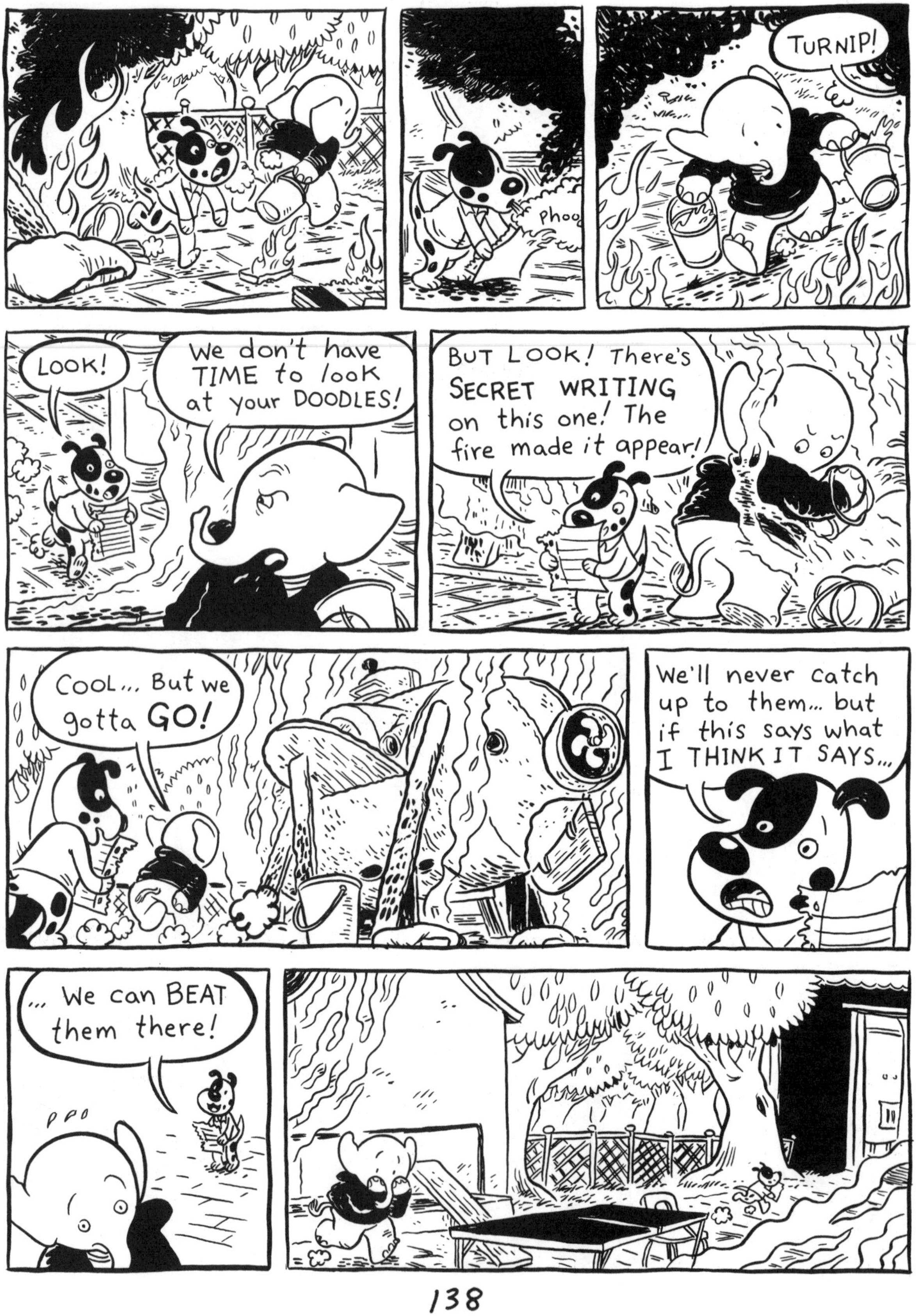
phoo
TURNIP!
LOOK!
We don't have TIME to look at your DOODLES!
BUT LOOK! There's SECRET WRITING on this one! The fire made it appear!
COOL... But we gotta GO!
We'll never catch up to them... but if this says what I THINK IT SAYS...
... We can BEAT them there!

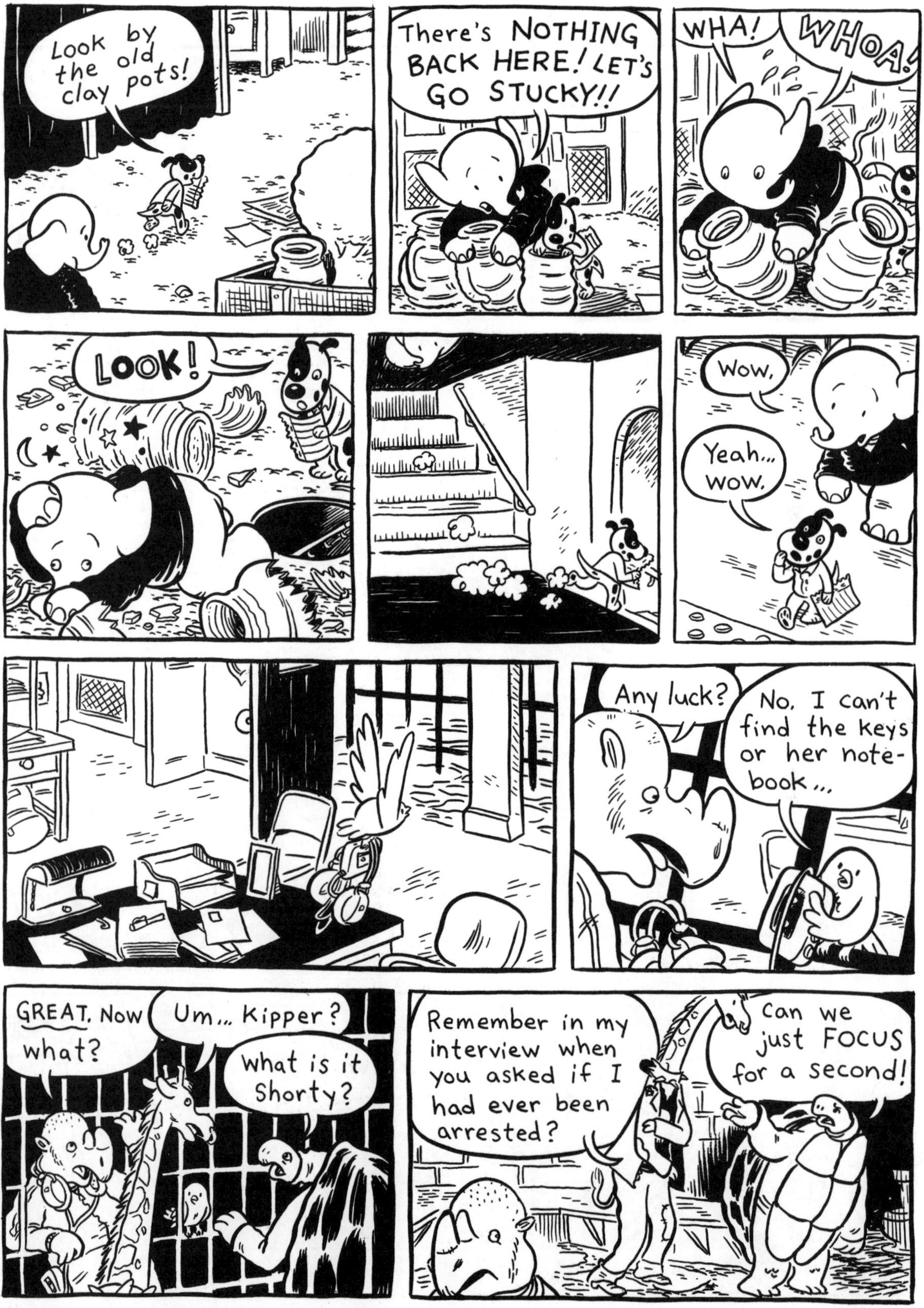
Look by the old clay pots!
There's NOTHING BACK HERE! LET'S GO STUCKY!!
WHA!
WHOA!
LOOK!
Wow.
Yeah... wow.
Any luck?
No. I can't find the keys or her note-book...
GREAT. Now what?
Um... Kipper?
What is it Shorty?
Remember in my interview when you asked if I had ever been arrested?
Can we just FOCUS for a second!

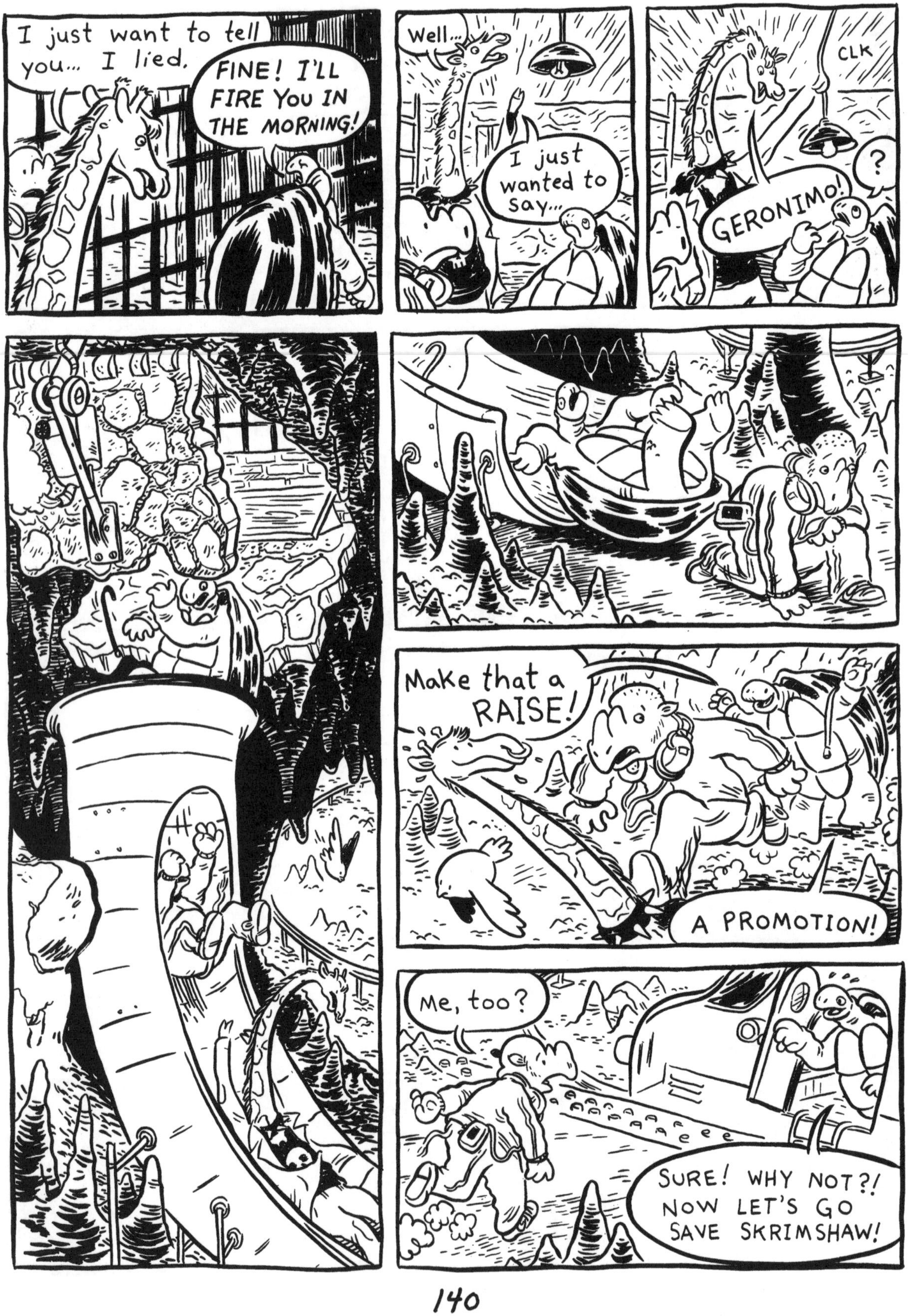
I just want to tell you... I lied.
FINE! I'LL FIRE YOU IN THE MORNING!
Well...
I just wanted to say...
CLK
?
GERONIMO!
Make that a RAISE!
A PROMOTION!
Me, too?
SURE! WHY NOT?! NOW LET'S GO SAVE SKRIMSHAW!

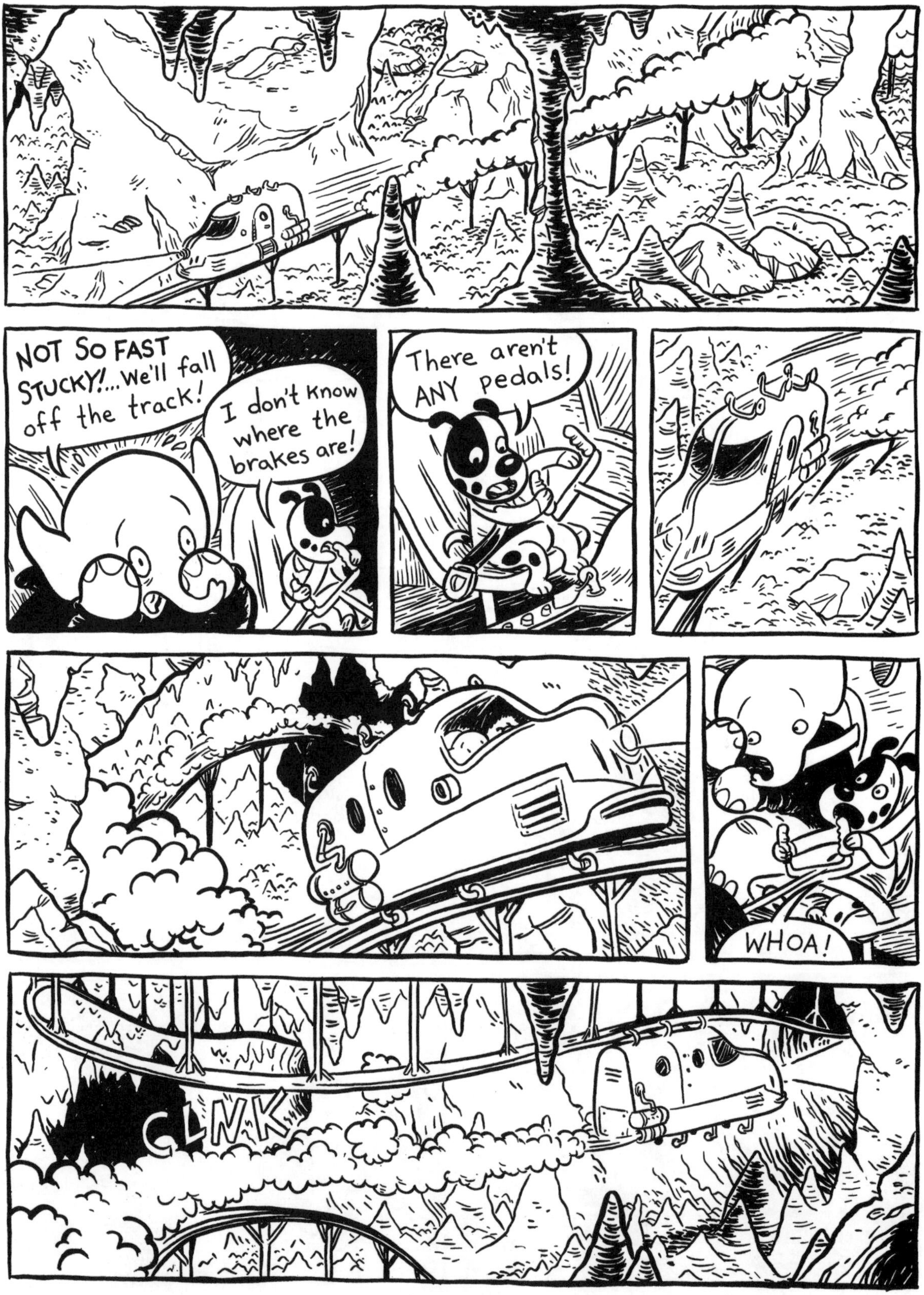
NOT SO FAST STUCKY!... We'll fall off the track!
I don't know where the brakes are!
There aren't ANY pedals!
WHOA!
CLNK

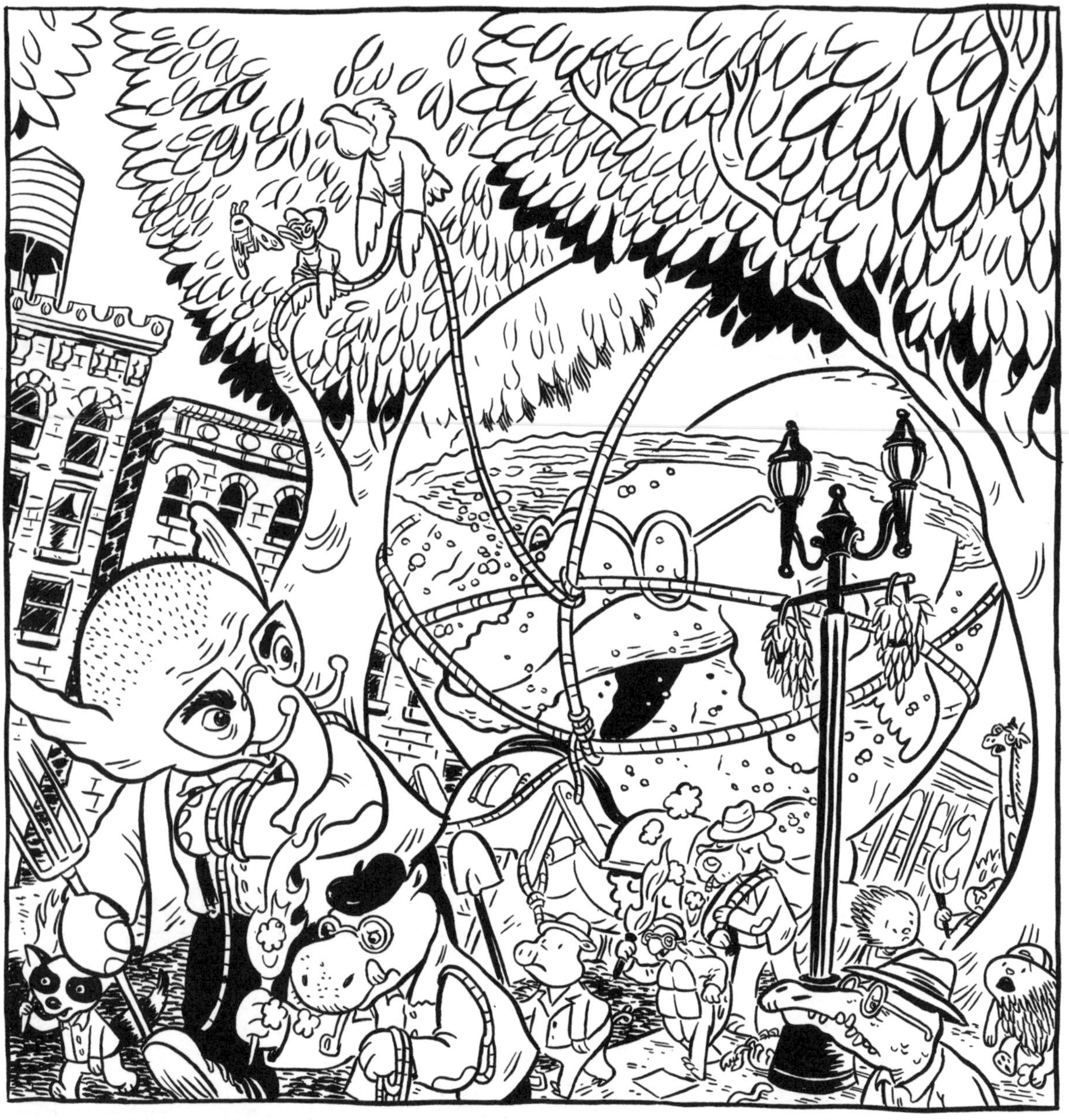

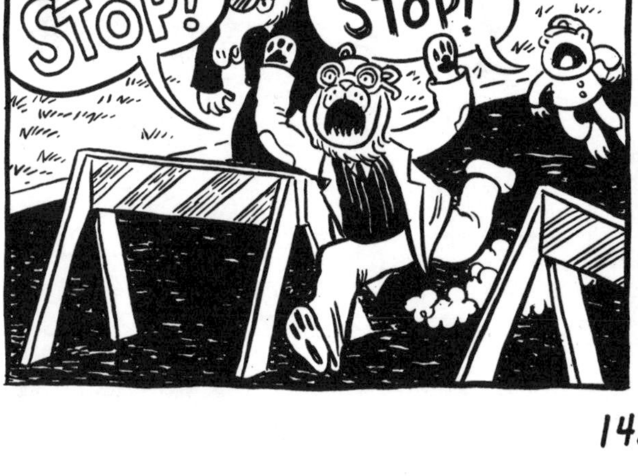
STOP!
STOP!

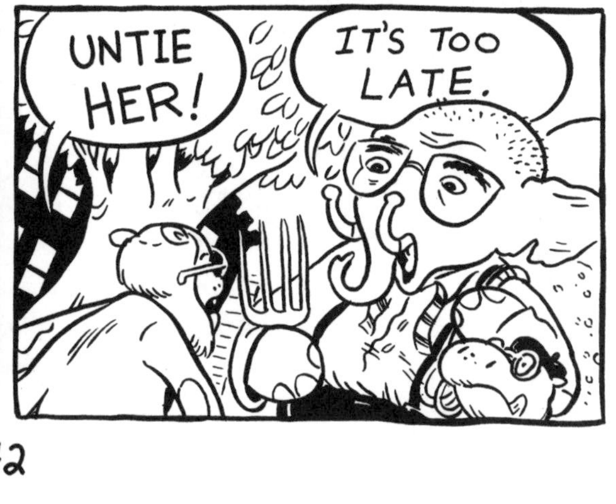
UNTIE HER!
IT'S TOO LATE.

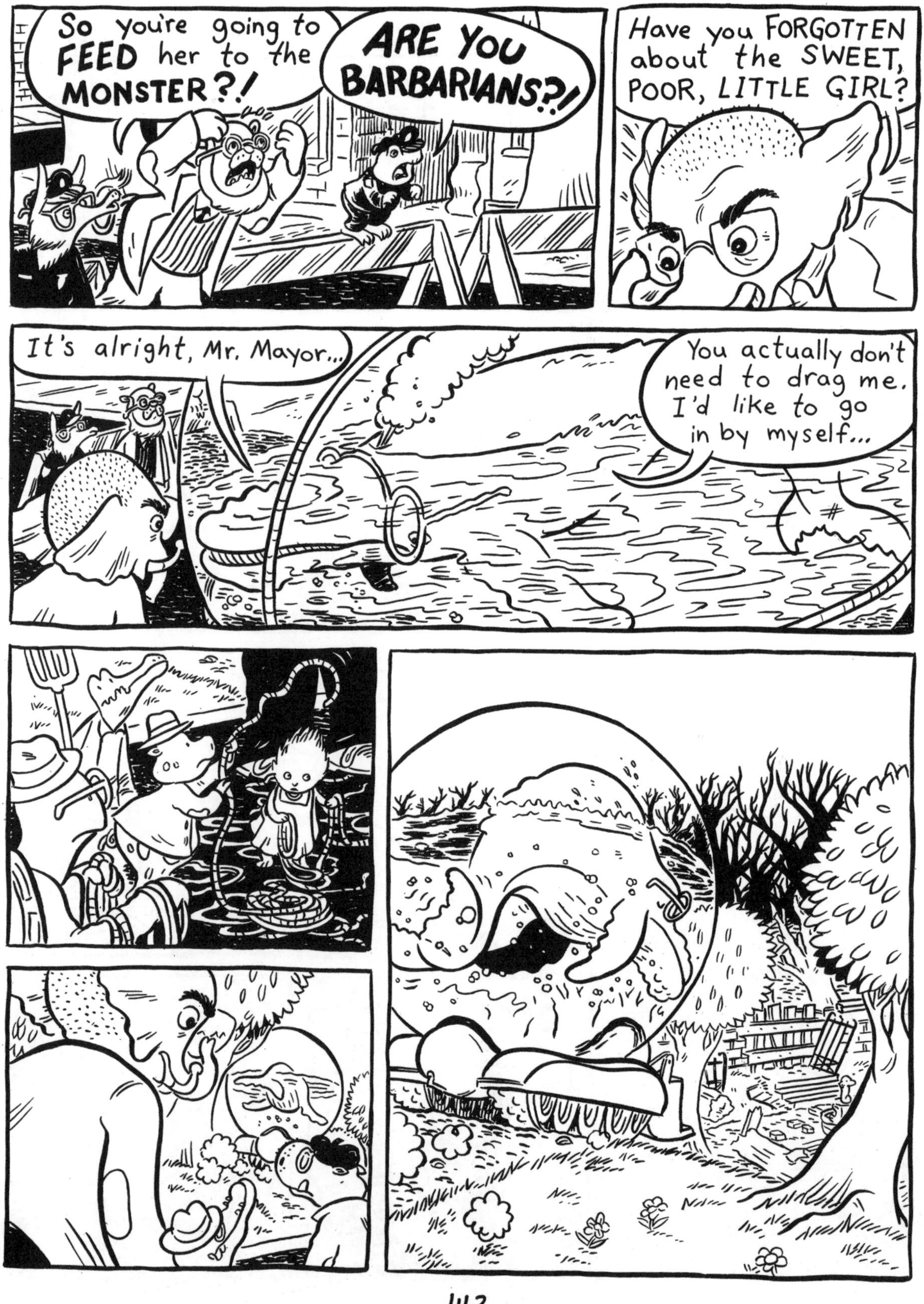
So you're going to FEED her to the MONSTER?!
ARE YOU BARBARIANS?!
Have you FORGOTTEN about the SWEET, POOR, LITTLE GIRL?
It's alright, Mr. Mayor...
You actually don't need to drag me. I'd like to go in by myself...

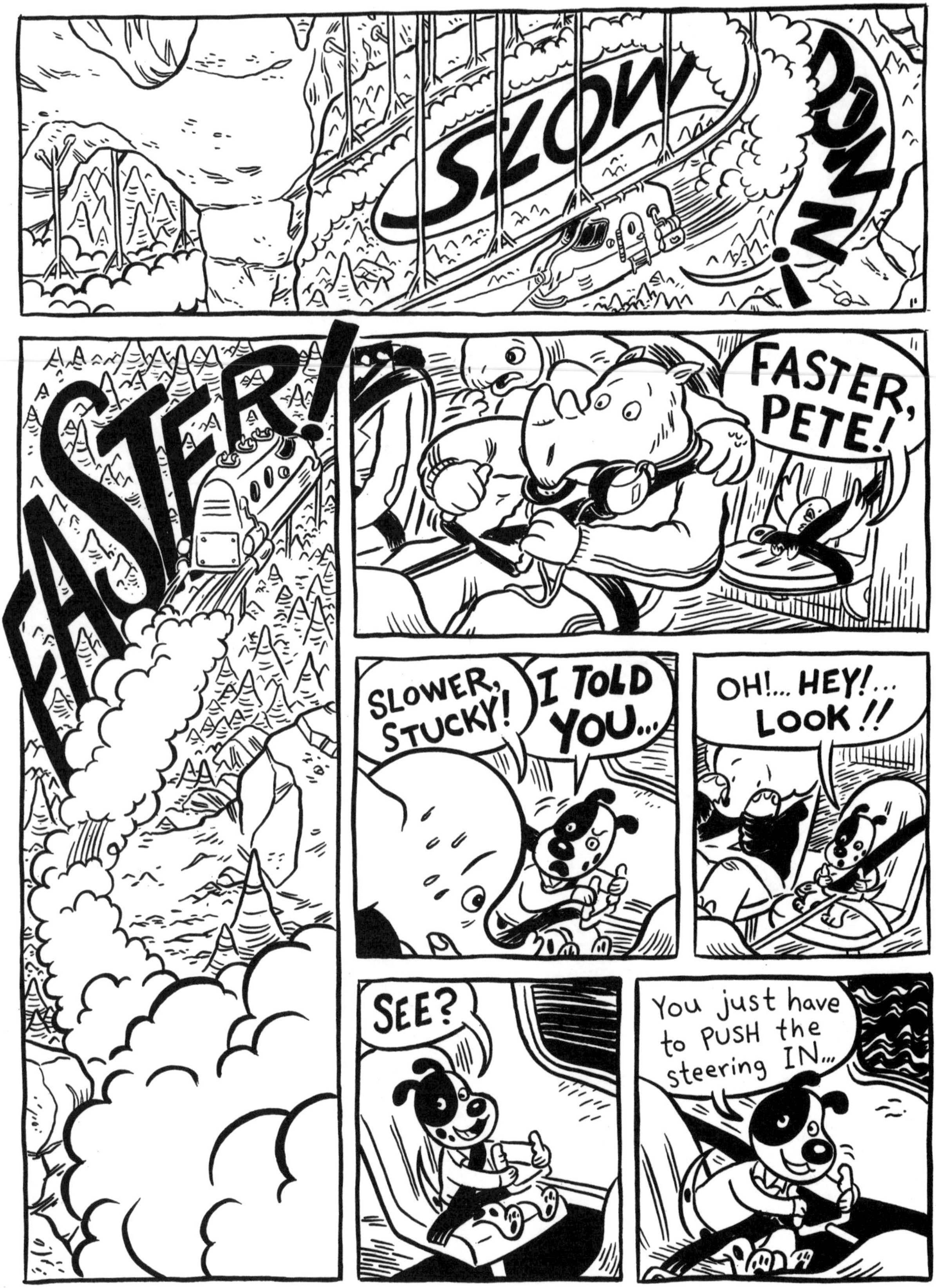
SLOW DOWN!
FASTER!
FASTER, PETE!
SLOWER, STUCKY!
I TOLD YOU...
OH!... HEY!... LOOK!!
SEE?
You just have to PUSH the steering IN...

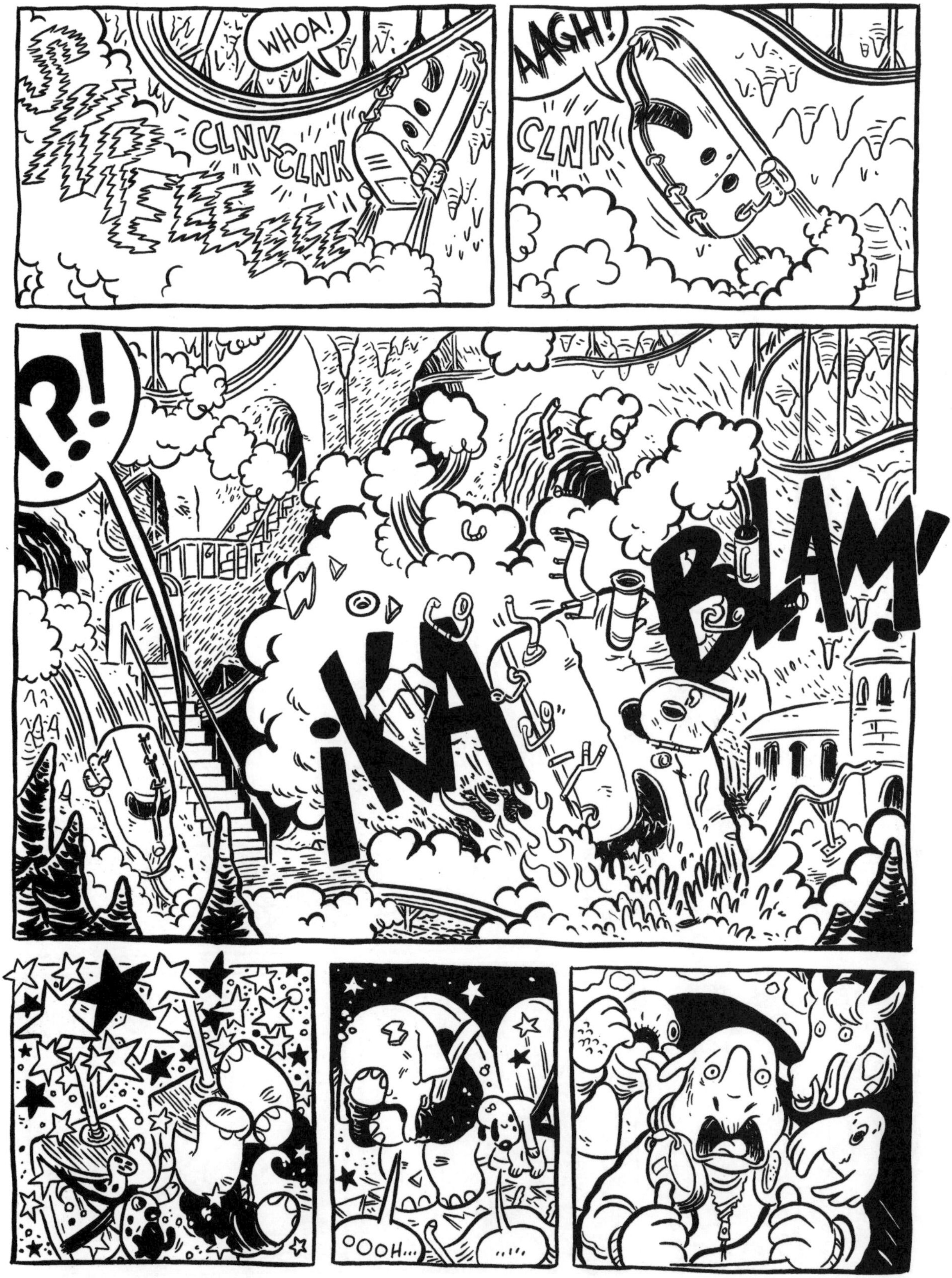
WHOA!
CLNK
CLNK
AAGH!
CLNK
!?!
KA
BLAM!
OOOH...

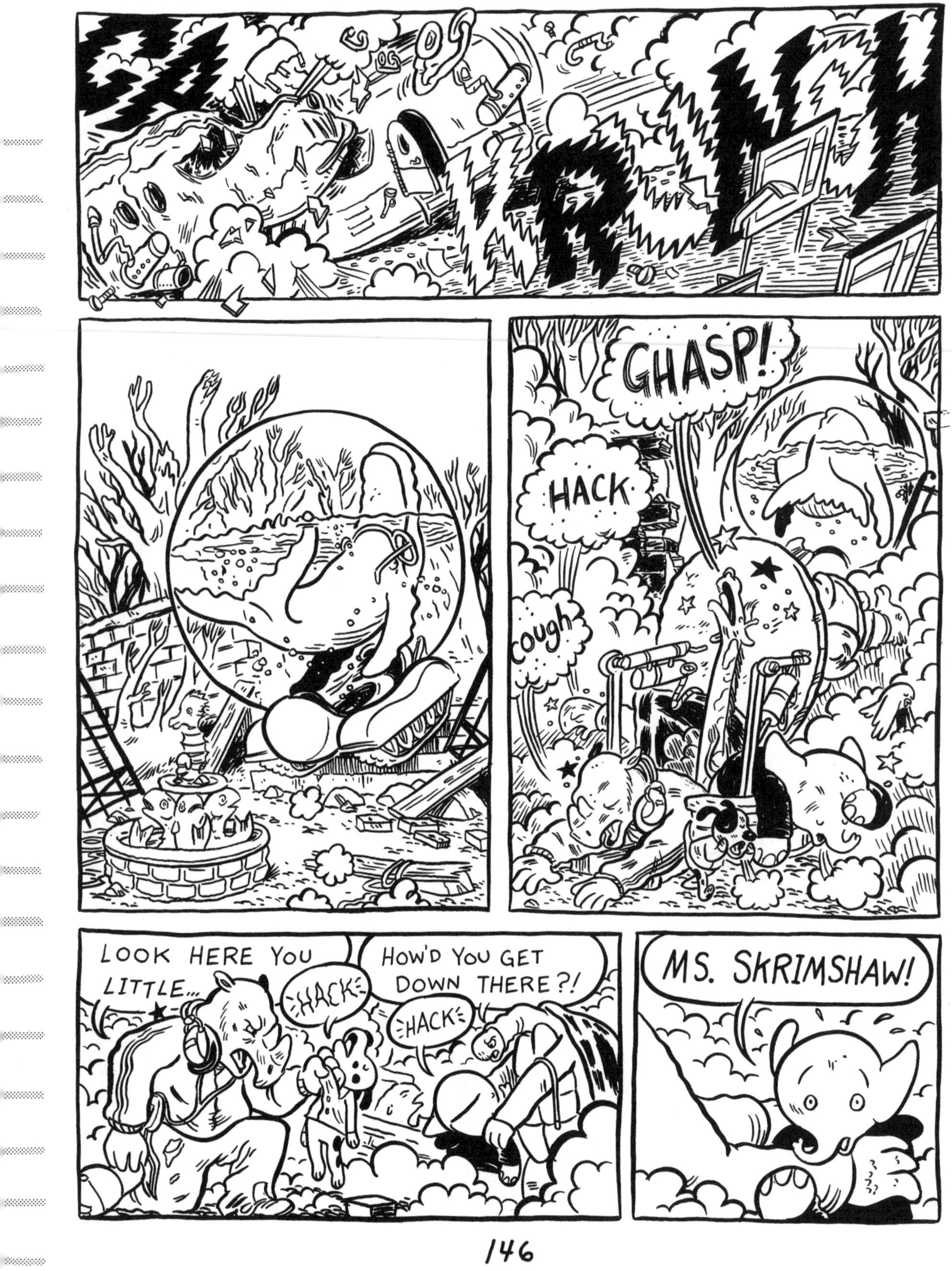
GHASP!
HACK
cough
LOOK HERE YOU LITTLE...
HACK
HOW'D YOU GET DOWN THERE?!
HACK
MS. SKRIMSHAW!

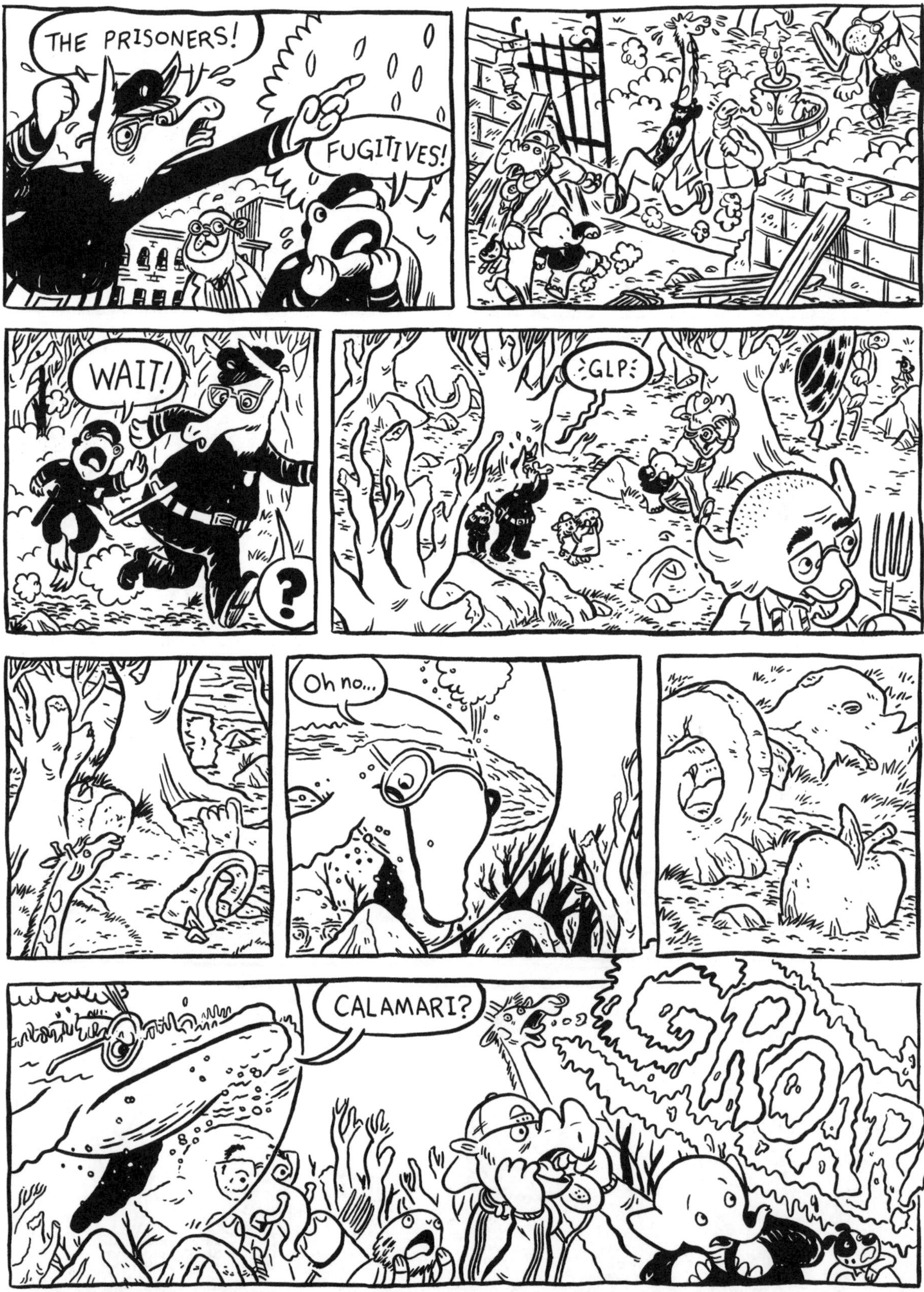
THE PRISONERS!
FUGITIVES!
WAIT!
?
GLP
Oh no...
CALAMARI?
GROAR!

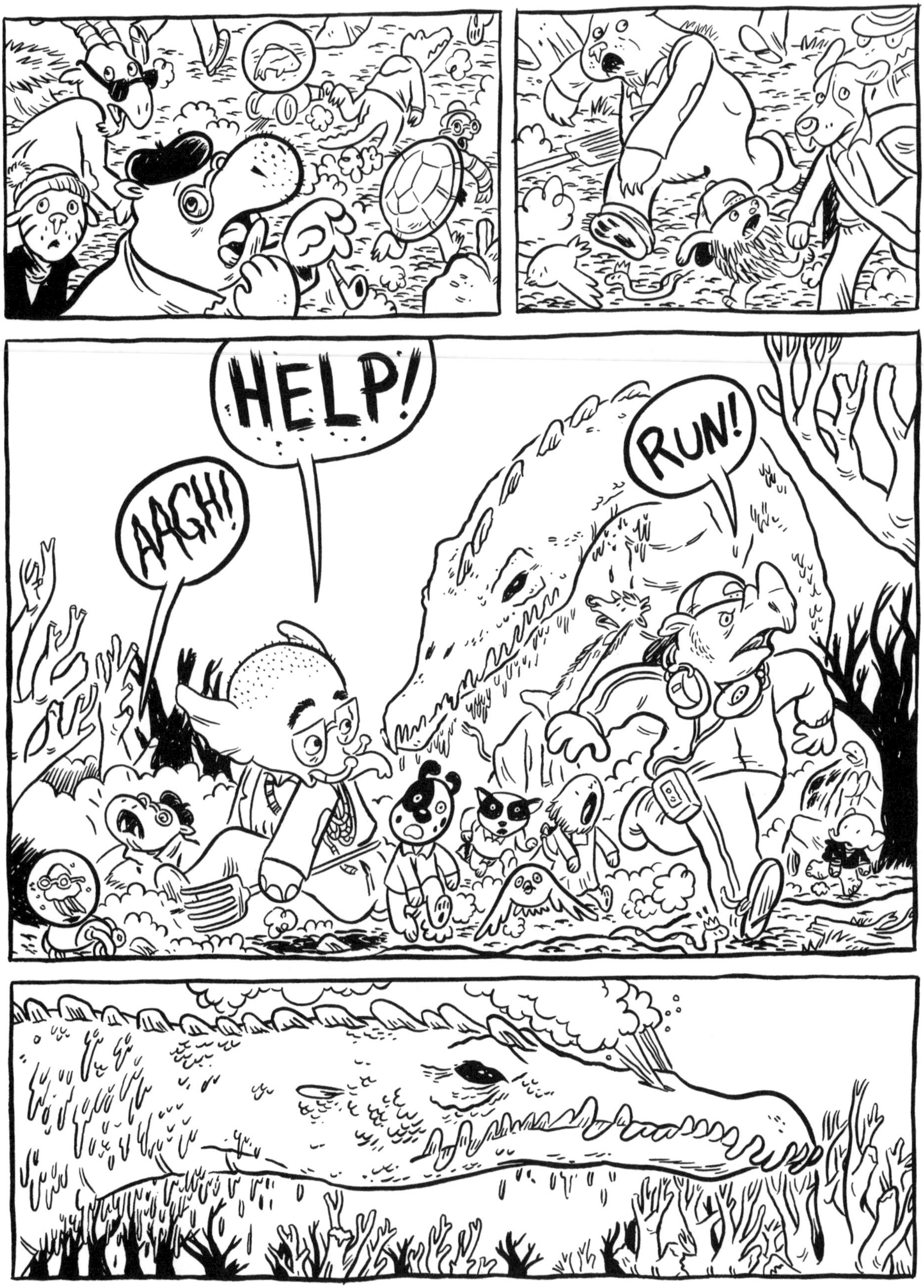
AAGH!
HELP!
RUN!

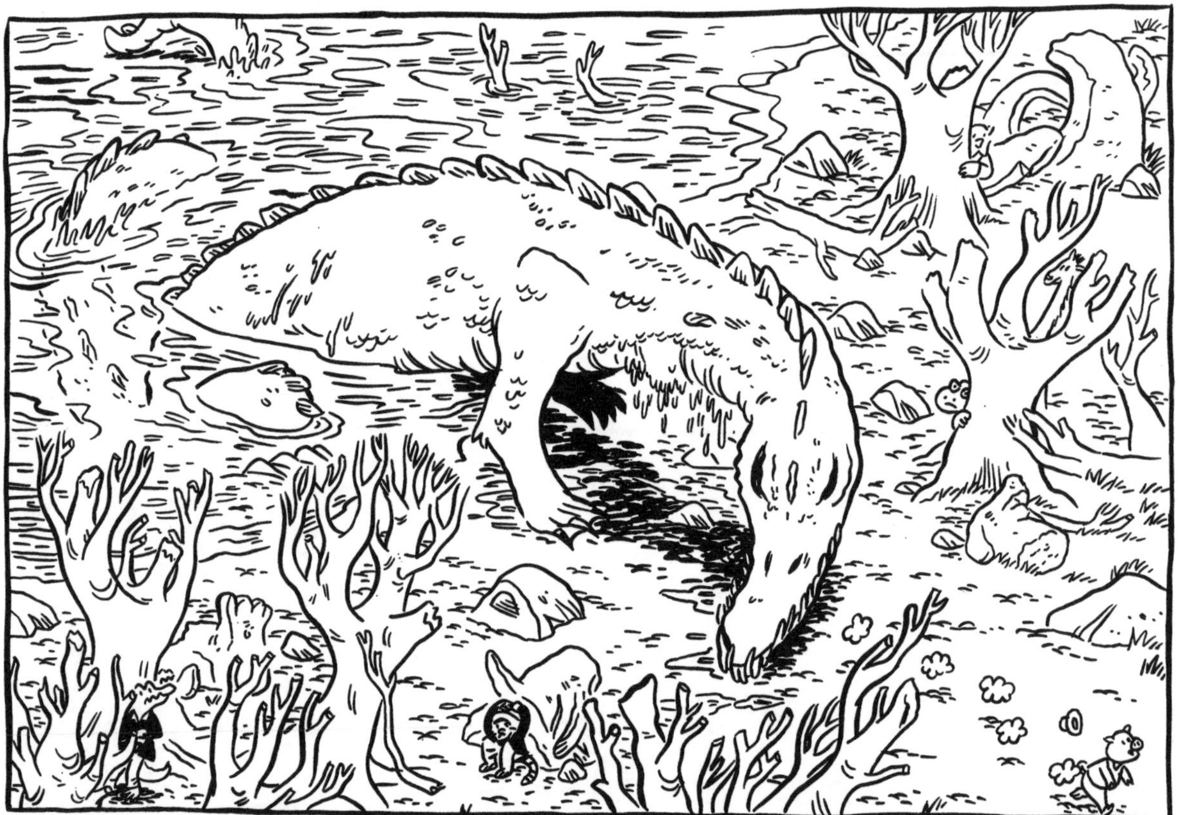

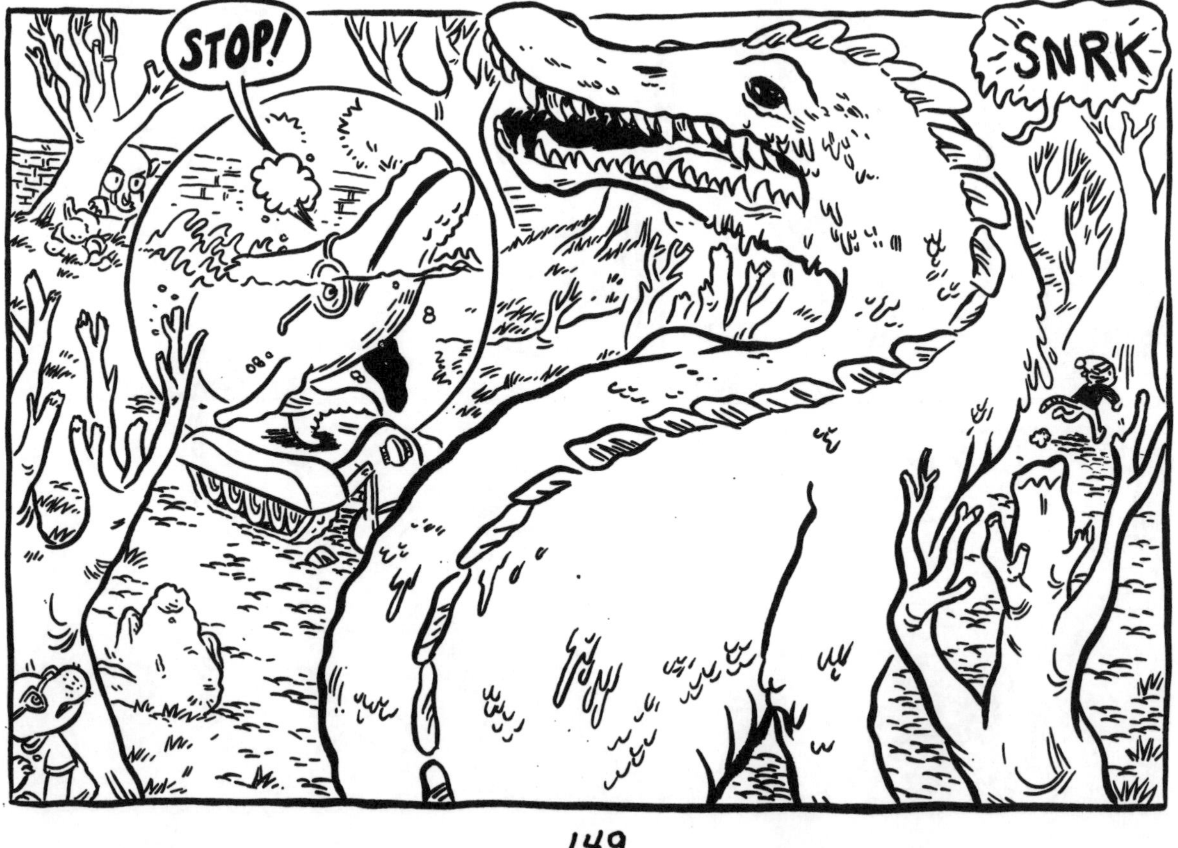
STOP!
SNRK

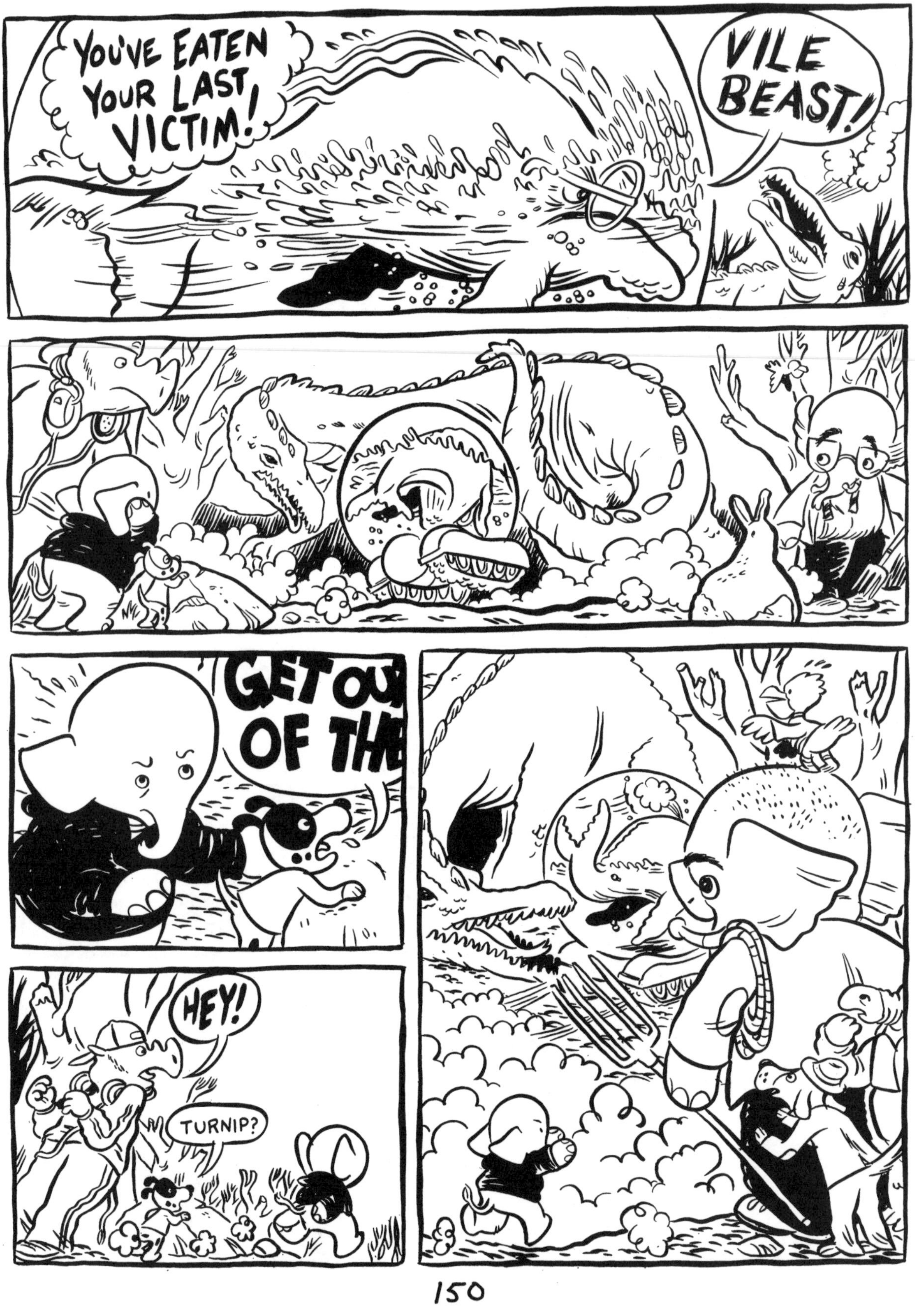
YOU'VE EATEN YOUR LAST VICTIM!
VILE BEAST!
GET OU OF TH
HEY!
TURNIP?

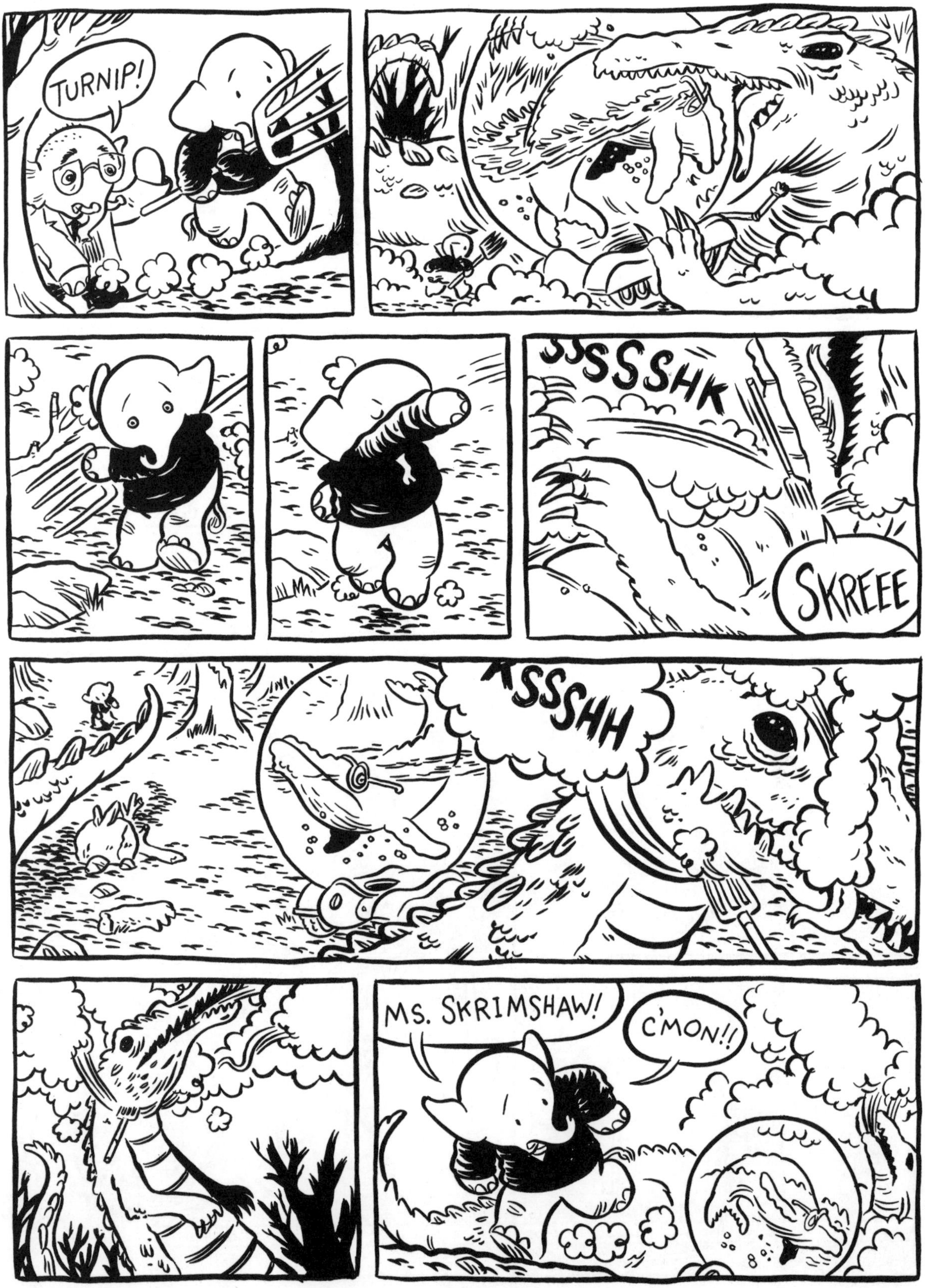
TURNIP!
SSSSSHK
SKREEE
ASSSHH
MS. SKRIMSHAW!
C'MON!!

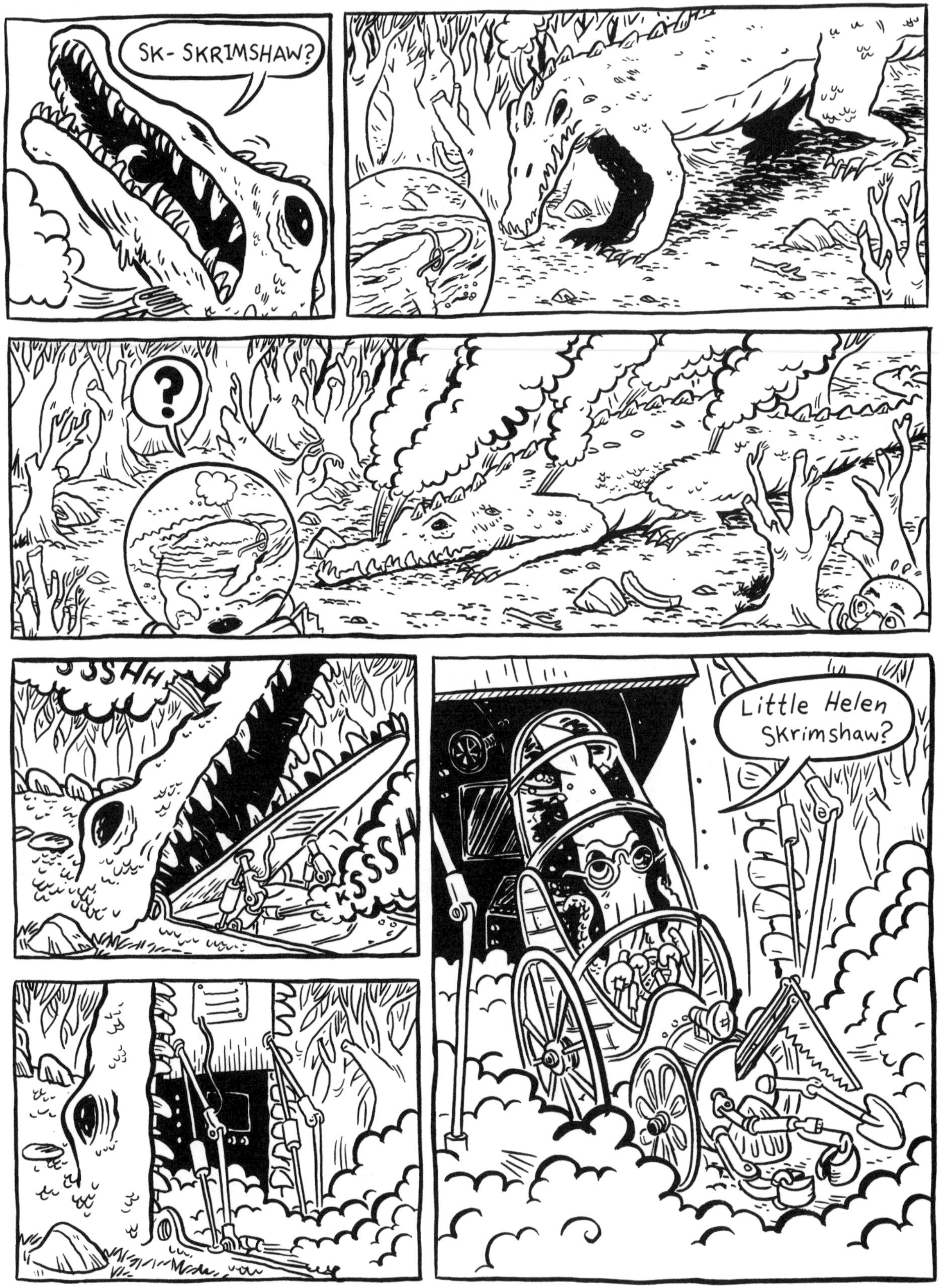
SK- SKRIMSHAW?
?
SSHH
KSSSH
Little Helen Skrimshaw?

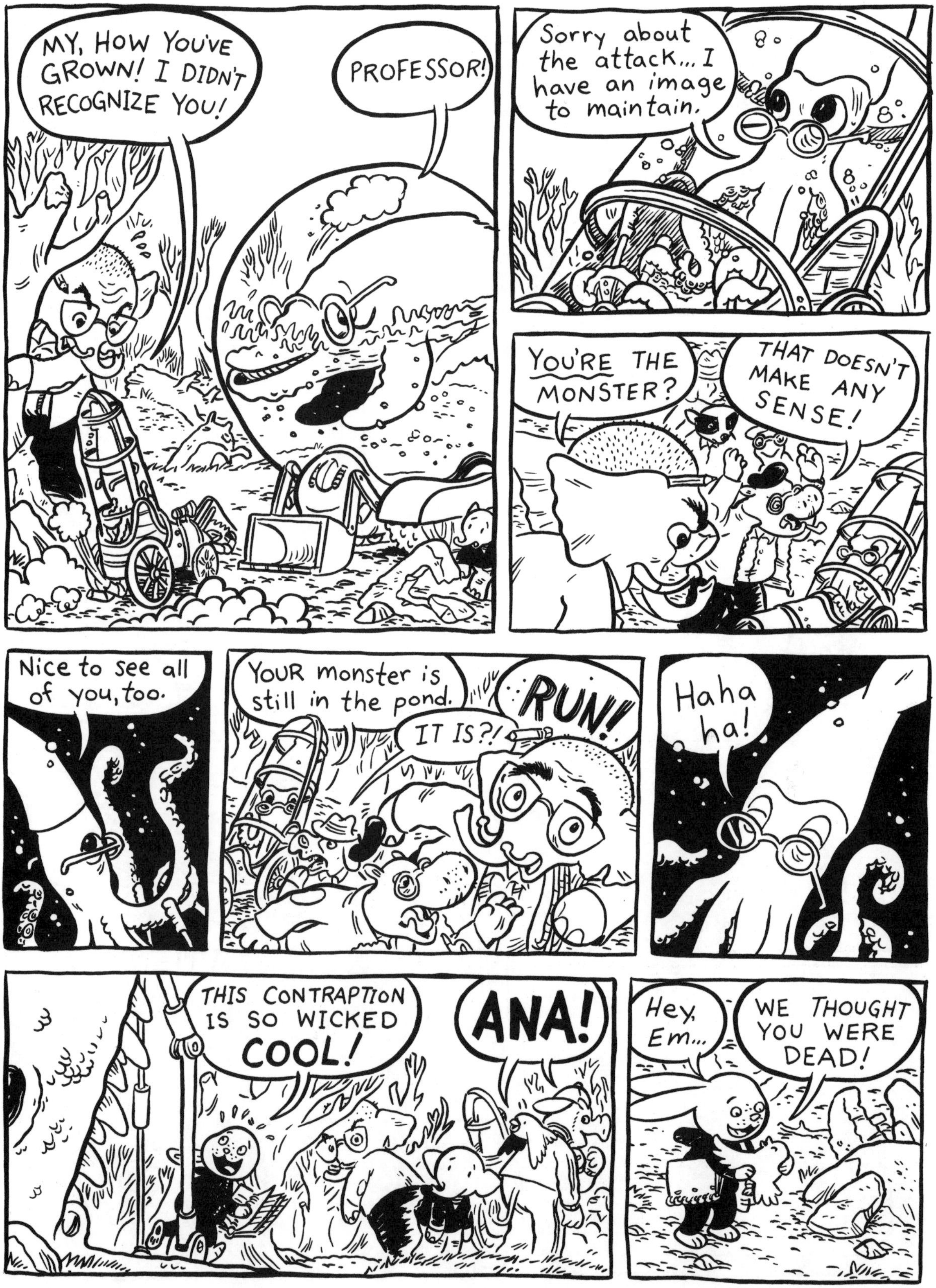

MY, HOW YOU'VE GROWN! I DIDN'T RECOGNIZE YOU!
PROFESSOR!
Sorry about the attack... I have an image to maintain.
YOU'RE THE MONSTER?
THAT DOESN'T MAKE ANY SENSE!
Nice to see all of you, too.
YOUR monster is still in the pond.
IT IS?!
RUN!
Haha ha!
THIS CONTRAPTION IS SO WICKED COOL!
ANA!
Hey, Em...
WE THOUGHT YOU WERE DEAD!

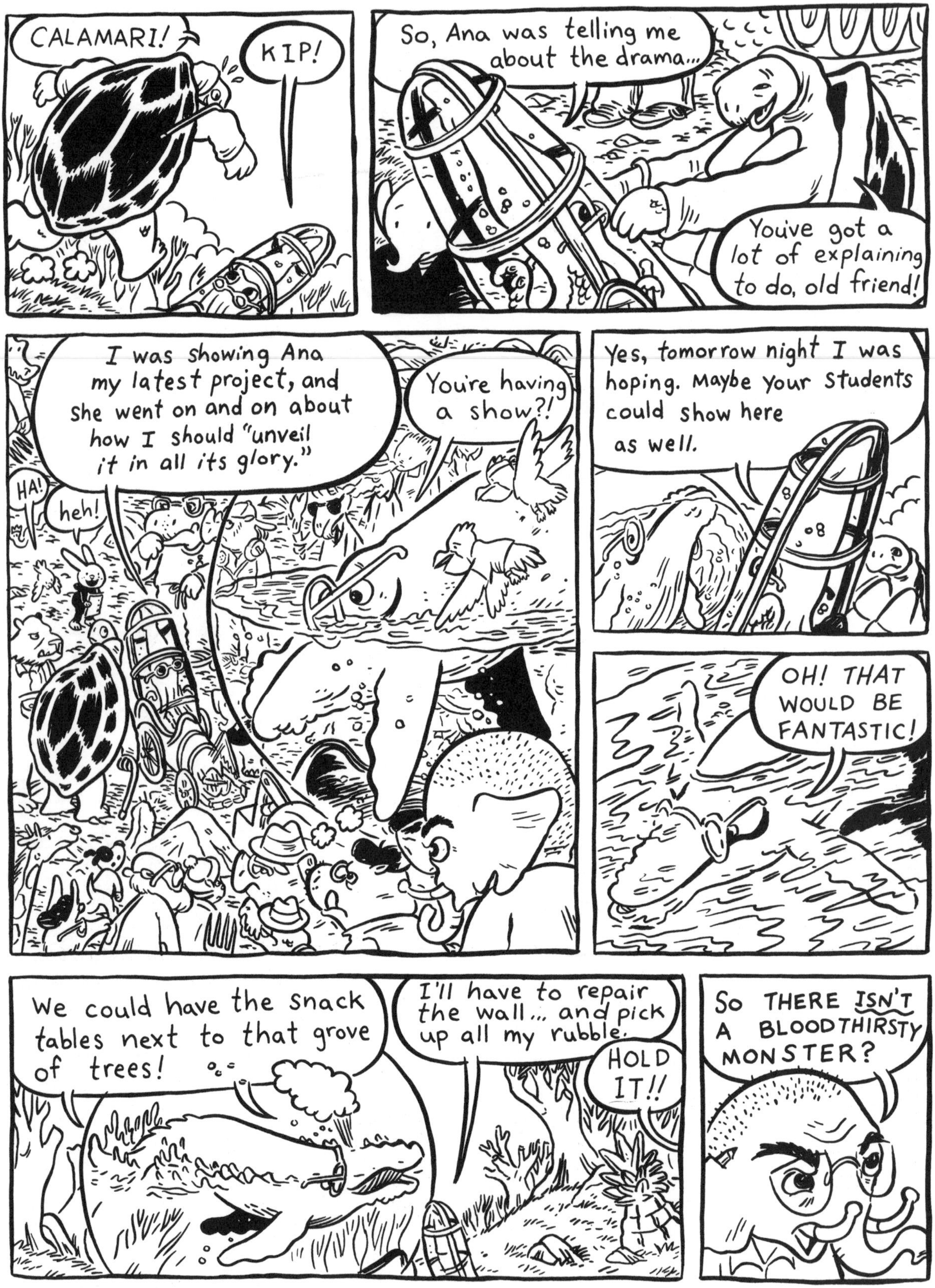
CALAMARI!
KIP!
So, Ana was telling me about the drama...
You've got a lot of explaining to do, old friend!
I was showing Ana my latest project, and she went on and on about how I should "unveil it in all its glory."
HA!
heh!
You're having a show?!
Yes, tomorrow night I was hoping. Maybe your students could show here as well.
OH! THAT WOULD BE FANTASTIC!
We could have the snack tables next to that grove of trees!
I'll have to repair the wall... and pick up all my rubble.
HOLD IT!!
So THERE ISN'T A BLOODTHIRSTY MONSTER?

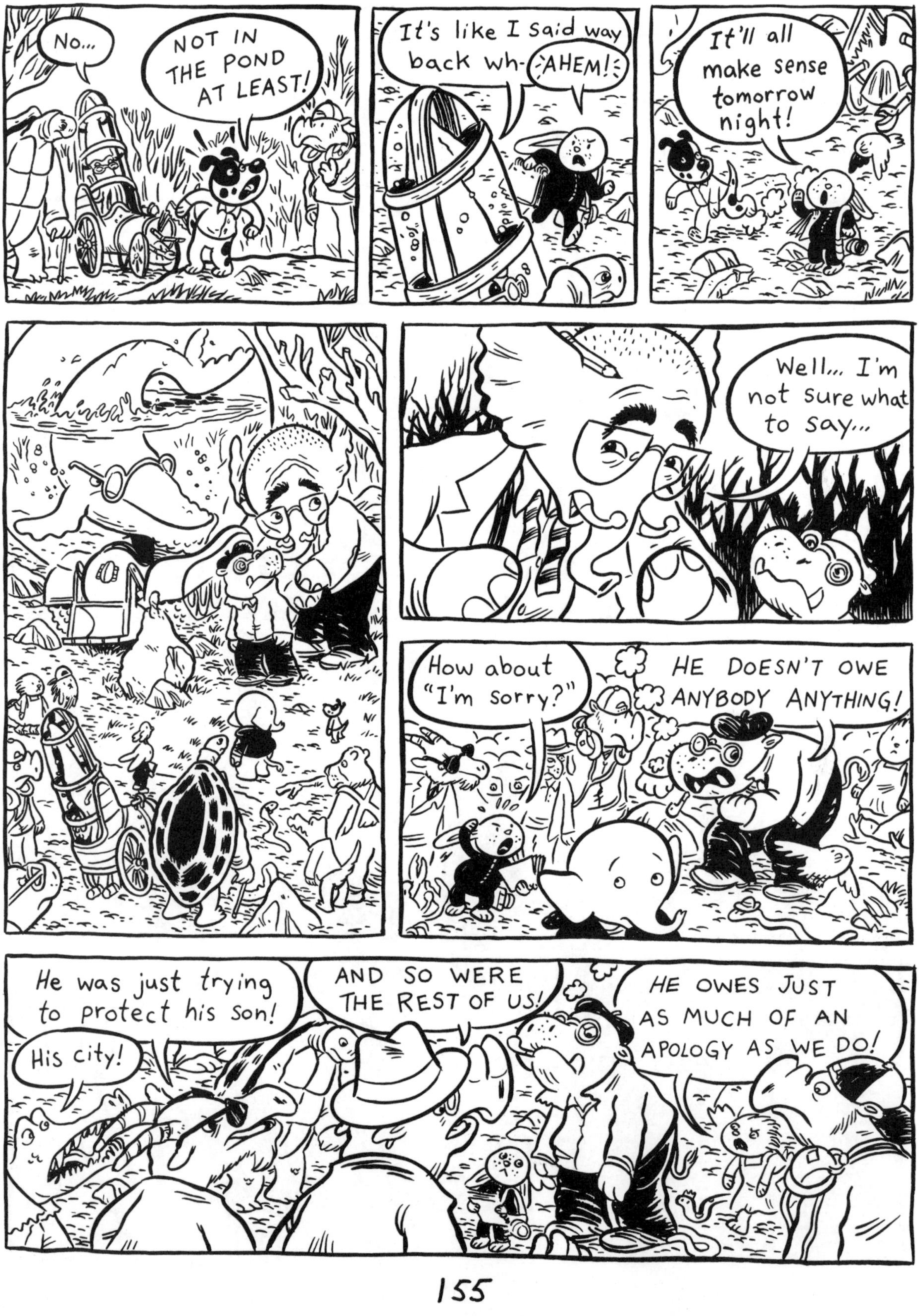
No...
NOT IN THE POND AT LEAST!
It's like I said way back wh-
AHEM!
It'll all make sense tomorrow night!
Well... I'm not sure what to say...
How about "I'm sorry?"
HE DOESN'T OWE ANYBODY ANYTHING!
He was just trying to protect his son!
His city!
AND SO WERE THE REST OF US!
HE OWES JUST AS MUCH OF AN APOLOGY AS WE DO!

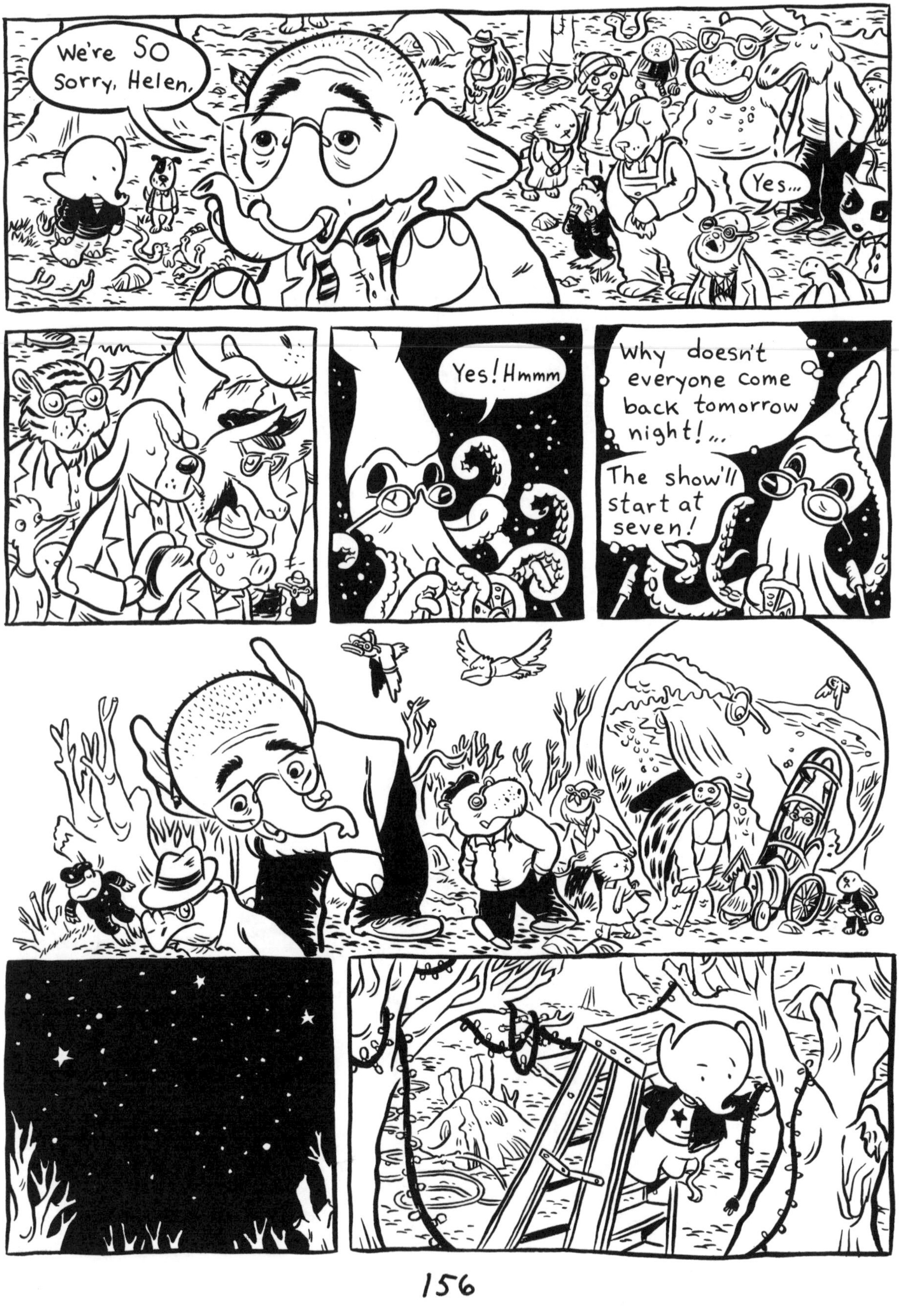

We're SO Sorry, Helen.
Yes...
Yes! Hmmm
Why doesn't everyone come back tomorrow night!...
The show'll start at seven!

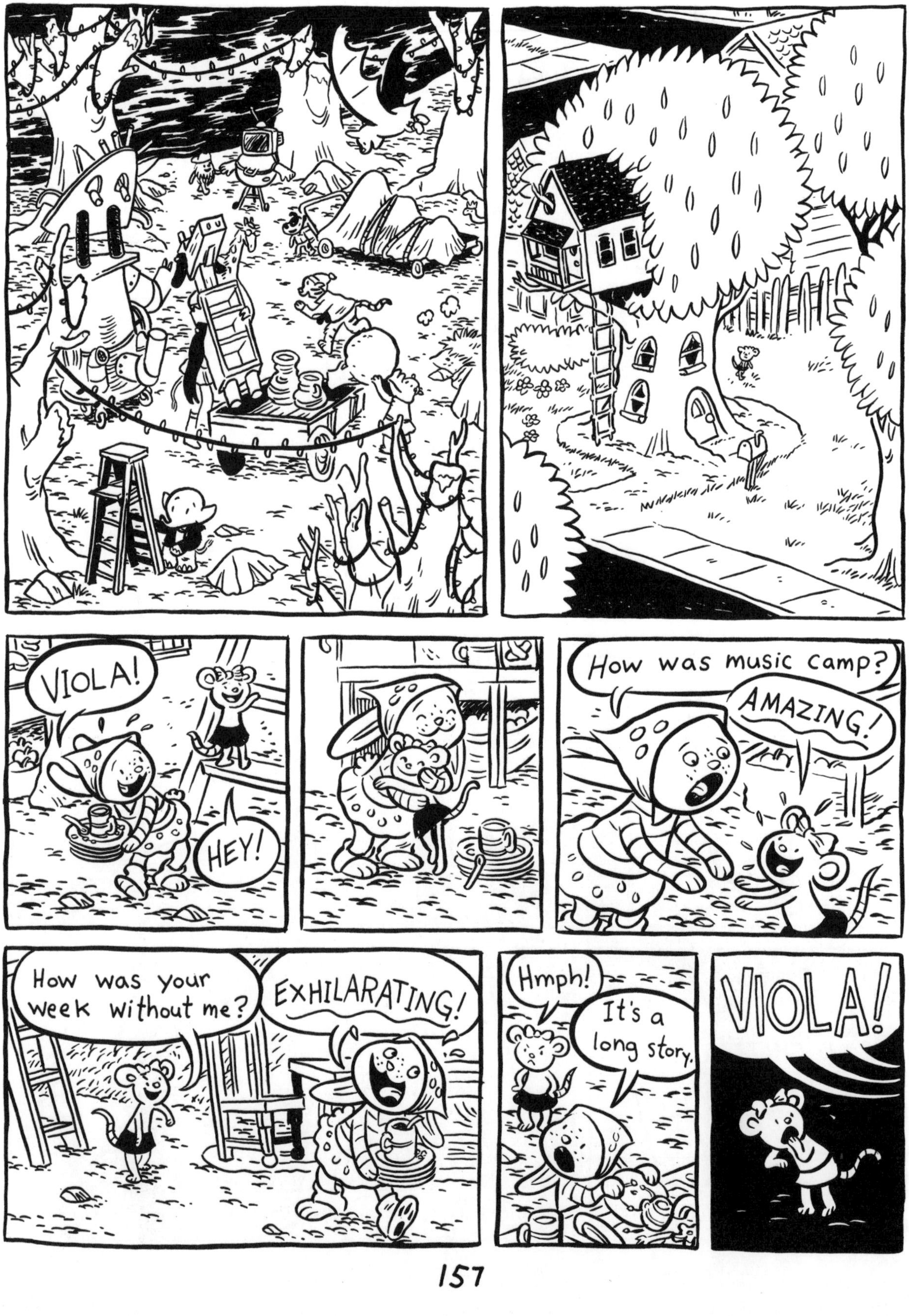
VIOLA!
HEY!
How was music camp?
AMAZING!
How was your week without me?
EXHILARATING!
Hmph!
It's a long story.
VIOLA!

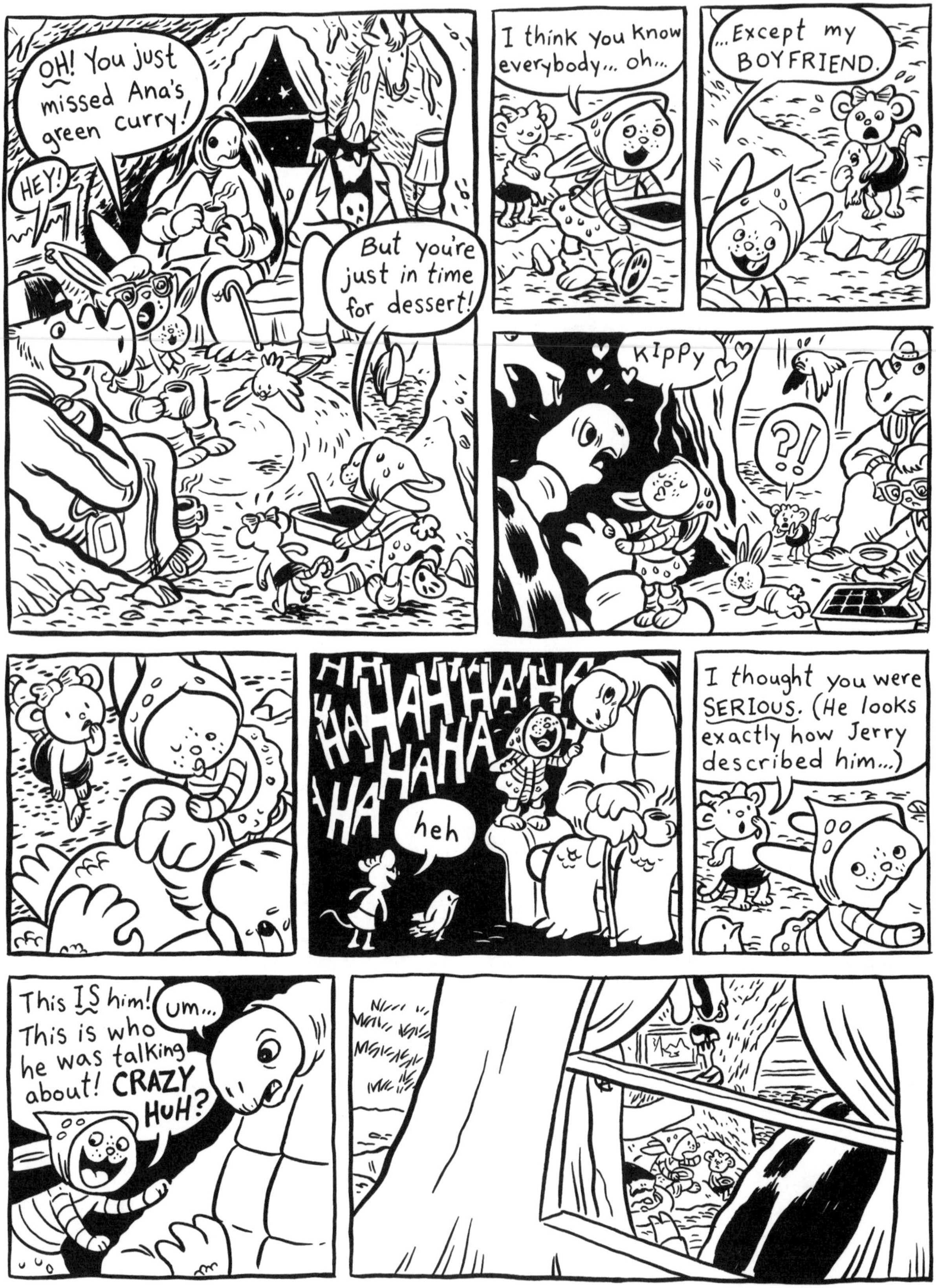
OH! You just missed Ana's green curry!
HEY!
But you're just in time for dessert!
I think you know everybody... oh...
...Except my BOYFRIEND.
KIPPY
?!
HAHAHAHAHAHAHAHAHAHAHAHA
heh
I thought you were SERIOUS. (He looks exactly how Jerry described him...)
This IS him! This is who he was talking about! CRAZY HUH?
um...

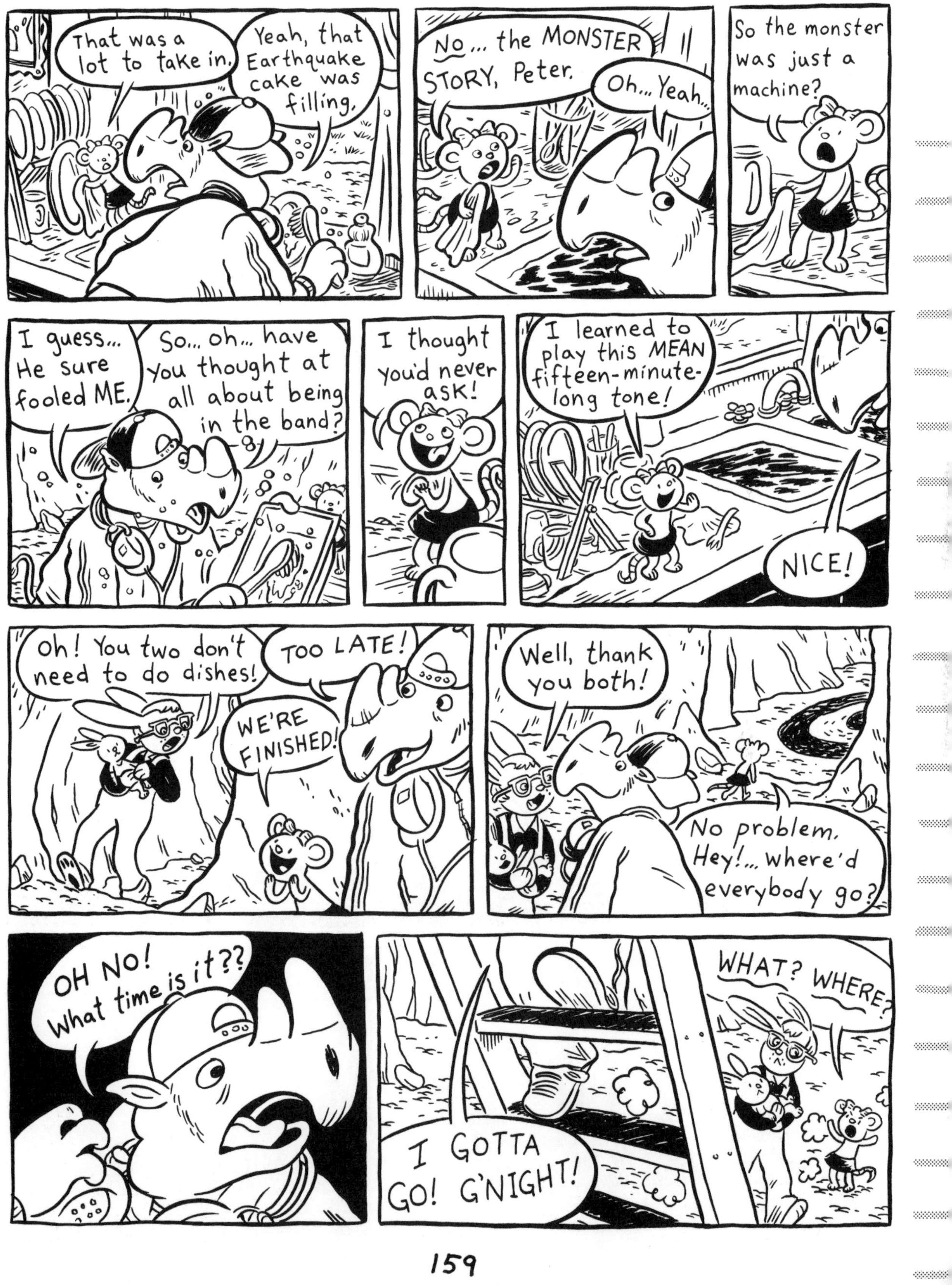
That was a lot to take in.
Yeah, that Earthquake cake was filling.
No... the MONSTER STORY, Peter.
Oh... Yeah...
So the monster was just a machine?
I guess... He sure fooled ME.
So... oh... have you thought at all about being in the band?
I thought you'd never ASK!
I learned to play this MEAN fifteen-minute-long tone!
NICE!
Oh! You two don't need to do dishes!
TOO LATE!
WE'RE FINISHED!
Well, thank you both!
No problem. Hey!... where'd everybody go?
OH NO! What time is it??
I GOTTA GO! G'NIGHT!
WHAT? WHERE?

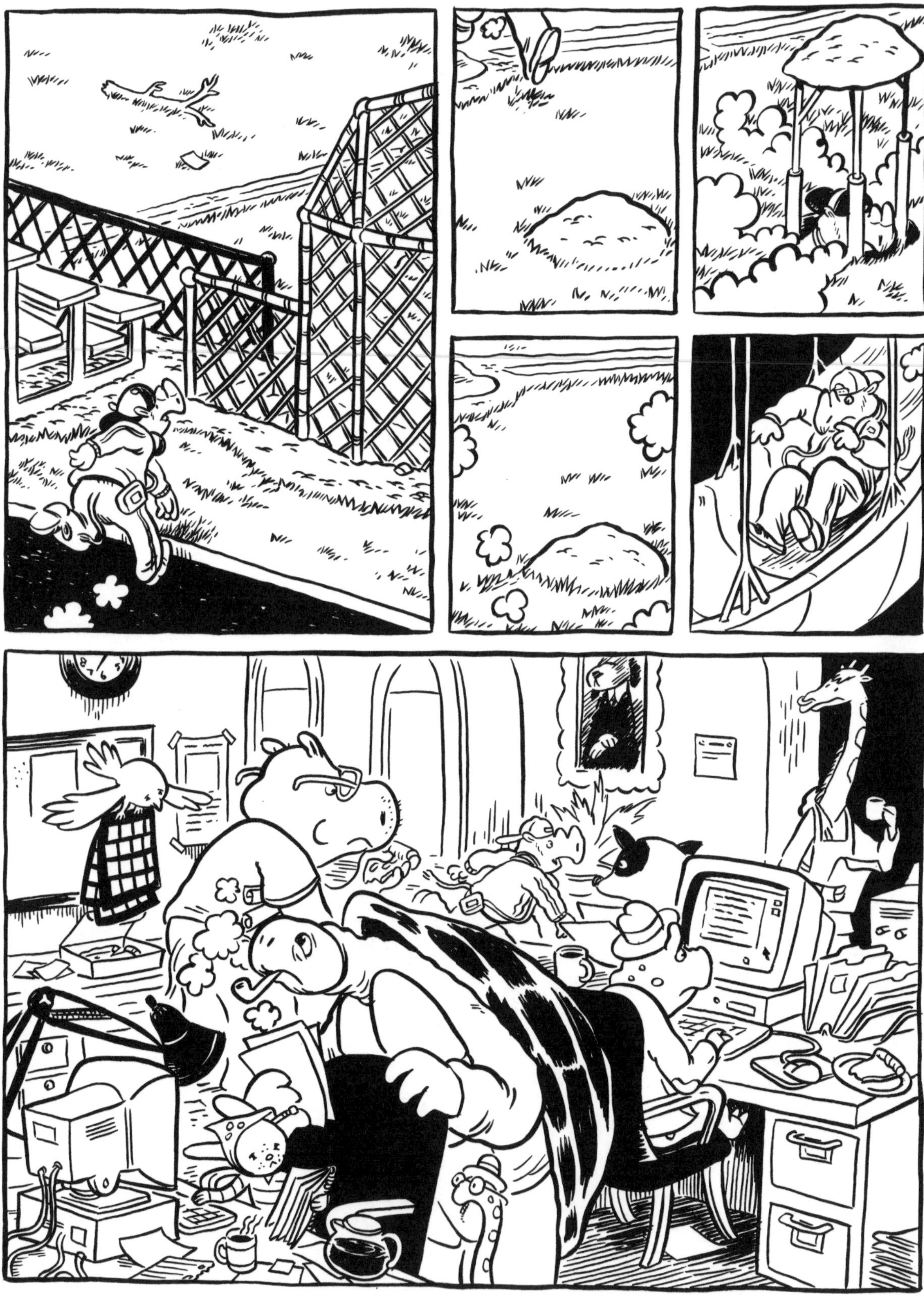

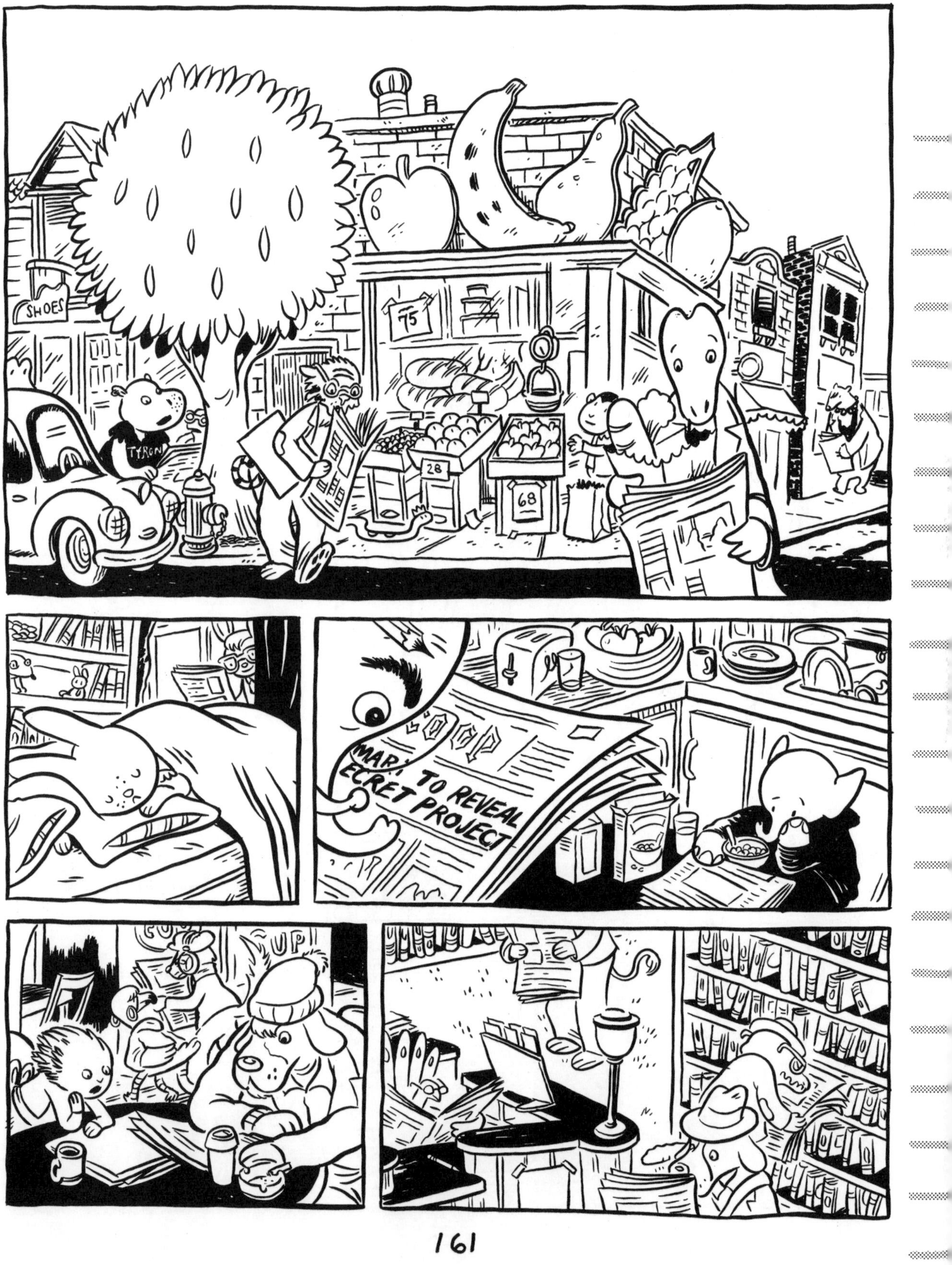
SHOES
TYRON
75
28
68
MAR. TO REVEAL
ECRET PROJECT

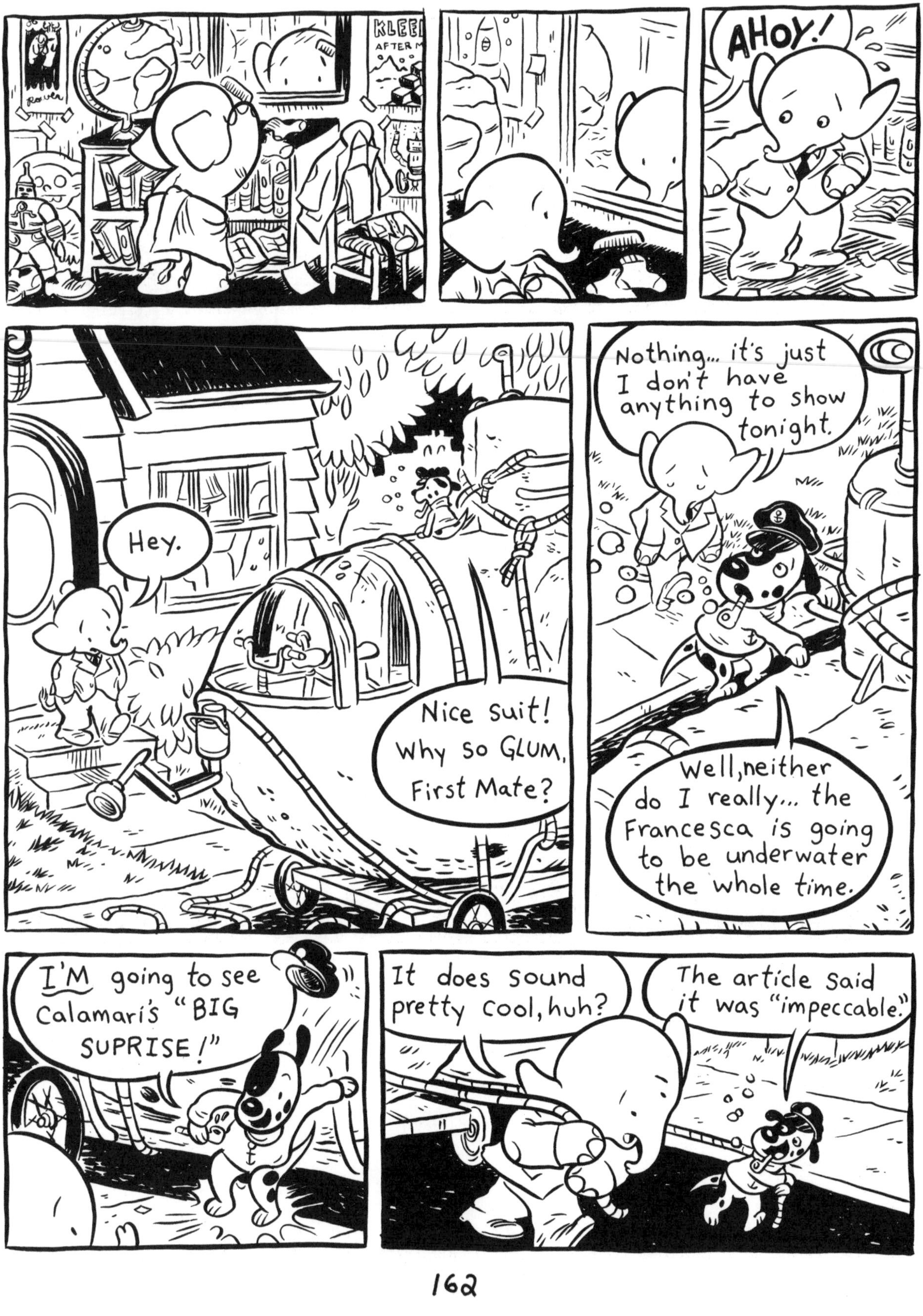
AHOY!
Hey.
Nice suit! Why so GLUM, First Mate?
Nothing... it's just I don't have anything to show tonight.
Well, neither do I really... the Francesca is going to be underwater the whole time.
I'M going to see Calamari's "BIG SUPRISE!"
It does sound pretty cool, huh?
The article said it was "impeccable."

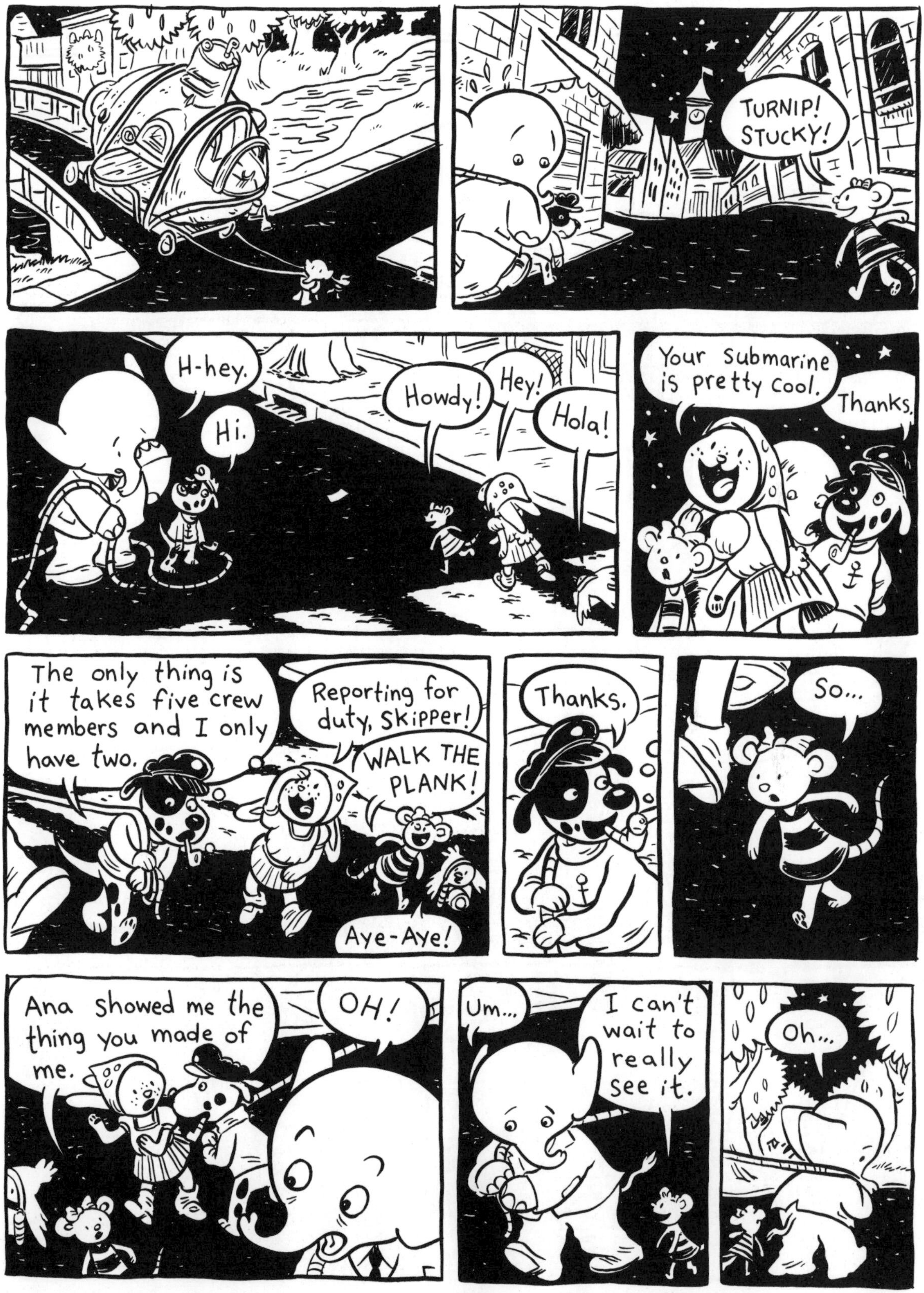
TURNIP! STUCKY!
H-hey.
Hi.
Howdy!
Hey!
Hola!
Your submarine is pretty cool.
Thanks.
The only thing is it takes five crew members and I only have two.
Reporting for duty, Skipper!
WALK THE PLANK!
Aye-Aye!
Thanks.
So...
Ana showed me the thing you made of me.
OH!
Um...
I can't wait to really see it.
Oh...

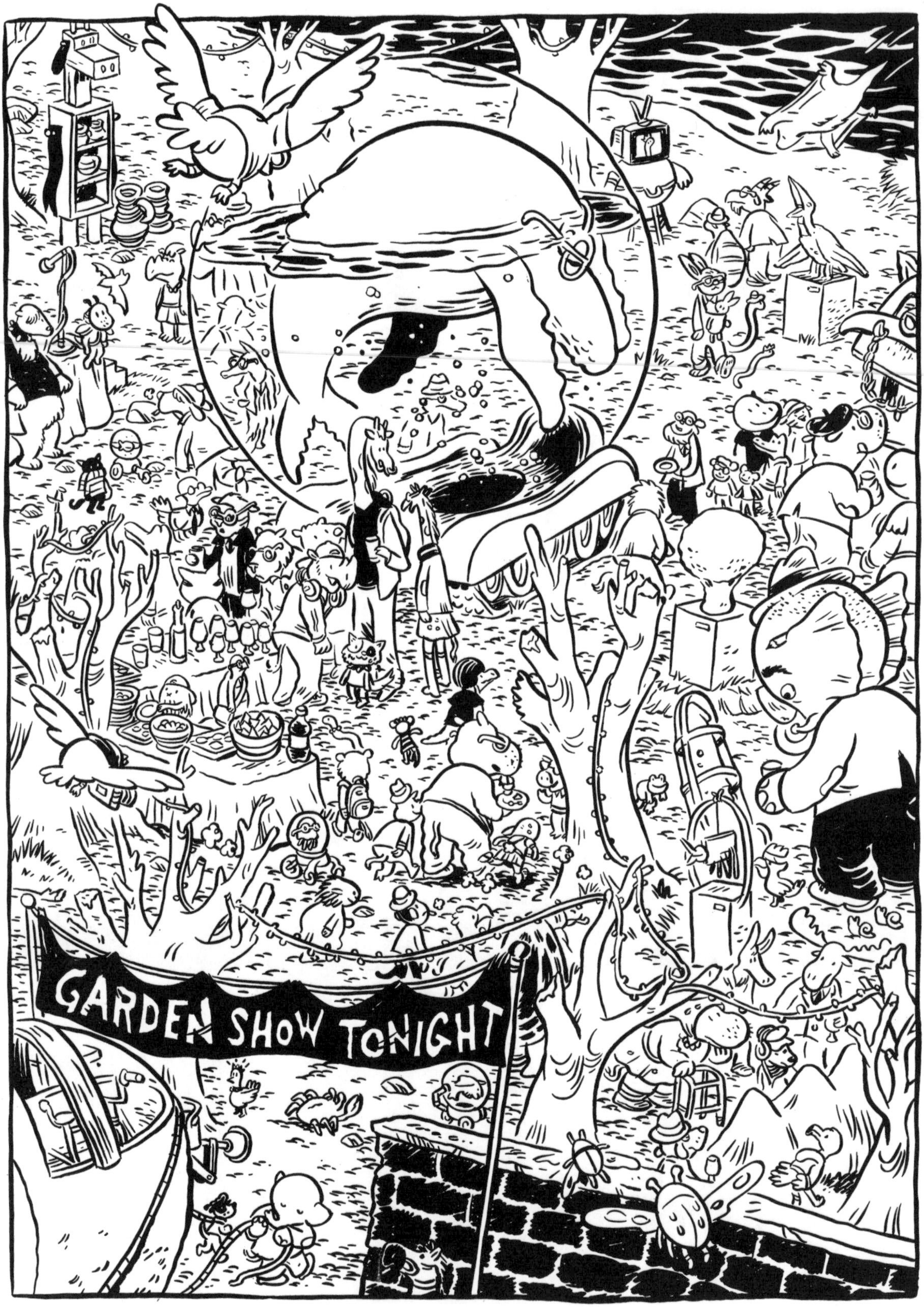
GARDEN SHOW TONIGHT

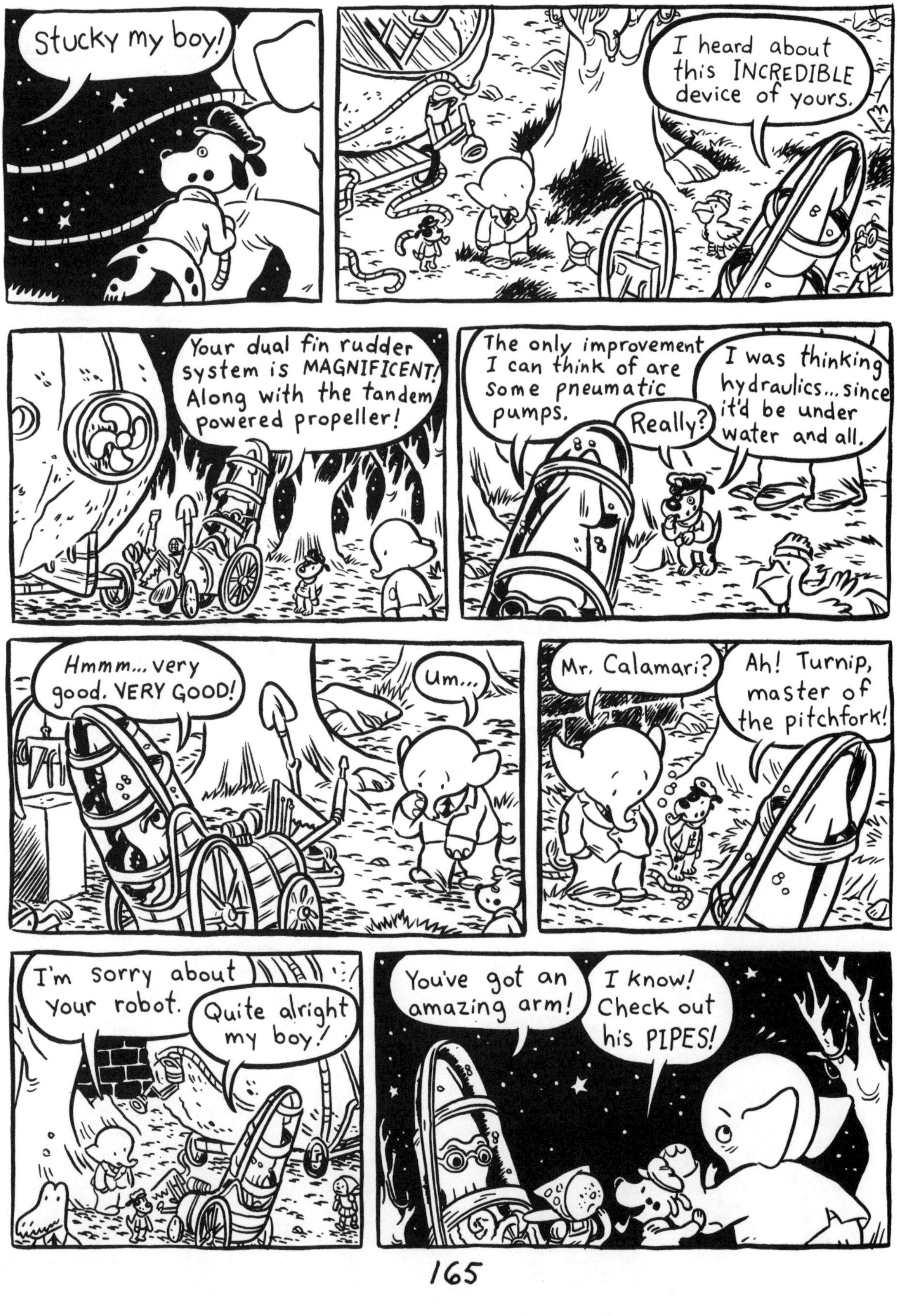
Stucky my boy!
I heard about this INCREDIBLE device of yours.
Your dual fin rudder system is MAGNIFICENT! Along with the tandem powered propeller!
The only improvement I can think of are some pneumatic pumps.
Really?
I was thinking hydraulics... since it'd be under water and all.
Hmmm... very good. VERY GOOD!
Um...
Mr. Calamari?
Ah! Turnip, master of the pitchfork!
I'm sorry about your robot.
Quite alright my boy!
You've got an amazing arm!
I know! Check out his PIPES!

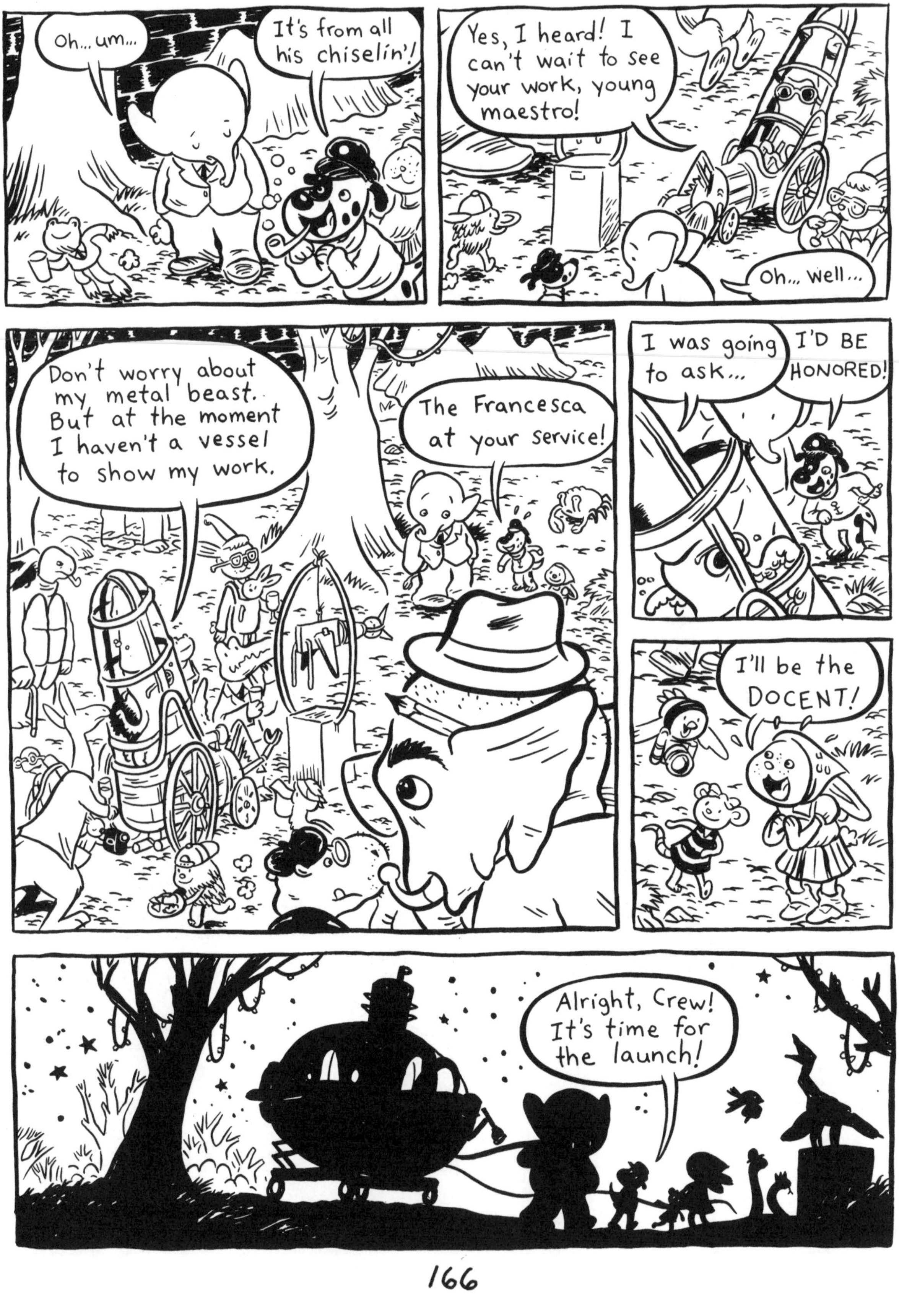
Oh... um...
It's from all his chiselin'!
Yes, I heard! I can't wait to see your work, young maestro!
Oh... well...
Don't worry about my metal beast. But at the moment I haven't a vessel to show my work.
The Francesca at your service!
I was going to ask...
I'D BE HONORED!
I'll be the DOCENT!
Alright, Crew! It's time for the launch!

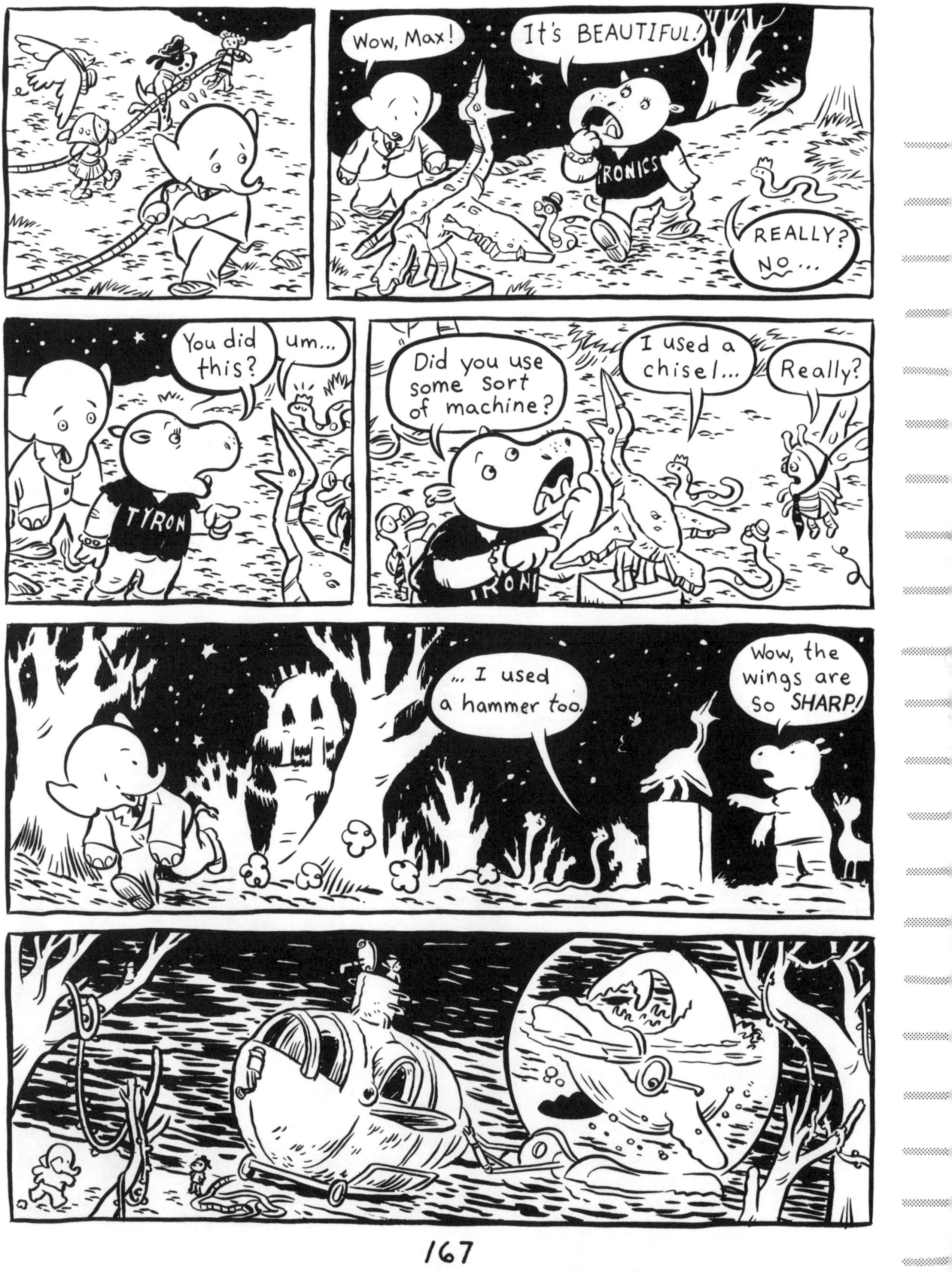
Wow, Max!
It's BEAUTIFUL!
REALLY? NO...
You did this?
um...
Did you use some sort of machine?
I used a chisel...
Really?
... I used a hammer too.
Wow, the wings are so SHARP!
TYRON

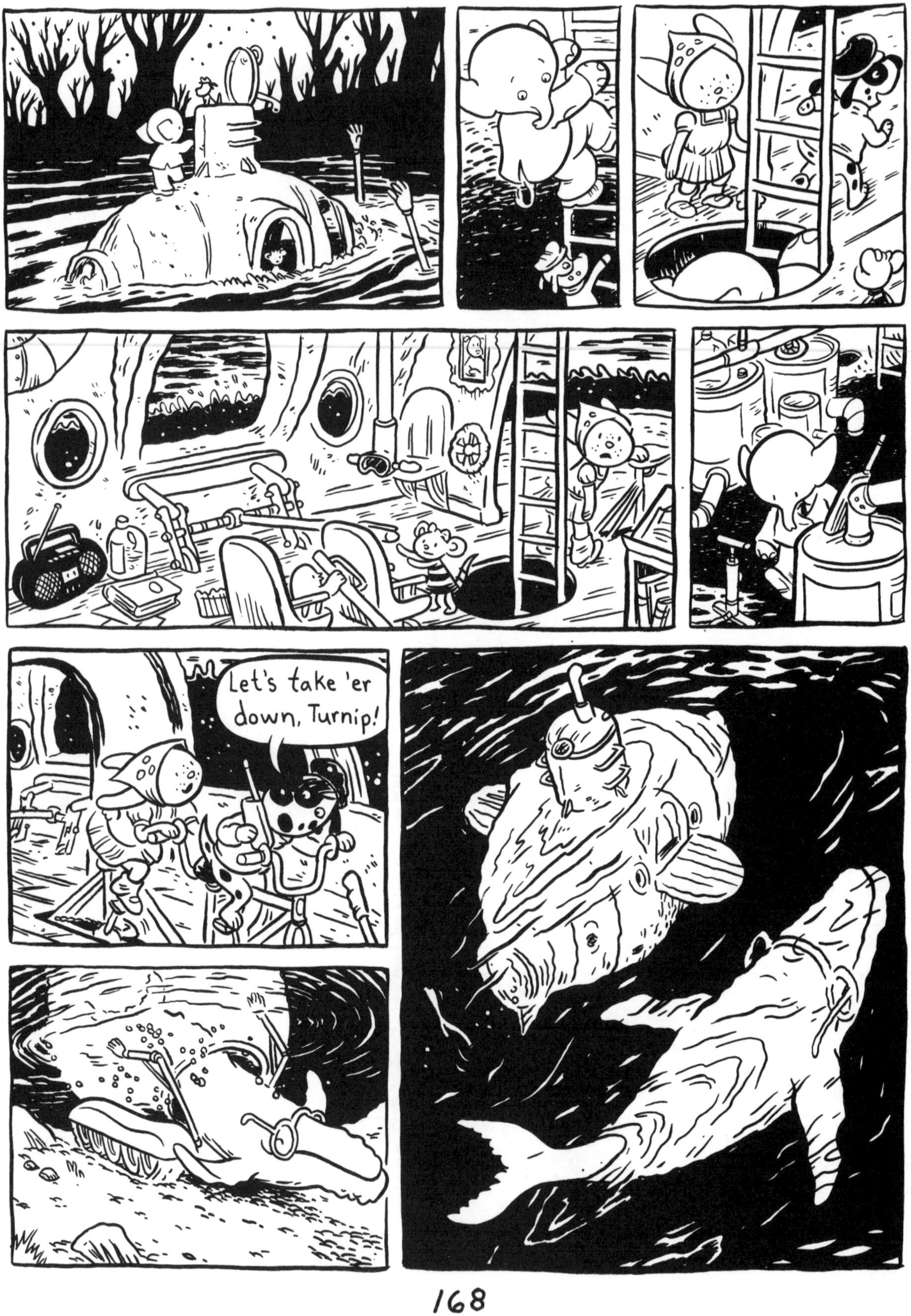
Let's take 'er down, Turnip!

LIGHTS!

CLK!

Did you see that creepy, sunken tree on our descent?

Yeah?

Well, that's what started the whole monster story. He originally built his robot to get close to the creature... but when he saw the tree he, knew he was completely alone.

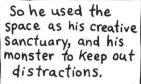

So he used the space as his creative sanctuary, and his monster to keep out distractions.

He decided what he really wanted to do was create something completely new. Breathe life into the pond again.

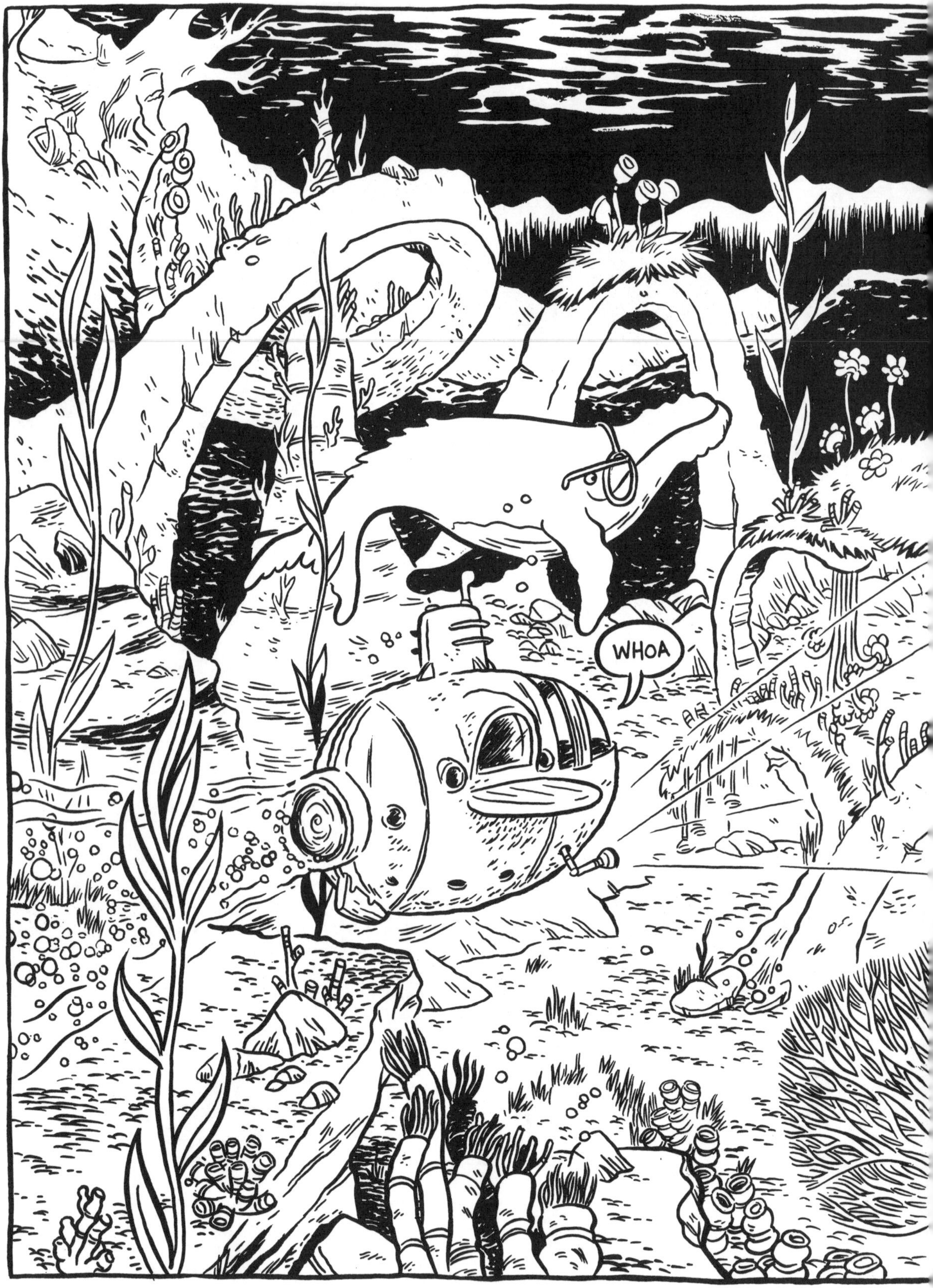
WHOA

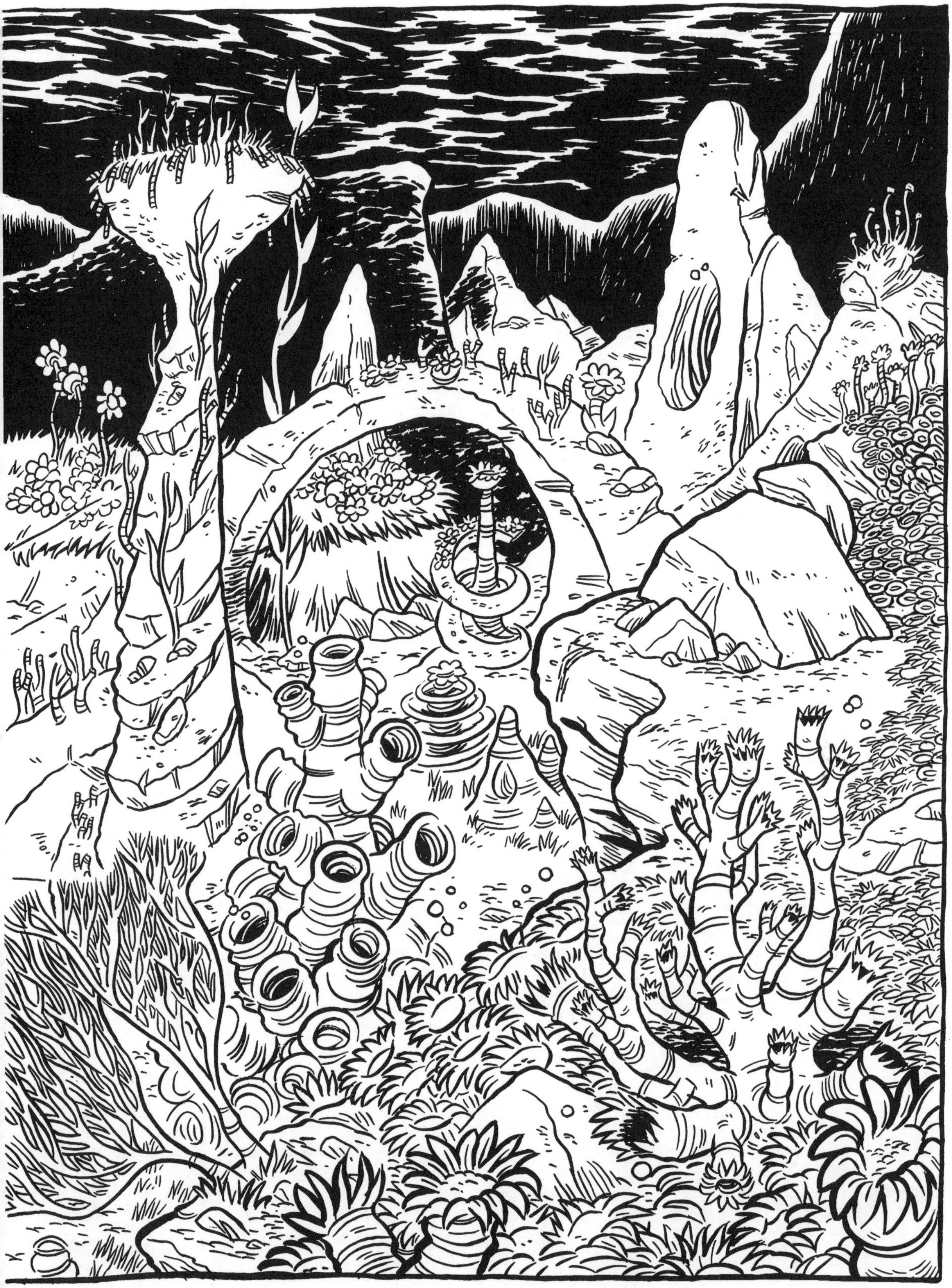

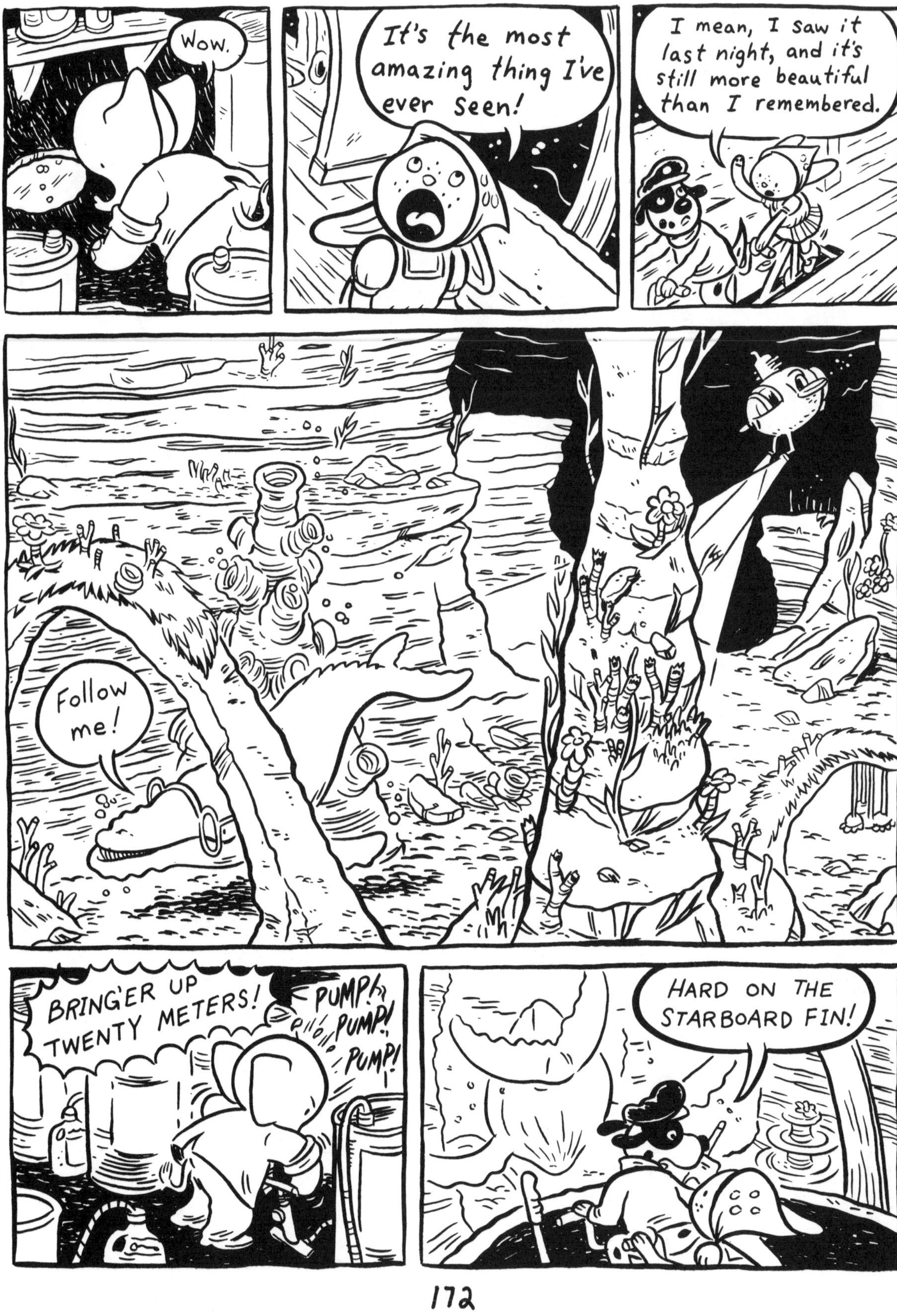
Wow.
It's the most amazing thing I've ever seen!
I mean, I saw it last night, and it's still more beautiful than I remembered.
Follow me!
BRING'ER UP TWENTY METERS!
PUMP!
PUMP!
PUMP!
HARD ON THE STARBOARD FIN!

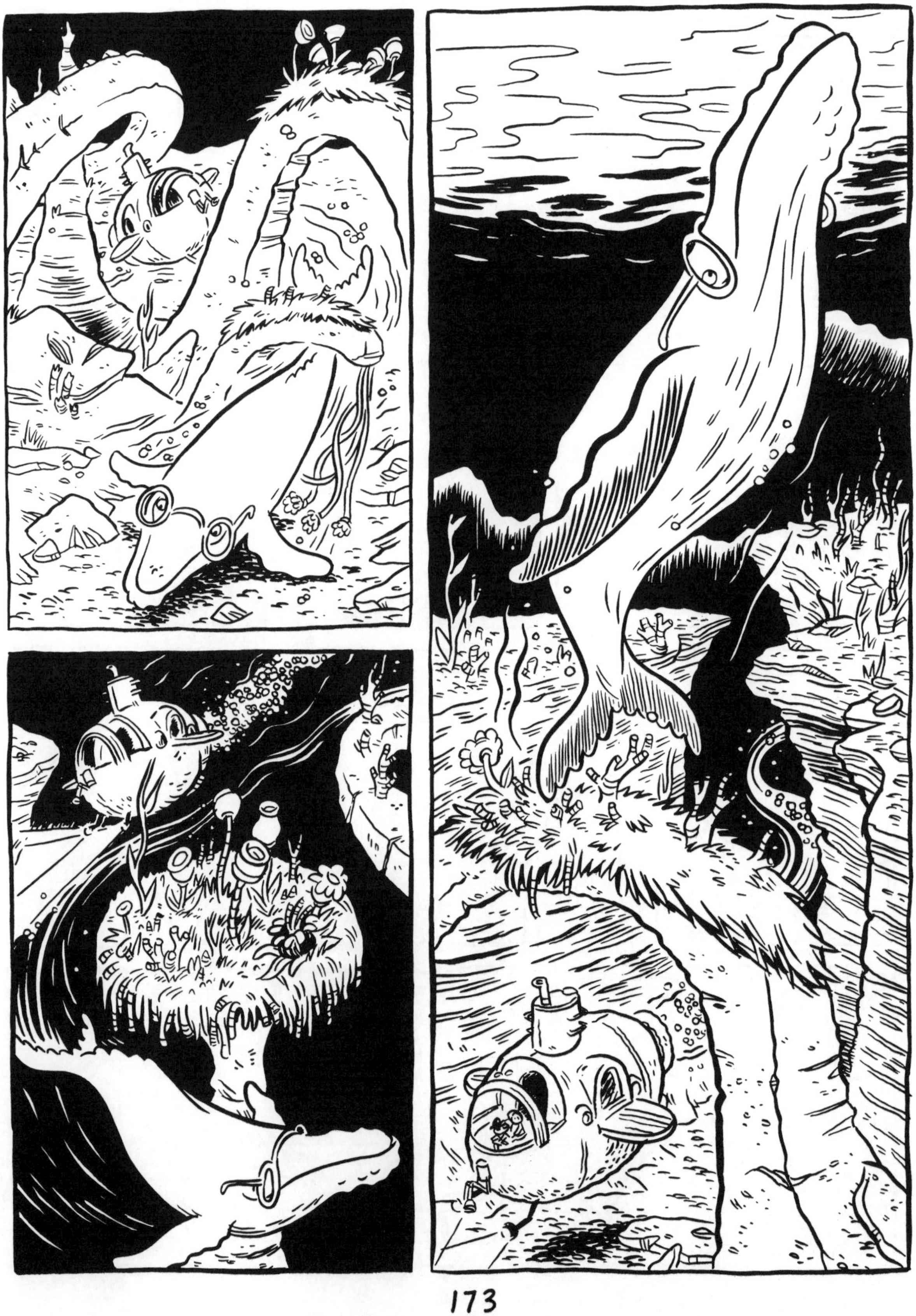

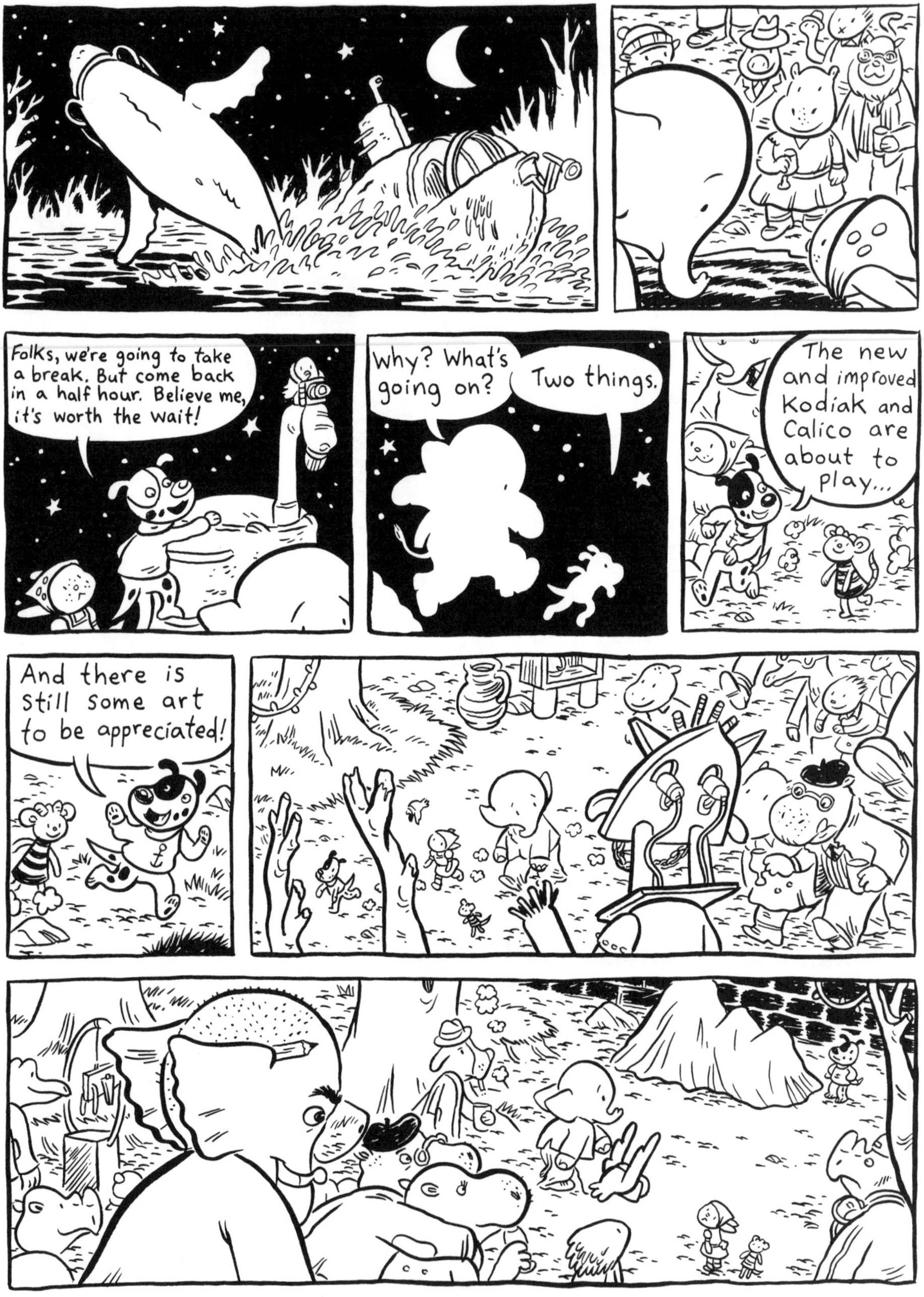
Folks, we're going to take a break. But come back in a half hour. Believe me, it's worth the wait!
Why? What's going on?
Two things.
The new and improved Kodiak and Calico are about to play...
And there is still some art to be appreciated!

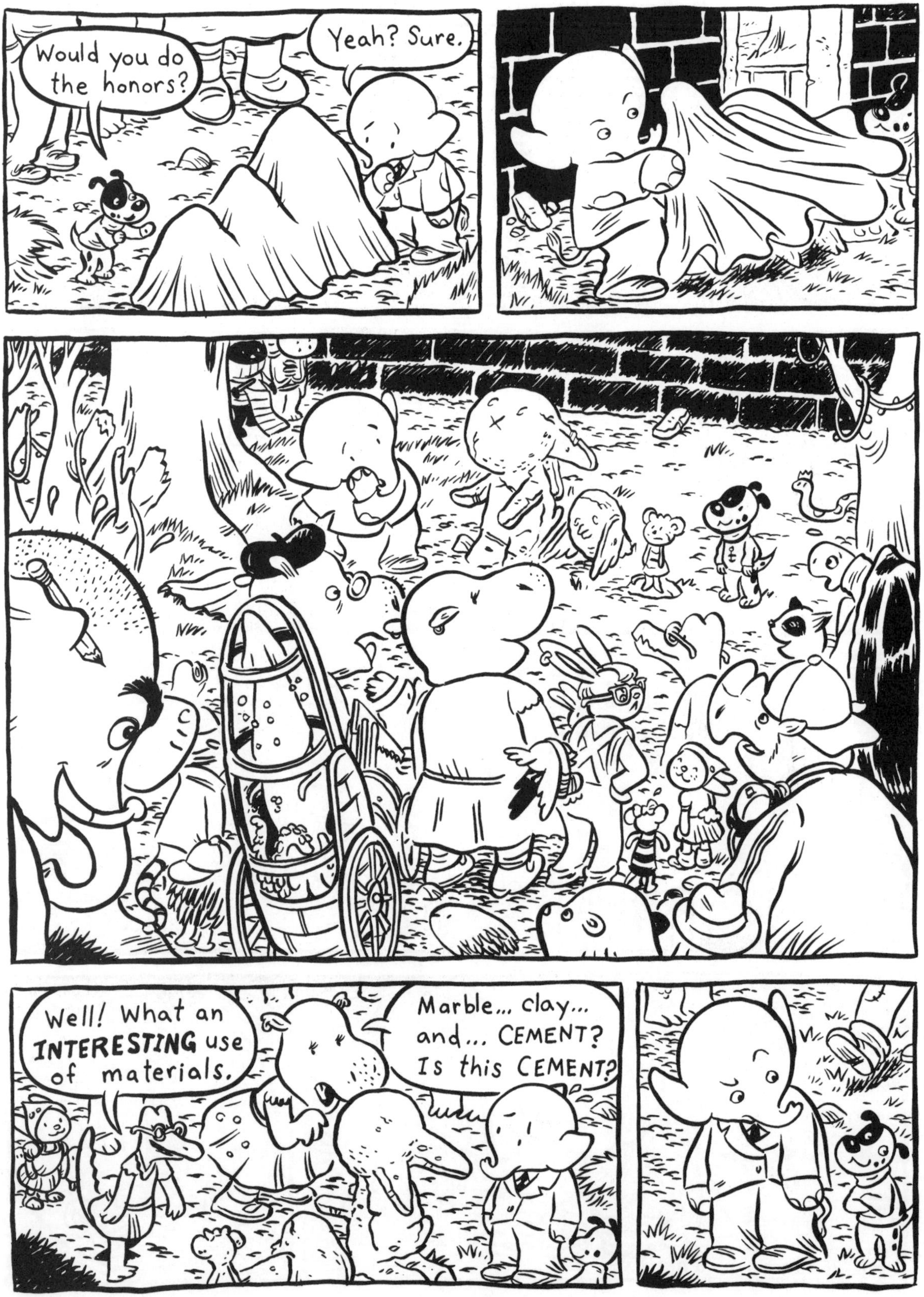
Would you do the honors?
Yeah? Sure.
Well! What an INTERESTING use of materials.
Marble... clay... and... CEMENT? Is this CEMENT?

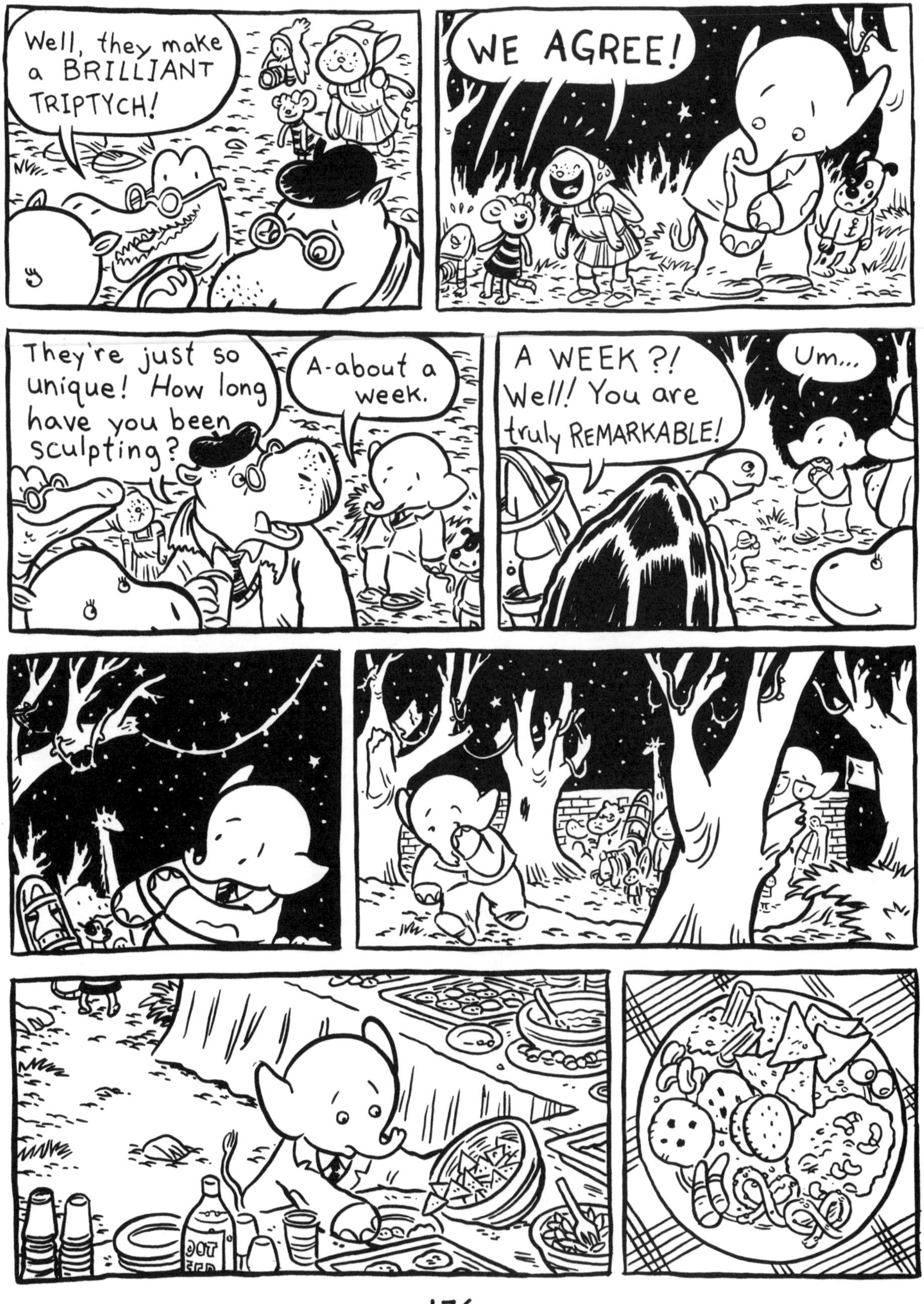
Well, they make a BRILLIANT TRIPTYCH!
WE AGREE!
They're just so unique! How long have you been sculpting?
A-about a week.
A WEEK?! Well! You are truly REMARKABLE!
Um...

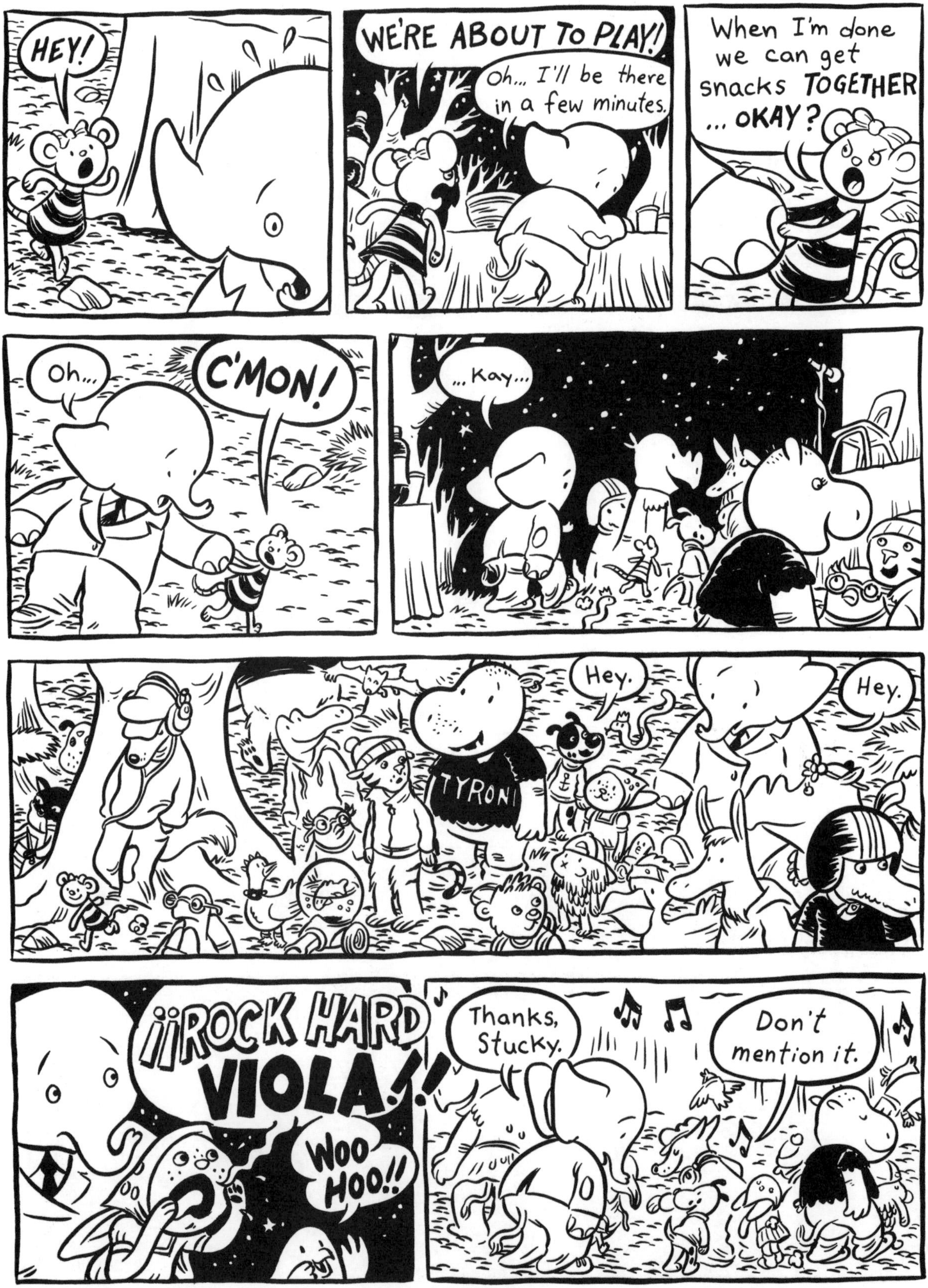
HEY!
WE'RE ABOUT TO PLAY!
Oh... I'll be there in a few minutes.
When I'm done we can get snacks TOGETHER ... OKAY?
Oh...
C'MON!
...Kay...
TYRON
Hey.
Hey.
¡¡ROCK HARD VIOLA!!
WOO HOO!!
Thanks, Stucky.
Don't mention it.

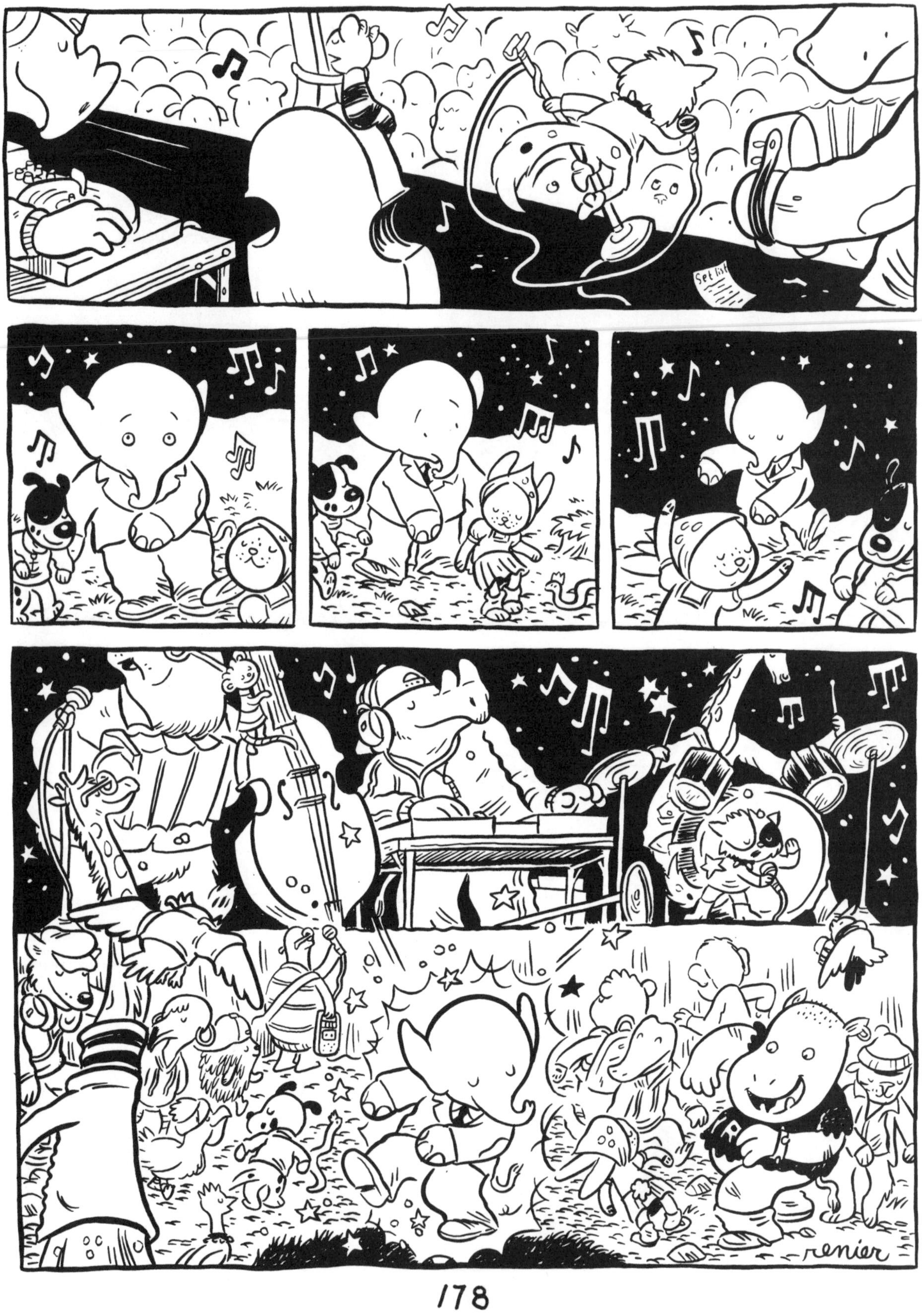
Set list
renier

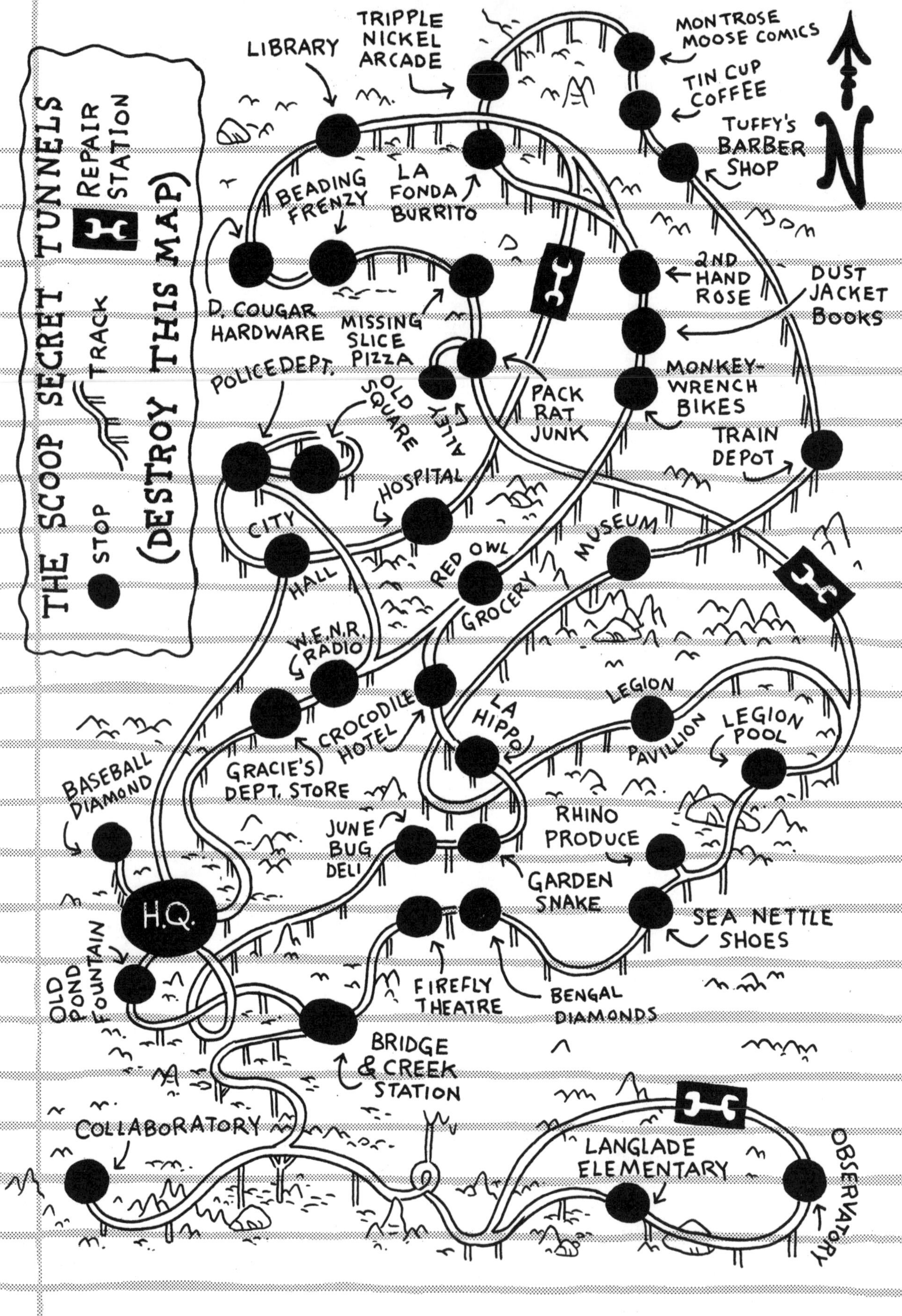
THE SCOOP SECRET TUNNELS
STOP
TRACK
REPAIR STATION
(DESTROY THIS MAP)
LIBRARY
TRIPPLE NICKEL ARCADE
MONTROSE MOOSE COMICS
TIN CUP COFFEE
TUFFY'S BARBER SHOP
BEADING FRENZY
LA FONDA BURRITO
2ND HAND ROSE
DUST JACKET Books
D. COUGAR HARDWARE
MISSING SLICE PIZZA
POLICE DEPT.
OLD SQUARE
ALLEY
PACK RAT JUNK
MONKEY-WRENCH BIKES
TRAIN DEPOT
HOSPITAL
CITY HALL
RED OWL GROCERY
MUSEUM
W.E.N.R. RADIO
CROCODILE HOTEL
LA HIPPO
LEGION PAVILLION
LEGION POOL
GRACIE'S DEPT. STORE
BASEBALL DIAMOND
JUNE BUG DELI
RHINO PRODUCE
GARDEN SNAKE
H.Q.
SEA NETTLE SHOES
OLD POND FOUNTAIN
FIREFLY THEATRE
BENGAL DIAMONDS
BRIDGE & CREEK STATION
COLLABORATORY
LANGLADE ELEMENTARY
OBSERVATORY